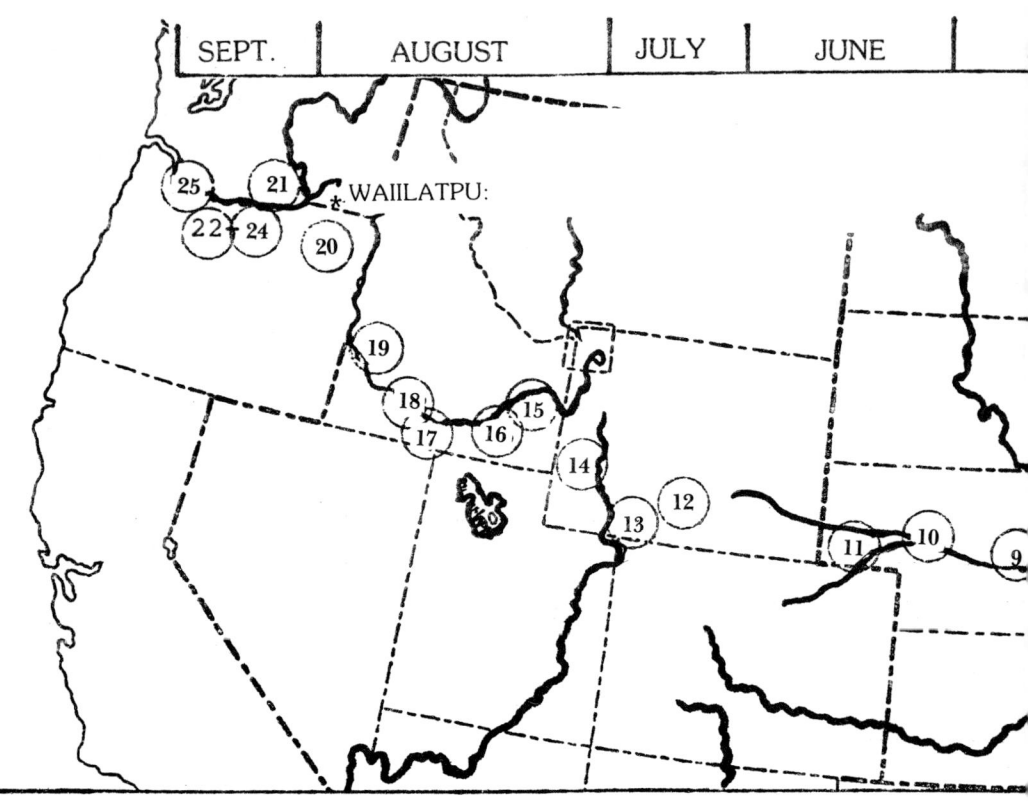

1.	Angelica, N.Y.	Narcissa Prentiss (age 28), & Marcus Whitman (age 34) were married in the Angelica Presbyterian Church, Thur. February 18, 1836. Departed Angelica, Fri., Feb. 19, for visits to Ithaca & Rushville before heading west.
2.	Rushville	Departed for Oregon Terr., Thur., Mar. 3.
3.	Williamsport	Sunday, Mar. 6.
4.	Pittsburgh	Sat., Mar. 12 - Tue., Mar. 15.
5.	Cincinnati	Thur., Mar. 17 - Tue., Mar. 22.
6.	St. Louis	Tue., Mar. 29 - Thur., Mar. 31.
7.	Liberty	Thur., Apr. 7 - Wed., Apr. 27.
8.	Platte River Crossing	Wed., May 18 - Fri., May 20.
9.	Joined Caravan	Thur., May 26 (1 a.m.).
10.	Forks Platte R.	Fri., June 3.
11.	Fort William (Fort Laramie)	Mon., June 13 - Tue., June 21.
12.	South Pass	Mon., July 4.
13.	Rendezvous	Wed., July 6 - Mon., July 18.

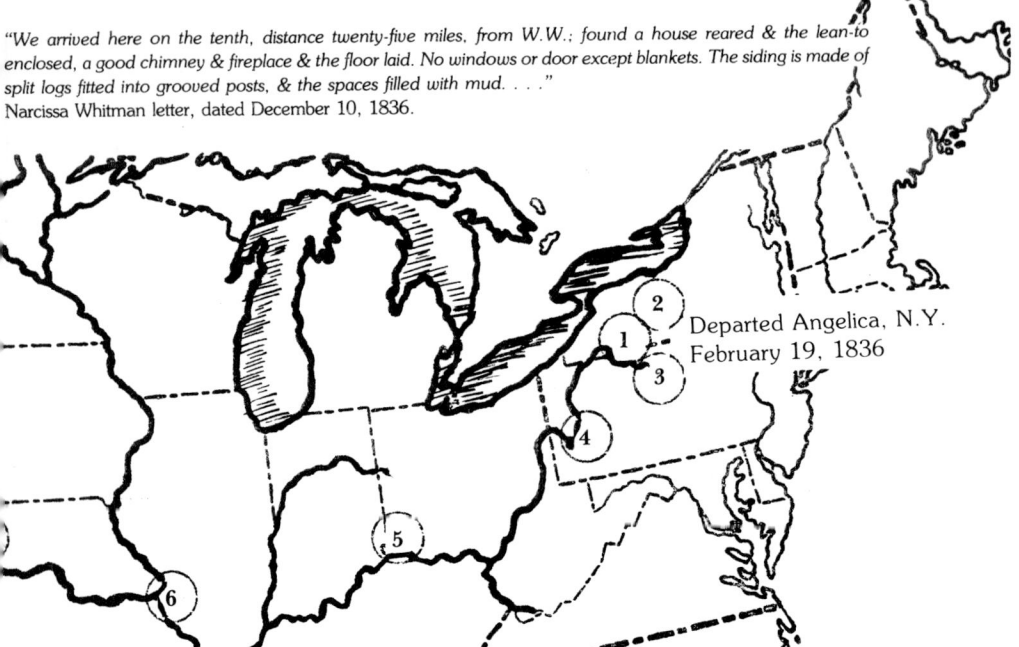

"We arrived here on the tenth, distance twenty-five miles, from W.W.; found a house reared & the lean-to enclosed, a good chimney & fireplace & the floor laid. No windows or door except blankets. The siding is made of split logs fitted into grooved posts, & the spaces filled with mud. . . ."
Narcissa Whitman letter, dated December 10, 1836.

14.	Soda Springs	Sat., July 30.
15.	Fort Hall	Wed., Aug. 3 - Thur., Aug. 4
16.	American Falls	Fri., Aug. 5.
17.	Salmon Falls	Fri., Aug. 12.
18.	Three Island Crossing Snake River	Sat., Aug. 13
19.	Snake [Boise] Fort	Fri., Aug. 19 - Mon., Aug., 22.
20.	Blue Mountains	Sun., Aug. 28 - Mon., Aug. 29.
21.	Fort Walla Walla	Thur., Sept. 1 - Tue., Sept. 6.
22.	The Chutes (Celilo)	Wed., Sept. 7.
23.	The Dalles	Thur. Sept. 8.
24.	The Cascades	Sun., Sept. 11.
25.	Fort Vancouver	Mon., Sept. 12 - Thur., Nov. 3.
	Fort Walla Walla	Sun., Nov. 13 - Sat., Dec., 10.
	Waiilatpu	Arrived Sat., Dec. 10, 1836.

After 295 days and about 2,500 miles, Narcissa Whitman arrived at her new home in the Walla Walla Valley.

The Letters of Narcissa Whitman

MRS. NARCISSA PRENTISS WHITMAN.

No authentic picture of Mrs. Whitman is in existence. This portrait of her has been drawn under the supervision of a gentleman familiar with her appearance, and with suggestions from members of her family. It is considered a good likeness of her.

The Letters of

Narcissa Whitman

1836 — 1847

by

Narcissa Whitman

Ye Galleon Press
Fairfield, Washington

Library of Congress Cataloging in Publication Data

Whitman, Narcissa Prentis, 1808-1847.
   The letters of Narcissa Whitman.

   Bibliography: p.
   1. Whitman, Narcissa Prentiss, 1808-1847—Correspondence. 2. Cayuse Indians—Missions. 3. Indians of North America—Northwest, Pacific—Missions. 4. Oregon—History—To 1859. 5. Pioneers—Northwest, Pacific—Correspondence. 6. Missionaries—Northwest, Pacific—Correspondence. I. Title.
F880.W615   1986   979.5'03'0924   86-13282
ISBN 0-87770-386-8

INTRODUCTION

Narcissa Prentiss Whitman was born at Prattsburg, Steuben County, western New York on March 14, 1808, to Stephen and Clarissa Prentiss, the third child in a family of nine. She attended public school in Prattsburg. On finishing the limited village schooling, she attended Franklin Academy for a year, then a seminary for women at Troy, New York. After this, she taught school, one of the very few respectable occupations open to women at that date. Miss Prentiss became interested in the missionary field after attending a meeting where the Reverend Samuel Parker made an appeal for money and missionaries to Christianize western Indians. This was in November of 1834, at which date the vast Oregon country was not part of the United States, but was held jointly by England and the U.S. England had been there first, with the Northwest Company, later with the Hudson's Bay Company that had been chartered by Charles the Second in 1660. U.S. fur traders quickly dominated the maritime fur trade, but were unable to compete successfully with the entrenched and experienced Honorable Company, Hudson's Bay. In 1835 Marcus Whitman and Samuel Parker had traveled to the fur trade "Rendezvous" in Wyoming. A decision was made that Parker, an older man and married with a family in the "States" would travel on to the Pacific Northwest while Whitman would return to recruit reinforcements. The agreement was that the two men would meet the following year, 1836, when Parker was to apprise Whitman of a suitable site for the proposed mission to save the heathens from perdition. Unfortunately, Parker did not honor this commitment, as he sailed on to Hawaii and later returned to the coast by sea. Marcus Whitman had none too much time in which to make all the arrangements to lead or take part in a missionary party to accompany the 1836 fur trade caravan to the Wyoming rendezvous. These arrangements needed to be completed by mid-February of 1836. Whitman left the Green River "rendezvous" August 27, 1835, taking with him two Nez Perce Indian boys. In the meantime Narcissa Prentiss had received no encouragement from the American Board and she apparently knew nothing of young Marcus Whitman but it was suggested that these two get together and they became engaged in February 1835, and Miss Narcissa Prentiss made application to the American Board to become a missionary to the heathens. On this same day Marcus Whitman started out on his westward journey with Samuel Parker. The American Board could now review her application to become a missionary confident that they would not be sending an unmarried female into the little-known and presumably wild inland Oregon country. Narcissa Prentiss now had to wait, wondering when Marcus Whitman would return from his westward travels or if he would return, but this he did, returning from the Green River rendezvous while Parker went on to Old Oregon. Marcus and Narcissa were married in the Angelica Presbyterian Church, Alleghany County, New York, leaving the next day on a 2500-mile journey to the Oregon Country. They traveled to Rushville, then Ithaca, where they picked up the two Nez Perce Indian boys, then on to Pittsburg. On March 12, 1836 they took passage on the 127-ton steamboat, *Siam*, later they traveled on other steamboats; *Junious*, *Majestic*, and *Chariton*, which landed them at Liberty, Missouri. While at Cincinnati the newly-married Whitmans were joined by a second couple, Henry Harmon Spalding and his wife, Eliza. The hundreds of miles of travel on four different river steamers was relatively pleasant to the point of luxury, but the 1900 miles of overland travel promised to be a summer of adventure. William H. Gray, a young man at the time unmarried, had also received an appointment from the American Board, but not until after the Whitman and Spalding party had left. He followed them and on April 19 managed to unite with them. Several days and something over 3000 dollars were spent at Liberty putting together an outfit for overland travel. A light wagon was obtained for the women and a heavier one to carry supplies and provisions. harness, saddles, guns, ammunition, food, trading goods, medical supplies, together with books, seeds, stationery and incidentals were taken in the wagons. Several head of cattle were added. As some of the cows provided milk on the overland journey, this seems a bit of good judgment.

The plan was to catch up with the American Fur Company caravan under guidance of Thomas Fitzpatrick. They overtook the fur trade caravan with considerable difficulty, fearing to travel through hostile Indian country without the protection afforded by the larger and more experienced party. Narcissa describes the caravan as a "moving village — nearly 400 animals with ours, mostly mules, and seventy men. The Fur Company has seven wagons and one cart drawn by six mules each, heavily loaded . . . ." Narcissa wrote the first of a long series of descriptive letters while descending the Ohio River from Pittsburg. The overland journey is described in some detail and occasionally with flowery nineteenth century English. The sighting of the first herds of buffalo is described and meetings with the first American native peoples, few of which had ever seen white women before. The heavier wagon was left at Fort William on the upper Platte River. This meant that Narcissa and Eliza would have to ride horses or mules the rest of the journey. On July 4th, 1836 the party crossed South Pass in the Rocky Mountains, the first white women to accomplish this. Mrs. Spalding carefully wrote: "Crossed a ridge of land today; called the divide, which separates the waters that flow into the Atlantic from those that flow into the Pacific."

Osborne Russell, an American trapper, wrote in his *Journal of a Trapper, or Nine Years in the Rocky Mountains, 1834-43,* "The two ladies were gazed upon with wonder and astonishment by the rude Savages, they being the first white women ever seen by these Indians and the first that had ever penetrated into these wild and rocky regions." Isaac P. Rose, another mountain man, who in 1884 published his *Four Years in the Rockies*, wrote, "Mrs. Whitman was a large, stately, fair skinned woman, with blue eyes and light, auburn, almost golden hair. He manners were at once dignified and gracious. She was by both nature and education, a lady, and had a lady's appreciation of all that was courageous and refined, yet not without an element of romance and heroism in her disposition strong enough to have impelled her to undertake a missionary's life in the wilderness. Mrs. Spalding, the other lady, was more delicate than her companion, yet equally earnest and zealous in the cause they had undertaken. The Indians would turn their gaze from the dark haired, dark eyed Mrs. Spalding to what was to them the more interesting golden hair and blue eyes of Mrs. Whitman, and they seemed to regard them as beings of a superior nature." Narcissa wrote that as soon as she dismounted from her horse, "I was met by a company of native women, one after the other, shaking hands and salluting me with a most hearty kiss."

As the American Fur Company caravan would be returning to the East after the conclusion of the Rendezvous, there was the problem of what route the missionary party should take to Oregon. The Nez Perce Indians present wished to return to their Idaho and Oregon country by the mountainous northern route, not possible for wagon travel. Traveling down the Snake River to the Columbia promised to be easier but was over much dry, hot country. The decision of which route to take was assisted by the arrival of a Hudson's Bay Company party under John L. McLeod and Thomas McKay. The Hudson's Bay Company had purchased Fort Hall in southern Oregon from Nathaniel J. Wyeth, and wished to take possession of this post.

The missionary party had a bit of good luck with the arrival of John McLeod and Thomas McKay commanding a small group of Hudson's Bay Company employees . . . sent to take possession of Fort Hall in southern Idaho. What really was a business transaction on the part of the Honorable Company seemed to the missionaries to be a matter of divine providence, so they placed themselves under the protection of this party to continue their journey westward. Perhaps in gratitude for this stroke of fortune, Narcissa's letters describing the journey from the Rendezvous on to Fort Vancouver are quite detailed. Travel with the wagon in the absence of any real roads was becoming a problem. On July 25th, 1836 the wagon twice upset on steep hillsides. When, three days later, a wagon axle broke, Narcissa hoped that this conveyance would be abandoned, but a stubborn Marcus Whitman made a cart of the rear portion of the wagon and lashed the front wheels to the cart, being determined to take the wagon on as far as possible.

Seventeen days out from the Rendezvous they reached Fort Hall, which Narcissa described in some detail, including the somewhat delapidated condition of the garden at the fort. Four days later Snake Fort was reached, really Fort Boise on the Big Wood River (Boise River). On being told that the route over the Blue Mountains was very bad, Marcus decided to leave the wagon, hoping he could return later to claim it. The decision was made in part because of the worn-down condition of their horses. The party continued on horseback over the Blue Mountains and down into the Grand Ronde Valley which Narcissa describes as delightful, although the descent onto the valley floor was difficult. Fort Walla Walla, the Hudson's Bay Company post at the confluence of the Walla and Columbia Rivers, was reached on September first, 1836. They were warmly welcomed by Pierre Chrysologue Pambrun, Chief Trader at the post, and the naturalist, John Kirk Townsend. After resting several days the party traveled down the Columbia in small boats, a voyage taking six days. While resting at The Dalles, Mrs. Whitman became well acquainted with black fleas which invaded "every plait of her dress." Narcissa and Mrs. Spalding elected to stay as guests of Dr. John McLoughlin at Fort Vancouver while their husbands returned upriver to build a rude house some twenty-five miles east of Fort Walla Walla and some seven miles west of the present city of Walla Walla.

Although Marcus and Narcissa worked hard to establish a mission at Waiilatpu for the benefit of the nearby Cayuse Indians, it was difficult for Narcissa to accept the established customs of the native peoples, who already possessed a rude form of Christianity. Narcissa had become pregnant in the course of her horseback journey over the Oregon Trail and on march 14, 1837 her daughter, Alice Clarissa was born. The little girl seems to have been highly intelligent and the parents were delighted with her, however her life was short; just twenty-seven months after her birth she drowned in the Walla Walla River.

While the Wailatpu Mission established to benefit Cayuse Indians in the end proved a disaster for the Cayuse people, the Whitman Mission became a way station on the Oregon Trail, and was politically important in assisting immigrants to travel to and settle in the Willamette Valley. The early domination of the Hudson's Bay Company inevitably gave way as more and more U.S. men and women traveled west on the Oregon Trail. The stream of immigrants disturbed the native people and great numbers of Cayuse Indians died of measles in the year of 1847, including children of chiefs. White people became ill as well as Indians, but the Indians had little resistance to diseases introduced by whites, the result being that a white person who became ill usually recovered and an Indian who became ill usually died, a most convenient matter for the white population that coveted

Indian land. Sometimes Indians died from introduced contagion who had never seen a white person. The Cayuse Indian, observing the rapid decline of their own numbers contrasted with the flood of incoming white immigrants overrunning the area believed that Dr. Marcus Whitman was poisoning them so they with some regret determined he must die. On November 29, 1847 Marcus and Narcissa were murdered along with eleven other whites living at the mission. Narcissa was the only woman killed It would appear that at least some of the Cayuse Indians hated her, or it is likely that she would have been spared. After some days of captivity Peter Skene Ogden, a Hudson's Bay Company officer, ransomed the remaining captives. Later, five Indian men were hanged at Oregon City for what is now called the Whitman massacre. It seems that one of the men who was hanged was not even present at the affair when the killings took place.

The Cayuse Indians have come out badly in history books, although actually they were proud, horseback, nomadic peoples who attempted to turn back the clock to what life was like for them before the Whitman Mission was established. The American Board of Commissioners for Foreign Missions which had sponsored and supported the Wailatpu Mission, closed the missions at Lapwai and Chimokain following the destruction of the Whitman Mission.

Although martyrdom may have to a degree enhanced the position of Marcus and Narcissa Whitman in western history, a fair judgment would be that these were courageous individuals who tried. Narcissa Whitman from descriptions that have come down to us was dignified, gracious, courageous, lady-like. She may have been the wrong personality in the wrong position, but she has an assured place in eastern Washington history; she was one of our true pioneers. Her detailed letters give us a window into early travel over the Oregon Trail and into pioneer life at the Waiilatpu Mission 1836 to 1847.

While there had been a white child born some years earlier to British parents at Spokane House located at the confluence of the Spokane and Little Spokane Rivers, and about which we know little, Alice Clarissa was the first white child born to U.S. parents in the Pacific Northwest.

Glen Adams
Fairfield, Washington
March, 1986

ON BOARD STEAMBOAT *SIAM*
March 15, 1836.

Dear, Dear Mother: — Your proposal concerning keeping a diary as I journey comes before my mind often. I have not found it practicable while traveling by land, although many events have passed which, if noted as they occurred, might have been interesting. We left Pittsburgh this morning at ten o'clock and are sailing at the rate of thirteen miles an hour. It is delightful passing so rapidly down the waters of the beautiful river. The motion of the boat is very agreeable to me, except while writing. Our accommodations are good; we occupy a stateroom where we can be as retired as we wish. Two boats left Pittsburgh before we did, but they are now in our rear. The captain of one of them became very angry because we attempted to pass, and shot into our path before us. For a time we thought injury would be done by their coming in contact but we passed her unhurt. The *Siam* was a very strong boat and might have sunk the other without much difficulty. It is an imposing scene to see the march of these stately figures as they pass us on the waters. Some are very large, and are swarming with inhabitants. It has been quite pleasant to-day, but too cold to be on deck much of the time. We have seen no snow since we left the Allegheny mountains.

March 28. — We have just come on board the *Majestic*. It is rightly named, for it is one of the largest boats on the river. We are now sailing on the waters of the great Mississippi. When I commenced this sheet we had just left Pittsburgh. We arrived in Cincinnati Thursday noon. Found Brother Spalding. Said he had been waiting for us anxiously for a fortnight; spent the remainder of the week in making arrangements for our journey, and on the Sabbath had a very interesting time with the disciples of Jesus there; felt strengthened and comforted as we left them, to pursue our journey into the wilderness. Much good feeling was manifested in the churches — a deep interest appeared to be taken in the missions. Especially our two Indian youth attracted the gaze and admiration of a crowd on Sabbath, but our expectations were not realized, and Saturday night found us on the waters of the Mississippi, eighty-nine miles from St. Louis. We felt it our duty not to

travel on the Sabbath, and determined to leave the boat, although many on board tried to persuade us to remain, and have preaching on the Sabbath, and of the number one was a Presbyterian minister from New York, who appeared quite anxious to detain us. At ten o'clock we landed at Chester, Illinois, and had a most delightful Sabbath of rest with the few disciples of Jesus we found there. An aged minister, who had been toiling in this part of the vineyard ever since the year 1817, we found of a kindred spirit. He preaches to several congregations. Said he had not had a brother minister to preach for him since he had been there; and to have a mission family call and enjoy the privileges of the Sabbath with him seemed like angels' visits. He had heard of their passing and repassing, often, Mr. Spalding preached in the forenoon, and in the afternoon my husband requested the children and youth to meet in a Sabbath school, and we distributed a number of books among them. Of the number we found one young man who professed to be a Roman Catholic—said he wanted to know our religion—had not a Protestant Bible, but if he had one would read it attentively. My husband gave him a testament, for which he appeared grateful.

Since we came on board we have come on very pleasantly; our accommodations are better here than on any previous boat—excellent cooks, and enough to eat—servants who stand at our elbows ready to supply every want.

Five o'clock.—We are now fast upon a sand-bar, but think we shall soon get off. It has rained all day—a dense fog covers the river, so that it is impossible to shun them. We shall be obliged to lie still to-night.

29th, Tuesday morning.—Fog very thick this morning, but now appears to be dispersing. We shall expect to see St. Louis to-day. Cold and damp, and am obliged to stay in my room. Can scarcely resist the temptation to stand out to view the shores of this majestic river. Varied scenes present themselves as we pass up—beautiful landscapes—on the one side high and rugged bluffs, and on the other low plains.

Evening.—We are now in port. Husband has been to the office, expecting to find letters from dear, dear friends at home, but find none. Why have they not written? seeing it is the very last, last time they will have to cheer my heart with intelligence from home, home, sweet home, and the friends I love. *But I am not sad.* My health is good. My mind completely occupied with present duty and passing events. St. Louis has a commanding situation. It is so late and foggy, our view of it as we come in is quite indistinct.

Wednesday, 30th.—A boat is in port, ready to take us up the Missouri, and will leave to-day. I intended to write several letters from here, expecting to spend some time, but as we made our purchases at Cincinnati, it is not necessary. When we were in Pittsburgh we heard that the Fur Company's steamboat *Diana* had left St. Louis. We then expected to make our journey from Liberty to Bellview by land, probably on horseback, 300 miles of which would have been the most difficult part of the journey, on account of the season and high water. But Providence has ordered it otherwise. Since we arrived here we learn that the *Diana* snagged herself and sunk, but in shallow water, so that no lives were lost. We have the promise of overtaking her before we reach Liberty. She is now lying up for repairs and drying her freight. We had a call from a gentleman this morning, who has resided in the mountains. Richard knew him very well. Is going back with us. He was formerly from Cincinnati. It seems to me now that we are on the very borders of civilization, although we shall pass many towns on our way to Liberty. At this moment my feelings are peculiar. I hardly know how to define them. I have not one feeling of regret at the step which I have taken, but count it a privilege to go forth in the name of my Master, cheerfully bearing the toil and privation that we expect to encounter. I intend to write home from Council Bluffs if I am not prevented, and give some statements which I cannot now. We could not pack all contained in that box sent us from Angelica. What we could not, Brother Whitman took home to sell for us, and sent the avails to St. Louis. How anxiously I looked for a line or two from some one of the dear family, in that box somewhere, but I saw none. Jane, don't forget to write to them for me. It is out of my power to write as much as I should like to. How often I think of the Christians in Angelica—those beloved sisters and brothers, with whom we have knelt before the altar of prayer. Surely, now I feel the influence of their prayers, although widely separated. Say to them we wish them to rejoice with us, and thank God for his kind protection, and the prosperity which has attended us since we left home; we are making arrangements for crossing the mountains, and shall expect to, unless prevented in the Providence of God. I think I should like to whisper in mother's ear many things which I cannot write. If I could only see her in her room for one-half hour. This much I can, mother. I have one of the kindest husbands, and the very best every way. Tell father by the side of his calomel he has taken a quarter of a pound of lobelia and a large quantity of cayenne, which will answer my purpose better than some of the apothecary medicines.

My husband unites with me in sending a great deal of love to dear friends there—G. and F. J., C.H.E. and N., and to father and mother. Mr. and Mrs. Spalding will go with us over the mountains. We send our Christian regard to Brother and Sister Hull, Brother and Sister Allen and Sister Patrick, and all who inquire. I have become very much interested in the Nez Perces lads; they are very affectionate and seem to wish to please us in everything. We think they will be of great service to the mission in various ways. We have just had a call from Dr. and Mrs. Misner. We expect the boat will leave us soon.

Farewell dear, dear parents. Pray for your unworthy children.

NARCISSA WHITMAN.

P.S.—Mother, I forgot to say that I heard Dr. Beecher in C., when I was there. Was introduced to Rev. Mr. Galliger, but did not hear him. My husband heard him in Pittsburgh—I was not able to go to church that day, because of a severe headache. Dr. B. appears the same in the pulpit that he does at a distance—I mean his preaching. He is a small man, quite indifferent in his appearance. I could hardly believe it was he when I saw him come.

N.W.

Mr. Stephen Prentice,
    Angelica, Allegheny Co.,
        New York.

Narcissa Whitman

ON BOARD STEAMBOAT *CHARITON*
Thursday, March 31, 1836.

Dear Sister Jane: — We did not leave last night as expected, and the day being very pleasant, gave me an opportunity of visiting the city. Received a call from our old acquaintance, Rev. Milton Kimball, and with him visited the cathedral. It was high-mass day.

We left the cathedral, after staying about an hour; called and made some purchases, then returned to the boat, and found that Mr. Lovejoy had called, to give us an invitation to dinner with him. Felt regret very much that I did not see him. My husband saw him. He wished to know when we were married, because he designed to publish it in the *Observer*. He still continues to edit his paper in St. Louis.

We left St. Louis immediately after dinner. Passed many delightful residences in Missouri, on the banks of the Mississippi, just as we leave the city. Dwellings situated upon mounds, and many remaining ones yet to be occupied — natural mounds, in appearance like that at Amity, only much larger. One of them is the situation of a female academy, now building. My next curiosity was Uncle Sam's toothpullers — two huge-looking boats lying to. They fearlessly run into danger, search out difficulties, and remove them. I should like to see them in operation, but shall not expect to now. Twilight had nearly gone when we entered the waters of the great Missouri, but the moon shone in her brightness. It was a beautiful evening. My husband and myself went upon the top of the boat, to take a more commanding view of the scenery. How majestic, how grand, was the scene! the meeting of two such great waters. "Surely, how admirable are thy works, O Lord of Hosts." I could have dwelt upon the scene still longer with pleasure, but Brother Spalding called us to prayers, and we left beholding the works of God for his immediate worship.

April 1st. — Nothing of much importance occurred to-day. My eyes are satiated with the same beautiful scenery all along the coasts of this mighty river, so peculiar to this western country. One year ago to-day since my husband first arrived in St. Louis on his exploring route to the mountains. We are one week earlier passing up the river this spring than he was last year. While the boat stopped to take in wood we went on shore, found some rushes, picked a branch of cedar, went to a spring for clear water (the river water is very rily at all times), and rambled considerably in pursuit of new objects. One of these circumstances I must mention, which was quite diverting to us. On the rocks near the river we found a great quantity of the prickly pear. Husband knew from experience the effects of handling them, and cautioned me against them, but I thought I could just take one and put it in my india-rubber apron pocket, and carry it to the boat. I did so, but after rambling a little I thought to take it out, and behold, my pocket was filled with its needles, just like a caterpillar's bristles. I became considerably annoyed with them; they covered my hands, and I have scarcely got rid of them yet. My husband would have laughed at me a little, were it not for his own misfortune. He thought to discover what kind of mucilage it was by tasting it—cut one in two, bit it, and covered his lips completely. We then had to sympathize with each other, and were glad to render mutual assistance in a case of extermination.

April 2nd, evening, ten o'clock.—We have come on well since we left St. Louis. Sailed all night last night, which is a rare thing on this river, on account of snags and sandbars. We are now at Jefferson City, about half way to Liberty from St. Louis. How long we stop here I do not know—perhaps all night.

Monday, 4th.—We passed the wreck of the Steamboat *Siam* to-day about noon. It is indeed a melancholy sight. She was not quite a year old. She ran upon a snag and sank, last winter. No lives lost. We stopped to-day at Chariton, about an hour. We went on shore and visited a steam sawmill. It was quite a curiosity, as well as the great engine that propels the boat upon the mighty waters.

Thursday, 7th.—Very pleasant, but cold. This morning the thermometer stood at 24° at nine o'clock. I have not seen any snow since we left the Allegheny mountains, before the 15th of March. I should like to know about the snow in New York. Is it all gone? How did it go, and the consequences? Mary, we have had a sick one with us all the way since we joined Dr. Satterlee. Mrs. Satterlee has had a very bad cough and cold, which has kept her feeble. She is now recovering, and is as well as can be expected. The rest of us have been very well, except feeling the effects of drinking the river water. I am an exception, however. My health was never better than since I have been on the river. I was weighed last week, and came up to 136 pounds. I think I shall endure the journey well—perhaps better than any of the rest of us. Mrs. Spalding does not look nor feel quite healthy enough for our enterprise. Riding affects her differently from what it does me. Everyone who sees me compliments me as being the best able to endure the journey over the mountains. Sister S. is very resolute—no shrinking with her. She possesses much fortitude. I like her very much. She wears well upon acquaintance. She is a very suitable person for Mr. Spalding—has the right temperment to match him. I think we shall get along very well together; we have so far. I have such a good place to shelter—under my husband's wings. He is so excellent. I love to confide in his judgment, and act under him. He is just like mother in telling me my failings. He does it in such a way that I like to have him, for it gives me a chance to improve. Jane, if you want to be happy get as good a husband as I have got, and be a missionary. Mary, I wish you were with us. You would be happy, as I am. The way looks pleasant, notwithstanding we are so near encountering the difficulties of an unheard-of journey for females. I think it would do your health good, as well as Lyman and Brother J.G., too.

This letter is free plunder. Jane, I will write to you again. What I say to one, I say to all. I should like to write to each of you, separately, but I wish to write so many ways that my time is so occupied that I cannot write as much as I want to. Since we have been here we have made our tent. It is made of bedticking, in a conical form, large enough for us all to sleep under—viz.: Mr. Spalding and wife, Dr. Whitman and wife, Mr. Gray, Richard Tak-ah-too-ah-tis, and John Altz; quite a little family—raised with a centerpole and fastened down with pegs, covering a large circle. Here we shall live, eat and sleep for the summer to come, at least—perhaps longer. Mary, you inquired concerning my beds and bedding. I will tell you. We five spread our India-rubber cloth on the ground, then our blankets, and encamp for the night. We take plenty of Mackinaw blankets, which answer for our bed and bedding, and when we journey place them over our saddles and ride on them. I wish you could see our outfit.

I had made for me, in Brother Augustus' shoe store, in Rushville, a pair of gentlemen's boots, and from him we supplied ourselves with what shoes we wanted. We have each of us a life-preserver, so that if we fall into the water we shall not drown. They are made of India-rubber cloth, air-tight, and when filled with air and placed under the arm will prevent one from sinking. Each of us take a plate, knife and fork and a tin cup. Mary, when we are under way I will describe the whole proceeding to you. When I see it before my eyes I can give a better description, for I shall have a better understanding of it. Husband has got me an excellent sidesaddle, and a very easy horse. He made me a present of a mule to ride, the other day, so I do not know which I shall like best—I have not tried the latter, Richard says "That's very bad mule—can't catch buffaloes." That is the test with him. An animal's speed makes him good, in his eye. I shall write you from Council Bluffs and at every opportunity, especially when Mr. Parker returns. We have lately received a letter from Mrs. Parker. O, what a spirit it breathed! When we were there she said if we could not get a minister to go with us we might keep Mr. Parker until one came, if we would only go on, and even now she has given permission for him to stay a year longer, and visit another tribe to the south. I wish I could show you her letter. You say Brother J.G. and his wife have been to Ithaca. Why did he not go when I was there? I had a good visit with Deacon and Mrs. Rolla, and a piece of a song, too, but not half enough. He sent me the "Missionary's Farewell," by Dr. Satterlee; music, by himself. Alas! my husband don't come to-night; the wind has blown so hard that I expect he has not been able to cross the river. Brother Gray is with him. I shall not feel so anxious about him on that account, so adieu for to-night. It is almost ten o'clock, and the family have all gone to rest.

I should like to tell you how the western people talk, if I had room. Their language is so singular that I could scarcely understand them, yet it was very amusing. In speaking of quantity, they say "heap of man, heap of water, she is heap sick", etc. If you ask, "How does your wife today?" "O, she is smartly better, I reckon, but she is powerful weak; she has been mighty bad. What's the matter with your eye?"

Letters

PLATTE RIVER, JUST ABOVE THE FORKS,
June 3rd, 1836.

Dear Sister Harriet and Brother Edward: — Friday eve, six o'clock. We have just encamped for the night near the bluffs over against the river. The bottoms are a soft, wet plain, and we were obliged to leave the river yesterday for the bluffs. The face of the country yesterday afternoon and today has been rolling sand bluffs, mostly barren, quite unlike what our eyes have been satiated with for weeks past. No timber nearer than the Platte, and the water tonight is very bad — got from a small ravine. We have usually had good water previous to this.

Our fuel for cooking since we left timber (no timber except on rivers) has been dried buffalo dung; we now find plenty of it and it answers a very good purpose, similar to the kind of coal used in Pennsylvania (I suppose now Harriet will make up a face at this, but if she was here she would be glad to have her supper cooked at any rate in this scarce timber country). The present time in our journey is a very important one. The hunter brought us buffalo meat yesterday for the first time. Buffalo were seen today but none have been taken. We have some for supper tonight. Husband is cooking it — no one of the company professes the art but himself. I expect it will be very good. Stop — I have so much to say to the children that I do not know in what part of my story to begin. I have very little time to write. I will first tell you what our company consists of. We are ten in number; five missionaries, three Indian boys and two young men employed to assist in packing animals.

Saturday, 4th. Good morning, H. and E. I wrote last night till supper; after that it was dark I could not see. I told you how many bipeds there was in our company last night; now for the quadrupeds: Fourteen horses, six mules and fifteen head of cattle. We milk four cows. We started with seventeen, but we have killed one calf, and the Fur Company, being out of provision, have taken one of our cows for beef. It is usually pinching times with the Company before they reach the buffalo. We have had plenty because we made ample provision at Liberty. We purchased a barrel of flour and baked enough to last us, with killing a calf or two, until we reached the buffalo.

The Fur Company is large this year; we are really a moving village — nearly 400 animals, with ours, mostly mules, and 70 men. The Fur Company have seven wagons drawn by six mules each, heavily loaded, and one cart drawn by two mules, which carries a lame man, one of the proprietors of the Company. We have two wagons in our company. Mr. and Mrs. S., husband and myself ride in one, Mr. Gray and the baggage in the other. Our Indian boys drive the cows and Dulin the horses. Young Miles leads our forward horses, four in each team. Now E., if you want to see the camp in motion, look away ahead and see first the pilot and the captain, Fitzpatrick, just before him, next the pack animals, all mules, loaded with great packs; soon after you will see the wagons, and in the rear, our company. We all cover quite a space. The pack mules always string one after the other just like Indians.

There are several gentlemen in the company who are going over the mountains for pleasure. Capt. Steward (Mr. Lee speaks of him in his journal — he went over when he did and returned) he is an Englishman and Mr. Celam. We had a few of them to tea with us last Monday evening, Capt. Fitzpatrick, Stewart, Major Harris and Celam.

I wish I could describe to you how we live so that you can realize it. Our manner of living is far preferable to any in the States. I never was so contented and happy before, neither have I enjoyed such health for years. In the morning as soon as the day breaks the first that we hear is the words, "Arise! Arise!"—then the mules set up such a noise as you never heard, which puts the whole camp in motion. We encamp in a large ring, baggage and men, tents and wagons on the outside, and all the animals except the cows, which are fastened to pickets, within the circle. This arrangement is to accommodate the guard, who stand regularly every night and day, also when we are in motion, to protect our animals from the approach of Indians, who would steal them. As I said, the mules' noise brings every man on his feet to loose them and turn them out to feed.

Now, H. and E., you must think it very hard to have to get up so early after sleeping on the soft ground, when you find it hard work to open your eyes at seven o'clock. Just think of me—every morning at the word, "Arise!" we all spring. While the horses are feeding we get breakfast in a hurry and eat it. By this time the words, "Catch up! Catch up," ring through the camp for moving. We are ready to start usually at six, travel till eleven, encamp, rest and feed, and start again about two; travel until six, or before, if we come to a good tavern, then encamp for the night.

Since we have been in the prairie we have done all our cooking. When we left Liberty we expected to take bread to last us part of the way, but could not get enough to carry us any distance. We found it awkward work to bake out of doors at first, but we have become so accustomed to it now we do it very easily.

Tell mother I am a very good housekeeper on the prairie. I wish she could just take a peep at us while we are sitting at our meals. Our table is the ground, our table-cloth is an India-rubber cloth used when it rains as a cloak; our dishes are made of tin—basins for teacups, iron spoons and plates, each of us, and several pans for milk and to put our meat in when we wish to set it on the table. Each one carries his own knife in his scabbard, and it is always ready to use. When the table things are spread, after making our own forks or sticks and helping ourselves to chairs, we gather around the table. Husband always provides my seat, and in a way that you would laugh to see. It is the fashion of all this country to imitate the Turks. Messrs. Dunbar and Allis have supped with us, and they do the same. We take a blanket and lay down by the table, and those whose joints will let them follow the fashion; others take out some of the baggage (I suppose you know that there is no stones in this country' not a stone have I seen of any size on the prairie). For my part I fix myself as gracefully as I can, sometimes on a blanket, sometimes on a box, just as it is convenient. Let me assure you of this, we relish our food none the less for sitting on the ground while eating. We have tea and a plenty of milk, which is a luxury in this country. Our milk has assisted us very much in making our bread since we have been journeying. While the Fur Company has felt the want of food, our milk has been of great service to us; but it was considerable work for us to supply ten persons with bread three times a day. We are done using it now. What little flour we have left we shall preserve for thickening our broth, which is excellent. I never saw any thing like buffalo meat to satisfy hunger. We do not want any thing else with it. I have eaten three meals of it and it relishes well. Supper and breakfast we eat in our tent. We do not pitch it at noon. Have worship immediately after supper and breakfast.

Noon.—The face of the country today has been like that of yesterday. We are now about 30 miles above the forks, and leaving the bluffs for the river. We have seen wonders this forenoon. Herds of buffalo hove in sight; one, a bull, crossed our trail and ran upon the bluffs near the rear of the camp. We took the trouble to chase him so as to have a near view. Sister Spalding and myself got out of the wagon and ran upon the bluff to see him. This band was quite willing to gratify our curiosity, seeing it was the first. Several have been killed this forenoon. The Company keep a man out all the time to hunt for the camp.

Edward, if I write much more in this way I do not know as you can read it without great difficutly. I could tell you much more, but as we are all ready to move again, so farewell for the present. I wish you were all here with us going to the dear Indians. I have become very much attached to Richard Sak-ah-too-ah. 'T is the one you saw at our wedding; he calls me mother; I love to teach him—to take care of him, and hear them talk. There are five Nez Perces in the company, and when they are together they chatter finely. Samuel Temoni, the oldest one, has just come into the camp with the skin and some of the meat of a buffalo which he has killed himself. He started this forenoon of his own accord. It is what they like dearly, to hunt buffalo. So long as we have him with us we shall be supplied with meat.

I am now writing backwards. Monday morning.—I begun to say something here that I could not finish. Now the man from the mountains has come who will take this to the office. I have commenced one to sister Hull which I should like to send this time if I could finish it. We have just met him and we have stopped our wagons to write a little. Give my love to all. I have not told you half of what I want to. We are all in health this morning and making rapid progress in our journey. By the 4th of July our captain intends to be at the place where Mr. Parker and husband parted last fall. We are a month earlier passing here than they were last spring. Husband has begun a letter to pa and ma, and since he has cut his finger so it troubles him to write to the rest. As this is done in a hurry I don't know if you can read it. Tell mother that if I had looked the world over I could not have found one more careful and better qualified to transport a female such a distance. Husband says, "stop."

Farewell to all.

NARCISSA PRENTISS.

Letters

ON PLATTE RIVER, 30 MILES ABOVE THE FORKS,
June 4th, 1836.

Dear Father and Mother Prentiss: — You will be anxious to hear from us at this distance and learn our situation and progress. We have been greatly blest thus far on our journey. We have had various trials, it is true, but they have mostly been overruled for our good. Narcissa's health is much improved from what it was when she left N.Y. We failed of going from Liberty to Bellevue as was expected in the Fur Co's. steamboat. We were waiting at Liberty for the boat for some time and though we would go on with our cattle, horses and wagons, and let Mr. Allis from the Pawnee agency stay with the ladies and go on the boat. Accordingly Messrs. Spalding and Gray went on and I was to join them at Cantonment Leavenworth. In the meantime Mrs. Saterlee died and the boat passed but refused to stop for us. Mr. Spalding wrote me he would wait eight miles the other side of garrison until I came up, so that when the boat passed I did not send an express as I otherwise should have done, but proceeded to hire a team to take us on; but when we arrived at the garrison he had crossed the river and gone directly on for Bellevue and had been gone for three days, which caused me to have to send an express for him, which did not overtake him until they were within forty miles of the Platte. I followed with the women and baggage, with a hired team. We met our teams the fourth day on their return. From that on we were greatly favored with fair weather, never having to encounter any rainstorm or serious shower. We have not been once wet even to this time, and we are now beyond where the rains fall much in summer.

We had several days delay from my going ahead to see Maj. Dougherty's brother, who was very sick and sent for me when he learned I was coming. It was Sabbath and we were within 18 miles of the Otto Agency, which is on the Platte, where Mr. Dougherty lives. On Monday I sent the man, who came for me, after the party, and I went to see Fitzpatrick, the leader of the Fur caravan, with whom we were to travel. I found him encamped ready for a start on Thursday morning, about twenty-five miles from the Otto Agency. When I returned our party had not arrived and did not come until Wednesday, the man who was to pilot them having lost his way.

We had great difficulty in crossing the Platte which, together with repairs to our wagons, detained us until Saturday noon, May 21st, and he (Fitzpatrick) had been gone from Sunday. We felt much doubt about overtaking them, but we pushed on, and after ferrying the Horn in a skin boat and making a very difficult ford of the Loup, we overtook the Company at a few miles below the Pawnee villages on Wednesday evening. We then felt that we had been signally blessed, thanked God and took courage. We felt it had been of great service to us that we had been disappointed in these several particulars, particularly as it tested the ability of our ladies to journey in this way. We have since made good progress every day, and are now every way well situated, having plenty of good buffalo meat and the cordial co-operation of the company with whom we are journeying.

June 6th. — We have just met the men by whom we can send letters and have to close without farther particulars or ceremony.

With Christian regards to your family, farewell.

Yours affectionately,

MARCUS WHITMAN.

Narcissa Whitman

PLATTE RIVER, SOUTH SIDE, SIX DAYS ABOVE THE FORT LARAMIE FORK, NEAR THE FOOT OF THE ROCKY MOUNTAINS, June 27, 1836.

Dear Brother and Sister Whitman: — We were in perplexity when we left Liberty, but it has been overruled for good. I wrote Mother Loomis from the Otoe Agency. We were in still greater perplexity there, while crossing our baggage. Husband became so completely exhausted with swimming the river on Thursday, May 9th, that it was with difficulty he made the shore the last time. Mr. Spalding was sick, our two hired men were good for nothing; we could not obtain much assistance from the Otoes, for they were away from the village; we had but one canoe, made of skins, and that partly eaten by the dogs the night before. We got everything over by Friday night. We did not get ready to start until Saturday afternoon. By this time the [American Fur] company had four and a half days the advance of us. It seemed scarcely possible for us to overtake them, we having two more difficult streams to pass, before they would pass the Pawnee villages. Beyond there we dare not venture more than one day. We were at a stand; but with the advice of brethren Merrill and Dunbar—missionaries among the Pawnees—after a concert of prayer on the subject, we decided to start and go as far as it would be prudent for us. Brother Dunbar kindly consented to become our pilot, until we could get another. He started with us and came as far as the Elkhorn river, then the man Major Dougherty sent for, for us, came up, and Mr. Dunbar returned. We had passed the river on Monday morning and taken down the rope, when our pilot and his Indian came up. It was with difficulty we crossed him and returned Mr. Dunbar. While on the opposite shore, just ready to leave us, he called to us to receive his parting advice, with a word of caution which will never be forgotten. Our visit with him and Brother Merrill's family was indeed refreshing to our thirsty spirits—kindred spirits rejoicing in the self denials and labors of missionary life.

The next day, in the morning, we met a large party of Pawnees going to the fort to receive their annuities. They seemed to be very much surprised and pleased to see white females; many of them had never seen any before. They are a noble Indian—large, athletic forms, dignified countenances, bespeaking an immortal existence within. When we had said what we wished to them, we hurried on, and arrived at the Elkhorn in time to cross all our effects.

Here I must tell you how much good Richard, John and Samuel—Pacific coast Indian boys whom Dr. Whitman had taken to New York with him the year before—did us. They do the most of driving the cattle and loose horses. Occasionally husband and myself would ride with them as company and encouragement. They came up to the river before us, and seeing a skin canoe on the opposite side, they stripped themselves, wound their shirts around their heads, and swam over and back again with the canoe by the time we came up. We stretched a rope across the river and pulled the goods over in the canoe without much difficulty.

Monday and Tuesday we made hard drives—Tuesday especially. We attempted to reach the Loup Fork that night, and a part of us succeeded. Those in the wagons drove there by 11 o'clock, but it was too much for the cattle. There was no water or feed short of this. We rode with Richard and John until 9 o'clock, and were all very much fatigued. Richard proposed to us to go on and he and John would stay on the prairie with the cattle, and drive them in in the morning. We did not like to leave them, and so we concluded to stay. Husband had a cup tied to his saddle, in which he milked what we wanted to drink; this was our supper. Our saddle blankets, with our India rubber cloaks, were our beds. Having offered up our thanksgiving for the blessings of the day and seeking protection for the night, we committed ourselves to rest. We awoke in the morning much refreshed and rode into camp before breakfast—five miles. The Fur Company was on the opposite side of the river, which we forded, and, without unloading our wagon much, were ready to move again about noon. We wished to be with the company when they passed the Pawnee village. This obliged us to make a day's drive to the camp in half a day, which was too bad for our horses. We did not reach them until 1 o'clock at night.

The next day we passed all their villages. We, especially, were visited by them both at noon and at night; we ladies were such a curiosity to them. They would come and stand around our tent, peep in, and grin in their astonishment to see such looking objects.

Since we came up with the camp, I rode in the wagons most of the way to the Black Hills. It is astonishing how well we get along with our wagons where there are no roads. I think I may say it is easier traveling here than on any turnpike in the States.

On the way to the buffalo country we had to bake bread for ten persons. It was difficult at first, as we did not understand working out-doors; but we became accustomed to it, so that it became quite easy. June found us ready to receive our first taste of buffalo. Since that time I have had but little to do with cooking. Not one in our number relishes buffalo meat as well as my husband and I. He has a different way for cooking every piece of meat. I believe Mother Loomis would give up to him if she were here. We have had no bread since. We have meat and tea in the morn, and tea and meat at noon. All our variety consists of the different ways of cooking. I relish it well and it agrees with me. My health is excellent. So long as I have buffalo meat I do not wish anything else. Sister Spaulding is affected by it considerably—has been quite sick.

We feel that the Lord has blessed us beyond our most sanguine expectations. We wish our friends at home to unite with us in thanksgiving and praise for His great mercies to us. We are a month earlier this year than husband was last, and the company wish to be at Rendezvous by the 4th of July. We have just crossed the river and shall leave here tomorrow morning.

Now, Sister Julia, between you and me, I just want to tell you how much trouble I have had with Marcus, two or three weeks past. He was under the impression that we had too much baggage, and could not think of anything so easy to be dispensed with as his own wearing apparel—those shirts the ladies made him just before he left home, his black suit and overcoat—these were the condemned articles. Sell them he must, as soon as he gets to the fort. But first I would not believe him in earnest. All the reasons I could bring were of no avail—he still said he must get rid of them. I told him to sell all of mine, too; I could do without them better than he could. Indeed, I did not wish to dress unless he could. I finally said that I would write and get Sister Julia to plead for me, for I knew you would not like to have him sell them, better than I should. This was enough; he knew it would not do to act contrary to her wishes, and said no more about it.

July 16th. — When I wrote this letter I expected to send it immediately, but we did not meet the party expected, and have had no opportunity since. We are now at the Rocky Mountains, at the encampment of Messrs. McLeod and McKay, expecting to leave on Monday morning for Walla Walla. It seems a special favor that that company has come to Rendezvous this season; for otherwise we would have had to have gone with the Indians a difficult route, and so slow that we should have been late at Walla Walla, and not have had the time we wanted to make preparations for winter. Husband has written the particulars of our arrival, meeting the Indians, etc., to Brother Henry.

One particular I will mention, which he did not. As soon as I alighted from my horse, I was met by a company of matrons, native women one after another shaking hands and saluting me with a most hearty kiss. This was unexpected and affected me very much. They gave Sister Spalding the same salutation. After we had been seated awhile in the midst of the gazing throng, one of the chiefs, whom we had seen before, came with his wife and very politely introduced her to us. They say they all like us very much, and thank God that they have seen us, and that we have come to live with them.

It was truly pleasing to see the meeting of Richard and John with their friends. Richard was affected to tears. His father is not here, but several of his tribe and brethren are. When they met each took off his hat and shook hands, as respectfully as in civilized life. Richard does not give up the idea of again seeing Rushville.

Your affection sister,
NARCISSA.

July 18th. — Under the protection of Mr. McLeod and his company we left the Rendezvous and came ten miles in a southwesterly direction. The Flatheads and some of the Snake Indians accompanied us a short distance. We make but one camp a day.

On the 22nd we had a tedious ride, as we traveled till half-past four P.M. I thought of mother's bread, as a child would, but did not find it on the table, I should relish it extremely well; have been living on buffalo meat until I am cloyed with it.

Have been in a peaceful state of mind all day. Had a freedom in prayer for my beloved parents; blessed privilege that such a sinner as I may have access to a mercy seat, through such a Saviour as Jesus Christ. It is good to feel that he is all I want, and all my righteousness; and if I had ten thousand lives I would give them all for him. I long to be more like him — to possess more of his meek spirit.

25th. — Came fifteen miles to-day; encamped on Smith's creek, a small branch of Bear creek. The ride has been very mountainous — paths winding on the sides of steep mountains. In some places the path is so narrow as scarcely to afford room for the animal to place his foot. One after another we pass along with cautious step. Passed a creek on which was a fine bunch of gooseberries, nearly ripe.

Husband has had a tedious time with the wagon to-day. It got stuck in the creek this morning when crossing, and he was obliged to wade considerably in getting it out. After that, in going between the mountains, on the side of one, so steep that it was difficult for horses pass, the wagon was upset twice; did not wonder at this at all; it was a greater wonder that it was not turning somersaults continually. It is not very grateful to my feelings to see him wearing out with such excessive fatigue, as I am obliged to. He is not as fleshy as he was last winter. All the most difficult part of the way he has walked, in laborious attempts to take the wagon. Ma knows what my feelings are. [This was the first wagon that ever came west of Fort Hall.]

26th. — Did not move camp today. Mr. McKay has been preparing to send out trappers from this place. Husband has been sick to-day, and so lame with the rheumatism as to be scarcely able to move. It is a great privilege that we can lie still to-day on his account, for he needs rest.

27th. — Had quite a level route to-day — came down Bear river. Mr. McKay sent off about thirty of his men as trappers to-day. Several lodges of Indians also left us to go in another direction, and we expect more to leave us to-morrow. They wish to go a different route from Mr. McLeod, and desire us to go with them; but it would be more difficult and lengthy than Mr. McLeod's. We are still in a dangerous country; but our company is large enough for safety. Our cattle endure the journey remarkably well. They supply us with sufficient milk for our tea and coffee, which is indeed a luxury. We are obliged to shoe some of them because of sore feet. Have seen no buffalo since we left Rendezvous. Have had no game of any kind except a few messes of antelope, which an Indian gave us. We have plenty of dried buffalo meat, which we have purchased from the Indians — and dry it is for me. It appears so filthy! I can scarcely eat it; but it keeps us alive, and we ought to be thankful for it. We have had a few meals of fresh fish, also, which we relished well, and have the prospect of obtaining plenty in one or two weeks more. Have found no berries; neither have I found any of Ma's bread (Girls, do not waste the bread; if you knew how well I should relish even the dryest morsel, you would save every piece carefully.) Do not think I regret coming. No, far from it; I would not go back for a world. I am contented and happy, notwithstanding I sometimes get very hungry and weary. Have six week's steady journey before us. Feel sometimes as if it were a long time to be traveling. Long for rest, but must not murmur.

Feel to pity the poor Indian women, who are continually traveling in this manner during their lives, and know no other comfort. They do all the work and are the complete slaves of their husbands. I am making some little progress in their language; long to be able to converse with them about the Saviour.

28th. — Very mountainous all the way to-day; came over another ridge; rode from 8 A.M. to 2 P.M. We thought yesterday the Indians were all going to leave us, except two or three; but not one has. They fear to, on account of the Blackfeet tribe, who would destroy them all, if they could. One of the axle-trees of the wagon broke to-day; was a little rejoiced, for we were in hopes they would leave it, and have no more trouble with it. Our rejoicing was in vain for they are making a cart of the back wheels, this afternoon, and lashing the fore wheels to it—intending to take it through in some shape or other. They are so resolute and untiring in their efforts they will probably succeed.

Had some fresh fish for breakfast and some antelope for supper, sent us by Mr. McLeod and other friends in camp. Thus the Lord provides, and smoothes all our ways for us, giving us strength.

July 29th.—Mr. Gray was quite sick this morning and inclined to fall behind. Husband and I rode with him about two hours and a half, soon after which he gave out entirely. I was sent on, and soon after husband left him to come and get the cart; but I overtook an Indian, who went back and soon met husband, and both returned to Mr. Gray. The Indian helped him on his horse, got on behind him, supported him in his arms and in this manner slowly came into camp. This was welcome relief, and all rejoiced to see them come in; for some of us had been riding seven hours, others eight, without any nourishment.

The next sheet of the journal is missing, which contains the account of their arrival at Fort Hall, where, she says, We were hospitably entertained by Captain Thing, who keeps the fort. It was built by Captain Wyeth, a gentleman from Boston, whom we saw at Rendezvous on his way east. Our dinner consisted of dry buffalo meat, turnips and fried bread, which was a luxury. Mountain bread is simply coarse flour and water mixed and roasted or fried in buffalo grease. To one who has had nothing but meat for a long time, this relishes well. For tea we had the same, with the addition of some stewed service berries.

The buildings of the fort are made of hewed logs, with roofs covered with mud brick, chimneys and fireplaces also being built of the same; no windows, except a square hole in the roof, and in the bastion a few port holes large enough for guns only. The buildings were all enclosed in a strong log wall. This affords them a place of safety when attacked by hostile Indians, as they frequently are, the fort being in the Blackfeet country.

Since dinner we visited the garden and corn fields. The turnips in the garden appeared thrifty—the tops very large and tall, but the roots small. The peas looked small; but most of them had been gathered by the mice. Saw a few onions, that were going to seed, which looked quite natural. This was all the garden contained. He told us his own did extremely well until the 8th of June, when the frost of one night completely prostrated it. It has since came up again, but does not look as well as it did before. This is their first attempt at cultivation.

The buildings at Fort William, on Laramie Fork of the Platte, are made the same, but are larger and more finished than here. Here we have stools to sit on—there we had very comfortable chairs, bottomed with buffalo skin. Thus you see we have a house of entertainment almost or quite as often as Christian of the Pilgrim's Progress did. We expect one more before we get to Walla Walla; that is Snake Fort [Boise], belonging to Mr. McKay, who is journeying with us.

From this on our company will be small. The Indians all leave us to-day except one or two who go with us to assist in driving the cattle—Kentuck, who went with Mr. Parker last year, and the chief, Rottenbelly. The whole tribe are exceedingly anxious to have us go with them. They use every argument they can invent to prevail on us to do so—and not only argument but strategy. We all thing it not best; we are very much fatigued, and wish to get through as soon as possible. To go with them would take us two months or more, when now we expect to go to Walla Walla in twenty-five days. When we get there rest will be sweet to us; so will it be to the Christian when he gets to Heaven. Will father and mother get there before I do? If so, then they will be ready to greet me on the threshold. Here we have raised our Ebenezer saying, "Hitherto the Lord hath helped us." Now we leave it and pass on. Our animals are nearly ready. It is now half-past two and we expect to go but a short distance and encamp.

Aug. 5th.—Morn; came all of ten miles last evening, and did not arrive here till after dark. Mr. McLeod and his company started earlier than we did, intending to come but a little way. We could not get ready to come with him, and the man who piloted us led us wrong—much out of the way. Those on whom we depended to drive cattle disappointed us. Husband and myself fell in behind them to assist John Alts, who was alone with them. This made us later into camp than the rest of our company. We came through several swamps, and all the last part of the way we were so swarmed with mosquitoes as to be scarcely able to see—especially while crossing the Port Neuf, which we did, just before coming into camp. It is the widest river I have forded on horseback. It seemed the cows would run mad for the mosquitoes; we could scarcely get them along. Mr. McLeod met us and invited us to tea, which was a great favor. Thus blessings gather thick around us. We have been in the mountains so long we find the scenery of this valley very grateful to the eye—a large stream on my right and one on my left, skirted with timber. At Fort Hall was our first sight of Snake river. We shall follow the south side of it for many days. We have passed many places where the soil is good, and would be fertile if there were frequent rains; but usually the country is barren, and would be a sandy desert were it not for the sage brush.

Eve. We passed the American Falls on Snake river just after dinner. The roar of the water is heard at a considerabale distance. We stopped during the greatest heat for rest and dinner. Now that the Indians are no longer with us we shall expect to make two camps. I expect this to be a great mercy to us weak females, for it was more than we could well endure to travel during the heat of the day without refreshment.

Aug. 6th.—Route very bad and difficult to-day. We crossed a small stream full of falls. The only pass where we could cross was just on the edge of rocks above one of the falls. While the pack animals were crossing, both ours and the company's, there was such a rush as to crowd two of our horses over the falls, both packed with dried meat. It was with great difficulty they were got out, one of them having been nearly an hour much to his injury. We have a little rice to eat with our dry meat, given us by Mr. McLeod, which makes it relish quite well.

Aug. 7th.—Sabbath; came fifteen miles and camped at a fine place, with plenty of good grass for our weary animals, Thus are blessings so mingled that it seems as if there was nothing else but mercy and blessings all the way. Was there ever a journey like this performed where the sustaining hand of God has been so manifest every morning. Surely the children of Israel could not have been more sensible of the pillar of fire by night than we have been of that hand that has led us thus safely on. God had heard prayer in our behalf, and even now while I am writing on this holy day is the sweet incense of prayer ascending before the throne of Heavenly grace. Nor are we forgotten by our beloved churches, at home in the prayers of the Sanctuary, we are too sensible of its blessed effects to believe otherwise; and oh! how comforting is this thought to the heart of the missionary. We love to think and talk of home with such feelings as these. It warms our hearts and strengthens and encourages us in the work of our beloved Master, and make our journeyings easy.

Aug. 8th, Monday.—Snake river. We have an excellent camp ground to-night; plenty of feed for our horses and cattle. We think it remarkable that our cattle should endure the journey as well as they do. We have two suckling calves that appear to be in very good spirits; they suffer some from sore feet—otherwise they have come on well and will go through. Have come eighteen miles to-day and have taken it so deliberately that it has been easy for us. The hunters came in last night well loaded; they had been in the mountains two days after game and killed three elk and two antelope. This is the first elk meat we have had, and it is the last opportunity we expect to have of taking any more game. We are told that many have traveled the whole distance from Rendezvous to Walla Walla without any fresh meat. We think ours will last until we reach the salmon fishing at Snake Falls. Thus we are well provided for contrary to our expectations. Mr. McLeod has excellent hunters; this is the reason why we live so well. There is but little game and that is found at a great distance from the route.

11th.—Tuesday and Wednesday have been tedious days, both for man and beast—lengthy marches without water; rocky and sandy. Had a present to-night of a fresh salmon; also a plate of fried cakes from Mr. McLeod. (Girls, if you wish to know how they taste you can have pleasure by taking a little flour and water, make some dough, and roll it thin, cut it into square blocks, then take some beef fat and fry them. You need not put either salt or pearlash in your dough.) Believe me, I relish them as well as I ever did any made at home.

12th.—Friday; raised camp this morning at sunrise and came two hours ride to the salmon fishery. Found a few lodges of Diggers, of the Snake tribe, so called because they live on roots during winter, who had just commenced fishing. Obtained some and boiled it for our breakfast. Find it good eating; had we been a few days earlier we should not have been able to obtain any fish, for they had but just come up. They never go higher than these falls and come here every season.

Friday eve.—Dear Harriet, the little trunk you gave me has come with me so far, and now I must leave it here alone. Poor little trunk, I am sorry to leave thee; thou must abide here alone, and no more by thy presence remind me of my dear Harriet.

Twenty miles below the falls on Snake river this shall be thy place of rest. Farewell, little trunk, I thank thee for thy faithful services, and that I have been cheered by thy presence so long. Thus we scatter as we go along. The hills are so steep and rocky that husband thought it best to lighten the wagon as much as possible and take nothing but the wheels, leaving the box with my trunk. I regret leaving anything that came from home, especially that trunk, but it is best. It would have been better for me not to have attempted to bring any baggage whatever, only what was necessary to use on the way. It costs so much labor, besides the expense of animals. If I were to make the journey again I would make quite different preparations. To pack and unpack so many times, and cross so many streams where the packs frequently get wet, requires no small amount of labor, besides the injury of the articles. Our books, what few we have, have been wet several times. In going from Elmira to Williamsport this trunk fell into the creek and wet all my books, and Richard's, too, several times. The sleigh box came off and all of us came near a wetting likewise. The custom of the country is to possess nothing, and then you will lose nothing while traveling. Farewell for the present.

13th. — Saturday; Dear Harriet, Mr. McKay has asked the privilege of taking the little trunk along, so that my soliloquy about it last night was for naught. However, it will do me no good, it may him.

We have come fifteen miles and have had the worst route in all the journey for the cart. We might have had a better one but for being misled by some of the company who started out before the leaders. It was two o'clock before we came into camp.

They were preparing to cross Snake river. The river is divided by two islands into three branches, and is fordable. The packs are placed upon the tops of the highest horses and in this way we crossed without wetting. Two of the tallest horses were selected to carry Mrs. Spalding and myself over. Mr. McLeod gave me his and rode mine. The last branch we rode as much as half a mile in crossing and against the current, too, which made it hard for the horses, the water being up to their sides. Husband had considerable difficulty in crossing the cart. Both cart and mules were turned upside down in the river and entangled in the harness. The mules would have been drowned but for a desperate struggle to get them ashore. Then after putting two of the strongest horses before the cart, and two men swimming behind to steady it, they succeeded in getting it across. I once thought that crossing streams would be the most dreaded part of the journey. I can now cross the most difficult stream without the least fear. There is one manner of crossing which husband has tried but I have not, neither do I wish to. Take an elk skin and stretch it over you, spreading yourself out as much as possible, then let the Indian women carefully put you on the water and with a cord in the mouth they will swim and draw you over. Edward, how do you think you would like to travel in this way?

15th. — Yesterday Mr. McLeod with most of his men left us, wishing to hasten his arrival at Snake Fort, leaving us a pilot and his weakest animals to come in with us at our leisure. This is a relief to us, as it is difficult to bring our cattle up to the speed they wish to travel. We passed the hot springs just before noon, which was quite a curiosity. Boiled a bit of dry salmon in one of them in five minutes.

16th. — This eve found plenty of berries called hawthorn on the stream where we have encamped. They are large as a cherry and taste much like a mealy sweet apple. Our route on this side of Snake river is less hilly and difficult than on the south side, and said to be two days shorter.

19th. — Arrived at Snake Fort, Boise, about noon. It is situated on Bigwood river, so called because the timber is larger than any to be seen this side of the mountains. It consists chiefly of cotton wood and is small compared with timber in the states. Snake Fort is owned and built by Mr. Thomas McKay, one of our company, whom we expect to leave here. He, with Mr. McLeod, gave us a hearty welcome; dined with them. Mr. McLeod was ready to leave on the morrow, but said he would stay a day longer to give us the opportunity of doing some necessary work, for which we were thankful.

20th. — Saturday. Last night I put my clothes in water and this morning finished washing before breakfast. This is the third time I have washed since I left home — once at Fort Williams and once at Rendezvous. Mr. McLeod called this evening to see if we were ready to leave. He observed we had been so engaged in labor as to have no time for rest, and proposed for ourselves to remain over Sabbath. This I can assure you was a favor for which we can never be too thankful, for our souls need the rest of the Sabbath as well as our bodies.

21st. — Sabbath. Rich with heavenly blessings has the day of rest been to my soul. Mr. Spalding was invited to preach in the Fort at 11 o'clock. The theme was the character of the blessed Savior. All listened with good attention.

22d. — Left the Fort yesterday; came a short distance to the crossing of Snake river, crossed and encamped for the night. The river had three branches, divided by islands, as it was when we crossed before. The first and second places were very deep, but we had no difficulty in crossing on horseback. The third was deeper still; we dare not venture horseback. This being a fishing post of the Indians, we easily found a canoe, made of rushes and willows, on which we placed ourselves and our saddles (Sister Spalding and myself), when two Indians on horseback, each with a rope attached to the canoe, towed us over. (O! if father and mother and the girls could have seen us in our snug little canoe, floating on the water.) We were favorites of the company. No one else was priviledged with a ride on it. I wish I could give you a correct idea of this little bark. It is simply bunches of rushes tied together, and attached to a frame made of a few sticks of small willows. It was just large enough to hold us and our saddles. Our baggage was transported on the top of our tallest horses, without wetting.

As for the wagon, it is left at the Fort, and I have nothing to say about crossing it at this time. Five of our cattle were left there also, to be exchanged for others at Walla Walla. Perhaps you will wonder why we have left the wagon, having taken it so nearly through. Our animals were failing, and the route in crossing the Blue Mountains is said to be impassable for it. We have the prospect of obtaining one in exchange at

Vancouver. If we do not we shall send for it, when we have been to so much labor in getting it thus far. It is a useful article in the country.

Now, for Edward's amusement, and that he may know how to do when he comes over the Rocky Mountains, I will tell how we got the cattle over the rivers. Our two Indian boys, Richard and John, have had the chief management of driving them all the way, and are to be commended for the patience they have manifested. They have had some one or two to help usually, but none so steady drivers as themselves. When a stream is to be crossed, where it is necessary for the animals to swim, Richard comes to my husband and asks if he may go over with his horse and clothes, and then come back after the cows. Having obtained consent he rides over, accompanied by his fellow drivers, all stripped to the shirt. Then they return with their horses, if the stream is wide and difficult. If not they leave their horses, tie their shifts over their heads, swim back, collect the cows and drive them through, all swimming after them. If the stream is very wide, and they return with their horses, they drive them swimming on the horses behind them. This saves them from the too great fatigue of swimming the river twice. They love to swim, as they love to eat, and by doing so have saved me many an anxious feeling, for the relief it has given my husband many times. In this case all the horses and mules were driven across likewise. Usually the best Indian swimmer was selected and mounted the horse that was good for leading to go before the animals as a guide, while many others swim after them to drive them over. When once under way, such a snorting and halloaing you never heard. At the same time you can see nothing save so many heads floating upon the water. Soon they gain the opposite shore, triumphantly ascend its banks, shake themselves, and retire to their accustomed employment.

26th. — Friday. On account of our worn out cattle and horses, it was thought best to separate from Mr. McLeod's party, at least some of us, and travel more deliberately. Two mules and a horse have almost entirely given out. It is necessary that some of our party go to Vancouver immediately for supplies and see Mr. Parker before he leaves. It was thought best for my husband and Mr. Gray to go. As Mr. McLeod intended to make but a day's stop at Walla Walla, we came on with him, leaving Mr. and Mrs. Spalding, the hired men, with most of our baggage, and the Nez Perce chief, Rottenbelly, to pilot them in. We parted from them about 3 o'clock and came as far as the Lone Tree. The place called Lone Tree is a beautiful valley in the region of Powder river, in the center of which is a solitary tree, quite large, but the side of which travellers usually stop and refresh themselves. We left our tent for Mrs. Spalding, as we expect to be out only a few nights, while she might be out many. Mr. McLeod kindly offered his for my use and when I arrived in camp found it pitched and in readiness for me. This was a great favor as the wind blew quite hard and the prospect was for a cool night.

August 27th. — Came in sight of the hill that leads to the Grande Ronde. This morning Mr. McLeod remained behind in pursuit of game, and did not come into camp until we had made a long nooning, although we had begun to feel a little concerned about him, yet about 3 o'clock he came into camp loaded with wild ducks, having taken twenty-two. Now, mother, he had just, as he always did during the whole journey, sent over nine of them. Here also, Richard caught fresh salmon, which made us another good meal, and if we had been out of provisions we might have made dinner upon the fresh-water clams, for the river was full of them.

Girls, how do you think we manage to rest ourselves every noon, having no house to shelter us from the scorching heat, or sofa on which to recline? Perhaps you think we always encamp in the shade of some thick wood. Such a sight I have not seen, lo, these many weeks. If we can find a few small willows or a single lone tree, we think ourselves amply provided for. But often our camping places are in some open plain and frequently a sand plain, but even here is rest and comfort. My husband, who is one of the best the world ever knew, is always ready to provide a comfortable shade, with one of our saddle-blankets spread upon some willows or sticks placed in the ground. Our saddles, fishamores and the other blankets placed upon the ground constitute our sofa where we recline and rest until dinner is ready. How do you think you would like this? Would you not think a seat by mother, in some cool room preferable? Sometimes my wicked heart has been disposed to murmur, thinking I should have no rest from the heat when we stopped, but I have always been reproved for it by the comfort and rest received. Under the circumstances I have never wished to go back. Such a thought never finds a place in my heart. "The Lord is better to us than our fears." I always find it so.

28th. — This morning lingered with husband on the top of the hill that overlooks the Grande Ronde, for berries until we were some distance behind camp. We have now no distressing apprehensions the moment we are out of sight of the camp, for we have entirely passed the dangerous country. I always enjoy riding alone with him, especially when we talk about home friends. It is then the tedious hours are sweetly decoyed away.

We descend a very steep hill in coming into Grande Ronde, at the foot of which is a beautiful cluster of pitch and spruce pine trees, but no white pine like that I have been accustomed to see at home. Grande Ronde is indeed a beautiful place. It is a circular plain, surrounded by lofty mountains, and has a beautiful stream coursing through it, skirted with quite large timber. The scenery while passing through it is quite delightful in some places and the soil rich; in other places we find the white sand and sedge, as usual, so common to this country. We nooned upon Grande Ronde river.

The camas grows here in abundance, and it is the principal resort of the Cayuses and many other tribes, to obtain it, as they are very fond of it. It resembles an onion in shape and color, when cooked is very sweet and tastes like a fig. Their manner of cooking them is very curious: They dig a hole in the ground, throw in a heap of stones, heat them to a red heat, cover them with green grass, upon which they put the camas, and cover the whole with earth. When taken out it is black. This is the chief food of many tribes during winter.

After dinner we left the plain and ascended the Blue Mountains. Here a new and pleasing scene presented itself—mountains covered with timber, through which we rode all the afternoon; a very agreeable change. The scenery reminded me of the hills in my native county of Steuben.

29th. — Had a combination of the same scenery as yesterday afternoon. Rode over many logs and obstructions that we had not found since we left the states. Here I frequently met old acquaintances in the trees and flowers, and was not a little delighted; indeed, I do not know as I was ever so much affected with any scenery in my life. The singing of birds, the echo of voices of my fellow travelers, as they were scattered through the woods, all had a strong resemblance to bygone days. But this scenery was of short duration — only one day.

Before noon we began to descend one of the most terrible mountains for steepness and length I have yet seen. It was like winding stairs in its descent, and in some places almost perpendicular. The horses appeared to dread the hill as much as we did. They would turn and wind around in a zigzag manner all the way down. The men usually walked, but I could not get permission to, neither did I desire it much.

We had no sooner gained the foot of this mountain than another more steep and dreadful was before us. After dinner and rest we descended it. Mount Pleasant, in Prattsburg, would not compare with these Mount Terribles. Our ride this afternoon exceeded anything we have had yet, and what rendered it the more aggravating was the fact that the path all the way was very stony, resembling a newly macadamized road. Our horses' feet were very tender, all unshod, so that we could not make the progress we wished. The mountain in many places was covered with this black broken basalt. We were very late in making camp to-night. After ascending the mountain we kept upon the main divide until sunset, looking in vain for water and a camping place. While upon this elevation we had a view of the Valley of the Columbia River. It was beautiful. Just as we gained the highest elevation and began to descend the sun was dipping his disk behind the western horizon. Beyond the valley we could see too distinct mountains — Mount Hood and Mount St. Helens. These lofty peaks were of a conical form, separated from each other by a considerable distance. Behind the former the sun was hiding part of his rays, which gave us a more distinct view of this gigantic cone. The beauty of this extensive valley contrasted well with the rolling mountains behind us, and at this hour of twilight was enchanting and quite diverted my mind from the fatigue under which I was laboring. We had yet to descend a hill as long, but not as steep or as stony as the other. By this time our horses were in haste to be in camp, as well as ourselves, and mine made such lengthy strides in descending that it shook my sides surprisingly. It was dark when we got into camp, but the tent was ready for me, and tea also, for Mr. McLeod invited us to sup with him.

Dearest mother, let me tell you how I am sustained of the Lord in all this journey. For two or three days past I have felt weak, restless and scarcely able to sit on my horse — yesterday in particular. But see how I have been diverted by the scenery, and carried out of myself in conversation about home and friends. Mother will recollect what my feelings were and had been for a year previous to our leaving home. The last revival enjoyed, my visit to Onondaga and the scenes there — these I call my last impressions of home, and they are of such a character that when we converse about home these same feelings are revived and I forget that I am weary and want rest. This morning my feelings were a little peculiar; felt remarkably strong and well — so much so as to mention it — but could not see any reason why I should feel any more rested than on the morning previous. Then I began to see what a day's ride was before me, and I understood it. If I had had no better health to-day than yesterday I should have fainted under it. Then the promise appeared in full view: "As thy day, so shall thy strength be," and my soul rejoiced in God, and testifies to the truth of another evidently manifest, "Lo, I am with you always."

30th. — In consequence of the lengthy camp yesterday, and failure of animals, two of the company's men left their animals behind, with packs also. This occasioned some anxiety, lest the wolves should destroy their beaver. To-day they sent back for them, and we make but a short move to find more grass. On following the course of the stream on which we encamped last night we found cherries in abundance, and had time to stop and gather as many as we wished. They are very fine — equal to any we find in the States. When we arrived Mr. Gray had the dinner waiting for us. This afternoon the men rested and made preparations to enter Walla Walla. The men who went for the animals returned late. We all regretted this hindrance, for Mr. McLeod intended to see Walla Walla to-day and return again with a muskmelon for Mrs. Whitman (so he said.) He will go in tomorrow. It is the custom of the country to send heralds ahead to announce the arrival of a party and prepare for their reception.

31st. — Came to the Walla Walla river, within eight miles of the Fort (Wallula). Husband and I were very much exhausted with this day's lengthy ride. Most of the way was sandy with no water for many miles. When we left Mr. Spalding husband rode an Indian horse when he had never mounted before and found him a hard rider in every gait except a gallop, and slow in his movements, nor could he pace as mine did, so for the last six days we have galloped most of the way where the ground would admit of it.

September 1st, 1836 — You can better imagine our feelings this morning than we can describe them. I could not realize that the end of our long journey was so near. We arose as soon as it was light, took a cup of coffee, ate of the duck we had given us last night and dressed for Walla Walla. We started while it was yet early, for all were in haste to reach the desired haven. If you could have seen us you would have been surprised, for both man and beast appeared alike propelled by the same force. The whole company galloped almost the whole way to the Fort. The fatigues of the long journey seemed to be forgotten in the excitement of being so near the close. Soon the Fort appeared in sight and when it was announced that we were near Mr. McLeod, Mr. Pambrun, the gentleman of the house, and Mr. Townsend (a traveling naturalist) sallied forth to meet us. After usual introduction and salutation we entered the Fort and were comfortably seated in cushioned armed chairs. They were just eating breakfast as we rode up and soon we were seated at the table and treated to fresh salmon, potatoes, tea, bread and butter. What a variety, thought I. You cannot imagine what an appetite these rides in the mountains give a person. I wish some of the feeble ones in the states could have a ride over the mountains; they would say like me, victuals, even the plainest kind, never relished so well before.

After breakfast we were shown the novelties of the place. While at breakfast, however, a young rooster placed himself upon the sill of the door and crowed. Now whether it was the sight of the first white woman, or out of compliment to the company, I know not, but this much for him, I was pleased with his appearance. You may think me simple for speaking of such a small circumstance. No one knows the feelings occasioned by seeing objects once familiar after a long deprivation. Especially when it is heightened by no expectation of meeting with them. The door-yard was filled with hens, turkeys and pigeons. And in another place we saw cows and goats in abundance, and I think the largest and fattest cattle and swine I ever saw.

We were soon shown a room which Mr. Pambrun said he had prepared for us, by making two bedsteads or bunks, on hearing of our approach. It was the west bastion of the Fort, full of port holes in the sides, but no windows, and filled with fire-arms. A large cannon, always loaded, stood behind the door by one of the holes. These things did not disturb me. I am so well pleased with the possession of a room to shelter me from the scorching sun that I scarcely notice them. Having arranged our things we were soon called to a feast of melons; the first, I think, I ever saw or tasted. The muskmelon was the largest, measuring eighteen in length, fifteen around the small end and nineteen around the large end. You may be assured that none of us were satisfied or willing to leave the table until we had filled our plates with chips.

At four o'clock we were called to dine. It consisted of pork, cabbage, turnips, tea, bread and butter; by favorite dishes, and much like the last dinner I ate with Mother Loomis. I am thus particular in my description of eatables so that you may be assured that we find something to eat beyond the Rocky mountains as well as at home. We find plenty of salt, but many here prefer to do almost, and some entirely without it, on their meats and vegetables.

Sept. 2d. — Have busied myself to-day in unpacking my trunk and arranging my things for a visit to Vancouver. Mother will wonder at this and think me a strange child for wishing to add three hundred miles to this journey; not from necessity, but because my husband is going, and I may as well go as to stay here alone. If we were obliged to go on horseback, I think I should not wish to undertake it, but we are going in a boat and it will not take us more than six days to go there. A very agreeable change and I think I shall enjoy it as well as to stay here. I feel remarkably well and rested — do not need to lounge at all, and so it is with us all. I can scarcely believe it possible of myself, but it is true, I feel as vigorous and as well able to engage in any domestic employment as I ever did in my life.

I have not yet introduced you to the lady of the house. She is a native, from a tribe east of the mountains. She appears well, does not speak English, but her native language and French. The cooking and housework is done by men chiefly. Mr. Pambrun is from Canada, and much of the gentlemen in his appearance.

Sept. 3d. — Messrs. McLeod and Townsend left for Vancouver to-day, but Mr. McLeod is so loaded as not to be able to give us a comfortable passage. Mr. Pambrun is going by himself next week and offers us a passage with him.

About noon Mr. and Mrs. Spalding arrived with their company, having made better progress than was anticipated. Here we are all at Walla Walla, through the mercy of a kind Providence, in health and all of our lives preserved. What cause for gratitude and praise to

God! Surely my heart is ready to leap for joy at the thought of being so near the long-desired work of teaching the benighted ones the knowledge of a Savior, and having completed this hazardous journey under such favorable circumstances. Mr. Pambrun said to us the day we arrived, that there had never been a company previous to ours, that came into the Fort so well fed as ours for the last days of the journey. All our friends of the East company, who knew anything about the country, dreaded this part for us very much. But the Lord has been with us and provided for us all the way, and blessed be his holy name. Another cause for gratitude is the preservation of our animals, in this difficult, dangerous and lengthy route, while many parties previous to ours have had every animal taken from them, and been left on foot in a dangerous land, exposed to death. Two horses have given out with fatigue and have been left, two have been stolen or lost, but most that we have now, have come all the way from the settlements, and appear well. Two calves only have been lost. The remainder came on well except those we left at Snake Fort.

Sabbath, 4th. — This has been a day of mutual thanksgiving with us all. Assembled at the Fort at 12 o'clock for worship, our feelings are better imagined than described. This first Sabbath in September, a Sabbath of rest; first after completing a long journey, first in the vicinity of our future labors. All of us here before God. It is not enough for us alone to be thankful. Will not my beloved friends at home, the disciples of Jesus, unite with us in gratitude and praise to God for his great mercy? It is in answer to your prayers that we are here and are permitted to see this day under such circumstances. Feel to dedicate myself renewedly to His service among the heathen, and may the Lord's hand be as evidently manifest in blessing our labors among them, as it has been in bringing us here, and that, too, in answer to your prayers, beloved Christian friends.

5th. — Mr. and Mrs. Spalding have concluded to go with us to Vancouver, so nothing can be done by either of the parties about location until the Indians return from their summer's hunt. Expect to leave tomorrow. Have had exceedingly high winds for two days and nights past, to which the place is subject. Our room shakes and the wind makes such a noise that we can scarcely hear each other converse.

Sept. 7, 1836. — We set sail from Walla Walla yesterday at two o'clock p.m. Our boat is an open one, manned with six oars, and the steersman. I enjoy it much; it is a very pleasant change in our manner of traveling. The Columbia is a beautiful river. Its waters are clear as crystal and smooth as a sea of glass, exceeding in beauty the Ohio; but the scenery on each side of it is very different. There is no timber to be seen, but there are high perpendicular banks of rocks in some places, while rugged bluffs and plains of sand in others, are all that meet the eye. We sailed until near sunset, when we landed, pitched our tents, supped our tea, bread and butter, boiled ham and potatoes, committed ourselves to the care of a kind Providence, and retired to rest.

This morning we arose before sunrise, embarked and sailed until nine o'clock, and are now landed for breakfast. Mr. Pambrun's cook is preparing it, while husband and myself are seated by a little shrub, writing. We are this moment called. Farewell.

8th.—Came last night quite to the Chute (above The Dalles), a fall in the river not navigable. There we slept, and this morning made the portage. All were obliged to land, unload, carry our baggage, and even the boat, for half a mile. I had frequently seen the picture of the Indians carrying a canoe, but now I saw the reality. We found plenty of Indians here to assist in making the portage. After loading several with our baggage and sending them on, the boat was capsized and placed upon the heads of about twenty of them, who marched off with it, with perfect ease. Below the main fall of water are rocks, deep, narrow channels, and many frightful precipices. We walked deliberately among the rocks, viewing the scene with astonishment, for this once beautiful river seemed to be cut up and destroyed by these huge masses of rock. Indeed, it is difficult to find where the main body of water passes. In high water we are told that these rocks are all covered with water, the river rising to such an astonishing height.

After paying the Indians for their assistance, which was a twist of tobacco about the length of a finger to each, we reloaded, went on board, sailed about two miles, and stopped for breakfast. This was done to get away from a throng of Indians. Many followed us, however, to assist in making another portage, three miles below this.

Sept. 9th.—We came to The Dalles just before noon. Here our boat was stopped by two rocks of immense size and height, all the water of the river passing between them in a very narrow channel, and with great rapidity. Here we were obliged to land and make a portage of two and a half miles, carrying the boat also. The Dalles is the great resort of Indians of many tribes for taking fish. We did not see many, however, for they had just left.

Now, mother, if I was with you by the fireside, I would relate a scene that would amuse you, and at the same time call forth your sympathies. But for my own gratification I will write it. After we landed, curiosity led us to the top of that rock, to see the course of the river through its narrow channel. But as I expected to walk that portage, husband thought it would be giving me too much fatigue to do both. I went with him to its base, to remain there until his return. I took a handful of hazelnuts and thought I would divert myself with cracking and eating them. I had just seated myself in the shade of the rock, ready to commence work, when, feeling something unusual on my neck, I put my hand under my cape and took from thence two insects, which I soon discovered to be fleas. Immediately I cast my eyes upon my dress before me, and, to my astonishment, found it was black with these creatures, making all possible speed to lay seige to my neck and ears. This sight made me almost franctic. What to do I knew not. Husband was away, sister Spalding had gone past hearing. To stand still I could not. I climbed up the rock in pursuit of my husband, who soon saw and came to me. I could not tell him, but showed him the cause of my distress. On opening the gathers of my dress around my waist, every plait was lined with them. Thus they had already laid themselves in ambush for a fresh attack. We brushed and shook, and shook and brushed, for an hour, not stopping to kill for that would have been impossible. By this time they were reduced very considerably, and I prepared to go to the boat. I was relieved from walking by the offer of a horse from a young chief. This was a kindness, for the way was mostly through sand, and the walk would have been fatiguing. I found the confinement of the boat distressing, on account of my miserable companions, who would not let me rest for a moment in any one position. But I was not the only sufferer. Every one in the boat was alike troubled, both crew and passengers. As soon as I was able to make a change in my apparel I found relief.

We made fine progress this morning till 9 o'clock, when we were met with a head wind and obliged to make shore. We met the crew last night with the Western express. This express goes from and returns to Vancouver twice a year.

Eve.—Have lain still all day because of the wind. This is a detention, as we intended to have been at Vancouver by to-morrow evening. A party of Indians came to our camp this eve. Every head was flattened. These are the first I have seen near enough to be able to examine them. Their eyes have a dull and heavy expression.

10th.—High winds and not able to move at all to-day.

11th.—We came to the Cascades for breakfast—another important fall in the river, where we are obliged to make a portage of a mile. The boat was towed along by the rocks with a rope over the falls. This is another great place for salmon fishing. A boat load was just ready for Vancouver when we arrived. I saw an infant here whose head was in the pressing machine. This was a pitiful sight. Its mother took great satisfaction in unbinding and showing its naked head to us. The child lay upon a board between which and its head was a squirrel skin. On its forehead lay a small square cushion, over which was a bandage drawn tight around, pressing its head against the board. In this position it is kept three or four months or longer, until the head becomes a fashionable shape. There is a variety of shapes among them, some being sharper than others. I saw a child about a year old whose head had been recently released from pressure, as I supposed from its looks. All the back part of it was a purple color, as if it had been sadly bruised. We are told that this custom is wearing away very fast. There are only a few tribes of this river who practice it.

Sept. 12th.—Breakfasted at the saw mill five miles from Vancouver, and made preparations for entering it. You may be surprised to hear of a saw mill here when I said that there was no timber on the Columbia. Since we passed the Cascades the scene is changed, and we are told there is timber all the way to the coast.

Eve.—We are now in Vancouver, the New York of the Pacific Ocean. Our first sight, as we approached the fort, was two ships lying in the harbor, one of which, the Neriade, Captain Royal, had just arrived from London. The Columbia, Captain Dandy, came last May, and has since been to the Sandwich Islands, and returned. On landing we first met Mr. Townsend, whom we saw at Walla Walla. He is from Philadelphia, and has been in the mountains two years. He is sent here by a society to collect the different species of bipeds, and quadrupeds, peculiar to this country. We brought a parcel of letters to him, the first he had received since he had left home. Mr. Townsend led us into the fort. But before we reached the home of the chief Factor, Dr. McLoughlin, we were met by several gentlemen, who came to give us a welcome, Mr. Douglas, Mr. Tolmie and Dr. McLoughlin, of the Hudson's Bay Company, who invited us in and seated us on the sofa. Soon we were introduced to Mrs. McLoughlin and Mrs. Douglas, both natives of the country—half breeds. After chatting a little we were invited to walk in the garden.

What a delightful place this is; what a contrast to the rough, barren sand plains, through which we had so recently passed. Here we find fruit of every description, apples, peaches, grapes, pears, plums, and fig trees in abundance; also cucumbers, melons, beans, peas, beets, cabbage, tomatoes and every kind of vegetable too numerous to be mentioned. Every part is very neat and tastefully arranged, with fine walks, lined on each side with strawberry vines. At the opposite end of the garden is a good summer house covered with grape vines. Here I must mention the origin of these grapes and apples. A gentlemen, twelve years ago while at a party in London, put the seeds of the grapes and apples which he ate into his vest pocket. Soon afterwards he took a voyage to this country and left them here, and now they are greatly multiplied.

After promenading as much as we wished, and returning, we were met by Mrs. Copendel, a lady from England, who arrived in the ship Columbia last May, and Miss Maria, daughter of Dr. McLoughlin, quite an interesting young lady. After dinner we were introduced to Rev. Mr. Beaver and lady, a clergyman of the Church of England, who arrived last week in the ship Neriade. This is more than we expected when we left home—that we should be privileged with the acquaintance and society of two English ladies. Indeed, we seem to be nearly allied to Old England, for most of the gentlemen of the Company are from there or Scotland.

We have not found Rev. Samuel Parker here, to our great disappointment. He went to Oahu in the ship Columbia, a few weeks before we arrived. We have mourned about it considerably, for we thought it would be so acceptable to our dear parents and friends at home to hear him say that he had seen us alive here, after completing this long, unheard-of journey. Besides, I wished to send home many things which I cannot now. More than all this, his counsels and advice would have been such a relief to us, at this important time, as to location, character of the Indians, and the like. But it is wisely ordered, and we submit. He appears to have been a favorite here, and to have done much good.

The Messrs. Lee left Vancouver on Saturday last for their station on the Wallamet. Mr. Daniel Lee has been out of health, and for the year past has been at Oahu. He returned on the Neriade, benefited by his visit.

Sept. 13.—This morning visited the school to hear the children sing. It consists of about fifty-one children, who have French fathers and Indian mothers. All the laborers here are Canadian French, with Indian wives. Indeed, some of the gentlemen of the company have native wives, and have adopted the custom of the country not to allow their wives to eat with them. French is the prevailing language here. English is spoken only by a few.

Just before dinner we went on board the Neriade, the first ship I ever saw. She is a man-of-war, and goes to the Northwest coast soon. The Columbia returns to London this fall. The Company have lost three ships on the coast.

Sept. 14.—We were invited to a ride to see the farm. Have ridden fifteen miles this afternoon. We visited the barns, stock, etc. They estimated their wheat crops at four thousand bushels this year, peas the same, oats and barley between fifteen and seventeen hundred bushels each. The potato and turnip fields are large and fine. Their cattle are numerous, estimated at a thousand head in all the settlements. They have swine in abundance, also sheep and goats, but the sheep are of an inferior kind. We find also hens, turkeys, and pigeons, but no geese.

You will ask what kind of beds they have here. I can tell you what kind of bed they made for us, and I have since found it a fashionable bed for this country. The bedstead is in the form of a bunk, with a rough board bottom, upon which are laid about a dozen of the Indian blankets. These with a pair of pillows covered with calico cases constitute our beds, sheets and covering. There are several feather beds in the place made of the feathers of wild ducks, geese, cranes and the like. There is nothing here suitable for ticking. The best and only material is brown linen sheeting. The Indian ladies make theirs of deer skin. Could we obtain a pair of geese from any quarter I should think much of them.

Sept. 16th.—Every day we have something new to see. We went to the stores and found them filled above and below with the cargo of the two ships, all in unbroken bales. They are chiefly Indian goods, and will be sent away this fall to the several different posts of the company in the ship Neriade. We have found here every article for comfort and durability that we need, but many articles for convenience and all fancy articles are not here.

Visited the dairy, also, where we found butter and cheese in abundance—saw an improvement in the manner of raising cream. Their pans are an oblong square, quite large but shallow, flaring a little, made of wood and lined with tin. In the center is a hole with a long plug. When the cream has risen they place the pan over a tub or pail, remove the plug, and the milk will run off leaving only the cream in the pan. I think that these must be very convenient in a large dairy. They milk between fifty and sixty cows.

On visiting the mill we did not find it in a high state of improvement. It goes by horse power and has a wire bolt. This seemed a hard way of getting bread, but better so than no bread, or to grind by hand. The company have one at Colville that goes by water, five days ride from Walla Walla, from whence we expect to obtain our flour, potatoes and pork. They have three hundred hogs.

Dr. McLoughlin promises to loan us enough to make a beginning and all the return he asks is that we supply other settlers in the same way. He appears desirous to afford us every facility for living in his power. No person could have received a more hearty welcome, or be treated with greater kindness than we have been since our arrival.

Sept. 17th.—A subject is now before the minds of certain individuals, in which I feel a great interest. It is that we ladies spend the winter at Vancouver, while our husbands go to seek their locations and build. Dr. McLoughlin is certain that it will be the best for us, and I believe is determined to have us stay. The thought of it is not very pleasant to either of us. For several reasons, I had rather go to Walla Walla, where, if we failed to make a location, or of building this fall, we could stay very comfortably, and have enough to eat, but not as comfortably, or have as great a variety as here; besides, there is the difficulty of ascending the river in high water, not to say anything of a six months' separation, when it seems to be least desirable; but all things will be ordered for the best.

Sept.18.—Mr. Beaver held two services in a room in Dr. McLoughlin's barn to-day.

Enjoyed the privilege much. This form of worship, of the Church of England, differs in no way from that of the Episcopalians in the States. The most of the gentlemen of the fort are Scotch Presbyterians, very few being Episcopalians. The great mass of the laborers are Roman Catholics, who have three services during the Sabbath, one of which is attended at this house, at which Dr. McLoughlin officiates in French. He translates a sermon or a tract, and reads a chapter in the Bible and a prayer. The singing in Mr. Beaver's church was done by the children, some of their tunes having been taught them by Rev. Mr. Parker, and others by the Mr. Shepherd, of the Methodist mission.

Sept. 19.—The question is decided at last that we stay here about four or five weeks. There is so much baggage to be taken up now, that the boat will be sufficiently loaded without us. Have the cheering promise that our husbands will come for us in a short time if prospered. One thing comforts us. They are as unwilling to leave us as we are to stay, and would not if it were possible for us to go now. From this we are sure that they will make every effort to return for us soon. We are told that the rainy season will commence soon, and continue through the winter, and late in the spring, while at Walla Walla there is none. Vancouver, too, is subject to fever and ague. These are quite good reasons for preferring Walla Walla, even if we had to live in a lodge.

Have been making some necessary purchases for our two Indian boys, Richard and John, which we are glad to do, partly as a reward for their faithful care of the cattle during the journey. We left them at Walla Walla. They regretted our leaving them, and now I cannot feel willing to stay away from them all winter. Their anxiety to study continues the same, especially Richard. We love them both and feel deeply interested in their welfare, and shall treat them as our own as long as they deserve it.

Sept. 20th.—Dr. McLoughlin gave my husband a pair of leather pantaloons to-day. All the gentlemen here wear them for riding for economy. Riding horseback and carrying a gun is very destructive to cloth pantaloons.

Our husbands have been making preparations to leave us to-day, but have found so much to do that they could not get ready to leave much before night. They have concluded to start the boat a short distance and camp, while they, with Mr. Pambrun and Mr. Gray, remain in the Fort to leave early in the morning.

Sept. 21.—Our friends left us this morning early. One thing I should have mentioned, as decided upon before they left, was the propriety of making two stations. After consideration it was decided best to do so for sereral reasons. The Cayuses as well as the Nez Perces are very anxious to have teachers among them. They are a numerous tribe [not numerous, but wealthy and influential.—M. Eells] and speak the same language as the Nez Perces. There are other fields open ready for the harvest and we wish that there were many more laborers here ready to occupy them immediately. Several places have been recommended which our husbands intend visiting before they fix upon any place. You will recollect that we had Grande Ronde in view as a location when we left home. Our reasons for not fixing upon that place are insurmountable. The pass in the Blue mountains is so difficult and the distance so great that it would be next to impossible to think of obtaining supplies sufficient for our support. We could not depend upon game, for it is very scarce and uncertain. Mr. Parker recommends a place on the Kooskooska (Clearwater) river, six days' ride above Walla Walla. I hope to give you our exact location before I send this.

Sept. 22.—Dr. McLoughlin has put his daughter in my care and wishes me to hear her recitations. Thus I shall have enough to do for diversion while I stay. I could employ all my time in writing and work for myself it if were not for his wishes.

I have not given you a description of our eatables here. There is such a variety I know not where to begin. For breakfast we have coffee or cocoa, salt salmon and roast ducks with potatoes. When we have eaten our supply of them, our plates are changed and we make a finish on bread and butter.

For dinner we have a greater variety. First we are always treated to a dish of soup, which is very good. All kinds of vegetables in use are taken, chopped fine, and put into water with a little rice, and boiled to a soup. The tomatoes are a prominent article, and usually some fowl meat, duck or other kind, is cut fine and added. If it has been roasted once it is just as good (so the cook says), and then spiced to the taste. After our soup dishes are removed, then comes a variety of meats to prove our tastes. After selecting and changing, we change plates and try another if we choose, and so at every new dish have a clean plate. Roast duck is an everyday dish, boiled pork, tripe, and sometimes trotters, fresh salmon or sturgeon—yea, articles too numerous to be mentioned. When these are set aside, a nice pudding or an apple pie is next introduced. After this a water and a muskmelon make their appearance, and last of all cheese, bread or biscuit and butter are produced to complete the whole. But there is one article on the table I have not yet mentioned, and of which I never partake. That is wine. The gentlemen frequently drink toasts to each other, but never give us an opportunity of refusing, for they know that we belong to the Tetotal Society. We have talks about drinking wine, but no one joins our society. They have a Temperance Society here and at Wallamet, formed by Mr. Lee.

Our tea is very plain. Bread and butter, good tea, plenty of milk and sugar.

Sept. 30th.—We are invited to ride as often as once a week for exercise, and we generally ride all the afternoon. To-day Mrs. McLoughlin rode with us. She keeps her old fashion of riding gentleman fashion. This is the universal custom of Indian women, and they have saddles with high backs and fronts. We have been recommended to use these saddles, as a more easy way of riding, but we have never seen the necessity of changing our fashion.

I sing about an hour every evening with the children, teaching them new tunes, at the request of Dr. McLoughlin. Thus I am wholly occupied, and can scarcely find as much time as I want to write.

Oct. 18th.—The Montreal Express came this afternoon, and a general time of rejoicing it is to everyone. News from distant friends, both sad and pleasing.

Mr. Spalding has come with it and brought a letter from my husband, filled with pleasing information. The Lord has been with them since they left us, and has prospered them beyond all expectations. They have each selected a location. My husband remains there to build, while Mr. Spalding comes after us. Cheering thought this, to be able to make a beginning in our pleasing work so soon.

My Dear Sister Perkins: — Your letter was handed me on the 8th. inst., a little after noon, and I must say I was a little surprised to receive a return so soon. Surely, we are near each other. You will be likely to have known opportunities of sending to us, more frequently than I shall your way, which I hope you will not neglect because you have not received the answer to yours. I do not intend to be so long again in replying as I have this time. When I received yours, I was entirely alone. My husband had gone to brother Spalding's to assist him in putting up a house, and soon after, we had the privilege of preparing and entertaining Mr. and Mrs. McDonald and family of Colville. They came by the way of brother Spalding's, spent nearly a week with them and then came here. They left here last Thursday, and are still at Walla Walla. Had a very pleasant, agreeable visit with them. Find Mrs. McDonald quite an intelligent woman; speaks English very well, reads and is the principal instructor of their children. She is a correspondent, also, with myself and sister Spalding. She appears more thoughtful upon the subject of religion than any I have met with before, and has some consistent views. What her experimental knowledge is, I am unable to say. It would be a privilege to have her situated near us, so that we could have frequent intercourse; it would, no doubt be profitable.

You ask after my plan of proceedings with the Indians, etc. I wish I was able to give you satisfactory answers. I have no plan separate from my husband's, and besides you are mistaken about the language being at command, for nothing is more difficult than for me to attempt to convey religious truth in their language, especially when there are so few, or not terms expressive of the meaning. Husband succeeds much better than I, and we have good reason to feel that so far as understood, the truth affects the heart, and not little, too. We have done nothing for the females separately; indeed, our house is so small, and only one room to admit them, and that is the kitchen. It is the men only that frequent our house much. Doubtless you have been with the Indians long enough to discover this feature, that women are not allowed the same privileges as men. I scarcely see them except on the Sabbath in our assemblies. I have frequently desired to have more intercourse with them, and am waiting to have a room built for them and other purposes of instruction. Our principal effort is with the children now, and we find many very interesting ones. But more of this in future when I have more time.

Mr. Pambrun has sent a horse for me to ride to his place tomorrow. Mrs. Pambrun has been out of health for some time, and we have fears that she will not recover. As I have considerable preparations to make for the visit, must defer writing more at present. In haste, I subscribe myself,

Your affectionate sister in Christ,

NARCISSA WHITMAN.

P.S. — I long to hear from Mrs. Lee.

WALLA WALLA, 11th.

My Dear Sister: — I am still here. The brigade arrived yesterday and having time and opportunity to send home for this letter, both are sent by return boats. We have just received three or four letters from our friends at home, they being the first news received since we bade them farewell. Find it good to know what is going on there, although all is not of a pleasing character. Our Sandwich Island friends give us pleasing intelligence of the glorious display of the power of God in converting that heathen people in such multitudes.

Ever yours,
N. WHITMAN.

Rev. Mrs. H.K.W. Perkins,
    Wascopum,
        La Dalls.

My Dear Sister Perkins:—I did not think when I received your good long letter that I should have delayed until this time before answering it. But so varied are the scenes that have passed before me, so much company and so many cares, etc., besides writing many letters home, that I beg you will excuse me. Notwithstanding all this, I have often, very often, thought of you and wished for the privilege of seeing you. I must confess I do not like quite so well to think of you where you now are as when you were nearer. Why did you go? Some of our sisters might just as well as not have spent a short season with you this fall (for they have nothing else to do, comparatively speaking) rather than to have you and your dear husband lose so much time from your interesting field of labor; and besides we fear the influence of the climate of the lower country upon your health. Our prayer is that the Lord will deal gently with you and bless and preserve you to be a rich and lasting good to the benighted ones for whom you have devoted your life.

How changed the scene now with us at Wieletpoo from what it has been in former days. Instead of husband and myself stalking about here like two solitary beings, we have the society of six of our brethren and sisters who eat at our table and expect to spend the winter with us. This is a privilege we highly praise, especially when we come to mingle our voices in prayer and praise together before the mercy seat, and hear the word of God preached in our own language from Sabbath to Sabbath, and to commune together around the table of our dear Son and Saviour Jesus Christ. Those favors, dear sister, almost make us forget we are on heathen ground. Since I last wrote to you we have enjoyed refreshing seasons from the hand of our Heavenly Father in the conviction and conversion of two or three individuals in our family. Doubtless Brother Lee has given you the particulars, yet I wish to speak of it for our encouragement who have been engaged in the concert of prayer on Tuesday evening for the year past. I verily believe we have not prayed in vain, for our revival seasons have been on that evening, and I seem to feel, too, that the whole atmosphere in all Oregon is effected by that meeting, for the wicked know far and near, that there are those here who pray. We have every reason to be assured that were there more faith and prayer and consecration to the work among ourselves, we should witness in the heathen around us many turning to the Lord. If I know my own heart I think I, too, desire to be freed from so many worldly cares and perplexities, and that my time may be spent in seeking the immediate conversion of these dear heathen to God. O, what a thought to think of meeting them among the blood-washed throng around the throne of God! Will not their songs be as sweet as any we can sing? What joy will then fill our souls to contemplate the privilege we now enjoy of spending and being spent for their good. If we were constantly to keep our eyes on the scenes that are before us, we should scarcely grow weary in well doing, or be disheartened by the few trials and privations through which we are called to pass.

Dear sister, I have written in great haste and hope you will excuse me. Wishing and expecting to hear from you soon, of your prosperity and happiness, with much love and sisterly affection to you and yours, believe me,

Ever yours in the best bonds,

NARCISSA WHITMAN.

Rev. Mrs. H.K.W. Perkins,
    Wallamette.

WALLA WALLA, Dec. 5, 1836

My Dear Mother: — I have been thinking of my beloved parents this evening; of the parting scene, and of the probability that I shall never see those dear faces again while I live. Sweet as it used to be, when my heart was full, to sit down and pour into my mother's bosom all my feelings, both sad and rejoicing; now, when far away from the parental roof, and thirsting for the same precious privilege, I take my pen and find a sweet relief in giving her my history in the same familiar way. Perhaps no one else feels as I do. It would be, indeed, a great satisfaction to me to have my mother know how I do from day to day — what my employment and prospects are — but more especially the dealings, the kind dealings of my Heavenly Father towards us continually.

We left Vancouver Thursday noon, Nov. 3rd, in two boats — Mr. McLeod, myself and baggage in one. and Mr. S. in the other. We are well provided for in everything we could wish — good boats, with strong and faithful men to manage them; indeed, eight of them were Iroquois Indians, from Montreal — men accustomed to the water from their childhood, and well acquainted with the dangers of this river. Mr. McLeod's accompanying us was as unexpected as desirable. He only came into Vancouver two days previous to our leaving, from an expedition to the Umpqua, south of the Willamette. It rained some that afternoon, also on the 4th and 5th; the 6th it rained all day, nearly, and the wind was very strong, but in our favor, so that we kept our sail up most of the day. Our boat was well covered with an oilcloth. I succeeded in keeping myself dry by wrapping well in my cloak and getting under the oilcloth. At night, when a great fire was made, our tents pitched and the cloth spread for tea, all was pleasant and comfortable. I rolled my bed and blankets in my India-rubber cloak, which preserved them quite well from the rain, so that nights I slept warm and comfortable as ever. My featherbed was of essential service to me in keeping my health this rainy voyage. Did not expect to get one when I wrote from Vancouver.

On the morning of the 7th we arrived at the Cascades, made the portage and breakfasted. Had considerable rain. The men towed the boats up the falls, on the opposite side of the river. The water was very low, and made it exceedingly difficult for them to drag the boats up, in the midst of the rocks and noise of the foaming waters. Sometimes they were obliged to lift the boats over the rocks, at others go around them, to the entire destruction of the gum upon them, which prevents them from leaking. It was nearly night before all were safely over the difficult passage, and our boats gummed, ready for launching.

8th. — Breakfasted just below The Dalles. Passed them without unloading the boats. This was done by attaching a strong rope of considerable length to the stern of the boat, two men only remaining in it to guide and keep it clear of the rocks, while the remainder, and as many Indians as can be obtained, draw it along with the rope, walking upon the edge of the rocks above the frightful precipice. At the Little Dalles, just above these, the current is exceedingly strong and rapid, and full of whirlpools. Not recollecting the place particularly, at the request of the bowsman I remained in the boat, being quite fatigued with my walk past the other Dalles. It is a terrific sight, and a frightful place to be in, to be drawn along in such a narrow channel between such high, craggy, perpendicular bluffs, the men with the rope clambering sometimes upon their hands and knees upon the very edge, so high above us as to appear small, like boys. Many times the rope would catch against the rocks and oblige someone to crawl carefully over the horrible precipice to unloosen it, much to the danger of his life. When my husband came up, in passing this place, the rope caught in a place so difficult of access that no one would venture his life to extricate it, for some time. At last, an Indian ventured. When he had ascended sufficiently to unfasten it, he was unable to return, and did not until he was drawn up by a rope. They had another accident which threatened both the lives of some of them, and the property, and but for the protecting hand of God would have been lost. While the men with the rope were climbing up a steep and difficult ascent, the rope lodged upon a rock, which held it fast, and had it remained there until all hands had gained their point and commenced hauling, all would have been well; but one of the men above prematurely shoved it off. The current took the boat down stream rapidly, in spite of every effort to save it, prostrating all hands upon the rocks, and some of them were nearly precipitated down the precipice by the rope. The boat received no injury, but was safely moored below The Dalles, on the opposite shore. Our husbands, with the men, obtained an Indian canoe and crossed to the boat. Thus they were preserved. It was just night as we succeeded in passing this difficult place in safety, for which we desired to be grateful. Many boats have been dashed to pieces at these places, and more than a hundred lives lost. The water was very low at this time, which makes the danger much less in passing them. No rain to-day. Thursday we made the portage of the chutes, and were all day about it. While on land, had several heavy showers. Friday, also, was another soaking-wet day; the night, too. This was dreary enough. Saturday was much more pleasant—no rain. We arrived at Walla Walla early Sabbath morning, in health, with all our effects preserved to us, mercifully. I felt that I had great cause to bless and praise God, for so seasonable a return, and under such favorable circumstances. Husband come from our location on the 18th. Had succeeded in making a comfortable place for me, but because of Mr. Pambrun's earnest solicitation for me to remain a few weeks with his family, I did not return with him. Mr. and Mrs. P. are exceeding kind—appear to feel that they cannot do too much to make us contented and happy here. In the meantime, I am cheerfully engaged in teaching the wife and daughter to read. We consider it a very kind providence to be situated near one family so interesting, and a native female that promises to be so much society for me. She is learning to speak the English language quite fast. Mr. and Mrs. S. left Walla Walla for their location, on the 22nd of November, Mr. Gray going with them to assist in building, etc. This dear sister goes very cheerfully to her location, expecting to live in a skin lodge until her house is built; and this, too, in the dead of winter; But she prefers it to remaining here, and so should I.

Heard from husband last week, and of the death of Hinds, a colored man who came with us from Rendezvous on account of his health, being far gone with the dropsy. Already death has entered our house, and laid one low.

Dec. 8th. — Received intelligence that husband was coming tomorrow to remove our effects and myself to our new home. It is an agreeable thought to be so near a fixed location after journeying so long.

Dec. 26th. — Where are we now, and who are we that we should be thus blessed of the Lord? I can scarcely realize that we are thus comfortably fixed, and keeping house, so soon after our marriage, when considering what was then before us. We arrived here on the tenth — distance, twenty-five miles from Walla Walla. Found a house reared and the lean-to enclosed, a good chimney and fireplace, and the floor laid. No windows or door except blankets. My heart truly leaped for joy as I alighted from my horse, entered and seated myself before a pleasant fire (for it was now night). It occurred to me that my dear parents had made a similar beginning, and perhaps a more difficult one than ours. We had neither straw, bedstead or table, nor anything to make them of except green cottonwood. All our boards are sawed by hand. Here my husband and his laborers (two Owyhees from Vancouver and a man who crossed the mountains with us), and Mr. Gray, have been encamped in tents since the 19th of October, toiling excessively hard to accomplish this much for our comfortable residence during the remainder of the winter.

It is indeed, a lovely situation. We are on a beautiful level — a peninsula formed by the branches of the Walla Walla river, upon the base of which our house stands, on the southeast corner, near the shore of the main river. To run a fence across to the opposite river, on the north from our house — this, with the river, would enclose 300 acres of good land for cultivation, all directly under the eye. The rivers are barely skirted with timber. This is all the woodland we can see; beyond them, as far as the eye can reach, plains and mountains appear. On the east, a few rods from the house, is a range of small hills, covered with bunchgrass — a very excellent food for animals, and upon which they subsist during winter, even digging it from under the snow.

Letters

WI-EL-ET-POO, March 30, 1837.

Dear Parents, Brothers and Sisters: — Again I can speak of the goodness and mercy of the Lord to us in an expecial manner. On the evening of my birthday, March 14th, we received the gift of a little daughter — a treasure invaluable. During the winter my health was very good, so as to be able to do my work. About a week before her birth, I was afflicted with an inflammatory rash, which confined me mostly to my room. After repeated bleeding, it abated very considerably. Mrs. Pambrun had been with me two weeks previous to this, and has been much out of health. She, with my husband, dressed the babe. It would have made you smile to see them work over the little creature. Mrs. P. never saw one dressed before as we dress them, having been accustomed to dress her own in the native style. I was able to lend a helping hand and arrange the clothes for them, etc. Between us all, it was done very well. She slept very quiet that night, but the next night she cried very hard. All the reason of it was that she was hungry, and we did not think to feed her soon enough. On the second day I dressed her alone, sitting in the bed, and have ever since. I slept but little the two first nights, but since have got my usual sleep. She is a very quiet child, both night and day — sleeps all night without nursing more than once, sometimes not at all.

Thus you see, beloved sisters, how the missionary does in heathen lands. No mother, no sister, to relieve me of a single care — only an affectionate husband, who, as a physician and nurse, exceeds all I ever knew. He was excessively pressed with care and labor during the whole time of my confinement. I received all the attention I required of him. He had my washing and the cooking to do for the family. (Mrs. P. had two children with her, and, on account of her ill health, she could not give much assistence.) During the same week we were thronged with company, for the whole camp of Indians has arrived. Mr. Gray spent several days with us at this time; also, Mr. Pambrun and Mr. Ermatinger paid us a visit on Friday, and left on Saturday. All this, with the care of four men and two boys that know little or nothing about work, just at the commencement of plowing, etc., requires many steps for one man alone. It was a very great mercy that I have been able to take the whole care of my babe, and that she is so well and quiet. The little stranger is visited daily by the chiefs and principal men in camp, and the women throng the house continually, waiting an opportunity to see her. Her whole appearance is so new to them. Her complexion, her size and dress, etc., all excite a deal of wonder; for they never raise a child here except they are lashed tight to a board, and the girls' heads undergo the flattening process. I have not yet described my babe to you. I think her grandmother would willingly own her as one of her number of babies, could she see her. Her hair is a light brown, and we think will be like her aunts Jane and Harriet. She is plump and large, holds her head up finely, and looks about considerably. She weighs ten pounds. Fee-low-ki-ke, a kind, friendly Indian, called to see her the next day after she was born. Said she was a Cayuse te-mi (Cayuse girl), because she was born on Cayuse wai-tis (Cayuse land). He told us her arrival was expected by all the people of the country — the Nez Perces, Cayuses and Walla Wallapoos Indians, and, now she has arrived, it would soon be heard of by them all; and we must write to our land and tell our parents and friends of it. The whole tribe are highly pleased because we allow her to be called a Cayuse girl. We have beautiful weather here this month. Travel here is as pleasant as May in New York.

May 2nd, 1837.—The opportunity of sending home has come to hand, but I have been able to write but little. Mr. McLeod leaves soon with an expedition to Rendezvous, the same as last year. We can send letters very safely to Rendezvous, so long as this expedition goes, but the great uncertainty lies in the expedition of the American Fur Company. This year we are safe enough in sending. Mr. Gray has made up his mind to go home this fall. In my last date I mentioned his being here a few days. He assisted Mr. S. in building and returned to Walla Walla the first of January, to await Mr. Ermatinger's arrival from the Flathead country. He thinks of traveling with them, in company with Mr. E., for the purpose of learning their language, with a view to a settlement among them. When he left us, in March, he did not think of returning to the States until one year from next fall, so we expected to see him again. He has written us that he had determined to go this year. He will meet Mr. Leod at Rendezvous, if his life is preserved. It would have been agreeable for us to have known of his going, immediately when he went from here, that we might have sent some things home by him. We have been here so short a time, however, that we should not have been able to send many things. His present determination is to return in two years, when we shall expect letters in abundance. We are all very well at present. I believe I was up and dressed the day the babe was a week old, and in a day or two after was about the house, and the next Sabbath walked out of doors. The weather is very mild and beautiful—so much so, that I do not require a fire in my room but a small part of the time. Fine, healthy atmosphere—no danger of nervous affections here. I have not been troubled in the least as I used to be. Mrs. P. remained with me until Friday of the second week, when she left her daughter, about twelve years of age, with us, for the purpose of being taught to read, etc. It being impossible for me to obtain permanent help here, husband wrote to V. for an orphan girl. Dr. McLoughlin sent us one by express. She arrived the first of April. Is entirely unacquainted with every kind of work, neither can she speak the English language. Said to be sixteen, but she is not larger than a girl of twelve years. You have no idea how difficult it is to realize any benefit from those who do not understand you. During the winter, husband had two men only to assist him—Nina and Green. Green returns to the mountains again this spring, and Mr. Spalding has sent us Jack again. These two Owyhees will remain with us we know not how long. Here we are lost again, because they speak a different language. They are the best for labor of any people this side of the mountains. The Indians do not love to work well enough for us to place any dependence upon them. I find a peculiar tender feeling in my heart for these Islanders, in consequence of my acquaintance with Obakili's history. Hope you will remember them especially in your prayers, that they may learn a knowledge of the way of salvation. They have kind and tender feelings, and their attachments are strong. There are quite a number in the country. They make excellent cooks and house servants. Our men do their own cooking, and sometimes cook for me.

The third Sabbath after my babe was born, the weather was too cold to hold our meeting out of doors. So many Indians had come recently that it was impossible for all to get into our house. It was concluded best to go to the young chief Tow-en-too-e's lodge. I went, with the babe, to assist in singing. Found it a very convenient place, and completely filled. His part of it was remarkably clean and neat. Several families join their lodges together, making a long hall. In this way they hold great numbers. Their lodges are made of skins and rush mats, and, with a fire in the center, they are very warm and comfortable. The single lodges are put up in the same way. Mr. Dunbar describes them in his journal.

Indeed, I should not attempt to sing with them, were it not for the assistance my husband renders. You will recollect, when he was in Angelica, he could not sing a single tune. Now he is able to sing several tunes, and lead the school in them. This saves me a great deal of hard singing. I have thought many times if the singers in my father's family could have the same privilege, or were here to assist me in the work, how much good they could do. I was not aware that singing was a qualification of so much importance to a missionary. While I was at Vancouver, one Indian woman came a great distance with her daughter, as she said, to hear me sing with the children. The boys have introduced all the tunes they can sing alone into their morning and evening worship—these they sing very well. To be at a distance and hear them singing them, one would almost forget he was in a savage land.

May 3.—We had a short call yesterday from Mr. Douglass, of Vancouver. He was appointed to go with the express across the mountains this season, but, on account of the sickness of Mr. Henzie, and probable death, he was sent for, to take his place in the store. There has been much sickness, both at Vancouver, Walla Walla, and here, and some deaths. The Indians here had but just begun to break ground for planting, when many of them were taken sick with an inflammation of the lungs. This was severe upon them, and threw them in great consternation. The old chief Umtippe's wife was quite sick, and came near dying. For a season they were satisfied with my husband's attention, and were doing well; but when they would over eat themselves, or go into a relapse from unneccessary exposure, then they must have their te-wat doctors; say that the medicine was bad, and all was bad. Their te-wat is in the same species of juggling aspracticed by the Pawnees, which Mr. Dunbar describes—playing the fool over them, and giving no medicine. They employed them over and over again, but they remained the same. Soon they became weary of these, and must have a more noted one. Umtippe got in a rage about his wife, and told my husband, while she was under his care, that if his wife died that night he should kill him. The contest has been sharp between him and the Indians, and husband was nearly sick with the excitement and care of them. The chief sent for the great Walla Walla te-wat for his wife, at last, who came, and after going through several incantations, and receiving a horse and a blanket or two, pronounced her well; but the next day she was the same again. Now his rage was against the te-wat—said he was bad, and ought to be killed. When the te-wats were called, husband had nothing more to do with them. Their sickness commenced about the first of April, and, through the great mercy of God to us, none of them died to whom medicine was administered. Near the last of April, the old chief was taken sick, and, notwithstanding all his villainy, he came to my husband to be doctored. He was very sick, and we thought he would die; but the medicine given him soon relieved him. Last Saturday the war chief died at Walla Walla. He was a Cayuse, and a relative of Umtippe; was sick but six days; employed the same Walla Walla te-wat Umtippe sent for, but he died in his hands. The same day Ye-he-kis-kis, a younger brother of Umtippe, went to Walla Walla, arrived about twilight, and shot the te-wat dead. Thus they were avenged. Both Umtippe and his brother went from our house on the morning of the same day. It is but a few of the oldest men who are filled with so much war and bloodshed. If they should all die, a new character would at once be given the whole tribe. The younger ones naturally possess a different disposition, and manifest an eager desire to adopt the manners and customs of civilized life; but they are ruled by the chiefs, and feel themselves obliged to bow in subjection to them.

Notwithstanding all our trials, yet our situation is enviable to Brother and Sister Merrell's. We have not their difficulties to contend with. No alcohol here to destroy men's lives; neither do they steal, I have let my clothes remain out over night, feeling just as safe in doing it as I used to in Prattsburgh. There is another circumstance which makes our situation very agreeable. There is not a man, woman, or scarcely a child, but what is well covered, and many of them have changes of garments. Some are dressed entirely in cloth made in American style. Those who wear only a shirt and leggins, wear a blanket or Buffalo skin over their shoulders. The women and girls' dresses are made entirely of skin.

Plurality of wives exists among all the tribes here. Their excuse is, with many wives they have plenty to eat, but where they have but one they have nothing. The women are slaves to their husbands here, as well as in other heathen countries. The system of head-flattening exists among their people in a degree, but not to excess. The girls' heads only are flattened. They consider it a peculiar mark of beauty, and it makes them more acceptable in the sight of the men as wives. They raise but few of their children. Great numbers of them die. Those that live suffer a great deal from neglect, etc. I am often asked why I do not put my dear babe in a te-cash (this is the name of their cradle), and think it very strange that she should sleep with me without being tied up, so that I should not kill her.

But it is time for me to think of closing, as I am unable to write without her on my lap. She is now seven weeks old, and weighs thirteen pounds. We have given her the names of our mothers, Alice Clarissa. We both have a sister of the same name also. We think she resembles her grandmother Clarissa very considerably, as well as her mother. O, the responsibilities of a mother! To be a mother in heathen lands, among savages, gives feeling that can be known only to those who are such. You see our situation. If ever we needed your prayers and sympathies, it is at the present time. Ye mothers of the maternal associations, let me beg an interest in your prayers, especially for your unworthy sister, now she has become a mother, and for my little one. I feel utterly incompetent for the place, and were it not for the strong arm of the Lord I should sink under the responsibilities resting upon me. The present crisis is a trying one to our faith and confidence in God. The sickness continues yet among the Indians. We hoped that it had abated. Last week the whole camp left us, to go and dig their camas, a root upon which they place great dependence, and an excellent food for them.

Monday of this week Stick-as, an excellent Indian, came back very sick, and remains here yet. He has been taking medicine, and it appears to have relieved him, in a measure; but, because he is not all about immediately, he has become exceedingly uneasy and restless, and talks about the te-wats. He, with many other sensible ones in the tribe, and men of influence, too, are convinced that it is a deception, and not of God, yet no doubt feel a great struggle in their minds, to entirely renounce that in which they have so long had implicit confidence. So far they remain firm, and we hope soon to see its entire overthrow.

It has been, and still is the case with them, when one dies in your care they will hold you responsible for his life, and you are in great danger of being killed. The only way of pacifying them is to pay them well for the good you have endeavored to do them. Brethen Lees have found it so, and others have in this country, who have wished to do them good.

We have had no rain this spring, of any consequence. May 1st it commenced, and has continued most of the time since. The most of our planting was done previous to the rain.

I have not yet spoken of our eatables. We brought a good supply of pork, flour, butter, etc., from Vancouver with us, and corn and potatoes from Walla Walla. The Indians have furnished us a little venison—barely enough for our own eating—but to supply our men and visitors we have killed and eaten ten wild horses bought of the Indians. This will make you pity us, but you had better save your pity for more worthy subjects. I do not prefer it to other meat, but can eat it very well when we have nothing else. We have had milk since the first of February; two of our cows calved about this time.

But I *must* close. I cannot say how much we need your prayers and must beg of you again and again to pray unceasingly for us. If you would have us live, and not die, you must pray. Who will come over and help us? Weak, frail nature cannot endure excessive care and anxiety any great length of time, without falling under it. I refer more particularly to my husband. His labor this spring has affected his health considerably. His old complaint in his side affects him occasionally. We both fail of writing as much as we desire. He is unable to write to any of my friends, and so am I to his, and wish you would copy my letters and send to his friends. He has requested the same of them, with regard to his letters.

Our love to you all, and the dear church of Christ. Farewell.

NARCISSA WHITMAN.

P.S. — You are indebted to little Alice Clarissa's quiet disposition for this sheet. I have no cradle yet, and she has lain in my lap all day; for she does not like to be where she cannot see her mother, long at a time. She receives many kisses for her grandparents, uncles and aunts, every day. She is now in bed with her father, sleeping sweetly. She is pleasant company for me, here alone.

One o'clock, and I retire, leaving the sick Indian to himself the remainder of the night.

Letters

WIELETPOO, WALLA WALLA RIVER, OREGON TERRITORY,
March 14, 1838.

Very, Very Dear Parents: — More than two years have passed since I left my father's home and not a single word has been wafted hence, or, perhaps I should say, has greeted my ears to afford consolation in a desponding hour. This *long,* long silence makes me feel the truth of our situation, that we are far, very far removed from the land of our birth and Christian privileges. I am weary of writing so much about ourselves without receiving a response, and yet I am anxious that father and mother should know all about us. Our opportunities of sending are so very favorable that I cannot well deny myself the privilege of writing, although it is exceedingly difficult for me to write much. We send this by our excellent friend and kind benefactor, Dr. John McLoughlin, chief factor of the Hon. Hudson's Bay Company. He starts in a few days for England, crosses the mountains with the express on the northern route to Canada, from thence he goes to New York. He had written us a few days since saying that he will try and make it convenient to call at the missionary rooms, Boston. We shall be very happy to have him do so. Probably he will be unable to make any further calls as his business requires haste. We expect him to pay us a visit as he passes, although we are twenty-five miles out of the way. We wrote several letters last fall and sent them to the Sandwich Islands in the ship *Neriede,* but our last letters from Vancouver inform us that she only sailed the very last of February from Fort George (once called Astoria). She was detained longer than usual in consequence of the melancholy death of Captain Home. He with four seamen were drowned in crossing the river from the ship *Neriede* to Fort George by the oversetting of the long boat, which was at the time under a crowd of sail. They were expecting to sail for Oahu in a few days and only thought to take a ride of pleasure in the new boat before they started to try her proof in the time of danger, little thinking that death was so near. Suddenly a squall of wind and snow came upon them and before they could lay their hands on the rigging to lower the sails she filled and sank to the bottom. The people on shore saw her coming before the storm, but as she disappeared thought she must have returned to the ship as they were not expecting her, and it was not until a day or two after that they discovered their loss. The boat is still to be seen at the bottom of the river with her rigging untouched and the mast-top standing out of the water, after an unsuccessful attempt of the ship to take her up. O, the dangers of that river! Scarcely a year passes without the loss of several lives. We have just been told that the company have lost upwards of three hundred men in the Columbia.

Our last letters leave us in a state of preparation to make a journey to Brother Spalding's. We left our home November 8th about noon, and it rained considerably until nearly sunset. The next day was clear and we made a long day of it, and got very tired. Felt obliged to make all possible speed because we had been detained at home longer than was expected. It commenced raining that night and continued until near night the next day, and we only made a short move. The next morning the ground was covered with snow, but it was clear through the day and the snow nearly disappeared. But Saturday it commenced raining just as we got our horses up to start, after raining all night. We rode all day in the wind and rain and came to the Snake river about the middle of the afternoon and thought to stop, but it cleared away, and after making a fire and warming a little, we started again and came to the crossing place, and when the sun went down it found me sitting by the root of a large tree on stones with my babe in my arms, watching by moonlight the movements in crossing our baggage and horses. This was the only piece of wood in sight and with a few bunches of wild sage a fire was made against it to warm me while waiting to cross. Soon I was seated in a canoe with my babe and landed across safely. At a little distance from the shore we found lodges and were supplied by them with fire-wood and lodge poles. Just before reaching this place we received a line from Mr. Spalding wishing us to make all possible speed. This was Saturday night and for some time we were on the point of proceeding in the night as there was a good moon and we wished to reach there before the Sabbath. We had about twelve miles and perhaps more, but I felt too much fatigued to undertake it, for we had already a tedious day for us both, and concluded to remain and ride in the morning, leaving the baggage and men to come on Monday. We found Sister Spalding very comfortable and were not a little rejoiced to meet them after a separation of a year. On the morn of the 15th she became the mother of a fine, healthy daughter. We stayed with them three weeks and had the pleasure of seeing her up about the house before we left. Mr. Pambrun, of Walla Walla, and Mr. Ewing made them a visit while we were there. Mr. Ewing remained with them a short time after we left. Had much cold and snow while we were there and in returning. We left on the 2d of December; took a log canoe and came down the waters of the Clearwater and Snake rivers to Walla Walla; thought this would be a more comfortable way than to go over the hills on horseback. It was Saturday when we started. We spent the Sabbath at the junction of Clearwater with the Snake river, where Mr. Parker was when he wrote his last letter to us when we were coming to this country, and where we were the Saturday night before we reached Mr. Spalding's. We had a tedious journey home; almost every night we were obliged to clear away the snow to find a place to camp upon, and sometimes we sailed until it was quite late to find wood, fearing we should be under the necessity of spending the night without. But in these things and in other dangers the Lord brought us safely through and we arrived at our habitation in peace, after spending a day at Walla Walla, on the evening of the 9th, Saturday, just one year to day from my first removal to this place.

Mother will see from the date of this letter and remember with interest the events of it, thirty years previous, as I do but one year ago to-day. Our little daughter is just a year old. Have felt to make an unreserved consecration of her to God to-day and to seek for wisdom and grace to train her up for His glory. She has enjoyed unremitting health, for which I desire to be thankful. Her journey to Brother Spalding's, not withstanding the severity of the weather, did her no injury. She enjoyed it very much, particularly riding on horseback. She rode with her father all the way from Walla Walla (twenty-five miles) and we only stopped once to nurse and change her, which she did not relish quite so well as to be moving. It snowed quite fast nearly all day, particularly towards night, and our stopping place was by the first stream we crossed, about half way from Walla Walla; built a fire, threw down a blanket and sat upon the ground to rest and warm for a few minutes. It was some time after dark before we reached home and were not a little rejoiced to see it again.

Alice Clarissa enjoyed the visit equally as well as her parents. Sister Spalding was the only white woman she had ever seen besides her mother, and at times she appeared to realize no difference between them. She would play with her and kiss her with the same ardor of expression she would her mother, and when the little Eliza was born it appeared for a time as if she would devour her in her eager grasp with her hands and her mouth in her great joy to welcome her.

I am certain if she could see her grandmother and grandfather she would have many kisses to bestow on them as well as upon her aunts and uncles. She is beginning to talk considerably—says "Papa," "Manna," "Sarah," "Trim," "pussy," and when we are engaged in school she will take her book or a piece of paper and a little stick to point with and say her "A, B, C, I, J, K's" very distinctly. When we sing she shows her interest in it by beating time with her hand with the other children and trying to sing. I have kept her entirely off the floor this winter until within a fortnight past, and now she begins to think of using her feet in trying to walk. We have had a school ever since we returned from Brother Spalding's, and my kitchen has been filled with children morn and eve, which has made my floor very dirty, besides it is open and cold. She is as large and larger than some of the native children of two years old. Her strength, size and activity surprises the Indians very much. They think it is owing to theirs being laced in their te-cashes (as they call the board they use for them), motionless night and day, that makes their children so weak and small when compared with her. It is doubtless owing to this with many other causes.

Soon after I commenced this letter husband, self and baby walked about a mile to see a pair of twins born in the night of the 10th. They were both boys and appeared very well. We found the mother with them in a small lodge made of a single mat, about half as high as a man, scarcely room enough for three persons to sit in it comfortably, and without a fire. She had a plenty of dried grass for her bed with a few old skins. Both of her babies were laced to a board, as small as they were. Their comforts at such a time would be death to us. They usually go from the main lodge and build a temporary hut for their lying-in hospitals. Many infants die because their mothers have not milk for them, and they know not how to prepare food to feed them or have no means to do it. They usually nurse them until they are three or more years old. In January a child died about a year and a half old, and a few moments after its mother had another one born, and we afterwards found the death of the other child to be caused by starvation. Its mother had no milk for it and it was too young to eat their roots. Sister Spalding was obliged to feed her babe considerably Little Alice Clarissa has been very much favored; she has had enough to spare most of the time.

On the last Sabbath before we left Brother Spalding's we had the unspeakable satisfaction of giving away our dear babes to God in baptism and having the seal of that blessed covenant placed upon their foreheads. Surely, dear mother, if this is a comfort to mothers in a Christian land, it is doubly so in the midst of heathen. We also had the privilege of commemorating the dying love of the Saviour, a blessing which we have not enjoyed since we sat at the table with our beloved friends in Angelica on the eve of our marriage. O, ye privileged ones who can sit together in heavenly places and mount upon wings as eagles, little do you realize the feelings of the solitary missionary in the land of darkness, as Egyptian darkness itself. Truly God is with us; were it not for this we could not live. We could not endure the responsibilities resting upon us. We cannot tell you how much we want *help to pray* for ourselves and for these perishing souls.

28th.—*My Dear Parents;*—I have but a moment to write left me. We have been expecting Doctor McLoughlin to pay us a visit but yesterday he sent us word that he was behind his time and should not be able to, but wished to have the pleasure of seeing us at Walla Walla. To-day we got ready and started, but it commenced raining so hard we were obliged to return—that is Alice and her mother. Husband will go notwithstanding the rain and is waiting for this; therefore I am in haste. I expect to write soon by another opportunity by the way of Rendezvous. We are all well. We want very much to hear from our dear parents and hope soon to have the privilege. Please accept our love and give a portion to any who are interested in our welfare and the cause they and we love. Farewell.

As ever your affectionate daughter,

NARCISSA WHITMAN.

Letters

WIELETPOO, WALLA WALLA RIVER, OREGON TERRITORY,
April 11, 1838.

My Dear Parents: — My last letter, of March 14th, I was obliged to close and send off before I had finished it. I sent it by Doctor John McLoughlin, Esq., Chief Factor, etc., etc., of the Hon. Hudson's Bay Company, who has been a resident of this country for fifteen years. I wish it were possible for some of our friends to see him. I did not see him as I passed, as I expected to. Husband did, and he asked of him letters of introduction to my friends. He takes the northern route across the mountains to Montreal, from there to New York and Boston, then across the Atlantic to England. Wm. McKay is expected to go to the States to complete a medical education, and we have given him letters of introduction and recommendation to the medical college of Fairfield, Herkimer county, N.Y. He is son of Mr. Thomas McKay, clerk of the same company, the gentleman who rendered us so many kind attentions in our journey to this country. A daughter of his has been living with us this winter, and probably will for some time. She is a very good girl, for one who has had so few advantages, and renders me much assistance in my domestic labors. The little girl of whom I wrote last fall is with me yet — Sarah Hall. She has been a great comfort to me so far, as well as the other one, but I am daily looking for trouble, and know not as we shall be able to keep her. Her father is a very wicked, troublesome man. How long he will be contented to have her stay, I know not. We do not wish to take children into our family as boarders, and dress them, for we do not think it the best way. We have many applications, but refuse all except one or two who are willing to labor. The Indians are not easily satisfied. They are so impressed with the idea that all who work are slaves and inferior persons, that the moment they hear of their children doing the least thing they are panic-stricken and make trouble. We have had a school for them for about four months past, and much of the time our kitchen has been crowded, and all seem very much attached. We shall soon commence teaching them to read their own pages, which Mr. Spalding intends to send to the Sandwich Islands, to get it printed, by the next ship that leaves Vancouver. We appear to have every encouragement missionaries could possibly expect, for the short time we have been here. We see a very great improvement in them, even in the short space of one year. That old chief, Umtippe, who threatened my husband's life last spring, is especially changed, particularly in his deportment to us, and about the house. And, besides, we are becoming familiar with their language, so that husband is able to give them a greater amount of truth with the satisfaction that they understand what is said to them; and we have every evidence to believe that they feel the force of divine truth upon their minds. For several Sabbaths past, our worship with them has been very interesting. All seem to manifest a deep interest in the instruction given them. Some feel almost to blame us for telling them about eternal realities. One said it was good when they knew nothing but to hunt, eat, drink and sleep; now it was bad. We long to have them know of a Saviour's pardoning love. The most interesting exercise is the Sabbath School in which we assemble — the youth and children at five o'clock P.M. The aged ones appear to be as much interested as the children. We have been teaching them the Ten Commandments, with which they are very much pleased. There are many very interesting children, both among the Nez Perces and Cayuses. We have generally given names to those that have attended school. One boy about ten years old we have given the name of Edward—a bright, active boy, and loves his book. He has a brother, a young man whom we call David, who is very promising; he has been to school steadily all winter, and is remarkably sedate and sober—very different from all other young men of the tribe. He, with his father, is making a large quantity of land ready for planting. He is the Indian Teloukike, that gave our baby the name of Cayuse tenni, spoken of in a former letter. His little daughter we call Jane. She attends school, also—all very good looking children, and quite handsome. Pa and Ma will see that I have my Jane, my Mary, and my Harriet, too.

My Clarissa is my own little companion from day to day, and dear daughter. My Harriet is Mr. Pambrun's little daughter, the gentleman who has done us so many favors. She was born last August. She, like all the other children of this country, was doomed to be laced to a board for the first three months of her life, but, on being released for a short season, she learned the blessed privilege of liberty, and they could not tie her up again. I am expecting her, with her mother, to make me a visit this week. I hope Harriet will remember her namesake, for I am at a loss many times to repay them for their kindnesses, for they will set no prices for anything they do. They have recently sent me a rocking-chair, and a little chair for Alice Clarissa. We are astonished, and can weep with gratitude to God for the innumerable kind favors we continually receive from the inhabitants of this country. In January we had a present of twelve fine pickled buffalo tongues, sent from Colville by Mrs. McDonald, 250 miles up the Columbia river, and the first of March we ate some apples sent us by Dr. McLoughlin. His daughter, Marian, was married this spring to Mr. Rae, a gentleman of the Company. She is the young lady that recited her lessons to me while I was at Vancouver.

We have recently had a settler near us—Mr. Compo, the man who came from the mountains with Mr. Parker. There is so much good land near us on these streams, it is probable we shall not be long without many neighbors, and, besides, the Indians are making farms all about us, which to us is a very favorable omen. We are anxious to give them the means of procuring their provisions in a more easy way, and in abundance, so that there may be less starving ones during the winter. Many come from a great distance to obtain seed for planting, and many of those who have passed us, back and forth, this winter, and to whom we have given a little corn to eat.

Flannel dresses for Alice Clarissa, shoes, etc.—in short whatever of ready-made clothing for ourselves and babe you send us, will save so much of my time for teaching and writing, the latter of which I have a great deal to do, and, besides, my eyes suffer very much from weakness—more than formerly. Notwithstanding the winters here are mild, we find flannels very comfortable from the month of November to April. In the summer the heat is sometimes very great, and most of the time we require to wear very thin clothing. I mentioned in my letters last fall the articles of clothing most needed, probably you will not be able to send until you see this. In addition to what I then wrote, I would request that strong iron-bound casks or barrels be used for packing, instead of boxes.

The books, etc., sent by the Board last summer, were injured very considerably by the salt water. The only piece of flanel sent was nearly destroyed. They should not exceed 100 pounds weight, for the convenience of the portages, and besides we shall find a few barrels very convenient in housekeeping. Clothing well packed, even with crockery in the center, would come safe. Besides the portages, we are obliged to convey our supplies on horses to our station, and to be able to do this without unpacking will save much time, expense and trouble. I thank Sister Jane very much for those numbers of the *Mothers' Magazine*. I should have done so before. Nothing can be more acceptable than regular numbers of such valuable publications. I am much pleased with W.A. Alcott's publications, what few numbers I have seen, and think them very useful, especially for mothers. If mothers need help in training up their children in Christian lands, surely we do here, in the midst of heathen, without one savory example before our eyes.

Were it not for the indelible impressions made upon my own heart, the influence of dear mother's precepts, prayer and example, which still retain their force, I should often be lost in my treatment of our dear daughter. I never can be sufficiently thankful for my education, and may it continually stimulate me to unwearied diligence for the good of others.

May 10th. — Under date April 11th, I spoke of old Umtippe's appearance. He seems to be declining fast. Last Saturday he came here, he said on purpose to spend the Sabbath. Said he had had recently three fainting turns, and felt that he should not live a great while. He had been very wicked, and did not know where his soul would go when he died — was lost about it. Sabbath noon, after the morning worship (Mr. Lee was here and preached, and husband interpreted), he said "The truth never appeared so clear to him before. Always, when he had attended worship, his mind had been on those about him, but now it had been on what was said to him. Before he came to meeting would not eat but very little, so that his mind might be clear to hear good." Never can a person manifest a greater change. That selfish, wicked, cunning and troublesome old chief, now so still and quiet, so attentive to the truth, and grateful for favors now given! Surely, naught but the spirit of God has done this. We are not yet satisfied how much he understands of the atonement, or whether he has any correct views of salvation through Jesus Christ. But this we do know, that God is able by his spirit to take what little truth we are able to give, and impress it upon the hearts and consciences of the most benighted minds.

Mr. Lee has spent much time with us, and we have been greatly refreshed with his prayers and conversations. I wish he could call, on his way to New York, and pay you a visit, but it will be very doubtful.

I have made two small kegs of butter, one for Mr. Lee, and one for Mr. McKay, to take to the mountains.

Our prospects are very flattering in every respect. The Indians have planted a good deal of land this spring, and nothing keeps them from settling about us but the want of the means of cultivation. If you wish to know more upon this subject, you can by obtaining husband's letters to Brother A. Whitman and Squire Gray, of Wheeler.

The time is at hand when I must bid you adieu once more for a season, but before writing again I hope I shall have received letters from some or all of you. May heaven's richest blessing rest upon you, my beloved parents, and the smiles of that adorable countenance be your joy continually. So prays your affectionate daughter,

NARCISSA WHITMAN.

P.S.—I have one more request to make. That is, that the name of Alice Clarissa Whitman, born at Wieletpoo, O. Territory, March 14, 1837, be placed in father's family Bible. Also, that a copy of the family record be sent us when convenient.

N.W.

Letters

WIELETPOO, WALLA WALLA RIVER, OREGON TERRITORY,
September 18, 1838.

My Dear Jane: — You know not with what feelings of inexpressible joy I received your letter dated January and August, 1837, and sent from Leroy. It came to hand, together with one from Brother Judson, the 11th of July, and had I received it four days sooner I might have sent you the answer, which by this time you would have received, and learned what our circumstances are, down to that period. I wrote Sister Whitman at that time, by the express sent to Mr. Lee, occasioned by the death of his beloved wife and our dear sister, whose loss we all deeply deplore, although I never have seen her, but was an interested correspondent. It is nearly two years and five months since I left, and have not heard a lisp from you, except one from Brother Judson, while at Liberty.

It would, indeed, have been a consolation, very great, to have received your letter sent to St. Louis, containing the accounts of which you speak, in relation to Angelica, for it was what I expected and wished to hear about you. And can it be that Mr. Dryer has at last heard and believed what Christ has been saying for so *long a time* to him? Well may he tremble and adore that grace and salvation that has snatched him from the jaws of the bottomless pit. I should, indeed, like to hear him pray, and to rejoice once more with that beloved sister that has so long wept and prayed over him; but to find him in heaven will be joy complete, unutterable. Of the thirty added to the church with him, I should like to know if Robert Waight was of the number. We have received no letters from Brother or Sister Hull or Bridgeman, and from all the letters received at that time, no one has informed us where Brother Rudd is. Your letter by Brother Gray is also received. He and his wife reached here the 14th of August. They left their company about 100 miles the other side of Snake Fort, and came on, with but one man to accompany them.

Letters received from Mr. Greene in July caused our hearts to sink, and we gave up all hopes of a reinforcement very soon joining us. But the Lord was better to us than our fear, and we feel to admire and adore his great kindness and love to us and these interesting heathen, that he has disposed the hearts of his dear people to send us helpers in this glorious work so soon. Yes, and all excellent ones, too. Mr. Walker and Mr. Eells are destined to form another station. Mr. Gray and Mr. Roberts go to assist Brother Spalding, and Mr. Smith remains with us. Mrs. Smith looks enough like sister Clarissa to be her, almost, except she is not quite as tall.

Yes, Jane, you cannot know how much of a comfort our little daughter, Alice Clarissa, is to her father and mother. O, how many melancholy hours she has saved me, while living here alone so long, especially when her father is gone for many days together. I wish most sincerely that her aunts could see her, for surely they would love her as well as her parents. She is now eighteen months old, very large, and remarkably healthy. She is a great talker. Causes her mother many steps and much anxiety. She is just beginning to sing with us in our family worship. The moment singing commences, if she is not in her mother's arms, she comes to me immediately and wishes me to take her, especially if it is a Nez Perces hymn that we are singing. We have but three or four of them, and sing them every day, and Alice has become so familiar with them that she is repeating some part of them most of the time. Situated as I am, I know not how I shall succeed in training her as I ought. So many Indians and children are constantly in and about our house, and recently I discover her much inclined to imitate and talk with them, or they with her. It makes them very much pleased to think she is going to speak their language so readily. They appear to love her much. The old chief Cut Lip says "he does not expect to live long, and he has given all his land to her."

I regret you could not have seen Mr. Gray, on your own account as well as ours, and, besides, I should like to have seen those papers you wished to send. Recollect, I have seen no papers of any kind since I left the States, except a few numbers of the *New York Observer* for the year 1836. If any of you wish to do us an incalculable favor, please send our address to the editors and request them to send us the numbers regularly, by way of the Sandwich Islands, and pay for them. I requested, before I left home, that I might have the *New York Evangelist* sent me. I have not seen but one number since. This will be the cheapest way for us to know what is going on in our beloved native land—for to remain as ignorant as we now are is a great shame. I will leave you to select what papers are most interesting for us. I can think of no better way to learn the news of home, in the present manner of letter-writing—each of you careful to send us only one sheet at a time. I cannot say who are the most hungry—you, who are saturated daily with every kind of intelligence, or us here, who can hear but little else than what passes in our little world, west of the Rocky Mountains, up and down the Columbia river.

So far as I can learn, you seem not to complain of the postage upon my letters, when I send sheets upon sheets even—for, really, I cannot find one large enough to contain all I wish to have you know about us. Now, what would be most cheering to us is to have you as liberal for our good, as for yourselves, and pay the postage on as many sheets to us as we sent you. You ought, in reality, to write much more, for you have more to write about, and far more time than a solitary missionary, overwhelmed with cares and labor, and ready to sink under them.

But whither am I running? My sheet is full before I am aware, and I have not begun to tell you my story. You speak of these children, singing sweetly, and of my hearing the voice of prayer more sweet; yes, dear Jane, it is true. The Lord has heard prayer for some immortal souls around us. One dear boy, who has been living with us little more than a year, gives pleasing evidence of a change of heart, and the lispings of his desires to God in prayer are like the first prattlings of an infant child—for all that he has learned of the English is since he has been here. His name in Mongo Mevway, his mother a native and father a Sandwich Islander. He has recently heard that his father is dead, which makes him feel very bad, and he cries; then he goes to Jesus and prays, and feels comforted. I should think he was about eleven years old. You see, Jane, Alice has come and laid her dirty hands on this letter, and given it a fine mark. I send it as it is, so that you may have some of her doings to look at, and realize, perhaps, there is such a child in existence.

For the remainder, see Sister Mary Ann's letter.

I hope you will all be particular in acknowledging our letters when and where written—so that we may know what letters are received. Do, all of you, write often, and send to Boston, for opportunities frequently occur of sending to the Sandwich Islands, and we can always get them from there once or twice a year. I thank you for your proposed visit to come and take my children home. I wish very much to see you; hope you will be persuaded to come and spend your life here in the same work in which we are engaged, and not only you, but many others I know of. I hope to receive letters from each of them, especially Mr. and Mrs. Hull, Mr. and Mrs. Brigman, Mr. and Mrs. Patrick, etc., etc. How refreshing letters would be from them, as well as from all of my brothers and sisters. I cannot see, for my life, why you do not write. I am sorry my journal cost you so much. I would not have cut the sheets had I supposed it would have made any difference. I regret you should have it printed, or any of it, for it never was designed for the public eye. You mistake Alice's Indian name. Not Cayuse Jo, but Kayuse Ten-ni—accent on the last syllable.

Ever your affectionate sister,
NARCISSA WHITMAN.

Narcissa Whitman

WIELETPOO, WALLA WALLA RIVER, OREGON TERRITORY,
September 25, 1838.

My Dear Mary Ann: — It gives me great satisfaction to have this opportunity of answering letters from beloved friends at home — a privilege I have not before enjoyed since I have been here. I am sorry you or sister Jane should hesitate so about writing me; true, it takes some time for your letters to reach me, but they are, nevertheless, interesting, and you must recollect that three years must elapse from the time of your writing, to receiving the answer, if sent by way of the Islands. You cannot be more anxious to hear from me than I am to hear from you. Dear father has written quite a long letter, and you know not how precious it is to us, and I fondly hoped dear mother would have said something, too; but she allowed her place to be filled by another hand.

When the contemplated railroad over the Isthmus of Darien shall have been opened, which is expected to take place within two or three years, I hope communications will be more frequent than they are at the present time. What you have written about the individual members of our family is much more particular than in any letters I have received, and therefore very acceptable. You cannot be too particular, for I am as interested to know about your prosperity or adversity now as while with you, both spiritually and temporally, and hope you will never hesitate again. I regret to hear of Clarissa's ill health, and of the loss of her babe. Hope she and Brother Kinny will write us soon, for I should like to know something more about them.

You speak of coming very near crossing the Rocky Mountains this spring. My dear sister, I wish most sincerely that yourself and husband were here, and Jane, too, and her husband; for there is not enough for all to do. Seeing you came so near coming, I think it is best to give up looking for you until you do come, which I hope will be soon.

Our hearts are truly refreshed by the present reinforcement. They are truly worthy people. The ladies are all with us except Mrs. Gray and will probably stay the winter. Mrs. Smith is sister to Mrs. Tracy, of Singapore. She and her husband are stationed with us for the present. I hope you will have the satisfaction of seeing Rev. Mr. Lee, who is now in the States. It will do you good to learn about us from him. Dear afflicted brother, he was not permitted to witness the sufferings his beloved wife was called to endure just before her death. She called Dr. White Thursday morning, June 21st, and lingered along until Saturday evening, at nine, her pains nearly all subsiding, which obliged him to introduce the forceps, and at half-past ten she was delivered of a living child — a son — much to the joy of all the anxious sisters present. She appeared quite well during the Sabbath, and no one doubted her recovery except the doctor, who had not been without his fears. Monday evening the babe died, and on Tuesday morning she awoke very happy and exclaimed, "I am going to my rest." And, just as the sun was rising, she sweetly breathed out her soul, into the hands of her Saviour. We all mourn her loss greatly, and feel as if the Lord had come very near to us. And again have they afflicted them, quite recently. Mrs. White, in paying a visit with Mr. Leslie to Mrs. Perkins, at the Dalles, who is expecting to be confined soon, in her return in an Indian canoe, with Indian pilots, got upset. She was taken up by the Indians, and hung to the canoe, which was bottom upwards. Mr. Leslie was taken up in the same way, but her little son, about eight months old, could not be rescued until life had become extinct. They floated for more than a mile, with their bodies in the water, before they were taken to land. Thus, you see, dangers stand thick on every side. Mrs. Lee was contemplating a visit to us, with Dr. and Mrs. White, this fall.

Now to come home. I have been to Walla Walla twice this summer, in company with my husband, to visit Mrs. Pambrun, who has been sick for a long time, and most of the time dangerously so. In the spring, when Mr. Spalding met Mr. Lee here, before he left he quite persuaded my husband to believe that he needed a house more than we did, and prevailed on him to go over and assist in building, notwithstanding he had more work on hand than he could possibly attend to, besides his own building. He left here tne first of June and was gone two weeks. I am a little before my story. Quite early in the spring, Charles Compo, Mr. Parker's interpreter, came here and put himself under our protection, and went to cultivating land here, and assisting my husband in his cares. He is an excellent man, and we feel as if the Lord had sent him here. Husband left him in charge when he went to Mr. S.'s, having got all the crops in. Imagine, if you can, the care and constant watch necessary to preserve a farm exposed to every depredation, without a fence, and not only our own stock, but the Indians', too, far and near.

His stay there was not as long as expected, in consequence of Mr. McDonald and family, from Colville, visiting them and us. Stayed a week at each station. Found them very interesting people. They went to Walla Walla from this place, and stayed until the Brigade arrived from Vancouver, which brought our letters from you—the first we had received. I was there at the time of their arrival. Letters from the Board at this time gave us the first intelligence of its embarrassments, and little or no encouragement of Mr. Gray's return with more associates.

Soon after our return, Sarah Hull, my little Indian girl, that had been living with me for little more than a year, was taken sick with a lingering sickness, and died August 11th, much regretted by us all. For a week before she died, she was helpless and speechless. On Tuesday, the 7th, husband was sent for by an express from The Dalles, to visit Mrs. Perkins, who was in a critical situation, and did not return until Monday evening. She died on Saturday evening, and was buried on the Sabbath. If ever I felt the presence of my husband necessary to sustain me, it was while passing through such a scene. But the Lord sustained and comforted me, especially during the exercises on the Sabbath. Mrs. Pambrun came up to assist about the burial. Had a general attendance. Sang, prayed and tried to talk a little to them, and but a little, for I cannot do much more than stammer yet in their language. Dear Sarah, how we all loved her, especially little Alice. She used to play with her so prettily, and divert her for hours together, and watch her so carefully when out of my sight. I never expect her loss to be made up to me in this respect, for it is rare to find one so good as she was; and besides, she understood English so well that she seldom used any other language to my babe. She was one of the number who had begun to read at our family worship. We did not get that evidence of a change of heart in her case that would have been desirable. She appeared lamentably indifferent to the subject of religion, just before her sickness, and during the former part of it; but toward the last she seemed to be more sensible, and said she thought of Jesus, and prayed to him, but was afraid to die. These were the last words we understood her to say. Her disease centered in her head, and after this she appeared not to have her reason all the time. But she is gone, and a just God has done it, and although we cannot see the reason why she should be thus taken away, when light had just begun to dawn upon her soul, yet this we know and believe, that the Hand that dealt the blow does all things well, and blessed be His holy name. Two or three of the same family died while at Mr. Lee's school at the Willamette. She was named for Mrs. Hull by her request.

Dear sister, my sheet is full, and story only half told; but I must say a little to your dear husband, for I do not know that my husband will be able to write a single letter this fall. Please give my love to your father and mother Judson. Tell her I often think of her, and should like to receive a letter from her.

Little A.C. is quite sick—has a high fever, and her mother is full of anxiety about her—so much so that she cannot sleep, for her dear father is more than 300 miles from home—now at Vancouver, and will not be home in much less than four weeks.

Ah, dear sister, you know not what it is to be a mother in heathen lands, so full of anxiety and constant care, and no kind sister to lend a helping hand. But still it is a privilege, too. I should not know how to spare her, but the Lord knows what is for the best, and I desire always to say, "Pray for me and mine, my dear sisters and brothers." As ever, and for ever,

Your affectionate sister.
NARCISSA WHITMAN.

Mrs. Mather has written me a very kind letter. I hope some of the sisters will write her. Brother J.G. has written me, and I intend to write him a long letter. Farewell dear sister.

Letters

WIELETPOO, WALLA WALLA RIVER,
Oregon Territory, Sept. 28, 1838.

My Dear Father: — The reception and perusal of your kind letter made us exceedingly happy, as, also, to hear that our dear parents are still alive and in the enjoyment of health and other favours of a kind Providence.

Nothing we hear from our beloved native land is so cheering to us as the news of revivals, repeated and extended revivals of religion. I confidently expected Angelica would be blessed of the Lord when I left. "He that watereth shall be watered," so saith the Lord, and if the sending forth of one was the means of such a blessed work, what would be the result if many of her sons and daughters were to go and preach to the heathen? Surely no one would refuse, from this consideration only, the happiness enjoyed in being thus engaged, were there no other inducement, so it seems to me. But this is a difficult truth to believe when one is surrounded with all the comforts and splendour this earth affords. Home has no attraction for me, compared with the satisfaction and enjoyment every day affords in living here and extending a silent and gentle influence upon these benighted minds, aside from the more public labours of teaching, etc. O, that I could persuade my brothers and sisters thus to consecrate themselves to this heavenly work.

As we are situated we must till the land in order to live by the fruits thereof. We are very much in want of a farmer for ourselves and to teach the Indians to cultivate. This we have asked of the Board. If dear father and mother were here they would find plenty to do and as much pleasure in doing it as they now think they would have. I sometimes almost persuade myself to think that I shall some day enjoy the privilege of seeing them here.

The Lord only knows what he has for us to pass through in this world. Frequently I feel as if our stay would not be long here. The Lord has come near our Methodist friends with death. Mrs. Lee, the wife of Mr. Lee, now in the states, died in June under painful circumstances. About two days before she died, she became the mother of a living son. After a protracted labour the child was taken from her with forceps and lived but two days. Dr. White, physician. She was deeply lamented by all who knew her, and what rendered the case more trying, her husband was absent. An express was sent immediately to the states across the mountains, to inform him of his great loss. I do hope father will see him. He can give much information about us, for he was here three weeks before he left us in passing.

Recently Mrs. White lost her babe by drowning, in returning in an Indian canoe from Mr. Perkins'.

All of our number have been mercifully preserved so far, and so have the reinforcement we have been permitted to receive this fall, all arriving here in safety and in health, quite unexpectedly, but much to our joy.

Mr. and Mrs. Smith are stationed with us. Messrs. Walker and Eells go to Colville to form a station somewhere in the Flat Head language. Mr. Gray and wife and Mr. Rogers are with Mr. Spalding. Mrs. Walker finds a home with us this winter. We have had one house full of company most all summer, and shall probably always have considerable in the future.

We have had some precious meetings with the natives the season past, and of some we are almost encouraged to hope they are Christian. We sent for Mr. S. and held meetings every day with them for a week. Hope some good was done. I have written the particulars to Brother Judson and the two sisters, which probably all will have an opportunity of seeing.

My dear husband is not at home now. He has gone to Vancouver, 300 miles from here, on business for our mission. He has already been gone nearly two weeks and will not return for two weeks more. I am feeling very anxious for his return on account of our dear babe, she has been sick ever since he left and continues to be more so, we have neither of us had a quiet night's rest for some time. I feel exceedingly anxious for her, perhaps more so than the case demands. She has always enjoyed such perfect health, probably I feel it more on that account. Her body is covered with a rash much resembling the one I had just before she was born; has considerable fever and coughs a good deal. She is so large and heavy I find it just as much as I am able to do to take care of her, and need her father's help very much. She is so accustomed to see no other ones but her parents for so long a time that she is never contented out of my sight for a moment. Dear child, I fear I love her too well, she has always been such a comfort to us. The Lord only knows what trials he has for me to pass through and my only desire is to be submissive to his will. For this reason I shall not be able to write as much as I wished, and husband's absence will prevent his writing, also.

I am sorry dear mother did not write me. I wish very much to hear her say something to me again; it will be so precious, seeing I may never see her again. I hope no one will hesitate to tell me particulars about every member of the family, spiritually and temporally, adverse and prosperous, for I am still one of your number and desire to feel and sympathize with you in everything. How I should rejoice if dear brother's affliction should finally be the means of his becoming a missionary, as he knows he ought to be. Then would he not say "Before I was afflicted I went astray, but now have I kept thy word"?

O, how I am disappointed in not hearing that Edward, by this time, is prosecuting his studies for the ministry and missionary work. I shall never feel as if all was right at home until more of the dear ones are thus wholly given up to the work of the Lord. I cannot bear the idea that either of them are living for themselves in such a day as this. The Lord will not prosper them; they are the children of too many prayers and consecration to the work thus to live and be contented with this world's portion and applause.

How was I struck to hear of the death of Giles Cornish and rejoice to think that I was permitted to deal thus faithfully with his soul while with them. I long to hear more particulars about them.

Why do not Harriet and Edward write me? Could they not tell me, if they were to see me, many things about father and mother, themselves and friends, that would do me good to hear? Why not take their paper and sit down and write them to me? It would be just as acceptable. Now, if they wish me to write to them they must all write to me, for you have far more time to write than I have. You ought, all of you, to feel it your duty and privilege thus to comfort your solitary missionary sister and brother, and begin to say something to little Alice, for if she lives she will soon understand about her uncles, aunts and grand parents.

Farewell,

NARCISSA.

Please remember me to all dear friends in Angelica. I shall try to write Sister Dryer, if I have time. While the sisters were all here we formed a Maternal Association and I am its corresponding secretary, and of course have more letters to write than usual.

It is a great satisfaction to know that we have an interest in your prayers. We hope you all will be encouraged to pray yet more and more for us, for we feel that the present is the harvest season for these perishing Indians. The Lord spares the old chief his life yet, for wise reasons we hope. He has been serious all summer and we are in hopes he will yet become a Christian.

With much love to father and mother, brothers and sisters, I am, dear parents, ever your affectionate daughter,

NARCISSA WHITMAN.

HON. STEPHEN PRENTISS,
    Angelica, Allegany Co., N.Y.

Does Sister Clarissa and her dear husband ever think of us here? Why do they not write often and send to Boston? It is just as easy for me to get your letters as for you to get mine, if you will only write. We receive letters twice a year at least and have the opportunity to just as often as you do from us. If you should all write, and write many letters, too, you would not begin to satisfy the inquiries I wish to make about you.

Narcissa Whitman

WIELETPOO, WALLA WALLA RIVER, OREGON TERRITORY,
October 3, 1838.

My Dear Mrs. Parker:—Your truly welcome letter I received, at the hand of Mr. Gray, and sincerely thank you for it. The letters we have received from our beloved native land, although but few, as yet, have been exceedingly refreshing to us, expecially when bearing such welcome news as repeated and extended revivals of religion. Oh! may we continue to be thus cheered, until the whole land is deluged with them, and not an impenitent sinner be left to go to the dark regions of despair from under the full blaze of gospel light and privileges, such as are enjoyed in the land of our birth. For truly these poor Indians will say of those who refuse, "Could we have known of the doom that awaits the incorrigible, and have been shown a crucified Saviour with outstretched arms and a bleeding heart, waiting to receive us, we never should have come to this place of torment." The tearful eye, the solemn countenance, and the anxious heart bursting forth with the inquiry, "What must I do to be saved?" are scenes which my eyes loved to behold while in the home of my childhood. But, dear sister, to be permitted to witness the same scenes here, in this land of spiritual darkness and heathenism, causes feelings indescribable, and emotions too big for utterance. This we have seen, although in but few instances yet. Our desire and earnest prayer to God is, that the cases may multiply in extent, until multitudes, both natives and the more privileged inhabitants of this country, shall become interested in the salvation which Jesus, the blessed Saviour, died to purchase.

Mr. Parker doubtless remembers his interpreter, Charles Compo. The good seed which he was permitted to sow in his heart has not been lost. He came here early last spring, took a piece of land near us to cultivate, and remained here for the summer, and assisted my husband essentially in his labors on the farm, etc. We have employed him to take charge of the farm, etc., and find him very faithful and trusty. His superior knowledge of the language makes him truly a helper in our work. He has been a regular attendant upon our family social and Sabbath worship, and given much attention to the study of the Holy Scriptures since living here. Sometime in June, we observed him to be unusually solemn, and, upon inquiry, found him in deep anxiety for the salvation of his soul. Most joyfully did we point him to the suffering risen Saviour as the only way of escape from impending ruin, and as joyfully did he embrace him as his all-sufficient Saviour, and now can say, "The pleasures of this world have no charms for me."

Husband sent for Mr. Spalding to come and hold a protracted meeting with the Indians at our station. At the close of it, we formed ourselves into a little church. We had two laborers sent from the Sandwich Islands—Joseph Mahi and wife, both members of Mr. Bingham's native church. These, with ourselves and Compo, made our number seven. He requested to become a member, and on Sabbath, in the presence of the people, was regularly married and received to our little number, and sat down to the table of the Lord with us, for the first time celebrated at Wieletpoo. He was baptized and afterwards gave his little son to God in baptism. The season was a refreshing one to us. Mr. Pambrun was here and spent the Sabbath, and went away not a little affected with the scenes. We gain satisfactory evidence for one of the boys living in our family, as having found the pearl of great price. A young man living at Walla Walla, who was here during the meeting, expresses a hope likewise. And there are two or three of the Indians who appear to be unusually serious, and sometimes we almost feel as if they were of the number who have obtained mercy of the Lord.

A most important transaction during the meeting was the formation of a temperance society for the benefit of the Indians. All of the chiefs and principal men of the tribe who were here, readily agreed to the pledge, and gave in their names to become members of the society. I have recently been informed that two of them have been tempted to drink, but have refused and turned their backs upon it, saying they would never drink again. They are truly an interesting people. We love them most sincerely, and long to see them turning unto the Lord. It grieves us very much that you should think or hear that John is spoiled by your indulgence "or that we think so." No, my dear sister, it is not so—far otherwise. John is the same unassuming, humble, obedient lad that he was while at Ithaca, possessing many excellent traits of character different from many of his countrymen. The last time we saw him (which was in the spring, when he made us a visit), husband, in conversation with him, thought he gave good evidence of a change of heart. But he is not long for this world, if he is still alive. Nearly one year ago he was taken with the most afflicting disease I ever saw—the swelling of the joints. He came here for medical attention. He was so disfigured it distressed us very much to see him. The middle finger on each hand at the knuckles, and knee joints, were very much swollen. We urged him to stay with us—told him we would take good care of him and teach him, etc., but he was afraid to stay, fearing the Doctor would find it necessary to perform some surgical operation upon him. He left us, and I know not that we ever shall see him again in this world, and if we are permitted to meet him in heaven it will be, no doubt, in consequence of the prayers and instructions received while at Ithaca. He says he used to pray with Henry and others there, and no doubt their example was the means of his praying with and teaching his fellow mates to pray and sing the praises of God most sweetly, as I used to hear them when I was on a visit to Mrs. S. last fall. And two of the number are already numbered with the dead, leaving satisfactory evidence that they had given their hearts to the Saviour, and were going to meet him in heaven. Bright, healthy, promising girls when I saw them last fall. They had received the names of Martha and Mary, and were baptized just before they died. Truly, these are choice mercy drops to cheer us in our toilsome work here, for which we would be unfeignedly grateful.

Really, my sheet is full nearly, and I have not said half yet. It is a matter of great joy to us that we are so soon and so bountifully reinforced, and so unexpectedly, too. Mr. and Mrs. Gray join Mr. S. in their work. We are much pleased with our acquaintance with Mrs. G.—think her a most excellent person, and will, no doubt, be a great blessing to our missions. Mr. and Mrs. Walker, Mr. and Mrs. Eells, locate somewhere in the range of the Flathead language.

•

John's father lives many miles from us, and several from Mr. Spalding's. Before he was taken sick he was very attentive to his book, and assisted Mr. S. in cultivating, and his father, also; since, he chooses to be with his parents all the time. It has a happy effect upon his mind to remind him of his Ithaca friends, and when I asked him if he remembered the verse Mrs. Parker used to teach him, "For God so loved the world," etc., said he did, and brought me his Testament and wanted me to find it for him. I did. He took it and studied it a long time, very thoughtfully. It would be very desirable to have him near some of us, so that we might instruct him more, but this is denied us.

We were considerably disappointed not to receive letters from Mr. Parker. Hope he will not forget us. Please write, all of you. Miss McLoughlin is married to Mr. Rae. Her father has gone to England. As Mr. Lee is now in the States, you will probably hear all the news about Vancouver from him.

Messrs. W. and E. have gone to explore, and letters from them, recently received, say the Big Head's land, the chief of the Flatheads, situated near the Spokane Falls, is the place recommended by Mr. McDonald as the most favorable for a station—had not yet decided—intended to visit several other places. Their ladies will probably remain with us during the winter, particularly Mrs. Walker. My husband is now at Vancouver, in business for the mission, and probably will not be able to write as many letters to his friends as usual. With much love to you, dear husband, self and family, I am, dear sister, affectionately yours, in Christian love,

N. WHITMAN.

Saturday, 6th.—I have just heard from John. Richard has just come from his father's—says he is very sick and near dying, but he is praying and reading his testament all the time, and loves to think of Jesus. O, that I could see him once more! We love him tenderly, and always have, and Richard, too. He has come here well dressed, and wished to stay and go to school; how long he will stay contented I know not, but feel inclined to keep him.

NARCISSA WHITMAN.

Rev. Mrs. Samuel Parker,
    Ithaca, Tompkins Co., New York.

Letters

WIELETPOO, Feb. 18th, 1839.

My Dear Sister:—I received your letter last week, although written in Dec. We had some time ago the pleasure of reading of your husband's visit to the Willamette, in an account which he gives the particulars relative to the protracted meeting there. Be assured we rejoiced with you and angels in heaven at such a glorious display of the power of our God, and stretch out our hearts to desire a like blessing upon ourselves and our heathen neighbors.

I am much interested in the people at Vancouver, and am pleased to hear of the ladies' improvement, and earnestly hope the good work may extend to that place also, and that your detention there may result in great good to many souls.

The Lord will take care of those Roman priests there. It is doubtless for some wise purpose he has permitted them to enter this country. May we be wise and on the alert, and show ourselves true, faithful, energetic in our Master's work as they do, and we shall have no cause for fear, for there are more of us, their presence in this country; at least we feel it our duty to use every possible effort to obtain the language of the people, and not having as good an opportunity amid the cares of our family as we could wish, we, husband, self and little Alice, left our dwelling and went about sixty-five miles to a camp of Indians, in January, and was gone nearly three weeks, and received much benefit. Previous to this, husband had been over to Brother S.'s to attend a protracted meeting, held at the same time with yours at the W. And now we are on the eve of another departure. We expect tomorrow morn to start on a visit to Brother S.'s to attend a meeting of the mission, and also another protracted meeting with the Indians, when it is expected that nearly all the Nez Perces will be present. We feel deeply anxious for our people, and it seems sometimes as if the blessing was almost within reach for them, but it is withheld, and doubtless because the Lord sees that we are not prepared to receive it. O, for that deep humility, strong faith, repentance and union of soul in prayer which was the secret of success in your meeting, and which characterizes every revival of religion. But I must be excused from writing more at this time. Shall want to hear from you as soon as you shall have arrived home. Should judge from sister Walker's letter from you that the dear little babe, Henry Johnson, had got considerable hold of its mother's affections already. Precious trust, that, dear sister—an immortal mind to rear for Eternity. The Lord bless you and give you grace and wisdom to train that child for His glory, both in this world and hereafter, and make you feel continually that, what ever you do for him, you do it as belonging to the Lord, as given to Him and only a lent blessing to you, to train up for Him. But more of this another time.

With kind regards to your husband and Brother Lee, who we hope is again cheered with the society of his fellow associates by this time, and a kiss for the little one,

I am your affectionate sister,

N. WHITMAN.

P.S.—Mrs. W. will tell you her story herself as she has more time than I at present.

Rev. Mrs. Perkins,
    Wascopum.

Care of
    Lieut. P.C. Pambrun,
        Fort Walla Walla.

My Dear Sister:—Yours of the 8th inst. I received the evening of my return to this place from Clearwater. It had been waiting me but a day or two, I believe. I am happy to hear that you are once more so near us again. I received a hint from Sister White in her last letter that yourself and husband were on the way, or soon would be, to pay us a visit. I fear my last letter informing you of my absence has discouraged your coming. Had I received the least intimation that it were possible for you to visit us while our sisters were all here, I would have been at home without fail. The open winter and spring had made it more favorable for the them to leave for the upper station much earlier than was expected. They left the first of March just before I returned. We met them, however, on the Palouse, after they had been our five days. All was well; the babe was enduring the journey as well as could be expected. I hope you will still think of coming this season. We shall be happy to see you.

I visited Mrs. Pambrun on Monday of this week—found her in much better health than I once feared she ever would be again. She certainly talks English very well. I found myself able to obtain all the information concerning Vancouver I could wish. Maria has been with me a short time, and for her sake I would have been happy to have had her remain longer; but she could not be persuaded to stay from her mother any longer. We have a daughter of Mr. McKay's with us now—for little more than a year. She improves very much and promises to make a valuable person if she can be kept long enough.

You wished me to write something about my little girl. I do not know what to tell you than to say she is a large, healthy and strong child, two years old the 14th of this month. She talks both Nez Perces and English quite fluently, and is much inclined to read her book with the children of the family, and sings all our Nez Perces and English quite fluently, and is much inclined to read her book with the children of the family, and sings all our Nez Perces hymns and several in English. Her name is Alice Clarissa. You dreamed of seeing her you say. I hope it will be a reality soon, for I am very anxious to see young Henry Johnson, too. I am glad he learns to bear the yoke so well, not in his youth, but in his infancy. Exposures in journeyings in this country appear to be a benefit rather than an injury to our children. I have taken several with Alice, and they have generally been in the winter. When she was nine months old we went to Brother Spalding's to attend upon our sister at the birth of their child. It was in November, and we returned in December by way of Snake river, in a canoe. It was a tedious voyage, but we neither of us received any injury.

We intend to be very free from worldly cares this season, and apply ourselves entirely to the missionary work of studying the language and teaching. After our successful trial of last winter's encamping with the Indians, husband feels that he has no excuse for not taking me again and again, and I can make no objection, notwithstanding it would be far easier for me to stay at home with my child, and perhaps better for her; but the roving habits of the Indians make it necessary for us either to do so, or else spend the greater part of our time alone, during their absence from the Station. Husband is appointed to commence an out-station on the Snake river at the mouth of the Tukanon, and besides spending some time there during the fishing season, we intend to go to Grand Round with the Kayuses.

Brother and Sister Smith will probably go somewhere in the heart of the Nez Perce country, beyond Brother Spalding's, in order to commence translating the Scriptures immediately. We find work enough to do for all hands, and our daily prayer is that God will pour out His spirit on these benighted minds and turn their darkness into light, and make them His.

I hope you will continue to write often and freely. I do not see how you get along and learn so many languages. What is the particular benefit? We hear many spoken, but we intend to learn only one, and make that the general one for the country. We are all enjoying good health. Received a letter from Sister Spalding saying that Sister Gray was happily the mother of a little son—had a remarkable short and easy sickness and is doing well. The babe weighed nine pounds.

Please give my kind regards to your husband and Brother Lee. Hope he finds the monotony of Wascopam much changed by the return of its former occupants, particularly when there is such a pleasing addition.

Yours in love,

N. WHITMAN.

Rev. Mrs. Perkins,
    Wascopam.

Narcissa Whitman

WIELETPOO, WALLA WALLA RIVER, OREGON TERRITORY,
May 17th, 1839.

My Dear Jane: — This is a late hour for me to commence my home correspondence. Yesterday Mr. Ermatinger, who commands the expedition instead of Mr. McLeod and McKay, left here, after spending a night with us, for the mountains. We have felt much uncertainty about letters sent this way reaching you, this year. There is some doubt in Mr. E.'s mind about his being able to go as far as the American Rendezvous; if he does not, there probably will be no one to take them and bear them on, and it must be a known hand, too, for it is not safe to trust letters to those reckless beings who inhabit the Rocky Mountains. Besides this reason, we have been so much on the wing since the first day of January, that it has not been easy to write. If you have received my fall letters, they will show you where and how we were situated for the winter. In December, just three months after the arrival of the re-enforcement, Mrs. Walker gave birth to a fine son, here in our house. Mr. Smith had but just removed into the new house built last fall and winter after my husband's return from Vancouver. She did not recover without three relapses; suffered much from sore breasts and nipples, and what to me would be the greatest affliction, no nipples at all. Her poor babe had to depend upon a foreign native nurse or milk from the cows.

Mrs. Gray had a son born in March, the twentieth — recovered in a short time.

I said to you that we had been on the wing. January the first day, husband started to go to Brother Spalding's to attend a protracted meeting; after the close, and on his return, he formed a plan of going and living with the Indians for the benefit of having free access to the language and to be free from care and company. He had no difficulty to persuade me to accompany him, for I was nearly exhausted, both in body and mind, in the labor and care of our numerous family. Accordingly we left home on the 23rd of January. It was about fifty miles from our place; we arrived on the third day; had a pleasant journey and quite warm for the season of the year; we slept in a tent and made a fire before the mouth of it. We had not been there but two or three days before it became very cold and snowed some. This with the smoke made Alice cry some, and we were obliged to put up a lodge around the fire at the mouth of the tent to prevent the smoke from troubling us. While there I attempted to write you about us, but was soon obliged to give it up. I will make one extract from what I did write:

"Sab. at Tukanon, Jan. 27, 1839. — This has been a day of peculiar interest here. Could you have been an eye witness of the scenes you would, as I do, have rejoiced in being thus privileged. The morning worship at daybreak I did not attend. At midday I was present. Husband talked to them of the parable of the rich man and Lazarus; all listened with eager attention. After prayer and singing, an opportunity was given for those who had heavy hearts under a sense of sin, and only those, to speak if they wished it. For a few moments all sat in silence; soon a prominent and intelligent man named Timothy broke the silence with sobs weeping. He arose, spoke of his great wickedness, and how very black his heart was; how weak and insufficient he was of himself to effect his own salvation; that his only dependence was in the blood of Christ to make him clean and save his soul from sin and hell. He was followed by a brother, who spoke much to the same effect. Next came the wives of the first and of the second, who seemed to manifest deep feelings. Several others followed; one in particular, while confessing her sins, her tears fell to the ground so copiously that I was reminded of the weeping "Mary who washed her Saviour's feet with her tears." All manifested much deep feeling; some in loud sobs and tears; others anxious and solemn countenance. You can better imagine my feelings than I can describe them on witnessing such a scene in heathen lands. They had but recently come from the meeting at Brother Spalding's. We know not their hearts or motives of action, but our sincere prayer is that they all may be gathered to His fold as the children of His flock.

"O, my dear Jane, could you see us here this beautiful eve, the full moon shining in all her splendor, clear, yet freezing cold, my little one sleeping by my side, husband at worship with the people within hearing, and I sitting in the "door of the tent" writing, with my usual clothing except a shawl, and handkerchief on my head, and before me a large comfortable fire in the open air. Do you think we suffer? No, dear Jane; I have not realized so much enjoyment for a long time as I have since I have been here. I know mother will say it is presumption for them to expose themselves and that child to the inclemencies of such a season. We are all much better prepared to endure and secured from the cold than any we see about us, and ought not to say we suffer; and besides, Alice's health has improved since she left the house. But the advantages we expect to derive form associations with and benefiting them will more than compensate us for the little inconvenience we now experience. The meeting is closed and I write no more."

I was not able to write more after this. We stayed into the third week and were necessarily called home sooner than we expected. We had been home but just a week when husband was called to attend the meeting of our mission. I was permitted to accompany him. We started on Tuesday noon in a rainstorm, and reached there on Friday a little after noon, making 110 miles in three days on horseback, Alice riding with her father. This was in Feb. In March we returned, but not in the same way. Here I think I must stop, for if I should go into particulars it would take more time than I can command at present.

Mr. Hall and wife have arrived from the Sandwich Islands. They have come for the benefit of Mrs. H.'s health; brought a printing press, which is stationed at Mr. S.'s, and next week husband expects to go there to make arrangements for the benefit of Mrs. H.'s health. She is affected with a spinal irritation and appears just like L. Linsley; sits up but very little; was carried there in a boat up the Snake river. He thinks he can cure her. He has had several cases since he has been here, all with good success. Others write us if Mrs. Hall is benefited, they will probably come. We feel closely united to that mission. Our number of correspondents increase. Mrs. Judd and Mrs. Whitney write to me.

The Indians we encamped with were Nez Perces. The most of them were not so hardened in sin; or, rather, they were not so proud a people as our people, the Wieletpoos, are; the most of ours have been absent during the winter, and returned just the time we returned from Tukanon. Husband spent more than usual time in worship and instructing them, and instead of yielding to the truth they oppose it vigorously, and to this day some of them continue to manifest bitter opposition.

You know now how much we are expecting Brother and Sister Judson, and if we do not see him in July by the ship, I shall feel that he is coming across the mountains with

Brother Lee. We need help very much, and those who will pray, too. In this we have been disappointed in our helpers last come, particularly the two Revs. who have gone to the Flatheads. They think it not good to have too many meetings, too many prayers, and that is it wrong and unseemly for a woman to pray where there are men, and plead the necessity for wine, tobacco, etc; and now how do you think I have lived with such folks right in my kitchen for the whole winter? If you can imagine my feelings you will do more than I can describe. To have such dampers thrown upon us when we were enjoying such a precious revival season as we were when they came, is more than I know how to live under. This, with so much care and perplexity, nearly cost me a fit of sickness; and I do not know but it would have taken my life had it not been for the journey I was permitted to take the last of the winter. What I write here had better be kept to yourselves lest it should do injury.

We have just this moment received the news that the ship from England had arrived, but had brought no letters for us from our dear friends, because the ships had not arrived from the States to the Islands when she passed. We know not when we shall hear from home. I do not know where to send this because you say you visit Onondage next summer. O, how I long to hear about them there. O, that you would all write me, and each take a different subject, so as to tell me all the news you can.

With much love from husband, Alice and myself to you all and all with whom you are concerned, adieu.

    Your sister, in haste,
          NARCISSA WHITMAN.

P.S.—A.C. talks much, sings much, loves to read her book, and every morning at worship repeats her verse as regularly as morning comes; and appears to take a part in the worship, especially in the singing, as if she was as old as her mother; and often is very much disappointed if we do not give the tunes she is acquainted with; and she and her mother often talk about her relatives in the States. I might write half a sheet about our dear daughter, but have not time. Mr. Hall says much to us about the evils of allowing her to learn the native language, as well as our correspondents there. I can assure you we feel deeply for her. We know not what is our duty concerning her. In order to prevent it it appears that I must take much of my time from intercourse with the natives. I cast myself upon the Lord. I know He will direct in every emergency, and so farewell. Pray for us and the heathen. We hope and pray for a revival of religion. If our own hearts were united and right we should see it soon, and a general one, too.

                M.W.
                N.W.
                A.C.W.

Miss Jane A. Prentiss,
  Quincy,
    Illinois.

Letters

WIELETPOO, June 25th, 1839.

My Dear Sister:—Your letter of April inst. I received but a few days ago, or it would have been answered much sooner. You make some important inquiries concerning my treatment of my precious child, Alice Clarissa, now laying by me a lifeless lump of clay. Yes, of her I loved and watched so tenderly, I am bereaved. My Jesus in love to her and us has taken her to himself.

Last Sabbath, blooming in health, cheerful, and happy in herself and in the society of her much loved parents, yet in one moment she disappeared, went to the river with two cups to get some water for the table, fell in and was drowned. Mysterious event! We can in no way account for the circumstances connected with it, otherwise than that the Lord meant it should be so, Husband and I were both engaged in reading. She had just a few minutes before been reading to her father; had got down out of his lap, and as my impression, was amusing herself by the door in the yard. After a few moments, not hearing her voice, I sent Margaret to search for her. She did not find her readily, and instead of coming to me to tell that she had not found her, she went to the garden to get some radishes for supper; on seeing her pass to the water to wash them, I looked to see if Alice was with her, but saw that she was not. That moment I began to be alarmed for Mungo had just been in and said there were two cups in the river. We immediately inquired for her, but no one had seen her. We then concluded she must be in the river. We searched down the river, and up and down again in wild dismay, but could not find her for a long time. Several were in the river searching far down. By this time we gave her up for dead. At last an old Indian got into the river where she fell in and looked along by the shore and found her a short distance below. But it was too late; she was dead. We made every effort possible to bring her to life, but all was in vain. On hearing that the cups were in the river, I resolved in my mind how they could get there, for we had not missed them. By the time I reached the water-side and saw where they were, it came to my recollection that I had a glimpse of her entering the house and saying, with her usual glee, "Ha, ha, supper is most ready" (for the table had just been set), "let Alice get some water," at the same time taking two cups from the table and disappearing. Being absorbed in reading I did not see her or think anything about her—which way she went to get her water. I had never known her to go to the river or to appear at all venturesome until within a week past. Previous to this she has been much afraid to go near the water anywhere, for her father had once put her in, which so effectually frightened her that we had lost that feeling of anxiety for her in a measure on its account. But she had gone; yes, and because my Saviour would have it so. He saw it necessary to afflict us, and has taken her away. Now we see how much we loved her, and you know the blessed Saviour will not have His children bestow and undue attachment upon creature objects without reminding us of His own superior claim upon affections. Take warning, dear sister, by our bereavement that you do not let your dear babe get between your heart and the Saviour, for you like us, are solitary and alone and in almost the dangerous necessity of loving too ardently the precious gift, to the neglect of the giver.

Saturday evening, 29, — After ceasing to restore our dear babe to life, we immediately sent for Brother Spalding and others to come and sympathize and assist in committing to the grave her earthly remains. Tuesday afternoon Mr. Hall reached here. Mr. S. and wife took a boat and came down the river to Walla Walla, and reached here Thursday morning, nine o'clock, and we buried her that afternoon, just four days from the time her happy spirit took its flight to the bosom of her Saviour. When I write again, I will give you some particulars of her short life, which are deeply interesting to me, and will be to you, I trust, for you, too, are acquainted with a mother's feelings and a mother's heart.

Probably we may return to Clearwater with Brother and Sister S., as it is necessary for my husband to go on business for the mission. Dear sister, do pray for me in this trying bereavement, for supporting grace to bear without murmuring thought, the dealings of the blessed God toward us, and that it may be sanctified to the good of our souls and of these heathen around us.

O! on what a tender thread hangs these mortal frames, and how soon we vanish and are gone. She will not come to me, but I shall soon go to her. Let me speak to you of the great mercy of my Redeemer toward one so unworthy. You know not, neither can I tell you, how much He comforts and sustains me in this trying moment. He enables me to say, "The Lord gave and the Lord hath taken away, blessed, ever blessed, be the name of the Lord."

Sister Spalding sends love to you and will write you soon.

In haste, as ever your affectionate, but now afflicted sister in Christ,

NARCISSA WHITMAN.

Rev. Mrs. H.K.W. Perkins,
    Wascopum.

Letters

WIELETPOO, July 26th, 1839.

Very Dear Sister:—You know now how like an angel's visit your dear husband's presence has been to me, now in my truly lonely situation, for my dear husband has been absent for a week. This added to the death of my precious Alice has almost overcome me. He proposes to leave early in the morning; I would gladly detain him if I could till my husband's return. I thought I must write a few lines to endeavor to persuade you to undertake a visit to us when he comes to go to the general meeting. I think I have removed all his objections and made it appear easy for him to carry your dear babe. Now if you knew how easy we get along in traveling with children, you would not hesitate for a moment. I need not say that I want to see you very much and shall expect you will come, and we will go together to brother Spalding's. Do come; it will do you good; it will do us all good to meet together and mingle our prayers and tears before the throne of grace.

I have been talking to your husband much about Alice. When I see you I can tell you all. I am not able to say anything about her now for want of time. It would do me much good to see little Henry, and I shall feel that you will come and will have no occasion to regret or feel that you have lost time by it. We shall expect to have a meeting of our National Association, which we anticipate will be interesting to us all, especially mothers.

You will excuse this hasty note, I trust. I will write more next time, if you do not come.

Believe me ever your affectionate sister in the Lord.

N. WHITMAN.

P.S.—I ought to have said before this that your kind and sympathizing letter was cordial to my afflicted heart. Remember me to Brother Lee and kiss the babe for me.

N.W.

Rev. Mrs. H.K.W. Perkins.
    Wascopum.

Narcissa Whitman

WIELETPOO, September 30, 1839.

My Dearest Father:—I never have found it so trying to commence writing to my friends home as at this time, simply because of the late afflictive dispensation of Providence towards us, which renders me almost incapable of writing, from excessive feeling, the moment my thoughts return to the subject.

You will, doubtless, before this reaches you, have heard, through the Board, of the melancholy death of our *most precious and only child, Alice Clarissa.* That we loved her most ardently is true, and it is no less true that we feel keenly the severe pangs of a separation from *her*, who was so much the joy and comfort of our hearts in our lonely situation. Yet, it is the Lord that hath done it, and he has dealt with us as a tender parent deals with the children whom he loves. O, how often have I felt and thought what a privilege it would be, if I could see and unburden to my dear parents the sorrows of my broken and bleeding heart, since we have been bereft of our dear, sweet babe. Although deprived of this inestimable consolation, yet, dearest father, I desire to ask you to unite with us in praise and gratitude to God that He has so mercifully sustained me, and that, when crushed to the earth because His hand lay heavily upon me, His grace was manifest to preserve and sustain my soul from murmuring or repining at His dealings with us. This unspeakable consolation is ours, that our daughter is at rest in the bosom of Him who said: "Suffer the *little children* to come unto me, for of such is the kingdom of heaven." We rejoice, too, that we have been permitted to become parents, and that she has been spared to us as long as she was, and for the pleasure we had in witnessing the development of her ardent, active mind. Young as she was, we could plainly see a manifest relish and enjoyment in singing and worship, and the last month of her life she commenced learning to read, and improved rapidly. Mrs. Judd's little daughter had just sent her one of Gallaudet's *Mother's Primers,* with which she was much pleased, and had learned to the eighteenth page, the whole of which she read twice the day she was drowned.

But I must haste to give you the particulars of her sudden, mysterious flight. In letters previous, I have spoken of the situation of our home on the bank of the Walla Walla river, a large and rapid stream emptying into the Columbia. We had often thought of the danger to which she was exposed in our being so near the water, when she should run about, and have watched her most carefully, and used every precaution to make her fear going near the brink, and, till then, thought we had succeeded. But, unfavorably for us and her, she had lost that timidity from seeing children who had been here on a visit, with their parents, just a week or two before, playing about the water and seeing others of the family going to that place for water. Friday afternoon, before she fell in, we were in the garden weeding, and she was with us, diverting herself in trying to assist us, as she often had been, and just as we were about to go to the house, her father pulled up a radish and threw it down. She took it and was out of sight in a moment, and we supposed she had gone to the house. We came along directly, and husband stopped at the river to wash his hands, and found her there, washing the radish, which both frightened and surprised us, as we had never known her to venture there before. Her father first thought to put her into the water, all over, but feared the effect upon her reason, it being so easy to frighten her. Although we were horror-stricken at seeing her there—it being the first time—we did not inflict any punishment upon her, but talked to her seriously of the consequence to her if she should fall in, and concluded, in our minds, if we ever saw her near there again, to take some course to make her fear to approach the forbidden place. But, when the next time came, it was too late. While conversing with her that evening, we told her that if she should fall in the water she would die, and then father and mother would have no little Alice. She had, a few weeks before, seen her father drown a little dog that she used to play with, because it was sick and we feared it would injure her; and she seemed to realize what it meant when we told her that she would die, like Boxer, and mamma have no Alice. Some minutes after, while sitting in my lap, she appeared to be in deep thought, and said to me, with inquiring looks, "Alice fall in water, Alice she die like Boxer—mamma have no Alice." I then repeated my commands, and talked to her for some time, but it soon passed from her mind, as the event of her death will show.

I would describe to you, if I could, her bright, lively appearance on Sabbath morning, the day of her death. She had always slept with me until just a week before her death, and that night she proposed of her own accord, to sleep on the mat on the floor. This gave me a very strange and singular feeling, for I never could persuade her to lie away from me, not even in her father's arms, before, and I could not divest myself of the feeling that she was laid away for the grave. It being very warm, and because she preferred it, I let her sleep on the floor all night—but did not sleep much myself. Ever after this, I made a bed for her up by the side of mine, where I could lay my hand upon her. When I used to take her into the bed with me, she would lie a little while and then wish to go back again. Thus she gradually went out of my arms to the grave, so that I should not feel is so severely as if torn from them at once.

Sabbath morning, as she lay sleeping, I kissed her; she immediately awakened, stretched up her arms and put them about my neck and hugged and kissed me for a long time. I then told her I would go and get some water in a tub, to wash her, and went out. While I was gone, I heard her calling to me, and her father, who was sitting in the room, said she appeared to be reasoning with me, trying to persuade me that it was not best for her to be washed, and when I came for her, she said she did not wished to have me wash her in the tub. The manner of her talking, and her objecting to be washed, was so singular and unusual that I did not know how to understand it. I did not yield to her, but put her into the tub and washed her. She mildly submitted, but there was something so plaintive in her entreaties with me that I have since been sorry that I did not listen to her. I did not know but that it was the Sabbath that made her feel so reluctant about it, for it had been my usual practice to wash her on Saturday.

Her appearance at worship in the family was deeply interesting. She had been in the habit of selecting the hymn she wished us to sing, for some time, and that morning her choice was "Rock of Ages, Cleft for Me," a hymn which she has been delighted in singing for some time. O, if dear father and mother could have seen with what animation she sang, and how her sweet voice soared above ours! when we had completed the first verse, she arose out of her little chair and said, "Mamma, should my tears forever flow?" as if to remind me which verse came next, and when we commenced it she sat down and sung on, as usual. Our worship with the Indians was about noon. There being but four or five here, the camp having left the week previous, we had them come into our house. Her appearance was solemn and attentive, and, to close, husband requested the same hymn to be sung as at family worship. She united with us again, with a clearness and distinctness we shall never forget, and with such ecstacy as almost to raise her out of her chair. And no wonder, for what words could have been more appropriate to her mind than these: —

> "While I draw this fleeting breath,
> When my eyelids close in death;
> When I rise to worlds unknown,
> And behold Thee on Thy throne,
> Rock of Ages, cleft for me,
> Let me hide myself in Thee."

Dear father, when you sing this hymn, think of me, for my thoughts do not recur to it without almost overcoming me, and bringing fresh to my mind how she appeared when she last sang it with us. She had begun to talk about her grandparents, uncles and aunts, considerably, and I had hoped she would live to see them before she died, or at least some of them.

Little did we think that young breath was so fleeting, or that those sparkling eyes would so soon be closed in death, and her spirit rise to worlds unknown, and that to behold on His everlasting throne of glory, Him who once said, "I will be a God to thee, and thy seed after thee."

This was the last we heard her sing. After this she read her lesson to us, and then her father took her out into the garden and picked a stalk of pieplant for her, which she was very fond of. She called it apple. She ate a part of it and then threw the rest down. We both of us were sitting near the door, and she was diverting herself in and about it, and Margaret had been ordered to set the table, and get supper. The moment I ceased to hear her voice, or to see her, I sent Margaret to find her, and so it had always been. I never felt easy the moment she was out of sight, and I did not hear her, or know her father had the care of her, and so it was this time. I sent M. for her, but she did not look for her but little, and then went into the garden for radishes and lettuce for supper, but she did not come and tell me that she could not find her.

This letter must answer for all of our friends, for it will be impossible for us to write all we could wish. I have been engaged in copying a dictionary for two or three weeks, besides attending to our school, which is a great reason why I cannot write more, and my eyes trouble me very much.

Letters

WIELETPOO, WALLA WALLA RIVER, OREGON TERRITORY,
October 9, 1839.

Dearest Mother: — I have written a whole sheet to father talking about our dear little daughter, and have just arrived to the scene of her death. It was half past two when we gave directions for supper, thinking to have it some earlier than usual because husband had not eaten anything since breakfast, when I sent Margaret to look for her. Mungo went out with her at the same time and went to the river, but came back immediately and said there were two cups in the river. This startled us at once and as I made the inquiry, "How did they come there?" husband said "Let them be and get them out to-morrow, because of the Sabbath." I asked again how they came there and what cups they were. He said "I suppose Alice put them there," and immediately went out and took some poles to get them out. Why I was not alarmed in an instant is to me astonishing. It was doubtless owing partially to my confidence in the girl I sent for her, because she did not come and tell me she could not find her. I trusted she had and had taken her with her to get radishes, etc. I looked to see if she was with her, husband at the same time going to see about the cups. I went to the other side of the house and inquired for her, but no one had seen her. Then it was pretty plain in my mind where she was, and by the time I got to the river's brink, it flashed across my mind like a dream, that I had had a glimpse of her, while sitting and reading, entering the house and on seeing the table set for supper, she exclaimed with her usual animation, "Mamma, supper is almost ready; let Alice get some water." She went up to the table and took *two cups* that set by her plate and Margaret's (for we drank water instead of tea) and disappeared. This was like a shadow that passed across my mind, passed away and made no impression. Strange as it seemed to myself, I did not recollect it until I reached the place where she had fallen in. And now where is she? We thought if we could find her immediately she would not be dead entirely, so but that we could bring her to again. We ran down on the brink of the river near the place where she was, and, as if forbidden to approach the spot, although accessible, we passed her, crossed a bend in the river far below and then back again, and then in another direction, still further below, while others got into the river and waded to find her, and what was remarkable, all entered the river below where she was at last found. Dear mother, you cannot tell what our feelings were at that time, neither can I describe them to give you any adequate idea. By this time all hopes of her life were given up for she had been in the water too long now to think of saving her. As we were coming towards the house, we saw an old Indian preparing to enter the river where she fell in. I stopped to see him swim under water until he passed me, and just a little below me he took her from the water and exclaimed "She is found." I ran to grasp her to my breast, but husband outran me and took her up from the river, and in taking her into his arms and pulling her dress from her face we thought she struggled for breath, but found afterwards that it was only the effect of the atmosphere upon her after being in water. We tried every means that could be used to bring her to life, for a long time, but to no effect. Her spirit had been called to rise to worlds before unknown, and I could only say, "Lord, it is right; it is right; she is not mine, but thine; she has only been lent to me for a little season, and now, dearest Saviour, thou hast the best right to her; 'Thy will be done,' not mine." I cannot wish her back in this world of sin and pain; her tender spirit was of too delicate material to remain here longer and be subject to the ills of this cruel and unfriendly world. Jesus' love for her was greater than mine. He saw it necessary for our good and in mercy to her to take her to Himself. For a moment I felt all the horrors of the reflections that perhaps it might not be well with my precious child, and what was the horror at that moment to my soul. I immediately flew to the promises of God's holy word. I thought of his everlasting covenant in which he has permitted us, as parents, to enter, and the consciousness of an entire consecration of her to God, and to train her up to him, and that when I had been distressed to see in her a heart defiled by sin and in need of the cleansing efficacy of the Saviour's blood, and was led with earnest prayer to seek for her that salvation which is onto life, and knowing that God hears prayer, I felt that it must be well with her and it was well with me, and well with my husband. These circumstances, together with her thoughtfulness and relish for worship and particularly her own attempts at prayer have removed all doubts from my mind and I have the fullest confidence and the unspeakable consolation to feel and believe that she is at rest in the bosom of the blessed Jesus and has hid herself in Him as the everlasting "Rock of Ages cleft" for the salvation of her soul.

After we had ceased exertions to restore life, I washed her and prepared her for the grave, while husband wrote and sent immediately for Mr. Spalding and Mr. Hall to come and assist in burying her.

I have forgotten whether I wrote in the spring about Mr. Smith leaving us to go into the heart of the Nez Perces country to be better able to learn the language. He left in May and she was drowned on June 23d, aged two years; three months and nine days.

I cannot describe what our feelings were when night came and our dear child a corpse in another room. We went to bed, but not to sleep, for sleep had departed from our eyes. The morning came, we arose; but our child slept on. I prepared a shroud for her during the day, and before evening Mr. Pambrun came, but was ignorant of her death until he arrived, although we had gone to inform him. Mr. Hall arrived on Tuesday evening, got the news Monday noon and started immediately. Mr. and Mrs. S. came down the river to Walla Walla because he had broken his ribs and was unable to ride. They arrived Thursday noon and we buried her that afternoon.

We kept her four days. She did not begin to change in her appearance much for the three first days. This proved to be a great comfort to me, for so long as she looked natural and was so sweet and I could caress her, I could not bear to have her out of my sight; but when she began to melt away like wax and her visage changed I wished then to put her in so safe, quiet and desirable a resting place as the grave — to see her no more until the morning of the resurrection.

Although her grave is in sight, every time I step out of doors, yet my thoughts seldom wander there to find her. I seem not to feel that she is there. I look above and with unspeakable delight contemplate her as enjoying the full delights of that bright world where her joys are perfect and she does not now, as formerly, need the presence of her much loved parents to make her happy. Her little prayer used to be: "O Lord, bless little Alice; may she be Thy child, may she love Thee, and when she dies, may she go to heaven and live with Jesus, and sing his praises, forever and ever. Amen."

Dear mother, I know you will forgive me for occupying so much room for this one subject. I wish I had time to say much more, but must take a little time to tell you about our present situation. After the funeral it was thought best for us to go home with Mr. and Mrs. Spalding and the members of the Nez Perces Mission to meet at Mr. Smith's to confer about the alphabet, many of them not being satisfied with the one Mr. S. had settled upon. The Indians all being away we concluded to go, and after spending the Sabbath at Mr. S.'s, he, with Mr. Hall, went with us to Mr. Smith's, about fifty miles beyond. We stayed there nearly two days and then returned to Mr. Spaldings, spent the Sabbath and on Tuesday started for home and arrived Friday morning. In the afternoon we received a letter from Mr. Eells that his wife was sick and did not expect she would live and wished my husband to go immediately. She has a spinal difficulty and a weakness which was considerably aggravated in the journey across the mountains. He left that night and traveled almost night and day until he reached there, which was on Sabbath eve.

And now the trial was upon me which I had dreaded more than anything else—to have my husband go from home and leave me alone. It was then that I realized the full reality of my bereavement. Husband gone night after night, the cheering presence of that dear daughter taken from me which had always been my relief in such lonely hours. Add to this the sickness and death of two interesting children of an Indian, and very sudden, too; the care of burying them and meeting with all the superstitious feelings and notions in regard to sickness and dying among the natives, and yet, dear mother, you can realize but a small part of the trying feelings to be endured under such circumstances. What I underwent at that time I cannot describe.

For a poor, weak female to spend the Sabbath alone among the heathen in ordinary circumstances and having them look to her for instruction and not to have the command of the language so as to converse satisfactorily with them in hardly the least degree, she would feel, unavoidably, a weight of responsibility almost insupportable. In addition to this, on this Sabbath after our return and husband's leaving—it being just four weeks from the day of the scene of Alice's death, and the first of my being at home—I could not divest myself of the impression that she was about me. I seemed to hear her voice—her footsteps near me all day long. Towards evening the news came that the little boy was dying. My feelings were such that I could not go to see him die. The next morning, as soon as I was up, the father came and told me his other little son had followed his brother in the night, and that without appearing much sick or being sick but a short time. Both had the dysentery. They both were sensible to the last that they were dying;—probably five and ten years of age. The youngest said, when told that he was dying, that it was not dying—this would be but for a little while and then he should always live. He said of his own accord, "I love God," and often repeated the name of God. His father asked him, "Is it true that you love God?" He replied, "Yes, I love Him more than anything else." He said again, "Is it true that you love God more than anything else?" He said, "Yes, it is true." When he had said this he drew his blanket up over him as if he would go to sleep and *died*. These two little boys were members of husband's Sabbath school last summer when he taught them the Ten Commandments.

On Monday we had a box made large enough to put them both in and buried them — all done principally by the members of our own family, there being but one family here besides the one afflicted. The mother was taken sick also, and one child, and they began to feel that they should all die, and many, on hearing of the sickness and death of the two boys, were afraid to come here, for fear they should die, too.

The suddenness of the death of the boy last taken was a great wonder to them — said perhaps it was the medicine I gave them (which was nothing but a small dose of salts). I had not dared to give them the least thing for fear of the consequences, knowing that they were always ready to take the advantage of everything. As it was, they were distracted with every false and superstitious notion they could think of, which is no small part of a missionary's trials. All these things together made me feel as I never felt before — I seemed to "sink in deep waters, where the floods overflowed me" — and at times lost sight of my Supporter, or rather had not strength to cast myself upon Him. Husband was gone until the next Saturday. Thursday evening Mr. Perkins, from The Dalles, came and spent the night and until Saturday morning, which was a great relief to me. Mr. Walker came home with husband.

The third week in August we were surprised with a call from two young men from the states, Mr. Geiger, formerly from Angelica, and Mr. Johnson, from New York, who were here to explore the territory. They stopped a few days with us and then went on to the Willamette.

The next week we had to go to Mr. Spalding's to attend the general meeting of the mission. Mr. and Mrs. Hall returned with us and will spend the winter here. We all came down the Snake river to Walla Walla and she was brought up the Walla Walla river to this place in a canoe to the lower part of our plantation, and the rest of the way she was brought on a hammock. They are interesting and lovely people and we find them a great assistance to us in encouraging us in our perplexing labors here.

Two missionaries from the Oberlin Institute have come here — I mean to Oregon — for the purpose of establishing a self-supporting mission. Rev. Mr. Griffin and wife, and Mr. Munger and wife. They will find it very difficult to get along, probably, upon that system. Mr. Munger has engaged to us to finish off our house — he is a carpenter and will make us a more convenient house than I ever expected to have here, or at least very soon. One room is already finished which will make Mrs. Hall very comfortable for the winter. Mr. Griffin and wife are at Mr. Spalding's and must labor for their food this winter.

Mr. Hall, when he came in the spring, brought us a printing press. I believe we wrote about it in our last. He has printed us a little book and we hope to have him do more for us before he leaves.

After our return from the meeting we commenced a school immediately. We have more than a hundred and twenty on the list, but they do not all attend at one time. Men, women and children all attend and appear much pleased with the new book in their language.

A Catholic priest has recently been at Walla Walla and held meetings with the Indians and used their influence to draw all the people away from us. Some they have forbidden to visit us again, and fill all of their minds with distraction about truths we teach, and their own doctrine; say we ought to have baptized them long ago, etc., etc. The conflict has begun—what trials await us we know not. We never had greater encouragement about the Indians than at the present time. Could they be left unmolested until their minds should become settled upon the great truths they have been permitted to hear about—our hope and trust is in the Lord—we desire not to be moved by all the opposition of earth and hell combined, but to stay our souls upon Him, and to labor faithfully and diligently and leave the event with Him.

I have not received a single letter from home for more than a year except one from Cousin Jeremiah Butler, who is now at Oberlin, which these people brought. We have heard of the arrival of a box of clothing for us sent from Rushville. It is now at Vancouver.

I shall not be able to write more than this letter now, but shall hope to be able to write to you all to send across the mountains next spring, which will be received three months later than this, probably. I hope all who write me will be particular to mention what letters and the dates of all the letters they have received from us, so that we may know what letters you receive and what fail.

Dearest father and mother, farewell once more. I wish I had time to say more, for my heart is still burdened. Perhaps you will think we cast reflections upon ourselves for neglect, or as being the cause of dear Alice's death. We cannot do it, although we see now how it might have been prevented, could we have known or anticipated it. What I have to say more is, do pray for us. O, how I long to hear from you. I know not but that you may be as deeply afflicted as we are. It will be but a few more days and then we shall meet in heaven. O, what a glorious thought! Again I say farewell.

We are, dear parents, your afflicted and bereaved children,

MARCUS AND NARCISSA WHITMAN.

We send much love to you all who are beloved in the Lord. Pray for the poor Indians here who are at their wits' end to know which is the right way to worship—our hearts bleed for them for they know not what they do in rejecting Jesus Christ and his salvation.

N.W.

What would dearest mother say to us now if she should see us? I wish she would write me that I may hear her voice once more. How is it with her soul? Is her faith and confidence strong in the Lord? O, I know my mother prays for us, and the Lord will reward her for it. I do not expect to see her again in this world, but sometimes I desire to very much. I used to want to have you all see Alice, but now that desire is taken away.

WAILLATPU, Jan. 1st, 1840.

My Dear Sister Perkins:—I have been trying to imagine a reason for so long a silence, for I have received no letters from you since writing my two last. Hope you have not been sick. You have had much company, I know, as well as we here. We hear from you, notwithstanding, and our hearts greatly rejoice to learn of the success of your labors there. Brother Hall has favored us wth the perusal of your husband's letters. O, that we could be with you in the gracious visitations. My soul longs, yea, thirsts, for seasons like many I have been witness and partaker of, in my native land. I am tired of living at this poor dying rate. To be a missionary in name and to do so little or nothing for the benefit of heathen souls, is heart-sickening. I sometimes almost wish to give my place to others who can do more for their good. With us we need more prayer and holy living. But with our hearts divided between our appropriate missionary work and getting a living, how can we expect it otherwise?—yet this is no excuse. We think of you often, and daily are you remembered at the Throne of Grace. We rejoice that our Indians attend your meetings. O, that their hardened hearts might be touched by the power of Divine Truth, and they be made to taste the dying and redeeming love. A very few are with us for the winter and I have a school of about twenty. Their being absent so much of the time is exceedingly trying to us. Do write me and let me learn how you enjoy the precious seasons your husband writes of.

How does young Henry do? Sweet babe, I should like dearly to see him and his mother, also. Sister Spalding has a son.

Kind regards to your husband and believe me as ever,
Your affectionate sister, in bonds of Christina love,
N. WHITMAN.

Letters

WIELETPOO, OREGON,
April 30, 1840

My Dear Father:—It is almost two years since we have received a single letter from home, and I have written several times since, but another opportunity has arrived for sending, and I cannot let it pass without writing, so I read over the old letters and answer them over again. I feel very anxious to hear from you all. Yet I know not what changes have been made in the space of two years. I almost fear to hear—lest death should have found his way and broken in upon the number. It has been so with us. The lovely tender plant which our Heavenly Father gave us to rear for Him He has transplanted to His own Paradise above. It is almost a year since He took her, yet our hearts do not cease to bleed at the fond recollections of her innocent smiles and fond caresses. We do not wish her to come to us again, but we shall soon go to her. I see more than ever a reason why the Lord saw fit to take her from us. Our situation and responsibilities require that most of my time should be spent in teaching school, which I could not do without her having been exposed to the contaminating influence of heathenism and very much neglected.

Since September last I have been in school almost constantly, considering my other duties, and this spring, besides the school, morn and eve worship with the people and a Bible class with the women which I attended every day until my health gave way, and I was obliged to omit part of them except when I was entirely laid aside. I do not think I should have been sick had it not been for our open house. Both the house we live in, which a part of the time has been our school house, and where I have recently met my school. We still live in the house we first built although we built one of adobe the year our re-inforcement arrived. Various hindrances prevented our getting into it, or attending to finish it. Indeed, there was no one to do it until last fall. The Lord sent us a good mechanic from Oberlin, Mr. Munger, and his wife. They came out as self-supporting missionaries. He, seeing we needed his assistance very much, engaged to finish our house for us, and is still with us. A part of the house is nearly finished and will be a very comfortable and clean house to what this has been. Father cannot realize the difficulty and hardship we have had in getting what timber we must have for doors, floors, shelves, etc., for our house. No durable wood near us of any kind except alder, which we are trying to make answer for our tables, bedsteads, etc. We go to the mountains fifteen miles and cut and draw pine on a sled on bare ground (for there has been scarcely snow enough to draw but three or four for the two past winters). The second winter we were here we sent to the mountains and sawed boards there and packed them on horses. All our boards are sawed by hand with a pit saw, which dear father must know is very hard work, and besides this, the smoothing, daubing and whitewashing of an adobe house is very tedious work and requires much time and labor. Husband is now engaged in it, preparing it for painting. We feel ourselves highly favored that we could obtain oil and paint enough and at a reasonable price, to paint the wood work and floors, so as to save my strength and labor.

We need fences for our corn and wheat fields, garden and door yards, but have no timber near, and we have not been able to send to the mountains as yet. High door yard fences we need very much, so as to keep the Indians from making a highway of every part of our house and breaking our windows. It is so difficult to obtain glass that we feel very choice of what we have obtained and intend to have Venetian blinds made to all our large windows to preserve them and our house when we are absent, which we are obliged to be often more or less every year; at least husband is, and I go with him sometimes because it is better for my health than to stay home alone, many times entirely alone, especially when all the Indians are away; I suffer from dejection considerably—feel the want of society, especially since the death of our dear Alice.

There is no lime stone to be obtained anywhere near us and our alternative is to burn clam shells, which we hope to make answer the purpose. Another great inconvenience we experienced is the want of a solid material for hearths. Our house, chimney, fireplace, oven and hearths are all made of mud—unburnt bricks called adobes. Perhaps this is saying enough about our worldly affairs. I intend to give father a view of the plan of our house. I have much to write about the people that would be interesting if I had time.

There has been much sickness among them this spring and several deaths—some of them were our firmest friends. Their sickness causes us a great deal of perplexity, care and anxiety. They are anxious to take medicine, but they do not feel satisfied with this alone—they must have their jugglers playing over them or they will surely die. We have two or three instances where some have died without being played over. They are such miserable nurses that they die by their own neglect. We have been kept much of the time occupied in visiting and preparing food and medicine for them. It has been an unusually interesting time with them this spring.

They have attended quite generally upon instructions—some to hear for the benefit of their souls and others for the gratification of their pride and vanity. The former receive the truth, however plain and forcibly it may be applied to their own hearts and consciences, as the truth. The latter regret every application made to the hearts and lives of the people and call it bad talk, mutter and often tell him to stop for they have heard enough. There seems to be but few of this class, and there are some old men who think they are safe and will go to heaven when they die. They complain because the young and common people are taught as well as themselves. They wish us to teach two or three of the principal chiefs and let them teach the people, as they used to do at the fort before we came. They love to hear something new and marvelous—scripture names and history, or any subject that does not touch the heart. These they will repeat day after day and night after night, as if their salvation depended upon it; indeed, they make it their religion and are displeased the moment you attempt to shake the foundations of their hopes. They are supremely selfish and would compel you to do everything for them, if they could, without compensation.

I have written this letter so blindly I fear father will be troubled to read it. I have many and constant interruptions and write in great haste.

N.W.

WIELETPOO, May 2, 1840.

My Dear Mother:—I cannot describe how much I have longed to see you of late. I have felt the want of your sympathy, your presence and counsel more than ever. One reason doubtless is it has been so long since I have received a single letter from any one of the dear friends at home. Could they know how I feel and how much good their letters do me, they would all of them write a great deal and write often, too, at least every month or two, and sent to Boston and to Westport, to the care of Rev. Joseph McCoy; they would surely reach us. Our associates receive them in great numbers, which does not make us feel any better for ourselves. We are daily expecting the arrival of Mr. Lee's ship, laden with associates for that mission, and we have the encouragement from the board to expect four or five families for our own mission. By them we hope to receive letters in abundance. It is a consoling thought to us that we are permitted the prospect of having other fellow laborers to join us again so soon. We feel that we cannot do our work too fast to save the Indian—the hunted, despised and unprotected Indian—from entire extinction.

A tide of immigration appears to be moving this way rapidly. What a few years will bring forth we know not. A great change has taken place even since we first entered the country, and we have a reason to believe it will stop here. Instead of two lonely American females we now number fourteen, and soon may twenty or _____ more, if reports are true. We are emphatically situated on the highway between the states and the Columbia River, and are a testing place for the weary travelers, consequently a greater burden rests upon us than upon any of our associates—to be always ready. And doubtless many of those who are coming to this mission their resting place will be with us until they seek and find homes of their own among the solitary wilds of Oregon.

Could dear mother know how I have been situated the two winters past, especially winter before last, I know she would pity me. I often think how disagreeable it used to be to her feelings to do her cooking in the presence of men—sitting about the room. This I have had to bear ever since I have been here—at times it has seemed as if I could not endure it any longer. It has been the more trying because our house has been so miserable and cold—small and inconvenient for us—many people as have lived in it. But the greatest trial to a woman's feelings is to have her cooking and eating room always filled with four or five or more Indians—men—especially at meal time, but we hope this trial is nearly done, for when we get into our other house we have a room there we devote to them especially, and shall not permit them to go into the other part of the house at all. They are so filthy they make a great deal of cleaning wherever they go, and this wears out a woman very fast. We must clean after them, for we have come to elevate them and not to suffer ourselves to sink down to their standard. I hardly know how to describe my feelings at the prospect of a clean, comfortable house, and one large enough so that I can find a closet to pray in.

As a specimen I will relate a circumstance that occurred this spring. When the people began to return from their winter quarters, we told them it would be good for them to build a large house (which they often do by putting several lodges together) where it would be convenient for all to attend worship and not meet in the open air. They said they should not do it, but would worship in our new house and asked us if there were not houses in heaven to worship in. We told them our house was to live in and we could not have them worship there for they would make it so dirty and fill it so full of fleas that we could not live in it. We said to them further, that they did not help us build it and that people in other places build their houses of worship and did not let one man do it all alone, and urged them to join together by and by and build one for themselves of adobe. But it was of no avail to them; they murmured still and said we must pay them for their land we lived on. Something of this kind is occuring almost all the time when certain individuals are here; such as complaining because we do not feed them more, or that we will not let them run all over the house, etc., etc.

They are an exceedingly proud, haughty and insolent people, and keep us constantly upon the stretch after patience and forbearance. We feed them far more than any of our associates do their people, yet they will not be satisfied. Notwithstanding all this, there are many redeeming qualities in them, else we should have been discouraged long ago. We are more and more encouraged the longer we stay among them.

They are becoming quite independent in cultivation and make all their ground look as clean and mellow as a garden. Great numbers of them cultivate, and with but a single horse will take any plow we have, however large, and do their own ploughing. They have a great thirst for hogs, hens and cattle, and several of them have obtained them already.

Our greatest desire and anxiety is to see them becoming true Christians. For this we labor and pray, and trust in God for the blessing on our labors. But the labor is great and we are weak and feeble, and sometimes are ready to faint. We need the prayers of our Christian friends at home and I trust we have them. Could they know just how we are situated and all our discouragement I know they would pray more ardently for us and more importunately for us.

Dear father, I will relate one more anecdote and then must close. Te-lou-ki-ke said to my husband this morning: "Why do you take your wife with you to Mr. Walker's? Why do you not go alone? You see I am here without my wife; why do you not go alone? You see I am here without my wife; why do you always want to take your wife with you when you go from home? What do you make so much of her for?" He told him it was good for me to go with him; that we were one, and that wives were given as companions. He replied "that it was so with Adam because a rib was taken from him to make his wife, but it was not so now; it was different with us." This has often been brought up by them; the way I am treated, and contrasted with themselves; they do not like to have it so; their consciences are troubled about it. May they be more and more so until a reformation is made among them.

Plan of the mission house at Wieletpoo, drawn by Asabel Munger. We have made it larger than it was originally intended at the suggestion of Mr. Hall, so as to be more convenient to accommodate the general meeting of the mission.

EXPLANATIONS.

A—Our own sleeping room. B—Parlor. C—Dining Hall. D—Indian Hall. E—Kitchen. F—Pantry. G—Sleeping room for Joseph and wife, our domestics. H—Cellar and room above for boys. I—Storehouse. K—Hen house. LL—Privy house—double. W—Clothes press. X—Chest of drawers set in the wall. P—Book case. O—Show case for natural curiosities, and the lower part for bed and table linen. The upper part of both of glass; also set in the wall. R—Cupboard. T—Stairs. U—Medicine case. V—Stove. Seven large windows, the remainder are small. A, I and K are yet to be built, probably this summer. M—Turkey house of wood and yard. This is all we have made.

We give you the probable plan of our yard, which we need very much; but it is yet to be built. N is the place where Alice Clarissa fell into the river, and but a short distance below, she was found. S is in the direction of her little grave, further off than is represented by this view. The exterior does not look as well as the interior. The roof is made of poles, straw and dirt thrown upon the top. It will look better when it is whitewashed on the outside. We paint the wood work a light slate color; the front door, outside, green; the floors with yellow ochre; pantry shelves the same.

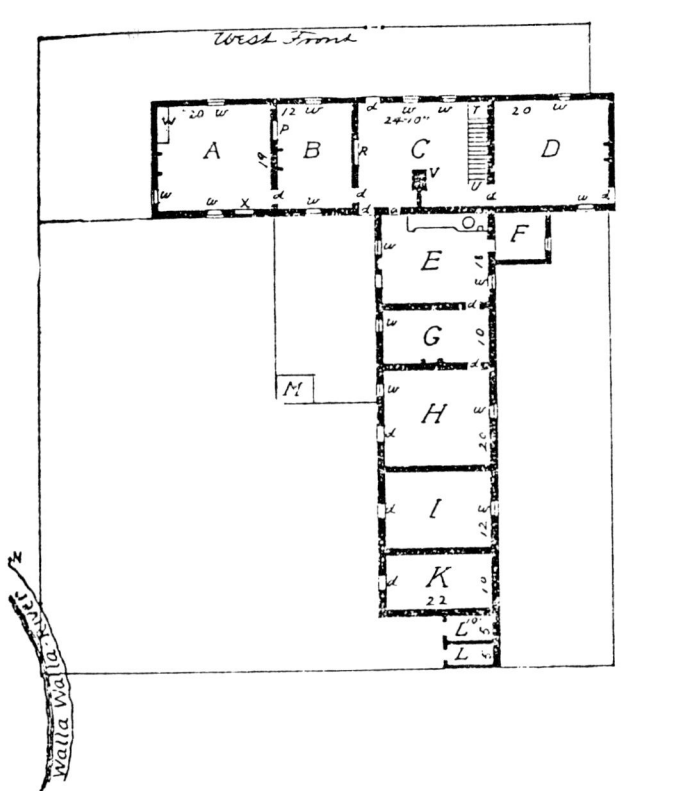

I do not know how many of my letters reach home or whether any of them. I write and send twice a year to some of them. I hope all who write will be careful to mention the reception of all our letters, so then we shall know what ones fail and what reach you.

Please give our love to all our friends who are interested in us, and accept much for dear father, mother and all the family.

Your affectionate daughter,
NARCISSA WHITMAN.

It seems as if the Lord's hand was in it in sending Mr. and Mrs. Munger here just at this time, and I know not how to feel grateful enough. My health has suffered considerably more than any winter before since we have been here. This is planting time and there is much to be done to the walls of the house to get it ready for painting the floors, and husband has but one week's time to complete it all so that Mr. M. can go on with his work. He wishes me to accompany him to Mr. Walker's to recover my health, and I have partly consented, although I feel as though the work needed my superintendence at home as soon as he can return.

Husband finds the responsibilities of a station too much for one man, in connection with his medical duties. He is pressed every moment, and often obliged to neglect, or but half perform, some part of his labors.

Our dear Brother and Sister Hall, who spent the last six months with us, were a great comfort to us, and their experience in the missionary life was also a help to us. They left us the first of March. Her health was much improved by her stay among us. I have written Sister Judson the particulars concerning her, and the birth of her babe.

O, how I wish I could look into that dear circle once more! Is dear father and mother well? Are they as strong as they were when I bade them farewell? Where are the children? Are they all scattered? If they are, but doing good in the world, it is well. How is it with Edward and Harriet? I do not hear a single word from them. What are their plans? Are they preparing to become missionaries? Notwithstanding all my trials here; notwithstanding I wish to see you all so much, yet I should not be willing to go home to see you. We often say so to each other. We do not wish to go home; we are contented and happy here, and here our thoughts centre. Our chief anxiety is to see these people choosing Christ—loving and serving him. It is for this we live and are willing to wear out our lives in endeavoring to persuade them to obey Christ. Sometimes we are ready to faint with the discouragements that beset our path; then again we look and take a fresh hold upon the arm of the blessed Saviour and go on. When I have felt the most desponding and cast down I have thought perhaps dear mother was not alive to pray for me any more. Then I think Jesus lives and He will not forsake me. He will not unless I forsake Him first. But my wicked heart is treacherous still and prone to leave him whom my soul loves. I often look up to that place of rest where my dear babe has gone and feel that I shall soon follow her.

Dear mother, when we meet there then we can converse together of all these things which are now trying to the flesh, and bless and praise God forever for them. Till then adieu.

Your affectionate daughter,
NARCISSA WHITMAN

Mrs. Clarissa Prentiss,
    Angelica, Allegany County, New York.

WAIILATPU, W. W. RIVER, OREGON TERRITORY,
Oct. 9th, 1840

My Dear Mother:—I cannot express the satisfaction we enjoyed in receiving, beholding and perusing dear mother's own letter; her own words and thoughts, written with her own hand. It arrived the first of June. An Indian brought it with other letters from Walla Walla after dark. We were in bed and had just got to sleep when he announced that letters had come. We could not wait until morning, but lighted a candle and read them. I received no other communications except what was contained in that sheet from father, mother and Harriet, from the States; but some from the Islands. It was enough to transport me in imagination to that dear circle I loved so well, and to prevent sleep from returning that night. I have long looked and longed for something that would seem like conversing with dear mother once more, and now it has arrived; I know not how to express my gratitude to her for it. O, could my dear parents know how much comfort it would be to their solitary children here, they would each of them fill out a sheet as often as once a month and send it to the Board for us. How I should like to know what each of them are doing and how they feel from week to week. It would be better to me than books, papers, or clothing. I have enough of everything and more than I can find time to read. If dear father can afford to pay the postage on my letters home and his own and mother's to me as often as I want to hear from them, we will be perfectly satisfied. I ask for nothing else. The Board are constantly sending us books and papers and boxes of clothing. There are two barrels now at Vancouver for us from Brother Judson, and have been since June; also one from Rushville and a box from Lysander. I expect we have letters in Brother Judson's barrel, which accounts for our not receiving any from them. We are looking for them up every day now. In some of my first letters I did ask for some clothing to be sent me. It was more because Mrs. Hull made me promise to write for what I wanted, than because I needed them. I do not need to have dear father send me anything, for others do, and what is not sent I can do without. We are well provided for; the churches take good care of their missionaries. Our chief desire is to be found faithful stewards in that which is committed to our trust.

    I received a letter in August from Sister Jane written in March. I am happy to hear that she and Edward are so wisely engaged. Hope they will let nothing interrupt them in their studies until E. becomes fitted for the ministry and the missionary field. Jane says she has had a call to go to the Sandwich Islands; I am glad she does not go. If she goes anywhere single, she must come and live with us; shall write to her to that effect. I wrote to father and mother in May last and sent them across the mountains; hope they have been received by this time. In that I mentioned we were about to state to Colville on a medical visit. Mrs. Walker has a little daughter—second child. We went and returned in little less than three weeks, 130 miles. This is hard riding for us. Husband is gone so much of his time and has so many important duties at home, being alone, that he feels as if he must perform his journeys as rapidly as possible. On our return we moved into our new house—find it very comfortable and much easier to do our work. Mrs. Munger was confined the 25th of June; recovered well—had a daughter. We left immediately for Mr. Spalding's to attend the general meeting of the mission. Soon after we returned the Lord was pleased again to visit our family with sickness and death. Mother will recollect that in the spring of 1838 we had a man and his wife sent us from the Sandwich Islands (natives) as missionaries. They came to assist us in our domestic labours. He was taken sick before we went to the meeting, but recovered and he and his wife went with us. He was sick and recovered several times, but every relapse brought him much lower than before. He died the 8th of August of inflammation of the bowels. Our loss is very great. He was so faithful and kind—always ready and anxious to relieve us of every care, so that we might give ourselves to our appropriate missionary work—increasingly so to the last. He died as a faithful Christian missionary dies—happy to die in the field—rejoiced that he was permitted to come and labour for the good of the Indians, while his heart was in heaven all the time. Who that could witness him in his dying moments and see the calm and sweet serenity of his countenance, but what would feel it a privilege to be a missionary—to be the means of saving one such soul from the midst of heathen darkness. His wife is just so faithful, but she is a feeble person. I know not how I could do without her; so we feel concerning him. But the Lord saw different. He had higher employment for him in heaven. Dear mother, we feel that the Lord means something by his repeated affliction; every year we have had a death in our family since we have been here. I feel as if it would be our turn soon and we know not how soon. In about a month after Joseph's death, I was taken with inflammation of the kidneys and was brought very low. But the Lord in mercy raised me up again and I got able to be about in a short time; but since that I got down again and have been ever since unable to see to my work. Have been taking medicine now for some time and begin to feel as if I should be quite well again; but do not expect to be able to engage in teaching again this winter. It is quite a trial to be laid aside when so much needs to be done. But missionaries wear out quick where they have always so much to do, and it will be so, so long as there are so few in the field.

    We are thronged with company now and have been for some time past, and may be through the winter. I often think of what mother used to say—"I wish Narcissa would not always have so much company." It is well for me now that I have had so much experience in waiting upon company, and I can do it when necessary without considering it a great task. As we are situated, our house is the missionaries' tavern, and we must accommodate more or less the whole time. Mr. Gray and family are removed from Lapwai (Mr. Spalding's station) and are now with us until they can build anew, or rather until after his wife's confinement. He has an Hawaiian wife lately from the Islands. Mr. Griffin and Mr.

Munger and their wives, who came out last summer as self-supporting missionaries, are here also. In August Rev. Mr. Clark, Philo Littlejohn, and Mr. Smith with their wives, arrived; they have come independent of the Board, also. We have no less than seven missionary families in our two houses. We feel that we need much patience and wisdom to get along with so many, and much strength, We are in peculiar and somewhat trying circumstances in relation to them. We are under the American Board and they have come out in opposition, or in other words to try to live independently of the Board. This they will find very difficult, or next to impossible to do, and some of them begin to see it so. We cannot sell to them, because we are missionaries and did not come to be traders; and if we did we should help them to establish an opposition Board. But we can give them, and report to the Board, which is not so agreeable to them. Their means are very limited and they will suffer before they can get help from the churches, if they have it at all. Those who have come this year are excellent people and we wish they were under the Board, for we need their labours very much. We should keep Mr. Littlejohn and his wife with us if we had any claim upon them. Ma is acquainted with them; he is Augusta's brother.

What a comfort it is to us that mother and father still live to pray for us, and may they long continue to. For they can never realize how much grace and wisdom, patience, forbearance, brotherly kindness, love and charity; yea, every Christian grace, meekness and humility, their daughter needs.

Once more, dear mother, farewell.

From your ever affectionate daughter.

NARCISSA.

P.S. — Your children both send much love. I had hoped that ma would have received a letter at this time from her son Marcus; but it is almost like hoping against hope, so long as his cares and duties are so complicated.

Narcissa Whitman

WAIILATPU, W.W. RIVER, OREGON TERRITORY,
Oct. 10th, 1840.

My Dear Father: — It does us a great deal of good to receive letters from our dear parents, although it is no oftener than once in two years. I am sorry my letters are so long in reaching home, and can see no good reason for it, especially after they get into the States. I write twice a year regularly many letters, but do not receive answers to all I write. I am happy to hear that father and mother have found a permanent resting place and did not move to the west. It is a pleasure to me to think of them as stationary and not moving about. It does us good to know all the particulars about those we love, and we may rest assured that the Lord will take care of them, and not leave them to suffer when old age is upon them. We have recently heard much about home and friends from Mr. and Mrs. Littlejohn, who are now with us. She was the Miss Sadler that lived at Brother Hall's, when I left. It makes me feel quite acquainted with home scenes once more. It is good to associate with warm-hearted revival Christians once more. We have none in our mission of as high-toned piety as we could wish, especially among those who came in our last re-enforcements. They think it is wrong for females to pray in the presence of men, and do not allow it even in our small circles here. This has been a great trial to me, and I have almost sunk under it. Mr. Clark and company have been with us now for nearly two months past, and we have had many precious seasons of prayer and social worship together, which seems like revival seasons at home that I used to enjoy.

We wish they had come out under the Board, both for our sakes, theirs and the mission cause. We fear they will suffer. At any rate, they cannot do any thing at present and for a good while to come, of missionary work, but take care of themselves. We hope no more will come in this way. Those who came last year got themselves into difficulty when they first started; it increased all the way, and they still are not reconciled and we fear never will be. They are living upon us; have done nothing yet but explore a little, and appear to know now what to do, but rather die than to give up their plans and say to the Christian world, it is wrong to go out in opposition to the Board.

Mr. Munger we have employed to finish our house. Men of great funds might go into the field and do good, but poor Christians cannot, even if they depend upon irresponsible churches. What the Lord will do with them we know not. Mrs. Griffin's health was poor when she came, and since she has been with us this summer she has been quite laid by with spinal complaint.

But enough of this. *Our trials* dear father knows but little about. The missionaries' greatest trials are but little known to the churches. I have never ventured to write about them for fear it might do hurt. The man who came with us is one who never ought to have come. My dear husband has suffered more from him in consequence of his wicked jealousy, and his great pique towards me, than can be known in this world. But he suffers not alone — the whole mission suffers, which is most to be deplored. It has nearly broken up the mission. This pretended settlement with father, before we started, was only an excuse, and from all we have seen and heard, both during the journey and since we have been here, the same bitter feeling exists. His principal aim has been at me; as he has said, "Bring out her character," "Expose her character," as though I was the vilest creature on earth. It is well known I never did anything before I left home to injure him, and I have done nothing since, and my husband is as cautious in speaking and thinking evil of him or treating him unkindly, as my own dear father would be, yet he does not, nor has he, received the same kindness from him since we have been missionaries together.

Every mind in the mission that he has had access to, he has tried to prejudice against us, and did succeed for a while, which was the cause of our being voted to remove any from a new station. This was too much for my husband's feelings to bear, and so many arrayed against him and for no good reason. He felt as if he must leave the mission, and no doubt would have done it, had not the Lord removed from us our beloved child. This affliction softened his feelings and made him willing to suffer the will of the Lord, although we felt that we were suffering wrongfully. The death of our babe had a great affect upon all in the mission; it softened their hearts towards us, even Mr. S.'s for a season. I never have had any difficulty with his wife; she has treated me very kindly to my face, but recently I have learned that she has always partook of the feelings of her husband. I have always loved her and felt as if no one could speak against her. The Lord in His providence has brought things around in such a way, that all see and feel where the evil lies, and some of them are writing to the Board and proposing measures to have an overture and settlement made, and it may require his removal or return to effect it; not so much for his treatment toward us as some others also. A particular charge brought against him is duplicity. It is painful for me to write thus concerning us here; and this is but a small item of what might be said. I have long had a desire to have some few judicious friends know our trials, so that they may understand better how to pray for us. If this mission fails, it will be because peace and harmony does not dwell among its members. Our ardent desire and prayer is that it may not fail. It is this state of things among us that discourages us. When we look at the people and the providence of God, we are more and more encouraged every year.

Since the return of the Indians this fall, it has seemed as if we were on the eve of a revival. Many of the principal Indians are deeply affected by the truth; some manifest it by bitter opposition, which does not discourage us, although faith is greatly tried.

19th—*Dear Father*:—I have been interrupted in writing this letter on account of ill health. It affects me unfavorably to write much; indeed, I am pretty much confined to my room, which is a very comfortable place, the most so of any I have found since I have been here. Since writing the above on the morning of the 16th, a message arrived and took my husband away as in a moment. It was from our Brother Smith, about a hundred and eighty miles from here. He wrote that the Indians were asking him to give them property and food, and wishing him to pay for the land he occupied. He told them he could not say anything about it; they became very angry and told him to move off to-morrow; he said he could not, but they still insisted upon it with great insolence, until he was obliged to tell them he would go. Sister Smith writes me that they are afraid for their lives and they ask for help immediately to come and remove them. Husband has gone and expects to be obliged to bring them away here. What the result will be the Lord only knows. The two principal instigators are brothers to the Indian who went to the United States for some one to come and teach them, that we read about as the first news west of the Rocky mountains. How transient is the missionaries' home. I believe we most of feel that "we have no abiding city here."

I seldom write home without speaking of one or both of us being absent or about to be. We journey a great deal and that, with other causes, has nearly worn me out, and my husband, too. I cannot say all I should like for want of time and strength. Part of the contents of this sheet, ought not to be circulated; it may do hurt. I do not wish it made public, for any one to make an ill use of it.

I am almost discouraged about Marcus ever finding time to write many letters to our friends at home; he has written none for a year past; he would if he could; he is away now and I do not know when he will return.

I began to write about the state of the people. Of late my heart yearns over them more than usual. They feel so bad, disappointed, and some of them angry because husband tells them that none of them are Christians; that they are all of them in the broad road to destruction, and that worshipping will not save them. They try to persuade him not to talk such bad talk to them, as they say, but talk good talk, or tell some story, or history, so that they may have some Scripture names to learn. Some threaten to whip him and to destroy our crops, and for a long time their cattle were turned into our potato field every night to see if they could not compel him to change his course of instruction with them.

These things did not intimidate us; it only drove us to a throne of grace with greater earnestness to plead for blessings to descend upon them. Our hearts only pant for time to have our whole minds given up to instructing them without being distracted with so many cares which are necessarily upon us, not for ourselves so much as for others. It has and still seems as if a rich blessing was near at hand for us and them, and sometimes I almost seem to grasp it. Why does the blessing stay? Is it because there is so few hands to labour and there is much rubbish to be cleared away? Or is it because of our unbelief and impiety of heart? Doubtless, both. O, for more deep and ardent piety in every heart; but particularly in my own and husband's. Will dear father pray that missionaries may be more holy and heavenly-minded, and less selfish. Could the churches at home be set down in heathen lands and see and know their missionaries as they know themselves, O how they would pray for them and feel and sympathize with them.

When will Christians cease to feel that their missionaries are such good people that they do not need to feel and pray for them as they pray for one another.

Dear Sister Jane writes that the Lord will do wonders for the heathen world this year, and we expect it, too, and may our hoped be realized.

I wish it did not hurt me so to write. I am very weak and feeble, and much thinking or excitement overcomes me. I should have got well long ago, I think, if it were possible for me to be quiet, with so many people about me and so much transpiring. Rest is not for us in this world. Dear mother says it seems as if she might see us again in this world. I do not know as I have such a thought; although it may not be impossible. I have long felt it more probable that we should never meet, and have thought more of meeting my friends in heaven than in this world, unless the Providence of God should make it necessary for us to leave the field. Our united choice would be to live and die here—to spend our lives for the salvation of this people. Yes, dear parents, we have ever been contented and happy, notwithstanding all our trials, and let come what will, we had rather die in the battle than to retreat, if the Lord will only appear for us and remove all that is in the way of His salvation; take up every stumbling block out of our hearts and from this mission, and prosper His own cause here. Our ardent prayer is, Lord let not this mission fail; for our Board says it is the last effort they shall make for the poor Indians:—and may the dear Christians at home feel to urge up their requests to God in our behalf. This is what we need more than anything else.

Once more, dear father, farewell. The Lord deal gently with my beloved parents in the decline of life; support them in death, and safely house them and us in His presence forever.

As ever, I remain, your affectionate daughter,

NARCISSA WHITMAN.

Hon. Stephen Prentiss,
    Angelica,
        Allegheny County
           New York, U.S.A.

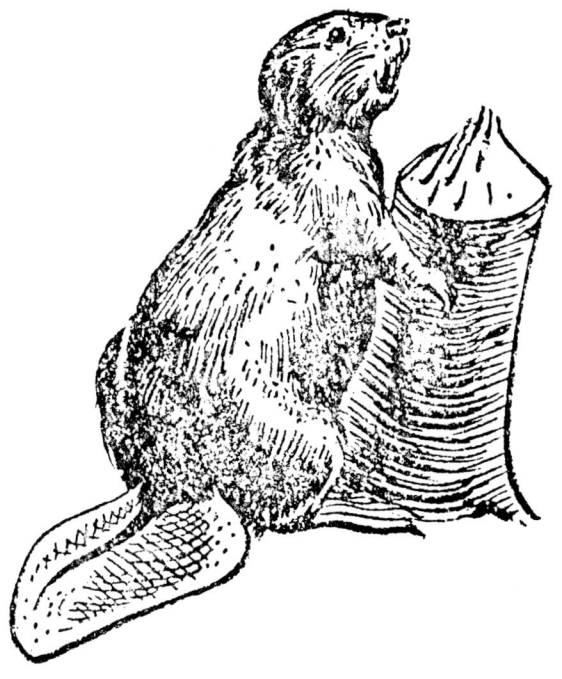

Narcissa Whitman

Oct. 20th, 1840.

My Dear Sister Harriet: — Your letter, although short, was very good and pleased me much; and now what do you think it would have been to me, how much good would it have done your brother and me, if it had been a whole sheet and well filled as I fill mine. I have written you separately a long letter, and one to Edward. You did not tell me that you had received any. Always tell me how many letters of mine you have received, and what their dates are, and then I shall know if you get all I write home. When I write you, I always wish to have you receive them, and if I know what you receive, then I shall know what you hear from me.

You did not tell me what you are doing, and what company you keep; what female meetings you attend, and whether you are doing good in the cause of Christ. What books do you read? Do you comfort ma by reading to her such books as Dwight's *Theology*, Doddridge's *Rise and Progress*, Milner's *Church History*, as Narcissa used to do in her younger days? What progress are you making in the divine life? You see there are many things I wish you to tell me — enough to fill more than one sheet. I am happy to hear that J. and E. have gone to prepare to become missionaries, and that you have a wish to be here with me. I should like to have you here very much, and I hope you will prepare yourself for it. I know dear mother would willingly give up Harriet to go to the heathen if the Lord should call her. This is what you ought to live for as well as me, for there is nothing so desirable. I may send for you yet, and you would do well to prepare yourself. I think of proposing to Jane to come and teach school here next time I write her. Dear Harriet, honour the Saviour everywhere you go; be entirely devoted to Him. You will never regret it. Do write me often and fully. Write a little oftener and send me more than one sheet a year. It will be good for you to cultivate the talent of writing. Yes, do more than I used to, and then you will not regret that you did not do it more, as I do now when I am obliged to write so often and so much. Those of the family that do not write me, I am afraid I shall forget to inquire after them, or write them. You all have more time than I, and more strength, too.

Your dear brother is not at home; if he was he would send much love. As it is I send it for him. Think of him traveling alone this cold weather. The first after he left his warm home, the wind blew very hard and cold, — he with but two blankets, sleeping on the ground alone; and since, it has rained almost every day, and sometimes snowed a little. I do not know when he will come home.

Farewell, dear Harriet. Pray much for your sister who loves you and send much love to you and all the brothers and sisters.

Tell me more about Stephen's children and H.'s and E.'s; you know, Harriet, mine is dead. Before this I have written all about her; tell me if you have seen it. Adieu,

Your affectionate sister,
NARCISSA.

Letters

WAIILATPU, March 2nd, 1841.

My Dear Sister:—We are in deep trial and affliction. Our Brother Munger is perfectly insane and we are tried to know how to get along with him. He claims it as a duty we owe him, as the representative of Christ's church, to obey him in all things. He is our lawgiver, as Moses was to the children of Israel. Last Sabbath was the accomplishment of all things to him—a glorious Sabbath; the bringing in of all things—the Judgment Day. Brother Perkins will recollect some features in his prayers while he was here, which we now see indicated a mind not sound on all points. Now don't let your faith in God be staggered by what has happened unto him. He has been thinking upon some points so long and so deeply that his mind has lost its balance. He has been nearly so before, his wife tells me, but not so entirely gone. Poor Sister M.—her trials are very great. To see him die in a happy state of mind would be, comparatively, a light affliction. He has been inclining this way so long we see but little or no hope he will ever be any better.

When your husband left us we were all of us at work with our own hearts to get them right for the blessing of God upon us. He was pleased to show some of us our hearts; at least me mine as I never saw it before, and I trust it has been a profitable lesson to me. The work seemed to go on gradually and we hope effectually, but frequently during this time we all felt our feelings destroyed by Brother Munger's prayers, and ventured to speak to him of it, but to our surprise he did not receive it with that Christian meekness and improvement we expected in him, but appeared to be more and more strengthened in his preconceived notions and feelings of himself, until he plainly convinced us by his strange actions that he was deranged.

Efforts have been made by my husband and Mr. Gray to restore him, but all prove ineffectual. He sent to be present at our family worship this morning, but we felt it would be no worship and deferred his coming until after, and now he is waiting for his troops to come in who, some of them, appear very unwilling to obey orders.

Brother Littlejohn has gone to see Mr. Clark at Mr. Smith's. We are expecting his return this week, also Mr. C. What will be done with him, we know not, but preparations must be made to take him home, if possible.

Do pray for his afflicted wife, and may the Lord teach us all a lesson for our profit, and show us the debt of gratitude we owe him for the merciful preservation of our reason to us.

I could say much more, but I have snatched this moment to write what I have, and must close.

Give much love to the Sisters Brewer and Lee, if with you.

Affectionately your sister in Christ,

N. WHITMAN.

Mrs. Elvira Perkins
    Wascopum.

Narcissa Whitman

WAIILATPU, May 30th, 1841.

My Dear Brother Edward: — Yesterday Mr. Ermatinger left us to go to Fort Hall and the Rendezvous, and we sent our package of letters to our friends by him. There being still another opportunity of writing, I embrace it for tomorrow. Husband is to send an Indian to overtake him on account of some business forgotten to be attended to while he was here. Mr. and Mrs. Munger, who I hope you will see, left more than three weeks ago with the main party who have the goods, and Mr. E. is to overtake them.

Since writing Jane's letter, much has transpired of interest to us. Mr. Pambrun, of whom you have often heard me speak, received an injury while riding out a little way from his fort by his horse losing the rope out of his mouth and running and surging, which threw him repeatedly upon the horn of his saddle and finally upon the ground. He was so bruised and maimed in the abdomen, that he was unable to move and was carried to the house on blankets. He died in four days after the journey, a most painful death. He died as he lived, saying that he was a Christian, but giving no evidence that he was one in heart. He was a Roman Catholic. Your brother went and stayed with him during his sickness until he died. He was so anxious to die to be relieved from pain and suffering, that he plead with the doctor to give him something to stupefy him so that he might die quick. When he was in the last agonies he insisted on having an emetic given him and when he could not prevail on the doctor or Mr. Rogers, who was with him when he was hurt and sick, he sent for his men to take and carry him out so that he might get it himself, but he did not succeed and gave up to die without it.

His poor family feel the loss very much; he was their main support; had nine children, the youngest an infant three weeks old. His wife is a half-breed. He gave me his little daughter, Harriet, the one named just before he died. We know not what the Lord means by this providence, but we hope good will result to His cause and his afflictions may be sanctified to the living.

Dear brother, this is the Sabbath day. At this time you are doubtless engaged in the worship of God in the sanctuary, a privilege I once enjoyed, but now am deprived of. Our minds suffer for the want of such privileges. Yet in our deprivation we have our enjoyments, for we can worship God in our own dwellings and find Him here present with us. At times the special presence of His Holy Spirit appears to be manifest, and he seems to be reaching down His hand filled with blessings to this dying people. The work is a great work; but how few and feeble are the labourers already in the field. Our earnest prayer is that more labourers might be sent to aid us in our work; men after God's own heart, and not easily discouraged.

The present is a time of unusual quiet — not an Indian is to be seen about us, all are scattered in little groups far and near, digging their kamas root, and taking salmon. Here is the missionary's trial in this country. The people are with him so little of the time, and they are so scattered that he cannot go with them, for but a few are in a place. Notwithstanding our discouragements, I feel that we would not be situated differently if we could. We would not be out of the field for any consideration whatever, so long as the

Lord has any work for us to do here. I wish Jane was here to help me. When I hear from you again I shall know what to do about sending to the Board to have her come, if Edward can spare her and will still go on with his studies. I hope you will remember what I have written to you in the other letter, and do as I have asked you to do, for your own sake as well as mine. You seem to be very near to us. It is almost June now, and I hope this letter will reach you in safety and speedily. Mrs. Littlejohn has become the mother of a fine Oregon boy; they will go home now as soon as they can get an opportunity by ship. Whether you see them or not, after they return I know not. Many others are getting discouraged and wishing to leave, and others are greatly disappointed in the country. I went to Walla Walla two weeks ago to attend Mr. P.'s funeral and spent about two weeks with the family. They sent for me to come home, for Mrs. Littlejohn was sick, but I did not get home until her babe was born. She is doing well and her babe also.

Dear Jane, I hear much of your watching and taking care of the sick. Do be more careful of your own health; I fear for you; you will wear out too soon. I have not been able to do much such work since I have been here.

Your brother often speaks of you and has intended to write you both, but has been pulled this way and that, so that he has not had time. Adieu; our love to you both. I have not written to pa and ma, as I intended, but husband has, which you may read if you see Mrs. Munger.

Your sister,
N. WHITMAN.

Narcissa Whitman

WIELETPOO, OREGON TERRITORY, October 1, 1841.

My Dear Jane:—I wrote you a folio sheet, as full as I could write it, to you and Edward, and sent it across the mountains with the almost certain assurance that it would reach you, at least by this time, if not sooner. But it has returned, with all the other letters we sent that way. We have now sent all our spring letters to Vancouver, to go by sea, so that it is doubtful when you will get them, if at all. I mentioned in my letter to you that Mr. Munger had become unbalanced in his mind, and it was thought best for him to return to his friends in the States. He had been prevailed upon to go, and accordingly started, with his wife and one child, to go across the mountains. To them we committed our letters, with the expectation that they would pass through Quincy on their way to Oberlin. They accompanied the H.H.B. Company's party to Fort Hall, and from thence to the place of the American Rendezvous, on Green River, and found that no party had come up from the States, and, from all that they could learn, no one was expected. They accordingly returned to Fort Hall, and concluded that there was no other alternative but to retrace their steps to this country again. Mr. M. was happy in doing so, but his poor wife did it very reluctantly, for her heart was very much set on going to her friends. They came down before the main party, and brought back our letters with them. They had not retraced their steps far before a large party of emigrants and Jesuits arrived from the States. But no one brought any letters from you or Edward; consequently, I was greatly disappointed, and must wait another year before hearing from you again.

The emigrants were twenty-four in number—two families, with small children, from Missouri. This company was much larger when they started. About thirty went another route, to California. The company of Jesuits were twelve in number, consisting of three priests, three novitiates, four laborers, and their pilot, started from St. Louis, one they found on their way. Their pilot is Fitzpatrick, the same person that commanded the party we came with from the States. This company came as far as Fort Hall. They then go with the Indians to the Flathead country, or Pend d'Oreille. It is not known where they will settle, but it is reported that they expect to locate themselves somewhere in that region, and in the same language that part of our mission are occupying.

Now we have Catholics on both sides of us, and, we may say, right in our midst, for Mr. Pambrun, while he was alive, failed not to secure one of the principal Indians of this tribe to that religion, and had his family baptized. He acts upon his band, and holds from us many who would be glad to come and hear us. And then, the Indians are acted upon constantly through the servants of the Company, who are all, scarcely without exception, Catholics.

We feel no disposition to retreat from our work, but hope to stand our ground, if such a thing is possible. Fitzpatrick is expected here when he has accomplished his piloting for that company, and is said to return to St. Louis this fall; if so, I hope to send this by him.

I may have mentioned the death of our kind neighbor at Walla Walla, Mr. Pambrun, in my letter this spring; although it was written before it transpired, yet it was not sent until afterwards. Early in May he received an injury from his horse, which caused his death in four days after he was hurt. Husband was with him all the time during his sickness and death. It was a most distressing scene. He was only anxious to die that he might be relieved of pain.

A short time before he was sick he got his mind upon marrying his daughter to one of our mission. I mean our Brother Rogers, who came out with the last reinforcement. This was a great trial to us, for we did not consider her worthy of him, besides being a half breed and a Catholic. She has had no education, except barely to learn to read and write. It was his subject of conversation by day and by night while he was alive, and in his will he appropriated more to her on his account, than to his other children, besides giving him much of his personal property, and willing him a hundred pounds sterling. This was that his wife and children might have a good home. In his mind the bargain was completed, and all the arrangements made, before he died. He was riding out with Brother Rogers when he was hurt. After his death the family was removed to Vancouver. We have since learned that she refused to marry Mr. Rogers, and he has returned the property willed to him. We think he has no reason to regret it on his own account. But the consequence of it all has been it has taken Brother R. out of our mission, and he has gone to settle for himself on the Willamette, or in that region.

We regret the loss very much, as he was a valuable member of our mission. This was not the only reason of his leaving us. He was stationed at Lapwai, with Mr. Spalding, and could not be contented to remain in that part of the mission after Mr. Smith left.

Feb. 2, 1842.—*Dear Jane:*—Since I commenced this letter much has transpired of deep interest, and is constantly transpiring that is of importance to this country, and those who are interested in her welfare. But I must talk to you a little before I tell about things here. I have just read your letter again, written in March, 1840, and it is now '42, and do you not think that is a long while to wait for letters from one's beloved sisters and friends? You have placed yourself so near us, I had hoped to receive letters from you every year, and even now I must wait until September before I can expect to hear from you again. Do, dear sister and brother, write a large parcel and have them ready—do not wait for an opportunity. It would be so comforting to get the history of you from one month to another, and from year to year. It would be such a treat that I should cry for joy over them. I suppose you feel the same about us. I write you all I possibly can—all that poor health and numerous cares will admit of. Besides, I have so many to write to, both here as well as to friends at home.

I wish you were here to comfort me with your society and aid me with your labors, for there is more work to do than we can do, although it is not with me now as it has been ever since we have been here. I am blessed with an excellent associate in Sister Gray, who is now located here. She is a sister, indeed. I love her much. It is not good to be alone—so many cares will wear out the health and life of any one, as we feel ours to be already, although we are recruiting some this winter.

Jane, I hear things about you that I do not like to hear. Sister L. says you watch with sick folks a *great deal*. You must stop it, or you will repent it when your health fails, and *it will fail*—you cannot always endure. Take care of yourself, for I want you to come here when you are through your care of Edward, if you do not marry. What do you think about it? How would you like to come? When I know your mind we can then make arrangements for your coming, by writing to the Board, etc. The missionary work is hard work, both for a body and mind, and requires health and strength. You say, "it is delightful work." So it is, when faith and love are in lively exercise, but where these are not in lively exercise, the work becomes burdensome, especially if health fails.

Feb. 4th.—I should like to give you the transactions of this day, and will if I can gather strength to do it. I was sick last night, with a severe headache, and have been so frightened to-day that I have not much strength of nerve left. The Indians are just now returning from their wintering quarters, and some of the Nez Perces have been serving the devil faithfully, especially those who spent their winter on the Columbia River below, in the region of the Des Chutes and Dalles. A young Nez Perces that had been to the Red River school died last summer. A brother of his, and three other principal men, managed to frighten the River Indians, as being the cause of his death, and compelled them to give many horses and much property, as a compensation, to keep them from other acts of violence upon them. Husband, learning of their base conduct, took advantage of their passing, on their way to Mr. S.'s station, to reprove them for what they had done. These men are all firm believers in the te-wats, or medicine men. This is a crying sin among them. They believe that the te-wat can kill or make alive at his pleasure.

Yesterday the mother of the young man that died was in to see me. She is an old medicine-woman, and as she had some of the horses and property thus basely obtained husband talked to her about it and told her it was her duty to give them back to those who stole them, as they had distributed among many. She at last said she would do it. Her talk aroused two others, as they were all that were here, who came in last evening and received the same plain admonition. They did not like such plain talk. They are great worshipers or at least feel and profess to be, and the man who would believe that they could do such great wickedness, and tell them of it and warn them of the consequences, was a bad man and would go to hell. One of them, more daring than the others, gathered twelve or fourteen of his friends and came in the forenoon to frighten us. One had a bow and arrows with iron points; another had a rope and another had the war club. When they first made their appearance these things were concealed under their blankets. The head man commenced the talk by saying that he was always good and that husband was bad and was always talking bad to them; that he had brought in his friends that were very powerful. This he said to frighten us and excite his allies. Soon husband spoke and told him to stop, and began to explain the conversation of last night. After a little, one of them took down a hair rope that was hanging near, and threw it down near the doctor, one of them that stood near put his foot on it. I began to be suspicious of that movement and thought they were intending to tie him. I told husband it was our rope and he picked it up and sent it out of the room. Soon a tall Indian advanced as the conversation increased in spirit—under his blanket I saw another rope and one behind him had a bow and arrows. I asked husband if I had not better call help, he said no, he was not afraid. I had not yet discovered the war club, but I had seen enough to excite my fears greatly. I went into another room, as slyly as I could, and called Packet, who is living in the Indian rooms, and told him what was going on; he went and got two other men and came in and seated themselves. (The gathering was in the kitchen.) The conversation continued and they soon saw that they had been led wrong by their leader, and their excitement died away. A native woman, a friend of ours, was in when they came in and I had just begun to read a chapter of the translation of Matthew to her. She was in yesterday, also, and was appealed to as a witness of what was said yesterday and was of service in quelling their rages. One of our men who came in first discovered the club, and the Indian was asked, when the excitement was over, what he came in with a club for? He flushed and put it around under his blanket out of sight. They all went away, ashamed of themselves and defeated. Their aim, doubtless, was to frighten us and cause the doctor to take back what he said yesterday; but *that* he would not do, but still said to them if he did not tell them plainly of their sins the Lord would be displeased with them. They said it would not do for him to talk so to Ap-ash-wa-kai-kin, their leader in wickedness, and the brother of the deceased young man; if he did, he would fight him. He told him that it was his duty to tell him that he had done wrong, and that he, as well as they, must make restitution to those whom they had so unjustly injured, and that he should not hesitate to tell them so.

March 23.—Him-in-il-ip-il-ip, one of the two that was so excited about his bad conduct being told him so plainly, promised before he left the place that he would restore the property he had so unjustly taken. About two or three weeks after the above transaction Ap-ash-wa-kai-kin came into camp. Husband was away at the time—he had gone about a day's ride to visit a sick woman, the wife of the Catholic, and spent the Sabbath with them, as there were many Indians there. He did not, however, after his return, find it convenient to converse with him under two or three days. But it was like a thunder-bolt to him, for it appeared that no one had told him of the transactions of the others. It was in the evening and we were alone with him—he raged and threatened and said he wondered how they had allowed him to escape—although husband had told him as mildly and affectionately as possible. He soon flew out of the house in great anger—leaving the door open behind him and went to his lodge and hid himself from us for several days. Before this conversation took place, he was eager to obtain a plough, but husband wished to see this business settled before he could oblige him. He finally promised before he left the place that he, also, would make restitution, and parted good friends.

I cannot give you the outrages of last fall. I have written them to our dear parents, if it reaches them you will doubtless have the perusal of it. That, with this, will give you some idea what we have to meet with, but we may say that these are no trials, comparatively, to what they would be if the full use of ardent spirits was introduced among them.

May 17th.—The time has at length arrived for sending off our letters, and it is the last moment. I have not written to any of our beloved friends in Angelica, you must send these letters when you have an opportunity.

Our general meeting is now convened. All the families of the mission are here except Mr. Spalding's who refused to attend. We are in deep waters, but we hope this meeting will decide our case as a mission in some way that will be a relief to our anxious minds. I cannot say much now, but the time will come when I hope to be able to speak freely.

Dear husband has not written a single letter to send home, nor can he, his mind is filled with so much labor, care and responsibility. He often speaks of you, but cannot write.

Mr. Munger, the man I wrote about in my letters of last spring as being deranged, has at last killed himself. He—after driving two nails in his left hand—drew out a bed of hot coals and laid himself down upon it, thrusting his hand into the hottest part of the fire and burnt it to a crisp, and died four days after. After they returned they went on to the Willamette, because we did not think it safe for him to remain here. This took place the last of December. I cannot enter into particulars as I would be glad to. My time, strength and thought are all occupied with the care of company, my children and the events of the meeting.

We have, I mean Mr. Spalding and us, just received a box of clothing from Prattsburgh.

I have seen only one letter and that is a joint letter to both families from O.L. Porter. By some hints in that and from other sources we learn that there is a party expected from that place to come out to our help, and perhaps to come next year. If it is so, it is through Mr. S.'s influence, unbeknown to the mission. If they come out unconnected with the American Board, it will be very trying to both us and them. Those who have already come can but just live, and I believe are obliged to abandon their object, because in this country it is as much as we can do to take care of ourselves if we have no help about.

I received a letter from H.P. and Livonia Prentiss, and right glad was I for it. It is the first we have received from them since we have been here. The box was directed to Mr. S. and consequently was not opened until it went to his place, and he delayed sending the things and letters so long and gave me no information of it until the time had arrived to send our letters off, consequently I have written only one letter to P. where I should have been glad to have written several.

What I have written in the first part of this sheet about our Brother Rogers, keep to yourselves. He is here now and we would be glad to have him join us again if the circumstances of the mission were a little different.

Letters

I send this letter by Edward Rogers, a young man who came out last fall and spent the winter with us. He has partly promised to call on you; I hope he will.

I sent Edward Mr. Smith's address on "The Mission Character." I hope he will read it very attentively and often; it is all true, and what he will have to meet if he becomes a missionary.

Please give my love to Mr. and Mrs. Beardsley. It would cheer me much if they would write us.

Mr. Clarke and all his party are in the lower country.

Mr. Littljohn has given up going home—he has not the means. We want him to come back and help us and have given him the invitation.

Love from us both to Jane and Edward.

Your sister, as ever,

NARCISSA.

Love to dear father and mother, and all the dear ones we love.

Farewell,   N.W.

Miss Jane Prentiss,
      Quincy, Illinois, U.S.A.

(Favor of Mr. Edward Rogers.)

Narcissa Whitman

WIELETPOO, OREGON TERRITORY,
October 6th, 1841.

My Dear Parents:—I have seated myself once more to write to my beloved father and mother, and a thousand thoughts rush into my mind so that I know not where to begin. I often feel and say: "O what would I give for one short hour of *conversation, counsel and prayer* with the dear object of earliest and continued affections, my father and my mother. And I know that if I could see you for an hour I should wish it prolonged and repeated until my heart's desire was satisfied; yet I do not know when that would be. Perhaps, never—until we meet where we hope to part no more. It is this thought, only, that satisfies my anxious mind and gives consolation.

Dear mother asks in her last communication, which we received about a month since, of September, 1840: "Do you never talk about visiting home for the sake of recruiting your exhausted strength." We often talk about the pleasure it would give us to see our friends and native land, but that we shall ever go home is uncertain. Indeed, we never expect to. We feel that our lives are too far spent to allow us to devote as much time as would be necessary to visit our friends and return. Yet such a thing may be. We know not what changes will take place.

Should our health require a change of circumstances it may not be considered necessary for us to go home unless some other object is to be accomplished by it for the good of the cause.

Mother also expresses a "hope that I do not regret the step I have taken and the sacrifice made for Christ in behalf of the perishing heathen." I have no occasion to repent, or the least cause to regret that I am here: but I wonder and am astonished, when I consider the qualifications necessary for the place I occupy, that I was permitted to come. I feel every day I live more and more that my strength is perfect weakness, and that I am entirely unfitted for the work, and have many gloomy, desponding hours, but that I wish myself back again, or that I had not come, I can safely say I have no such feelings, or that I would be in any other field than this, notwithstanding all our perplexities, trials and hardships. Yet I sometimes doubt my motive in this feeling, whether it is purely with a single eye for the glory of God or from some selfish principle. I find one of my most difficult studies is to know my own heart, the motive by which I am actuated from day to day, and feel more than ever to cling closely to the word of God as our *only guide* in this dark and dreary wilderness world.

Nov. 19th—I began this sheet some time ago, but was not able to finish it at that time. I have not enjoyed such a season as I have now for a few weeks past and as we expect to this winter since we have been here. So free from care and none in our house but my own family, which consists of self, husband, and our two little girls. Mrs. Gray has the care of all the laborers, etc., of the station, as my health would not admit of my doing it—being entirely without help.

Letters

It is useful and necessary for us, for we greatly need time for reflection and study, having not had any scarcely from the time we left home till the present, except what was filled with perplexing cares and trials. I feel that we have gained much in experience, but lost in mental culture, or, as it were, have been living on what we had stored up in our childhood and youth; and here I would speak of my feelings of gratitude to God for this unspeakable mercy of giving me such a mother to guide my youthful mind, directing my reading, and instead of allowing it to be filled with the light and vain trash of novel reading, I was directed to that which was more substantial and which treated the immortal mind and laid up in store a rich inheritance for this time of need.

Mother's desire that we should have been blessed with a precious revival among us and enjoying the privilege of seeing the natives beginning to speak forth the praises of dying and redeeming love has not yet been realized in all its parts. Last winter we had a breaking down in our own hearts and the blessing seemed ready to break upon the people, as it has seemed many times before, but was stayed and has been stayed for reasons known best to Him "Who ruleth all things well." The obstacles in the way of the conversion of this people are many and great with them as well as with their missionaries.

Mr. Smith and wife have left us now, on their way to the Sandwich Islands. She is sick with an irritation of the spine. Mr. Rogers has left the services of the mission, and gone to settle on the Willamette, so that our number and strength is greatly reduced. The state of the mission is somewhat known at the Islands, or rather, as it has been, which is the probable reason why our brethren who were sent to us decline coming. There has not been a very favorable opportunity as yet for them to come, as the only ship that has come in since was the *Peacock*, and she was wrecked on the sandbar in the mouth of the Columbia River; no lives lost. The lading of the ship was lost—everything except the papers. We are hoping that they will come in, in the spring vessels; if they do not we know not when we shall be again reinforced.

We hope to have better news to give when we write again, concerning our state. Several of the gentlemen of the U.S. Ex. Squadron visited us during the summer as they were exploring in this region. About twenty-five emigrants have gone past this fall, from Missouri, to settle on the Willamette. Two families with children, one of them very large—six in number—the parents upwards of forty years old. It was very pleasing to me to see such a mother with so many children around her, having come so far—such a dreadful journey.

Doubtless every year will bring more and more into this country. We have probably seen our most quiet time. Those emigrants are entirely destitute of every kind of food when they arrive here and we were under the necessity of giving them provisions to help them on. Our little place is a resting spot for many a weary, way-worn traveler and will be as long as we live here. If we can do good that way, perhaps it is as important as some other things we are doing.

We have changed our neighbor at the Fort—or rather the Lord has done it. Mr. Pambrun, the Catholic, died last May from an injury received from his horse. Our present neighbor is a Scotch Presbyterian, so that his influence is very different from the other in many things, and particularly in this one thing with the Indians. Mr. P. used to pay them when they made trouble, to quiet them—this one does not. The way chiefs have been made was by taking the most troublesome one among them and giving him property to make him quiet and pay him to keep the rest in order.

We had a few things burnt when the Fort was, such as salt, ploughs, etc., which had not been taken away. Messrs. Griffin, Clarke, Littlejohn and Smith, had nearly all their effects burnt, and are great sufferers. They had left them there to be sent down in boats. They have gone into the lower country and have settled below Vancouver and we hope will do much good to the few remaining Indians as well as to the settlers.

We have experienced much trial in Mr. Munger, who had been laboring for us—who came into the country with Mr. Griffin. The past winter he became unbalanced in his mind, called himself the representative of Christ's church, pretended to prophesy and said many insane things. We thought it best for him to return to the States because his wife was anxious to go to her friends. They accordingly started and went to Rendezvous, on the Green River, and because no one was going down they were obliged to return. We sent many letters by them but they all came back.

Although a party came up from St. Louis yet I did not hear from Jane and Edward as I had hoped. I see I must be contented with not hearing from my friends very often.

Mr. Munger and wife have gone to the Willamette and are among the Methodist missions. It was a trial for her to come back, but it pleased him very much. The journey appeared to do him good—he was more like himself when he passed here.

There are only two families of us now at this station. Mr. G., who is associated with us, and it is a great relief to have some one to share in the responsibilities of the work with us.

Adeline and Mr. Littlejohn told us much about our family that was news and interesting, and about Harriet's intended—we were pleased with her description of him and rejoice to think that we may think of her so well situated and so near our beloved parents. I hope they will both write us and tell me all about their situation. I was much pleased with Harriet's letter to me, but I could not see why she could not have filled out the whole sheet in the same way.

Father's account of Judge Hull and his family affected us very much. Adeline was here at the time it was received. This case seems a strange one. What on earth will ever induce him to forsake the ways of sin? Nothing but the power of Almighty God, and perhaps he will make even that impossible, by his rejection of the light. The condemnation of sinners in Christian lands will be far greater in the eternal world than that of these selfish Indians who have never known the light, and O, that they would feel it now and repent. What truth these Indians see and understand, they feel, and feel it keenly, too, but it is so painful to them that they get rid of it as soon as possible. All that is bad talk, to them, that shows them their own hearts.

From the commencement of this station until the present time, it has constantly been a point with some one or more of them to be arguing for property to be given them to keep them in subjection to others. First it was in the person of Um-tip-pi, now dead, and now in his two brothers, Wap-tash-tok-mahl and Ii-hich-kais-kais. We cannot but hope that this will open their eyes and cause them to feel that they have nothing to hope for from violence or any effort to frighten us to remove everything we could. They now feel that it is a very slight hold by which we are kept among them; we made them feel that not a thing we possessed was our own and that we lost nothing by leaving them, but on the other hand we were likely to feel it a privilege to work for our own support and emoluments—that if we left them it was only necessary to return to the Board what we held in trust and then labor for ourselves. It is difficult for them to feel but that we are rich and getting rich by the houses we dwell in and the clothes we wear and hang out to dry after washing from week to week, and the grain we consume in our families.

It is a remarkable fact that while we were talking with the Indians on Tuesday, the next day after the date of Mr. McKinlay's letter, that the intelligence came that Walla Walla Fort was burnt on that morning. I mentioned in my former letter that it was probably caused by sparks from the servant's chimney.

The Jesuit Mission, from St. Louis, under the care of Father Smith, late missionary to the Otoes, as I am informed, near Council Bluffs, has been established and houses are building, but the exact location I cannot give you. It yet remains to learn its effects.

If you see Mr. Hale or Mr. Drayton, of the U.S. Ex. Squadron (and perhaps others may tell you the same) they can describe the picture of a tree hanging in C.F. McLoughlin's room at Vancouver, which represents all Protestants as the withered ends of the several branches of papacy falling off down into infernal society and flames, as represented at the bottom. This gives a good idea of their manner of instruction to the Indians as drawn out in manuscript and given to them, accompanied with oral instructions of a similar character. The possession of one of these manuscripts by an Indian binds him not to hear any more the instructions of Protestants, so far as my observations can prove.

Thus much of the letter concerning the Indians. We would be glad if Harriet, or some one would copy it and send it to Brother Augustus Whitman. It is a great deal of writing for us to send so much to all our friends, we have so little time and strength. We expect to send this via Red River and St. Peter's. If father desired it he could send by way of Canada and we receive a letter every fall.

The remainder is concerning the fate of this Mission, which we hope will be kept in your own bosoms, at least until you hear from us again. We are in deep trials and would be glad to have our parents know them if they could. We dare not trust our own language to our friends — at least this is the way I feel — but will copy husband's to Mr. Greene, so that you may know some things they know concerning us. In the same letter he says:

"It is a great evil to this mission that the reinforcement promulgated their determination not to come on until they heard from the Board or this mission as shown in this country by the Scientific Corps of the *Peacock*. Father may not know that they arrived at the Islands in June last, during the sessions of the general meeting, and were designated to their several fields of labor the same as those who belonged to that mission. Our situation called only the more imperatively for them to come on and in no way could excuse their not coming. We are in no way unprepared for a reinforcement as we have no secret burnings. Whatever causes of complaint we have with each other are open and need in no case involve a third person. Nothing could have been more important than for them to come on. But I think any reinforcement will be very much unfitted for laboring in this field after passing the Islands and seeing the ease of their living and becoming impressed with the idea that the work there is so much more important than this, as held and maintained to them by that mission and the awakening influence of their representations of districts of many thousands yet vacant at the Islands, accompanied by discussions of whether it would be better for them to stop there where they may spend all their time in laboring for souls rather than to come here and labor for a few hundred and then be obliged to spend to much time in labor to procure their own sustenance. The last objection could not be true of Mr. Poris if he had come and been associated with me, but it was raised by him as having been urged at the Islands. You will know best what course to take in our case, to which we will most cheerfully submit. In the meantime, believe me to be your obedient fellow-laborer for the salvation of the Indians, white settlers and passers-by in Oregon.

M.W."

Again I would ask that this might not be circulated. It may do injury. Since I have been copying this page, husband came in and said he would rather I would not copy this, but I had begun before I knew he had any objections, and I could not well throw away the sheet. We hope this thing will be settled and not exist to be written about very long.

Their wandering habits, so little of the time at the station under the influence of truth, and their scattered situation in their wandering and want of time in their teachers to follow them. add to this, minds filled with perplexing care and labor necessary to sustain the body, in the few teachers they have among them, and perhaps what is the greatest obstacle, want of faith and a holy heart. This winter we hope will be different. Husband expects to visit around among them, and if I am not deceived, if I know what my feelings are, it is my prevailing, ardent desire to see the salvation of the Lord among them. What is before us we know not, nor how long we shall be permitted to remain among them. The missionary work is hard, up-hill work, even the best of it. There are no flowery beds of ease here, but it may be said to be so with Christians in my native land, but the danger of being deceived may be greater possibly there than here. We have meeting among ourselves besides the native worship. On the Sabbath a sermon is read. Tuesday evening is the Oregon concert of prayer observed by all the missionaries in the country, both of our number and among the Methodists. Besides the monthly concert, we have a Bible class, which is very interesting to us. We have our regular prayer meetings, a weekly one on Friday eve and the maternal meeting twice a month. In all the prayer meetings of this mission the brethren only pray. I believe all the sisters would be willing to pray if their husbands would let them. We are so few in number, it seems as if they would wish it, but many prefer the more dignified way. My husband has no objection to my praying, but if my sisters do not, he thinks it quite as well for me not to. But it seems sometimes, and has ever since we have been here, that if "these hold their peace, the very stones will cry out." The path of duty is the only path of safety, but it requires close watching to find that path under all circumstances.

My health has been poor for more than a year past and my many bodily infirmities doubtless causes my gloomy moments and unfits me for reading and reflection many times. I am in hopes I shall be better. The winter is a very trying season with me; I suffer so much with the cold. Husband was very sick last winter, but he is quite well now. I wrote to sister, Judson and Jane last spring, but did not write to father and mother, and sent it across the mountains, but the letters came back, as no one went to the States. I sent them this fall by ship. I shall write to Harriet next. I am obliged to any of my friends for writing me. I am sure if they knew how much good they do me they would write oftener. I wonder why brother H.P. and sister Livonia do not write me. I feel for their affliction very much. Where is Clarissa? Why does she not write and her husband? I should like to keep up my acquaintance with them. Brother Jonas G., where is he that he cannot write? It seems sometimes as if I might hear often from home. I hope father and mother will not stop writing, if all the rest do, for then my heart would break; I should not know how to be reconciled to it.

I should like to know more about the three grandchildren—are they good children? They must be some help to mother now, I should think. I hope to hear from Jane and Edward next summer. I have received one from them since they were in Quincy. I am obliged to use my spectacles while writing, or I could not write so much. When my health is poor my eyes are very weak. Please give my love to all the family and other friends who may inquire. Husband sends love, but gives no encouragement when he can write. His time and strength are so much taken up with the duties of his station. He scarcely writes a letter to any of his friends, except to Mr. Greene—to him he is obliged to write.

    Pray for your needy children,
                 M. & N. Whitman.

A regular way of sending letters to us would be to write every spring and direct them to the care of James Keith, Esq., Hudson's Bay Company, Lachine, Lower Canada, and paying the postage. It would reach us in the fall—October—without failure, generally—no other way is as sure, except by ship. Love to all from us both.

N.W.

Husband expects to go to Mr. Spalding's next week, to be gone some time. My two little girls are a comfort to me, in his absence, especially; they are both of them natives of the Rocky Mountains, and poor little outcasts when I took them. One of them is called Mary Ann and is the daughter of James Bridger, the man out of whose back the doctor cut an arrow point when he was up to the mountains the first time. She is six years old and has been with me but three months. The other is a child of one Meek, a mountain man, but who has now gone to the Willamette. Her name is Helen Mary and has been with us some over a year.

Seven hogs have been butchered to-day and it is a strange thing that I could keep writing all day and have nothing to do with it. We do not need to kill any more horses for meat, for we killed a very fat beef a short time ago, fed upon grass only, which yielded 148 pounds of tallow after it was tried. We have enough to live upon, but it costs labor to get it and take care of it—just as it does at home. Father and mother will have to get Harriet's eyes to read this; perhaps I fill my letters too full. If I do you must tell me. If I should take some that I received from friends as a pattern, mine would be too full.

Letters

WIELETPOO, Nov. 18, 1841.

My Dear Father:—I am permitted once more to address you. We received a letter from father, mother and Harriet last August, for which please receive our grateful thanks. We rejoice that health, so much comfort and strength of days are still added and enjoyed by our beloved parents. We bless God that you still live to pray for your children far away, as well as those that are near, and O may they be answered with answers of peace upon our souls.

My object in writing now is to copy a letter written by husband to Mr. Greene, giving an account of our late trials with the Indians. I can copy his letter better and do it much quicker than I can give it in my own language:

"REV. DAVID GREENE,
      "Sec. of the A.B.C.F.M.,

"*Dear Sir:*—I wrote you a few days since in which I promised to write again more fully, to be sent across the mountains via Red River and St. Peters.

"I went in July to attend Mrs. Eells in her confinement, Mrs. W. accompanying me, and were absent from the station six weeks, during which time the wheat was harvested by Mr. Gray's superintendence. In the meantime he had begun to build a house for himself of adobe. It is now roofed and the walls are being hewed and plastered, and in a short time it will be fit to dwell in, although not finished. Some of his lumber has been sawed by two white men lately from California. He has two others in his employ who came this year from Missouri. A man hired by Mr. Eells by the name of Packett (formerly at school at the Harmony Station), who could not at this time accompany Mr. E. on account of the health of his family, remains with us for the winter. Our Hawaiian woman, whose husband died a year ago, has gone to be in readiness to go home with Mr. Smith and wife. Mungo, the boy whom we brought up but who is now under engagement, has gone to assist Mr. Eells at that station. So that Mrs. W. and myself are alone with two small girls, one of three years and the other six, the first of which we have adopted as our own.

"In order to assist Mr. Gray to get on with his house I have taken the ordinary care of the station, and harvested the corn and potatoes, and sowed the wheat. Messrs. Walker and Eells have got their supplies of flour and meat from us since June. Mr. Spalding, also, has taken some twice, as his mill is not yet in order to run. The mill is a most valuable acquisition to this station. Its simple construction, its safe and durable water power make it a great labor-saving machine.

"The Indians at this station have been very quiet for the last year and a half, but from various causes which have been operating upon them, they were prepared for agitation, thinking this the best way to obtain property. I-a-tin, an Indian who had been to the Willamette settlement, undertook to embarrass Mr. G. In his building operations, forbidding him to cut timber without pay, and others joined him in talking of charging us for fire wood. There has often been talk of causing us to pay for the land we occupy. I-a-tin said he was told while at the Willamette that if any one came on the white men's land and he refused to go off, he was kicked off.

"The plantation of this station has been in common with the Indians, upon a point of land between two streams; as soon as our wheat was off the Indians put their horses in to the great injury of our garden, corn and potatoes. We have been hitherto unable to make fences for the want of timber and strength and time to do it; now we expect they will be able to do it in the spring, as Mr. G. is associated with us at this station, by digging a ditch around our fields, which answers the purpose of irrigation also, (none of our fields have any fences) as well as to that of some of the Indians.

"While Mr. Hale, of Boston, who belongs to the U.S. Exploring Squadron, was here, Til-ka-na-ik, another Indian, was most insolent because, when his horses were eating up our corn, I sent some Indians to catch them. He said I was likely to get the Indians whipped, for if I sent them to catch his horses he should beat them, and added that he put his horses there least they should stray, for he had no servant, and that was a shut up place, and that if I had them put out he would take one of our horses and ride him to hunt for his until he tired him out and then leave him. I then told him that I thought our field was a plantation and not for a horse pen; but if he thought it good to eat up our crops I had no more to say about it. He then said that this was his land and that he grew up here and that the horses were only eating the growth of the soil, and demanded of me what I had ever given him for the land. I answered "Nothing," and that he might depend upon it I never would pay him anything. He then made use of the word "Shame," which is used in Chinook the same as in English, and its parallel in Nez Perces. I requested him to wait while I spoke, and then told him of the original arrangement for us to locate here and that we did not come of ourselves, but by invitation from the Indians, and that the land was fully granted us. Here I left him; but in a short time after I was met by one of the chiefs who said it was troublesome to see those horses eating up the corn.

"I then related to him what had just passed with Til-ka-na-ik, and told him I had no intention to remove them. While we were talking he, Til-ka-na-ik, came along, having overheard us, and came up to me and asked me how many times I was going to talk, and struck me twice severly upon my breast and commanded me to stop talking. I told him I had been in the habit of talking from my childhood and intended to keep on talking. This Indian Til-ka-na-ik has for the year past been practicing the ceremonies of the Papists.

"Following this in order of time was another trial with I-a-tin, the first named Indian. His son had been employed to take care of our cattle and horses, but had been very unfaithful, having left them for four weeks, causing us to pay him off before his engagement had expired. I asked him how much I was to pay his son; he said just what I pleased. I then gave him the full value of what was agreed upon within five balls and powder. But it did not please him, and only caused him to raise a bitter complaint that he could not obtain justice. I then told him I would exchange some of the articles and give the full value of our first bargain in the things originally promised, and that then he would be in debt to me for the four weeks which his son neglected to take care of the cattle and for the unexpired time yet to be fulfilled in his bargain. I told him, also, that when, on the morning of the same day, I was grinding his wheat for him, I little thought he would treat me thus. At this he was much displeased and said to one in my family, and also in camp, that he would burn our mill. Mr. Gray is living in our old house, one part of which was in use as a work shop and kitchen. It was much used also as a place to store many small articles and tools, so that no Indian was allowed to go in there.

"One morning an Indian named Pitamianinmuksmuks went in and seated himself by the fire along with a hired man, the Hawaiian and an Indian who was there by order to cook for Indians who were laboring. The woman made complaint to Mr. G., and he desired him to go out; but he at once asked if he thought he would steal? Mr. G. told him many things had been stolen, and if he allowed one he must another, and that even if some would not steal, and if they were admitted, others would follow them, and on that account he wanted no one to come in there. Upon this, he became insolent and Mr. G. put him out of the room. He then went at once to the horse pen and threw his rope upon one of Mr. G.'s horses. Mr. G. followed him and cut his rope off and put him out of the pen. In the afternoon of the same day he came where I was at work and took the same horse in my presence.

"He was on a horse with another Indian and others had gathered around. I simply asked him if he made himself a thief how he could cleanse himself. His brother Sa-ki-aph said it would be good to kill our cattle. I told him he had now shown his heart, and if he thought so he could kill them. I then went to apprise Mr. G., who was at work upon his house. We soon saw Til-au-ki-ak, a relative of Pitamianinmuksmuks', with his young men coming toward the house. I requested Mr. G. not to answer him, but to allow me to do it. He came up to us in the building and began to address Mr. G., who took no notice of what he said, and he failed to create any excitement, but ordered Mr. G. to stop building and remove the next day. I told him it was the Sabbath and he could not go. It seemed strange to him to speak of reverence for the Sabbath at such a time. I then went down from the building and he soon followed me and began to complain of my taking the part of Mr. G., and said if he were to go to our country he should be very careful how he conducted himself lest he should be sent off. He said again that Mr. G. was laboring in vain for he must leave. I told him it was natural for us to labor, and we would not desist although we might labor in vain. I told him, also, that if Indians came into Mr. G.'s or my house and refused to do as we desired, it was right for us to put them out. He then took hold of my ear and pulled it and struck me on the breast, ordering me to hear—as much as to say, we must let them do as they pleased about our houses. When he let go I turned the other to him and he pulled that, and in this way I let him pull first one and then the other until he gave over and took my hat and threw it into the mud. I called on the Indians who were at work for Mr. G. to give it to me and I put it on my head—when he took it off again and threw it in the same place. Again the Indians gave it to me and I put it on. With more violence he took it off and threw it in the mud and water, of which it dipped plentifully. Once more the Indians gave it back to me and I put it on, all mud as it was, and said to him, "Perhaps you are playing." At this he left us. A day or two after this McKay, another Indian, made a violent speech and forbid all the Indians to labor for us.

"We intended to take no notice of these things, not even to mention them, but the superintendent of Fort Walla Walla, Mr. McKinlay, sent up his interpreter to inquire about it, as he had heard exciting stories from the Indians. I wrote him all was now quiet and we had no concern, but at the same time I gave him the last mentioned case and told him I feared Joe Gray, a half-breed Iroquois, for a long time a servant of the company, but who was in the camp of the Waiilatpu and Walla Walla Indians from April to September, contributed to cause this excitement, for I was told by an Indian after the affair that Joe Gray had told Til-au-ka-ik while at his camp and fishery that we were rendering the Indians miserable and that we ought to pay for the lands. This Gray is a Romanist and held worship in the forms of that church among the Indians.

"Mr. McKinlay espoused our cause warmly, and sent word to the Indians that he felt the insult offered to us as offered to himself, and that those who conducted themselves so much like dogs would not be permitted to see him with complacency. The interpreter added much to this, according to the Indians' stories. He told them that when Governor Simpson, of the Hudson's Bay Company, heard of the death of Chief Factor Black, who was killed at Thompson River Forts last winter in his own house by an Indian, he felt that it was not to have his people killed that he sent and had forts built and brought the Indian goods. He at once resolved to come himself and that he had gone past and was now in the lower country. He pointed to the fact of the company bringing a large number of men into the country, for a large party of settlers, as half servant to the company, were at that time at the fort on their way from the Red River to settle on the Cowlitz, and that the company had, during the last summer removed a large part of the cattle from the upper country, as evidence of a state of readiness to avenge Chief Factor Black's death, and that company were prepared and determined to avenge any other like outrage of the Indians, whether it occurred in one or two or three years, whether it might be here or among any other Indians. This excited them very much, for they did not know how to take it—they felt that they had committed themselves and been compared to dogs. After a meeting among themselves, they came to have a talk with us. Mrs. Whitman came and called me, as I was not in the house at the time, and Mr. G. and myself came in. They persisted in entering through the kitchen into the dining room and were seated when we came in. We invited such as were still in the kitchen into the dining room and let in all who presented themselves at their accustomed door. While we were talking, Pa-la-is-ti-wat, an old Indian, commenced threatening Mrs. W. at the window with a hammer, in order to force open the door, and at the same time Sa-ki-aph, who was in the house, was trying to unlock another door in order to throw open the house. I called on him to stop and also asked the chiefs to stop him, but called in vain.

"I then went and took the key from the door. He went directly into the kitchen, removed the fastening and opened the door, but I followed him and as he opened the door to let others in I put him out and fastened the door, returned and sat down. Having got the hammer from Pa-la-is-ti-wat he beat the door and the other took a large American ax, by which means they broke the kitchen door and a horde of lawless savages took possession of the house. At the same time Sa-ki-aph came in with the hammer and Pa-la-is-ti-wat with the ax to attack us. Mr. G. met the former and myself the latter and disarmed them. After I had got hold of the ax I did not excite myself to take it away until I had waited to see if the chiefs would speak to restore order, but waited in vain. After I took the ax away he held to my collar and struck me with his fist and tore my clothes. Mrs. W. took the ax from me while I was being held by the Indian, and Mr. G. put both ax and hammer upstairs. Sa-ki-aph soon returned with a club and advanced upon me. As I arose to take the club I dodged the blow he was leveling at me, for which I was greatly ridiculed by them as fearing death. While I was telling them I did not fear to die, if I did not partake of the sin of causing my death, Sa-ki-aph came in again with a gun and presented it to me and asked me if I did not fear to die. Our hired men were in the house by this time and one went and stood so as to command the gun. They persisted in saying that because I said I was not afraid to die that it was as though I had challenged them to kill me; but I told them "no" I did not challenge them nor did I want to suffer pain; but still I did not fear to die as I had just said. At the same time I showed them the consequence of killing us and sending us in advance of themselves into the presence of God.

"They now wanted us to say that we would not shut any of our doors against them, and said if we would do so we would live in peace. We told them that so long as we were allowed to live and occupy our houses we should order our doors, and if they wished to live in peace they must not oppose such regulations. Til-au-ka-ik now exclaimed that it was impossible to bully us into a fright.

"Wap-tash-tak-mahl next said that there was property in the house and that they were accustomed to have it given them when they had a difficulty. I told them they would not get the value of a single awl or pin for their bad conduct, and if they wanted property in that way they must steal it. He thought that was very hard language. I then told them that I felt that this was not an excitement of the moment but that it was the result of what Joe Gray had told them while on the Grande Ronde River. At first they were disposed to call me to an account for my authority, but Wap-tash-tak-mahl arose and said that it was true; he had told them so but had forbid them to tell of it lest he should be blamed. He then related what he had told them. That formerly the whites came on to the Iroquoise land, they killed two and drove them off; after that they killed two more, and then when the whites wanted to buy their land they loved them and said they wanted them for their children, but at last they bought them and gave a great sum of money and after that all lived together as brothers.

"They now broke up and went away, saying they would go and see if Mr. McKinlay would call them dogs. We thought best to apprise him of their intentions and sent accordingly to the Fort in the night.

"The next day was the Sabbath and it was a sad day to us. Many stayed away from worship and some went to the Fort carrying their arms. Others were insolent and reckless of evil. They did many violent acts, such as breaking our windows and troubling our animals. We now felt that we had showed the example of non-resistance as long as it was called for, and as we went to bed we put ourselves in a state of defence, should anything occur at the Fort and take our families and stay for a time, until we could either arrange to go away or return, as might seem best.

"On Monday I received a letter from Mr. McKinlay giving an account of their conduct there, a copy of which I will give you. Dated Walla Walla, Oct. 4th, 1841.

My Dear Sir:—I have the pleasure to inform you that there is every prospect of your being allowed to keep peaceful possession of your place and that you will not be further molested by the Indians (It was rumored that they intended to break into the fort Sabbath night which caused them to keep watch and mount all their guns, and cannons, and load them with nails, old pieces of iron, etc., to be ready in case they should need them.) Rogers would have told you how matters stood when he left. All, however, was quiet during the night. After breakfast this morning I sent for the Indians, and when they came into the hall, I told them I wished to know their hearts, and at the same time, tell the state of my own, for, although I sent for horses the other day, I would not trade one till such times as I knew whether we were to have war or not. That for my own part I did not care which. I dared them to take my fort from me, for that I had a sufficient number of men to protect myself, but that I could not protect you; but if they persisted in doing you harm that I would instantly send to Chief Factor McLoughlin, who would send up a sufficient number to avenge the whole and that the plunder of their horses would be considered sufficient payment for the trouble. That I knew they might kill you before assistance came, but that it afforded me great satisfaction they could not send you to hell. That it is the first time I have heard of Indians in any part of the country treating missionaries so, and that I never heard in any country of missionaries being obliged to pay for the lands they occupied. I concluded by saying that if you did I would do so, also. That spilling of blood was far from my wish, but that it was time we understood each other's hearts. Wap-tash-tak-mahl, McKay and Til-au-ka-ik all spoke, one after the other. It is unnecessary for me to tell you all that they said at present. Let it suffice, therefore, till we meet that what one and all of them said, expressed deep contrition for what had passed and many promises that they would conduct themselves well in future. In fact, they spoke most reasonably and acknowledged that they were altogether in the wrong. I then told them that I was very willing to blot from my memory their dogly conduct and that I was sure you would do so likewise. So I think you will find it to the advantage of all concerned to forget and forgive the past. But pray put your face against paying them for their bad conduct. In hopes that you will agree with me in my plans, I remain your sincere will-wisher,

'ARCHIBALD McKINLAY.'

"On Tuesday, the 5th, we called the Indians to hold a talk with them; the result of which was to gain a full acknowledgement of the first understanding we had with them before the establishment of the mission. This talk was fully interpreted to them by the interpreter at Walla Walla, and I do not know that it could have been more complete in all the relations required for the station. We told them plainly that unless they were ready to protect us and enforce good order, we would leave them; that we did not come to fight them, but to teach them. The first agitators were very full in their expressions of sorrow for their conduct, but Wap-tash-tak-mahl, who asked to be paid for their bad conduct and had pretended to be friendly, in this case also showed duplicity and how loth he was to relinquish the hope of getting property, as he has also at other times since. A brother of Iich-ish-kais-kais, not at the time at the station, but who soon after arrived, made a feast at which, as usual on such occasions, subjects of interest were discussed. He then proposed to require of us that we must distribute our cattle among them, or else they would require us to leave. Wap-tash-tak-mahl consented to the same, but Til-au-ka-ik, who had been the principal agitator before, entreated them not to do it, assuring them that they should not extort cattle by fear, and desired them not to follow in his bad track, for which he was justly censured by the superintendent at Walla Walla and incurred the name of a dog. It is said this brought tears into the eyes of Iich-ish-kais-kais, and a promise that he would not mention it again. Ka-mash-pa-hi, another who had arived since the disturbance, said he advised all to be still and say no more about causing themselves to be paid for the land, wood, water, etc. He did not think we expected such things when we located on the vacant lands.

"Yours truly,
"MARCUS WHITMAN."

Friday, 19th. — I wrote nearly all of this sheet yesterday afternoon and evening, and have written it so fast I fear my parents will find it difficult to read. We wish to send it today and it is the last opportunity for the present.

From your loving daughter,
N.W.

Narcissa Whitman

WAIILATPU, March 1st, 1842.

My Dear Jane and Edward:—I was busy all the forenoon in preparing my husband for his departure. He left about two o'clock p.m. to go on a professional visit to Brother Walker's, and I am once more left alone in this house with no other company than my two little half-breed girls, Mary Ann Bridger and Helen Marr Meek. Since he left I have copied a letter of one sheet and a half for him to Brother Spalding and written a short one to Sister S., besides which kept me until nearly dark, although I wrote all with all my might, for we had detained an Indian who was going that way, to take them, and before I could get them completed he began to be quite impatient. I, however, pacified him by giving him something to eat to beguile his time, and when he left gave him a good piece of bread to eat on the way. The Indians do us many favours in this way, and get as many from us in return, for they are always glad of something from us to eat on the way. Since I got my letters off I regulated my house some, got my own and my little girl's supper and some toast and tea for a sick man who has been here a few days, from Walla Walla to be doctored; attended family worship and put my little girls to bed, and have set me down to write a letter to Jane and Edward, my dear brother and sister that I left at home in Angelica more than six years ago. Since or just as I seated myself to write, Brother Gray came in to get some medicine for the sick man. He is in Packet's lodge a few steps from the door, and he is the man who attends to my wants, such as milking, getting water, wood, etc. He is a half-breed from the east side of the mountains and was brought up at Harmony mission, but came to the mountains about eight years ago and has since become a Catholic. Brother Gray has built him a new house and it is quite a piece from us. Thus lonely situated, what would be the enjoyment to me if E. and J. would come in and enjoy my solitude with me. Surely solitude would quickly vanish, as it almost appears to, even while I am writing. Jane, I wish you were here to sleep with me, I am such a timid creature about sleeping alone that sometimes I suffer considerably, especially since my health has been not very good. It, however, gives me the opportunity for the exercise of greater trust and confidence in my heavenly protector in whose hands I am always safe and happy when I feel myself there. My eyes are much weaker than when I left home and no wonder, for I have so much use for them. I am at times obliged to use the spectacles Brother J.G. so kindly furnished me. I do not know what I could do without them; so much writing as we have to do, both in our own language and the Nez Perces; and, besides, we have no way to feast our minds with knowledge necessary for health and spirituality without reading, and here the strength of the eyes are taxed again.

Out of compassion to my eyes and exhausted frame, dear ones, I must bid you goodnight. You may hear from me to-morrow, perhaps, if I am not interrupted with company.

2d—After attending to the duties of the morning, and as I was nearly done hearing my children read, two native women came in bringing a miserable looking child, a boy between three and four years old, and wished me to take him. He is nearly naked, and they said his mother had thrown him away and gone off with another Indian. His father is a Spaniard and is in the mountains. It has been living with its grandmother the winter past, who is an old and adulterous woman and has no compassion for it. Its mother has several others by different white men, and one by an Indian, who are treated miserably and scarcely subsist. My feelings were greatly excited for the poor child and felt a great disposition to take him. Soon after the old grandmother came in and said she would take him to Walla Walla and dispose of him, there and accordingly took him away. Some of the women who were in, compassionated his case and followed after her and would not let her take him away, and returned with him again this eve to see what I would do about him. I told her I could not tell because my husband was gone. What I fear most is that after I have kept him awhile some of his relatives will come and take him away and my labour will be lost or worse than lost. I, however, told them they might take him away and bring him again in the morning, and in the meantime I would think about it. The care of such a child is very great at first — dirty, covered with body and head lice and starved — his clothing is a part of a skin dress that does not half cover his nakedness, and a small bit of skin over his shoulders.

Helen was in the same condition when I took her, and it was a long and tedious task to change her habits, young as she was, but little more than two years old. She was so stubborn and fretful and wanted to cry all the time if she could not have her own way. We have so subdued her that now she is a comfort to us, although she requires tight reins constantly.

Mary Ann is of a mild disposition and easily governed and makes but little trouble. She came here last August. Helen has been here nearly a year and a half. The Lord has taken our own dear child away so that we may care for the poor outcasts of the country and suffering children. We confine them altogether to English and do not allow them to speak a word of Nez Perces.

Read a portion of the Scriptures to the women who were in today, and talked awhile with them. Baked bread and crackers today, and made two rag babies for my little girls. I keep them in the house most of the time to keep them away from the natives, and find it difficult to employ their time when I wish to be engaged with the women. They have a great disposition to take a piece of board or a stick and carry it around on their backs, if I would let them, for a baby, so I thought I would make them something that would change their taste a little. You wonder, I suppose, what looking objects Narcissa would make. No matter how they look, so long as it is a piece of cloth rolled up with eyes, nose and mouth marked on it with a pen, it answers every purpose. They caress them and carry them about the room at a great rate, and are as happy as need be. So much for my children.

I have not told you that we have a cooking stove, sent us from the Board, which is a great comfort to us this winter, and enables me to do my work with comparative ease, now that I have no domestic help.

We have had but very little snow and cold this winter in this valley. The thermometer has not been lower than 20° below freezing; but in every direction from us there has been an unusual quantity of snow, and it still remains. Husband expects to find snow beyond the Snake river, which he would cross today if he has been prospered, and may perhaps be obliged to make snow shoes to travel with. Last night was a very windy night, and the same today, but it is still now. Brother Walker is situated directly north of us, so that it is not likely that the snow will decrease any in going. It is uncertain when he will return if prospered and not hindered with the snow. He expects to be gone only four weeks. May the Lord preserve and return him in safety and in His own time, and keep me from anxiety concerning him. Goodnight, J. and E.

3d.—Dear Jane, this has been washing day, and I have cleaned house some; had a native woman to help me that does the hardest part. I am unable to do my heavy work and have been for two years past.

This evening an Indian has been in who has been away all winter. I have been reading to him the fifth chapter of Matthew. Every word of it seemed to sink deep into his heart; and O may it prove a savour of life to his soul. He thinks he is a Christian, but we fear to the contrary. His mind is somewhat waked up about his living with two wives. I would not ease him any, but urged him to do his duty. Others are feeling upon the subject, particularly the women; and why should they not feel?—they are the sufferers.

The little boy was brought to me again this morning and I could not shut my heart against him. I washed him, oiled and bound up his wounds, and dressed him and cleaned his head of lice. Before he came his hair was cut close to his head and a strip as wide as your finger was shaved from ear to ear, and also from his forehead to his neck, crossing the other at right angles. This the boys had done to make him look ridiculous. He had a burn on his foot where they said he had been pushed into the fire for the purpose of gratifying their malicious feelings, and because he was friendless. He feels, however, as if he had got into a strange place, and has tried to run away once or twice. He will soon get accustomed, I think, and be happy, if I can keep him away from the native children. So much about the boy Marshall. I can write no more tonight.

4th.—There has been almost constant high wind ever since husband left and increasingly cold. Feel considerably anxious concerning him, lest the deep snow and cold may make his journey a severe one. At the best it is very wearing to nature to travel in this country. He never has been obliged to encounter so much snow before, and I do not know how it will affect him. He is a courageous man, and it is well that he is so to be a physician in this country. Common obstacles never affect him; he goes ahead when duty calls. Jane and Edward, you know but little about your brother Marcus, and all I can tell you about him at this time is that he is a bundle of thoughts.

Met this afternoon for a female prayer meeting; only two of us—Sister Gray and myself—yet they are precious seasons to us, especially when Jesus meets with us, as He often does. I am blessed with a lovely sister and an excellent associate in Sister Gray, and I trust that I am in some measure thankful, for I have found by experience that it is not good to be alone in our cares and labours.

9th.—Last evening received a letter from Sister Walker dated Feb. 21st, in which she expresses some fears lest husband should not arrive in season on account of the deep snow. The probability is that he has had as much as one day on snow shoes if not more. We are having our winter now, both of cold and snow. During the last twenty-four hours there has been quite a heavy fall of snow in the valley, and it is doubtless doubled in the mountains.

Last eve I spent at Bro. Gray's, after the monthly concert. We opened some boxes that have just arrived from the Board to the mission, containing carding, spinning and weaving apparatus, clothing and books. Our goods often get wet in coming up the river, and we are often obliged to open, dry and repack again. We have abundant evidence that our Christian friends in the States have not forgotten us, by the donations we receive from time to time. My work last eve was such cold and damp work that it gave me many rheumatic pains all night, and besides it took us so long that I feel unable to write much more tonight. There is still another evening's work of the same kind, which must be done as soon as tomorrow. We take the eve because Bro. G. has so much labour during the day, and then our children are all in bed. Goodnight, Jane.

9th. — While I was thinking about preparing to retire to rest last eve, Bro. Gray came in to see if I could go over and see and aid in the arrangement of the other boxes. I finally mustered courage to go, because they were anxious to have it out of the way. Found it an easier job than was expected, because there was but one that needed drying.

Attended maternal meeting this afternoon. Sister G. and I make all the effort our time and means will permit to edify and instruct ourselves in our responsible maternal duties. Read this p.m. the report of the New York City Association for 1840, and what a feast it was to us! It is a comforting thought to us in a desert land to know that we are so kindly remembered by sister Associations in our beloved land. But the constant watch and care and anxiety of a missionary mother cannot be known by them except by experience. Sister G. has two of her own and I have three half-breeds. I believe I feel all the care and watchfulness over them that I should if they were my own. I am sure they are a double tax upon my patience and perseverance, particularly Helen; she wants to rule every one she sees. She keeps me on guard continually lest she should get the upper hand of me. The little boy appears to be of a pretty good disposition, and I think will be easy to govern. He proves to be younger than I first thought he was; he is not yet three years old — probably he is the same age Helen was when she came here. His old grandmother has been in to see him today, but appears to have no disposition to take him. She wanted I should give her something to eat every now and then, because I had got the child to live with me and take care of, also old clothes and shoes. So it is with them; the moment you do them a favour you place yourself under lasting obligations to them and must continue to give to keep their love strong towards you. I make such bungling work of writing this eve I believe I will stop, for I can scarcely keep my head up and eyes open. So good night, J., for you do not come to sleep with me, and I must content myself with Mary Ann.

11th. — Dear Jane, I am sick tonight and in much pain — have been scarcely able to crawl about all day. The thought comes into my mind, how good to be relieved of care and to feel the blessing of a sympathizing hand administering to the necessities of a sick and suffering body, and whose presence would greatly dispel the gloom that creeps over the mind in spite of efforts to the contrary. But I must not repine or murmur at the dealings of my Heavenly Father with me, for he sees it necessary thus to afflict me that His own blessed image may be perfected in me. O, what a sinful, ungrateful creature I am — proud and disobedient. I wonder and admire the long-suffering patience of God with me, and long to be free from sin so that I shall grieve Him no more. But there is rest in heaven to the weary and wayworn traveler, and how blessed that we may "hope to the end for the grace that shall be given unto us at the revelation of Jesus Christ." Pray for us, J. and E., for we need your prayers daily. Goodnight.

12th. — I would that I could describe to you what I have felt and passed through since writing the above. Before I could get to bed last night I was seized with such severe pains in my stomach and bowels that it was with difficulty that I could straighten myself. I succeeded in crawling about until I got something to produce perspiration, thinking that it might proceed from a cold, and went to bed. About two o'clock in the morning Sister Gray sent for me, for she was sick and needed my assistance. When I was waked I was in a profuse perspiration. What to do I did not know. Neither of them knew that I was sick the day before. I at last concluded that I would make the effort to go, casting myself for preservation on the mercy of God. Mr. Cook, the man who came after me, made a large fire for me in my room, and I was enabled to dress and dry myself without getting cold, the weather having moderated some from what it was a few days ago. I bundled myself pretty well and went with Mr. C.'s assistance, for I felt but very little better able to walk than I did the evening before, and Bro. Gray was washing it. In the meantime, after they were informed how I was, they sent me word not to come if I was not able. I took the babe and dressed it, and have been there all day with my children, although I have not been able to sit up all day. Both mother and babe are comfortable tonight, and I have come home to spend the night and Sabbath, leaving Mr. G. with the care of them tomorrow. They have a good Hawaiian woman, which is a great mercy.

Sab. Eve., 13th — Was kept awake last night by the headache considerably, and it has continued most of the day. Bro. G.'s house is very open, and the change from ours affects me unfavourable generally. Notwithstanding feeble health, this Sabbath has been a precious day to me. A quiet resting upon God is every thing, both in sickness and in health. My heart cries, O, for sanctifying grace that I may not become hardened under affliction.

14th. — I have this day entered upon my thirty-fifth year, and had my dear Alice C. been alive she would have been five years old, for this was her birthday as well as mine. Precious trust! She was taken away from the evil to come. I would not have it otherwise now. All things are for the best, although we may not see it at the time. Spent the day with Sister G., although not able to do much. Have been taking medicine and feel some better this eve, and hope to be better still tomorrow.

15th. — Have been with Sister Gray all day. There is so much there and all around us to call forth feelings of sympathy and care, that I have been so excited all day as not to scarcely realize my own state of health until I retire from it, and then I find myself completely exhausted. Thus it is that the missionary is so soon worn out, and his health fails and he is obliged to leave the field. He constantly sees work enough for his utmost time and strength, and much, very much that must remain undone for the want of hands to do it. We feel a merciful and timely relief in the association of Bro. and Sister Gray in our labours at this station. Had we continued much longer without help we should have been obliged, both of us without doubt, to have retired from the field as invalids. Yet still there is just as much as we all can possibly do, and more, too, for every year brings increased labours and demands upon us, and doubtless will continue to if there is much emigration to this country.

Edward, if you are thinking to become a missionary, you would do well to write a sermon on the word PATIENCE every day. Study well its meaning; hold fast on to patience and never let go, thinking all the time that you will have more need of her by and by than ever you can have while you remain at home. But I must stop before I exhaust myself, and gain strength for the duties of the morrow by rest.

21st. — It will be three weeks tomorrow since dear husband left, and I am feeling tonight almost impatient for his return. It has been stormy and cold every day since he left. Indeed, we have had our winter in this month, and now the rivers are so high that it is almost impossible to cross them without swimming. I feel that the Lord has mercifully and tenderly sustained and kept me from anxious feelings about him thus far during his absence. Doubtless he has suffered much, but the Lord will preserve, I hope, and return him again to me, filled with a lively sense of His goodness to us continually. The Indians feel his absence very much, especially Sabbaths. They are here so short a time they do not like to have him gone.

Today I have had the care of Sister G.'s two children and my three, which has been a hard day's work for me. I am more and more pleased with my little boy every day. He is so mild and quiet, and so happy in his new situation that I have not had the least regret that I took him in. He is learning to talk English extremely well — much faster than my two girls did. The second Sabbath he went about the room saying, "I must not work, I must not work," and also a part of a line of a hymn he had hear us sing," Lord teach a little child to pray," — all that he could say was, "a child to pray, a child to pray." He is learning to sing, also; he seems to have a natural voice, and learn quick. I think husband will have no objections to keeping him when he sees what a promising boy he is.

Sister Gray is recovering very fast; she came out into the kitchen yesterday to supper, and today she has dressed her babe, which is but ten days old. She took the advantage of me and dressed it before I could get over there this morning. She was going about her own room before it was a week old. Perhaps you will think we do as the natives do when we are among the natives. She certainly is very well, and we ought to be very thankful, and I trust we are. We all see so much to do that it is difficult to keep still when it is possible to stir. So goodnight, J. and E., for my sheet is full.

26th. — Husband arrived today about noon, to the joy of all the inhabitants of Waiilatpu. Mr. Eells came with him. His journey was prosperous beyond our most sanguine expectations, for the day that he would have been obliged to take snow shoes was so cold that by taking the morning very early they went on the top of the snow and arrived there in safety the Saturday after he left here. Sister Walker has a son, born on the 16th, four days after the birth of Sister Gray's. They call him Marcus Whitman. So it is, dear J. and E., that the Lord cares for and preserves us; and it seemed more than ever as if He sustained me from anxiety and gave me a spirit of prayer for him, and answered prayer in his safe return with improved health; and O, may the lives which He does so mercifully preserve, be devoted more entirely to His service.

Bro. Eells came for his boxes and will return next week. We are cheered with an occasional visit from one and another, which is a source of comfort to us in our pilgrimage here.

This sheet is full, and if you have trouble to read it, say so, and I will not do so again.

Your sister,

N. WHITMAN.

Dear Sister Jane: — It would be a pleasure to see you, and I am meditating how it could be, as you have come almost half way. I was just telling Narcissa what an interest I had taken in yourself ever since I was introduced to you at your father's house by Mr. Hamilton at the close of a prayer meeting. That was the first introduction to the family. From that moment my heart has been towards the family. But you smile, I suppose, and say it was Narcissa; no, it was Jane; Narcissa was in Butler. I presume you will have no recollection of the introduction; if so, let it rest on my recollection, which is vivid. I trust you are happily employed in aiding Edward. It is a noble work. Encourage him to study and toil. Tell him to finish his education before he gives his mind any liberty to rove. Let usefullness be his motto. Obstacles can be overcome. With much love to you both,

Your brother,

MARCUS WHITMAN.

I would send you some specimens of the country if it were not so difficult to pack them across the mountains.

May 17th, 1842. — I send this for the scrap my dear husband has written you, more than for what I have written. It may do you good to get even that from him who is so dear to your sister and to you, I trust. It was returned last spring, and I could not send it by ship. Rogers has just said that he would call on you, so that you can ask him as many questions as you can think of, and if he returns you can send by him next spring.

Adieu, dear E.

Your sister,

N.W.

WAIILATPU, July 22nd, 1842.

Mr Dear Mrs. Brewer:—I find the perusal of the Memoirs of Mrs. Smith so deeply interesting to myself, that I desire to ask the privilege of sending it, with your permission, to the different sisters of this mission, as one or two of them have begged the reading of it. It is most too precious a morsel to be enjoyed alone in this desert land. As I am unable to write to Sister Perkins this opportunity, I will just say I forward by this conveyance a few numbers of the *New York Observer*, containing several pieces from Dr. Humphries' pen on Education, which she requested in her last letter to me. We value them much and desire to preserve them.

I am happy to hear of your prosperity in the addition to your family of a little daughter. May she live long to cheer and bless you with her sweet smiles.

Hoping for the pleasure of receiving a letter from you, I am, dear sister, yours in Christian love.

NARCISSA WHITMAN.

Mrs. H.B. Brewer,
    Wascopum.

Narcissa Whitman

WAIILATPU, August 23, 1842.

Rev. Mr. and Mrs. Allen, Cuba, My Dear Christian Friends: — I have this morning been thinking upon our situation and wants as a mission, the spiritual condition of the native population, and the interests of the country at large as it respects the prosperity of the cause of Christ on the one hand and the extension of the powers and dominion of Romanism on the other. The thought occurred to me, I will sit down and write to this dear brother and sister, and solicit an interest in their prayers and those of their beloved charge for us; it may be it will give such a spring to the work that angels will strike their harps anew, and a song of praise be put into the mouths of many who are now in the broad road to ruin. Think, if you please, of the solitary missionary labouring and toiling, without a single Aaron or Hur to stay up his hands! What slow progress must he make, if any at all, where the preaching and praying are all to be done by the same individual! Perhaps you will say, and justly, too, that we do pray for you continually. My dear friends, let me entreat you to offer up special prayer in our behalf, for we need it more than I can express. In the first place, we need more missionaries, and those of us who are now on the ground need your prayers eminently, not as those who have already attained unto perfect men and women in Christ, but as greatly in want of an enlargement in every Christian grace, if not an entire renovation of soul to God.

The Kayuses, Nez Perces, Spokans, and all the adjacent tribes need your prayers, for they are a dark-minded, wandering people, having hearts, but understand not the truth. I will give you the language of one of them in a talk made three Sabbaths ago. After listening to an exposition of the truth in Proverbs, 5th chapter, he said: "Your instruction is good, the wise and discreet appreciate it; for the mass of us, we hear it, but it falls powerless upon our hearts, and we remain the same still." I felt it deeply as a reproof for our unbelief, and want of faithful, earnest prayer in their behalf. The present is the harvest time with them. We know not how soon ardent spirits will be introduced into the country to distract and impede our work. Settlers are beginning to come around us, and their influence will not be the most congenial, as they are mostly men living with native women, who have for many years been wandering in the deep recesses of the mountains, indulging themselves in every species of vice and wickedness until, as one of them frankly confessed to me a short time since, they were wickeder than the Indians around them. Perhaps most of them have received the elements of a christian education in their childhood years, and some have Christian parents. These, also, are eminently a subject for your prayers.

Romanism stalks abroad on our right hand and on our left, and with daring effrontery boasts that she is to prevail and possess the land. I ask, must it be so? Does it not remain for the people of God in this and Christian lands to say whether it shall be so or not? "Is not the Lord on our side?" "If He is for us, who can be against us?" The zeal and energy of her prients are without a parallel, and many, both white men and Indians, wander after the beasts. Two are in the country below us, and two far above in the mountains. One of the latter is to return this fall to Canada, the States and the eastern world for a large reinforcement. How true — "while men slept, the enemy came and sowed cares." Had a pious, devoted minister, a man of talent, come into the country when we did and established himself at Vancouver, to human appearance the moral aspect of this country would not be the same as it is now; at least, we think Papacy would not have gained such a footing. But the past cannot now be retrieved. It remains for us to redeem the time; to stand in our lines and fight manfully the battles of the Lord.

We send our imploring cry to you and ask, who will come to our help and who, remaining, will sustain us in the work by the mighty power of prayer? Without it, our work will be in vain, and perhaps worse than in vain.

We have a concert of prayer on Tuesday evenings, called the Oregon Concert, in which the members of this mission and our Methodist brethren and sisters in the lower country unite to pray for the success of the cause of Christ in Oregon.

It may be interesting to you to know something of what has been done since we came here. The missionaries in this field, as all Indian missions, have not only the spiritual wants of the people to attend to, but are obliged to provide for their own sustenance and comfort by cultivating land, building houses, mills, etc., and school houses, etc., for the people. These greatly divide his mind from his more appropriate mission work, and fill it with distracting cares, causing him to mourn and be filled with grief that so little is accomplished for the soul, the immortal part of man. Yet we have the satisfaction to feel that good has been and is done to them through this channel, and as well as the more direct way of instruction.

The Kayuses almost to a man, have their little farms now in every direction in this valley, and are adding to it as their means and experience increases.

[Remainder of this letter missing. — SEC'Y.]

Narcissa Whitman

WAIILATPU, Sept. 29th, 1842.

My Dear Jane and Edward: — I sit down to write you, but in great haste. My beloved husband has about concluded to start next Monday to go to the United States, the dear land of our birth; but I remain behind. I could not undertake the journey, if it was considered best for me to accompany him, that is to travel as he expects to. He hopes to reach the borders in less than three months, if the Lord prospers his way. It is a dreadful journey, especially at this season of the year; and as much as I want to see you all, I cannot think of ever crossing the mountains again — my present health will not admit of it. I would go by water, if a way was ever open; but I have no reason to think I ever shall.

If you are still in Quincy you may not see him until his return, as his business requires great haste. He wishes to reach Boston as early as possible so as to make arrangements to return next summer, if prospered. The interests of the missionary cause in this country calls him home.

Now, dear Jane, are you going to come and join me in my labours? Is dear Edward so far advanced as not to need your aid any more? Do you think you would be contented to come and spend the remainder of your life on mission ground? If so, make your mind known to husband and he will make arrangements for you at Boston to come. Count the cost well before you undertake it. It is a dreadful journey to cross the mountains, and becoming more and more dangerous every year; but if any mission families come, you will find no difficulty in placing yourself under their protection. Bring nothing with you but what you need for the way, and a Sunday suit, a Bible and some devotional book for your food by the way. Send the remainder by ship. When E. has well finished his education, I hope he will come, also, for there will be work enough here to do by that time. At any rate, if you do not come, spend, if you please, all the time you can in writing me until he comes back, for he wishes to return next summer. Now do not disappoint me, for I have not heard a word from either of you since March, 1840. I have written you much since that time, but it may not have reached you.

I shall be left alone at this station for a season, until Mr. Gray can send some one up from below to take the charge; and he has left the mission and goes to engage in a public school. I hope to have Mr. Rogers or Mr. Littlejohn to winter here — the latter wishes to return to the States in the spring.

Now, dear J. and E., adieu. I hope you will see husband long enough to have a good visit with him. I hope he will call as he goes along. If he has time, he will, but his business requires haste, if he returns next spring.

Please give much love to Mr. and Mrs. Beardsley; tell her I shall never cease to remember and love her, and ardently hope they will both write me. I should like to hear of the different members of her family with whom I used to be acquainted.

Gladly would I write more if I could, but must write a line to other friends. Pray for me and mine while we are separated from each other.

Much love from myself to you both.

Affectionately your sister,

N. WHITMAN.

P.S.—I have forgotten to speak of husband's company in travel. He is Mr. A.L. Lovejoy, a lawyer who came up from the States this summer, and now is willing and anxious to return for the good he may do in returning. He will probably come back again. He is not a Christian, but appears to be an intelligent, interesting man.

N.W.

Mr. Edward W. Prentiss,
    Mission Institute,
        Quincy, Illinois
Favour of Dr. Whitman   Care of Rev. Wm. Beardsley

WAIILATPU, Sept. 30th, 1842.

My Beloved Parents, Brothers and Sisters: — You will be surprised if this letter reaches you to learn that the bearer is my dear husband, and that you will, after a few days, have the pleasure of seeing him. May you have a joyful meeting. He goes upon important business as connected with the missionary cause, the cause of Christ in this land, which I will leave for him to explain when you see him, because I have not time to enlarge. He has but yesterday fully made up his mind to go, and he wishes to start Monday, and this is Friday. I shall be left quite alone at this station for a season as Mr. G. and family leave for the Willamette to engage in a public school, and is dismissed from this mission. I hope to have Mr. Rogers and wife to come and winter here, or Mr. Littlejohn, perhaps both, and next summer I intend going below and spending some time in visiting for the benefit of my health, that is to relieve myself from care so that I shall have an opportunity to recruit. Now, dear mother will wonder why I could not come with him. My health, the season of the year, the speed with which he expects to travel, and the danger of the way, are reasons which make it impossible for me to accompany him. As much as I do desire to see my beloved friends once more, yet I cheerfully consent to remain behind, that the object of his almost immediate presence in the land of our birth might, if possible, be accomplished. He wishes to cross the mountains during this month, I mean October, and reach St. Louis about the first of Dec., if he is not detained by the cold, or hostile Indians. O may the Lord preserve him through the dangers of the way. He has for a companion Mr. Lovejoy, a respectable, intelligent man and a lawyer, but not a Christian, who expects to accompany him all the way to Boston, as his friends are in that region, and perhaps to Washington. This is a comfort to me, and that he is not to go alone, or with some illiterate mountain man, as we at first expected he would be obliged to. He goes with the advice and entire confidence of his brethren in the mission, and who value him not only as an associate, but as their physician, and feel, as much as I do, that they know not how to spare him; but the interest of the cause demands the sacrifice on our part; and could you know all the circumstances in the case you would see more clearly how much our hearts are identified in the salvation of the Indians and the interests of the cause generally in this country.

I cannot write but little, as I wish to give several of my friends at least a line or two to encourage them to remember me when he returns. He hopes to come back next summer, and I do hope each one of my brethren and sisters will tell me their own story on paper themselves, for husband will have so much business on his mind to attend to that he will not remember half you say to him. And will not dear father and mother write me with their own hand long letters? It will be, indeed, such a compensation for our separation, and I trust I shall feel a sufficient reward for permitting him to leave me behind and to make his visit alone to you. Forgive me, dear mother, if he is the sole theme of this letter; I can write about nothing else at this time. He is inexpressibly dear to me. Once when Mr. Lee left his wife and she died in his absence, I thought I never could consent to be left so, but since the death of our beloved A. Clarissa, the sundering of that strong and tender tie has, I trust, loosened my affections to earthly objects, or in other words divided my heart by removing that tender object of a mother's love to my heavenly home, thus admonishing me to hold my affections more in subserviency to His blessed will for objects of earth, however strong the ties may be, and increased my attachments may be, and increased my attachments above. It seems we have another object added to increase our attachments to the home, which our Saviour has gone to prepare for us.

I have just heard of the death of Sister M.A. Judson, but know nothing of the particulars, but hope to this fall by ship. I long to know more about it. I hope Brother J. is supported.

I hope you will have a long visit with your son and brother, and a profitable one, and be cheered by it, and may he be preserved to return again. I can write no more. Adieu, my beloved parents, brothers and sisters. May the rich blessings of heaven rest upon us all, and we be so happy as to meet in heaven.

Affectionately yours,
N. WHITMAN.

P.S.—I hear that Sister H. is a mother. I hope she and her husband will write me, also sister Clarissa and her husband, and J.G. I have written to that brother, but have received none from him. I would write to brother J.G. if I had time. He and all others must receive my dear husband as my living epistle to them and write me by him.

N.W.

Hon. Stephen Prentiss,
    Angelica, Allegany Co.,
        New York.
Favour of Dr. Whitman

Narcissa Whitman

WIELETPOO, Oct. 4th, 1842.

My Dear Husband:—The line you sent me to-day by Aps did me great good. I thought I was cheerful and happy before it came, but on the perusal of it I found that it increased my happiness four-fold. I believe the Lord will preserve me from being anxious about you and I was glad to hear you say with so much confidence that you trusted in Him for safety. He v ill protect you I firmly believe. Night and day shall my prayer ascend to Him in your behalf and the cause in which you have sacrificed the endearments of home, at the risk of your life, to see advancing, more to the honor and glory of God. Mr. G and family did not leave until this morn; they spent the night here, which was a great relief to me. I am sorry we forgot your pencil, comb and journal. Aps brought back Mr. Lovejoy's—said you left it in camp. He told me quite a story about the Prince stopping you, and so did Ipuantatawiksa. Prince came in very pleasant this afternoon—said he wanted John to go up and help him to-morrow.

5th. In arranging the cupboard to-day, I found that you had not taken the compass as you designed to. I fear you will suffer for the want of it; wish I could send it to you with the other things you have forgotten. I intended to have spoken to you about purchasing one or two pair of spectacles. Perhaps you will think of it. Mr. G. and family had some trouble in getting to Walla Walla yesterday. The cart broke. Hannah had an ague fit and one of the children—Helen is recovering; she has appeared quite well to-day. I feel in much better health than when you left. You will see by this that I do not neglect the tree you have given me to cultivate. Where are you tonight, precious husband? I hope you have been prosperous to-day and are sleeping sweetly. Good night, my loved one.

7th. *My Dear Husband:*—I got dreadfully frightened last night. About midnight I was awakened by some one trying to open my bedroom door. At first I did not know what to understand by it. I raised my head and listened awhile and then lay down again. Soon the latch was raised and the door opened a little. I sprang from the bed in a moment and closed the door again, but the ruffian pushed and pushed and tried to unlatch it, but could not succeed; finally he gained upon me until he opened the door again and as I supposed disengaged his blanket (at the same time I calling John) and ran as for his life. The east dining room door was open. I thought it was locked, but it appears that it was not. I fastened the door, lit a candle and went to bed trembling and cold, but could not rest until I had called John to bring his bed and sleep in the kitchen. It was in such a time that I found he was too far off. Had the ruffian persisted I do not know what I should have done. I did not think of the war club, but I thought of the poker. Thanks be to our Heavenly Father. He mercifully "delivered me from the hand of a savage man." Mungo arrived in the night some time and came in to see me this noon. I told him about the Indian coming into my room—the first I spoke of it to any one. Soon after he went to Walla Walla and left his wife with me. I did not think to write by him. He returned this eve bringing letters from Mr. McKinlay and Mr. Gray, who it seems is not off yet, urging me to remove immediately to Walla Walla. Mungo told them of my fright last night; it alarmed them very much. Mr. McK. and wife were coming up here to-morrow and she was going to stay some time with me, but he says he will not do it now, but insists upon my removing there immediately. He has told Mungo to stay until he comes on Monday and tomorrow he sends back the wagon for me to be ready to go on Tuesday. I shall go if I am able. They appear so anxious about me; doubtless it is not safe for me to remain alone any longer. In talking to Mr. McKay and Feathercap about it, I told them I should leave and go below—I could not stay and be treated so. I told them I came near beating him with the war club; they said it would have been good if I had done so and laid him flat so that they all might see who he was. Some think there will be no further danger. I think it safer for me to go now, as our friends are so anxious about me, and Mr. and Mrs. McK. so kindly offer to prepare a room to make me comfortable, and Mrs. G. says "Bring a small stove with you." Mungo appears quite humble—says he is sorry for his bad conduct and wants I should teach his wife to write or rather have her work for me. He came near having a fight with the one that had the first claim upon her. In the first place the Indian stole one of his horses. M. went and took it back again. He was then met by him and others armed with bows and arrows. M. resorted to his pistol, but Charles told him not to shoot him. They settled it by his requesting some present and M. paying him a shirt. Messrs. W. and E. did not marry them, but sent him to you for your direction. M. gave for his wife 4 horses, 1 gun, 1 coat, vest, pantaloons, leggings, 2 shirts and 100 loads of ammunition and a blanket. The poor girl had everything taken from her but the dress she had on. Ask Deborah how she would like beginning in the world in that style. For my part I should prefer the winter just past rather than just begun for such a beginning.

My good woman did not go away as we expected when you paid her. She came in sick on Wednesday; I gave her some pills and this morning she came again and has washed for me. Pitiitosh's wife came also and I set her to work as I had enough to do before the day was gone. Feathercap's wife came in and set herself to work. She has done so before, since you left. Cleaned out the cellar and helped arrange the things brought from the other house. John ground for them to-day—our Indians.

Sat. eve, 8th—I do not feel as sad and lonely this eve as I always have formerly done when you have been away. The tree you had given me to cultivate no doubt has a good effect upon me. You could not have selected one so useful to me. I see plainly that it will not fail to test my affection for my dear husband in the end. I hope you do not have a sad moment about me. Where are you to-night, my love, preparing to spend the holy Sabbath. My heart has met thine at the mercy seat and I trust blessings are in store for you on the morrow, both for body and mind. Methinks you have taken leave of Monsieur Bayette and gone a comfortable day beyond. The Indians say more Americans are coming—perhaps I shall hear from you again. Again let me say, be not anxious for me—for the sympathies of all are excited for me the moment they hear you have gone. I shall be well taken care of and no doubt shall have more letters to answer than I am able to write. Received one to-day from Mr. Spalding expressing the kindest sympathy and concern, both for you and myself, and desire for the success of your undertaking. He is coming here next week; says Mr. Eells will be here at the same time. It is the Lord sustains me; I know it must be that or I should not feel as happy about you as I do, and I trust you feel no less his supporting hand than I do. O, may we continue to feel it until we are brought together again rejoicing in his goodness.

The Indians have been so engaged in singing their hunting songs for several days past that but few have come around the house until to-day. The bride has attracted them, I suppose. How will you feel, dear husband, when you seat yourself in Sister Julia's house, or with our mothers, and not see the windows filled with Indians, and the doors also; will you not feel lost? I can scarcely imagine how you will feel. Could it consistently with duty have been so I should rejoice to be a partaker with you of the feelings necessarily produced by a visit to those dear firesides — but I am happy in remaining, while you are permitted the prospect — and I hope for the reality of seeing those beloved objects once more.

Sabbath eve, 9th — My dear husband would like to know what kind of a Sabbath we have had here, for I know his heart is with the people. Ellice, who brought me Mr. Spalding's letter, was their minister to-day. This afternoon I had a Bible class in English with him, John and Mungo, besides the time I spent with the children. He read and appeared to understand very well. He thinks he loves the Saviour. I urged the duty of secret prayer in addition to his family worship, and showed him the passage in Matthew. He said he would in future attend to the duty daily. He told me yesterday that if he had been here he would have gone with you to the States. Although I am alone as to associates and my husband is gone, yet I have not been lonely to-day. The presence of the Saviour fills every vacancy. My little children appear thoughtful and solemn. Helen said, "Will father come home to-day?" when the people were assembling for worship. She is quite well now.

12th. — *My Dear Husband:* — I am now at Walla Walla — came here yesterday; was too unwell to undertake the journey, but could not refuse, as Mr. McKinlay had come on purpose to take me. He came in the wagon and brought the trundlebed and I laid down most all the way. To-day I have been scarcely able to get off the bed; feel a little better tonight, so I thought I must write a little to you, although it must be but a little, for the want of strength. The Indians did not like my leaving very well — seemed to regret the cause. I felt strongly to prefer to stay there if it could be considered prudent, but the care and anxiety was wearing upon me too much. Good night, beloved husband.

Friday eve, 14th. — *My Dear Husband:* — Your letter written last Saturday, the 8th, was handed me this afternoon by Raymond. I rejoice to hear of your prosperity so far, and hope by this time you are near Fort Hall.

17th. — I undertook to write to you last Friday, but was too sick to do it and had to give it up. Took a powder of quinine and calomel that night — the next day and yesterday could scarcely go or lie in bed. I suffered much for the conveniences of our dear home; think I received serious injury in sleeping on damp made blankets for a bed, for I have been sick ever since I have been here. I anticipated being not as comfortable here as at home, and could I have been left a week longer I should have preferred it, for I did not think I should be further molested, but Mr. McKinlay would not leave me there any longer. Mr. and Mrs. McKinlay are very kind, but they know not how to make one as easy and comfortable as Mr. Pambrun used to. It has been warmer for two days past and the stove is now up, so that I am pretty comfortably situated now.

But why should I say so much about myself? My dear husband does not give me such an example. Indeed, I wish to hear so much about your own and my other self, and hear so little when you do write, that I probably am more particular than I otherwise would be in speaking of myself.

Mr. McDonald arrived yesterday from Vancouver. The ship *Victoria* is not in. He says Mr. Ermatinger has become a Catholic. He wrote you and sent me a box of raisins.

Letters arrived today from Messrs. W. and Eells. They have no idea that you are at Fort Hall, as you probably are at this time. They wish an "invoice of property taken by Mr. G." but he has left none. I shall write him that they wish it.

Mr. Walker has written you. His closing remark is, "Be assured that whether you go or stay, you and Mrs. W. will have our prayers and best wishes for your peace and usefulness. May the Lord direct us all." The letters came to Wieletpoo and the mule was sent, but the bearers returned without coming here, and of course no opportunity of sending them the intelligence of your departure.

I have filled this sheet—perhaps I shall another before the express arrives. Mr. Perkins has sent word to have me come down there in the express boats without fail. I have not yet determined what I shall do. Should like to be relieved of the care of David if I could while you are gone, but do not know as I can. I want to see Mr. S. before then, if I conclude to go.

Your affectionate wife,

NARCISSA WHITMAN.

Narcissa Whitman

WALLA WALLA, Oct. 22, 1842.

My Dear Husband:—The word is given that the express is arriving and I hasten to write you my farewell for the present, praying earnestly that we may be permitted to meet again and spend many years together in love, serving the Lord and in building up his cause. Your letters, how they have cheered me, especially to see your confidence and trust in the Lord; both for yourself and me in the time of trouble and danger. I have made up my mind not to expect you until late next summer. Indeed, much as I shall and do want to see you, I prefer that you stay just as long as it is necessary to accomplish all your heart's desire respecting the interest of this country, so dear to us both—our home.

And especially do I wish you to stay long enough to visit all our dear relatives and friends, both for yourself and me. Will it not be too true, that while enjoying the society of those loved ones, my husband will wish dear wife was along to make her own visits and give zest to his? I surely have the vanity and the evidence to think so and am greatly comforted with it.

We have had a false alarm about the express. I am glad they have not come, for I am not ready for them yet. Think I shall go down to Mr. Perkins' if they do not arrive here and pass on the Sabbath.

Mr. Spalding is here; he came yesterday. He has had considerable trouble with the Indians which prevented his coming last week. Spends the Sabbath here.

Mr. McDonald left yesterday P.M. Have had a very interesting visit with him. He was greatly surprised to hear you were off. Spoke of you with interest—wished very much to see you, and from what I could infer, he intended to open his heart to you relative to his present and future situation. He manifested a great desire to read serious books and goes to-day to Waiilatpu to select from the library for his reading this winter. Notwithstanding his hilarity and glee, he is a man of deep thought and serious feelings. He has a praying sister who does not forget him in her anxiety for the salvation of his soul, and I feel constrained to join mine to hers, and O may the blessings of Abraham's God descend upon him!

He takes six bags of flour from the mill into the Snake country. He brought me a keg of fresh apples from Vancouver, and ever since we have been enjoying ourselves on apple pies. What would you think of having our friends send us some dried fruits from the States. Perhaps it is not warrantable to make the expense for the gratification of the taste.

Mrs. Eells expressed great anxiety for your comfort in the journey, sent you some dried apples to take along with you.

Mr. S. has opened a barrel, directed to you, and divided the contents equally among the four families. He has done it very exact and much to his own satisfaction.

My dear husband, what will you do about seeing Mrs. Munger's relatives while you are in the States? It would be a great kindness to them if you could see them and give them some account of her situation and trials here. It just came to my mind as I, in looking over my file of letters, saw her brother Hoisington's letter to you. I have heard nothing more from her since you left.

I hope you will see Mrs. Mather, if she is still living, and tell her how much I love her and thank her for her good, long letters, and hope she will write many more such.

I forgot — rather I mentioned in my other letter Tanatua's report from the priest. He says he promised to send one up from the States to settle on the Utilla next summer.

The Indians that met you beyond Grande Ronde appeared very happy to say that they had seen you and to hear something of your plans about returning, from yourself. Stik-as really mourns about you, that he did not come to see you before you left. I believe it is a great comfort to them to see me left behind. They tell me they are waiting to see where I go, before they decide where to go for the winter. The little children's eyes brighten when I speak of you and they love to have me do so. They say you are gone a long time and wish to know when you will come again.

Almost three long weeks have passed since we exchanged the parting kiss and many, very many, long weeks are yet to come before we shall be permitted, if ever in this world, to greet each other again. I think of you and feel as if you were in my heart continually. I follow you night and day, and shall through the whole journey, in my imagination and prayers. I as confidently believe and trust in the Lord concerning you, as I learn from your letter that you do, and it affords me unspeakable satisfaction to know that my heart is as your heart in this matter. I do believe we shall be permitted to meet again. I cannot feel otherwise, and I as confidently believe you will be blest in the object of your visit to the States.

If I go to Vancouver next summer I think I shall come back again so as to be here when you return. Mr. Grant is ordered to come down so that I shall expect to receive a letter from you about the first of January.

By this time I expect you are more than half way to Winter — so the distance widens between us — but I am thankful that it is our bodies only that are separated and that absence and distance cannot make a space between our hearts. "Love is stronger than death."

Read this letter, my husband, and then give it to my mother — perhaps she would like once more to take a peep into one of the sacred chambers of her daughter's heart — it may comfort her, seeing she cannot see her face again in the flesh. But my better self I hope she will be permitted to see, and delight her eyes and heart with the sight, to the satisfaction of her soul — and my beloved father, too. O, their precious lives! and may it give a thrill of joy to their hearts before unknown, to think they still have a child, though a poor, weak one, on heathen grounds.

My husband, what can I say more to you tonight? I wish you sweet sleep and a quiet rest under the shadow of Almighty love and to more mercy, and may the calm smile of the Savior's presence cheer you, and a Sabbath day's blessing be your portion and that of your companion in travel. So prays

Your ever affectionate wife,

NARCISSA W.

Letters

WASKOPUM, OREGON TER., Feb. 7, 1843.

Honored and Beloved Parents:—It is with peculiar feelings of interest that I think of the home of my childhood now. And why should I not, since *every* object I hold most dear on earth is there.

Last evening was monthly concert. Being too feeble to meet with the brethren and sisters here, I spent most of the evening in my room.

How can I describe the hallowed influence that seemed to be shed around me, the inward peace and sacred sense of the presence of God in my soul? I could think of nothing else but that surely beloved friends must be praying for me. This cannot be in answer to my own individual prayer that I receive all this. I felt as if in spirit I was in the midst of that loved circle, feeling the influence and enjoying its heavenly sweets with you, my father, my mother, my sisters and brothers and my beloved husband, too—what earthly objects can I name dearer to me than these. They are my all, yet widely separated from me. I speak as if you were enjoying the society of my dear husband at this time. If the Lord has spared his life and prospered him according to his and my expectations, you are. Beloved parents, what do you think of your lonely child in this lonely world? You pray for her, I know you must, or she would not feel the support—the almost constant support of the Saviour's presence—which is graciously granted under the trying circumstances in which I am placed. How do you like to see your son? How do you enjoy his society after so long an absence? Did you ever dream of seeing him there without me? I flatter myself that it would add a little to the happiness of you all if I was there with him. I am sure it would to mine. But if you enjoy his and make him happy I shall be satisfied.

I never have felt much as though I would see my friends again in the flesh. Since my husband has gone to see them without me I feel it less doubtful than ever. But we know not in what way the Lord will lead us. It is a great satisfaction to me to think that he will see them and be able to give me information concerning them which I could get in no other way and from no other source, should the Lord spare him to return to me.

You must feel some anxiety to know how I have endured and been situated since being left alone in our lonely house among a savage people. I wrote a full letter to Dr. Whitman and sent it by ship which I hope he will receive before he leaves you to return. That will give an account of what transpired immediately after he left and of my leaving Wieletpoo. The express boats that took the letter to the ship brought me to this place where I have been ever since. I was unable to ride to either of the stations of our mission and had determined to remain at Wieletpoo for the winter, it being the only place where I could remain the most comfortably. I was obliged to leave, very much against my feelings, because others judged it unsafe for me to remain—particularly the gentlemen in charge at Walla Walla.

Mr. Perkins sent me an invitation to come here. The unexpected delay of Mr. Littlejohn's arrival, and the more than probability that I should be obliged to spend the winter at Walla Walla or at Wieletpoo, without the society of a female friend, were reasons that determined me to come.

March 6th.—I have concluded to finish this letter and send it by the express which goes by way of Montreal, for it will reach its destination sooner than if sent by the mountains. I see my writing is very poor and I fear father and mother will not be able to read it. My eyes are almost gone—my poor health affects them materially and writing is very injurious to me. I can neither read, write or sew without spectacles, the most of the time, and sometimes with them I suffer considerable pain.

As I commenced giving some account of what has transpired since my dear husband left, I will go on. Waskopum in one of the stations of the Methodist Mission situated on the Columbia River just below The Dalles. The Dalles is the place, if you recollect, where I fought such a battle with the fleas on my first arrival in the country (see my journal). There are three families here, Revs. Lee and Perkins, and their wives, and Mr. and Mrs. Brewer, farmer. I am spending a very happy winter here and I trust it has been and will be for my spiritual good, for truly the society and prayers of such a company of living and growing Christians is very refreshing to me, after having lived so much alone, immerged in care and toil.

Soon after I came here Mr. McKinlay, of Walla Walla, wrote that the mill at our station was burnt and it was supposed to be set on fire by Indians. This was very afflicting news to me, for all our living came out of our mill principally, and not only ours at the station, but multitudes in the country, in different ways, were benefited by it. Probably there was more than two hundred bushels of wheat and corn burnt and some flour. The mill bolt and threshing mill, even to a part of the wheel, was burnt. My poor husband will feel this sadly—so much lost, and so much, too, that will save labor. I think, sometimes, if I had not left perhaps it would not have been burnt. But it will all work for the best to us and the poor Indians, too, I hope. As my health has been and is, I do not think it would have been best for me to remain there. I left a good man there, but he could do nothing alone as it was set on fire in the night and not discovered until it had made considerable progress. It is pretty difficult to ascertain whether it was the work of design or carelessness. It is said that two boys, and we know them to be "of malicious habits," were fishing and threw fire down on the bank of the river that communicated with the straw. The sensible part of the Cayuses feel the loss deeply, and they will feel it more when they want their wheat ground next fall. We hope it will be a good lesson to them and be one means of making them a better people.

Husband had prepared adobes to surround the mill before he left, but being called away so suddenly Mr. Spalding engaged to see them put up. He had arrived at Wieletpoo when I left Walla Walla and commenced the work, but was sent for in great haste as Mrs. S. was taken very sick and was unable to take care of herself or children. This left the mill unfinished or unprotected.

When I came here I felt anxious to meet Mr. and Mrs. Littlejohn on the way, or hoped he would arrive shortly after, but Mr. Gray was detained in going down, and he in coming up. Cold weather commenced much earlier than usual, and they were windbound on the river several days and did not reach this place until the middle of November, and as the mill and grain was burnt it was concluded best for Mrs. L. and myself to remain here until Mr. L. and Mr. Geiger should go up and see how things were. They were accompanied by Dr. White, the government agent for this country, and a small party who went up to visit the Indians, settle difficulties, to recommend the appointment of chiefs, and the institution of a code of laws among the different tribes. As our station was vacated by all its inhabitants, the Indians had all left for their wintering quarters, and some of them from indignation on account of the burning of the mill. A meeting was appointed, a few came, but could do nothing but make a few inquiries and appoint another meeting which is to be the 10th of May.

At Lapwai they had more successful meetings, appointed a high chief and other small chiefs of the different bands, framed laws which were translated and printed in the Nez Perces language.

Mr. Littlejohn, when he left the lower country, sold his property with a view to go to the States over the mountains this spring. While attending that meeting he became so interested in the Indians as to change his mind about going home and pledged himself to stay in the country and aid in teaching them. Mr. S. immediately invited him to come there and spend the winter and go to teaching; and because it was easier work than to stay and teach at our station, he consented to go and has gone, with his wife, there. Left our station with only Brother Geiger alone.

I intended to return and spend two or three months there this spring, but the same difficulty is in the way—no female companion at the station. Dr. White, however, insists upon my going up to be there at the meeting appointed, as there is no one in this part of the country, now husband is gone, and Mr. Gray likewise, that is much acquainted with the Cayuses. I expect to go up in about two weeks, and hope to return and make a visit at Vancouver and the Willamette, as I am very cordially invited. We made application to Mr. Rogers, who was in the Willamette and had just married, to come and take charge of the station during husband's absence, and had he got the intelligence soon enough he would have been happy to come, for he had just then entered into an engagement of another kind for a milling company to build a flour mill. This was a great disappointment to me and a trial to him that he did not know of it soon enough to come; his wife was very young and inexperienced in housewifery and on this account, as well as many others, he would have rejoiced to come. He came up with Dr. White as interpreter, and was of essential service; indeed, there is not another individual in Oregon that acquires the native language with so much facility and readiness, and no one more universally beloved by all who knew him, and especially the native inhabitants.

I have now come to the most trying and melancholy part of my intelligence, and how shall I write it? Brother Rogers, in his return from the upper country, spent several days here. I had an interesting visit with him, little thinking it would be what it has proved to be, the last we shall have in this world together. I was much encouraged to hope he would be able to make arrangements so that he could leave and go up this spring and take charge of the people and teach them, for no one in the country was more capable than he was. But such as he was and such as we valued him, the Lord took him as if he would say unto us, "Put not your trust in an arm of flesh." Before I heard of his death I had been thinking and feeling considerably about the result of the meeting in May with the Cayuses. Much talk has been going on among them since the meeting at Lapwai, which leads us to expect a very exciting time. Brother Rogers' wisdom and prudence as an interpreter, and his knowledge of Indian character, has led us to feel that his presence was absolutely necessary for a peaceful meeting, and without it we had better not have a meeting. But "the Lord's thoughts are not ours, neither are his ways our ways."

As I have said before, he had taken him from us, and what renders the affliction more aggravated, he was not alone in his departure from this vale of tears. He was drowned with five others at the same time in the Willamette River. Of this number was his beloved wife, her youngest sister aged two years and a half, Squire Crocker, recently from the States, and two Clatsop Indians. The circumstances of the melancholy disaster were these: Dr. White, Mr. Raymond of the Methodist mission, and the above named individuals, left the Butte for the falls in the mission's large canoe, on Wednesday, Feb. 1st. This was just a month from the time Brother Rogers left us at this place. They had made one portage on foot just above the main fall as far as the trail will admit, and got into the canoe, as is usually done, and the canoe was dropped down to the landing place with a strong rope. The landing place is within two rods of the main falls. All got in except Mr. Raymond and four Indians who had the management of the rope; they dropped down to the landing place in safety, and Dr. White stepped on a log and instantly the canoe took a sheer out into the current. Doctor had a paddle in his hand which Squire Crocker took hold of to haul the canoe back; at the same time they called to Mr. Raymond to haul, which he did, and it shot the canoe into the suction of the falls, which got such a possession of it at once as to sweep them over the frightful precipice in an instant, notwithstanding all their efforts at paddling to make the island on the other side. Two Indians were saved by plunging into the current and got an impetus which carried them through and they reached the island and were saved. What an awful scene! They were seen by individuals below the falls just as the canoe made the fatal plunge, who instantly came in boats to their relief. Four were seen swimming at first for a time, but three of them sank almost immediately; one of them continued swimming until the boat came within thirty yards of him when he sunk in a whirl "to rise no more." This was Brother Rogers. The letter giving us the intelligence was written four days after the dreadful disaster took place. At that time neither of the bodies had been found.

The river was very high, the current frightfully rapid, boiling and whirling in its course. The bow of the canoe was broken off at the rowlocks, and a piece split out of the bottom half the length of the canoe. O, how fatal to them was their security, for they had no setting poles out, neither had they fastened the canoe—a precaution which ought always to be taken upon these frightful rivers of Oregon.

Mrs. Rogers was the eldest of five daughters of Mr. Leslie, who has gone to the States with the two next eldest, their mother having died in the Willamette two years ago. The two youngest were in Mr. Rogers' family. Mrs. Rogers spent the time of her husband's absence in Mrs. Gray's family, with her two daughters. It seems they were in the act of returning to the falls when they were drowned, and providentially one of the sisters was left to be spared so melancholy a fate.

As an individual I feel that I have lost a friend—a brother. I had never seen Mrs. R., but was fondly anticipating an acquaintance in a few months. We are so few in number in this country that real friends are valuable, and their loss deeply felt; but to the country, to the missionary cause, the loss is very great.

My beloved parents, if the Lord has permitted you to enjoy a visit with my dear husband, you doubtless know more about us as a mission and our missionary work than you formerly have. I hope he will bring me full long letters from both dear fathers and mothers' own hand, and each of my sisters and brothers now living. I have not received a single letter yet giving any of the particulars of the dear one that is dead.

September, 1840, is my last date from home. I am expecting to hear soon when the ship comes in. I shall write again in about two months if my health permits. It is very trying to the feelings of the natural heart to be here in this desolate land without my husband, and were it not for sustaining grace I should sink under it. But the favors of the Lord are many and great in giving me so many friends to cheer and comfort me. My health is very poor; this increases the trial, because, in consequence I have too many gloomy and depressing hours, and evil forebodings, in which I have not strength of mind to rise above. The Lord gives me much of his gracious presence, and increased spiritual enjoyment in communion with him, for which I desire to be thankful.

My paper will not contain all that a full heart pants to pour forth into the bosom of dear, long-absent parents—a privilege which doubtless would be too much for my weak nature to endure. With pleasing delight do I look forward to that happy time when we may meet in yonder happy world and enjoy in full fruition what eye hath not seen nor ear heard—of things prepared for us.

I hope all will remember my most earnest request to write to me. I love you all increasingly and shall till I die. Dear Brother G., I feel and sympathize with him more than I can express. O, that he would write me, and Sister Clarissa likewise, and all of you. Brother Judson, the Lord has broken his heart, but he can bind it up. Shall I ever hear him speak to me again. My heart yearns over you all while I write farewell. May we all meet in heaven forever, prays your unworthy, your lonely but every loving daughter,

NARCISSA.

Believe me, dear friends, I am happy in making the sacrifice for Christ—it is for Him. We have made it and I rejoice in it, yea, and will rejoice, however trying to the flesh. I see no reason to regret my husband's going home without me; nor shall I, if I suffer loss in all things.

Hon. Stephen Prentiss,
    Cuba, Alleghany Co., N.Y.

Letters

WASKOPUM, March 11th, 1843.

My Dear Harriet: — I have just been reading your letter, written more than two years ago. I have been thinking all day of writing you, but can scarcely find courage enough; even now, I feel more like taking my bed rather than writing, much as I long to commune with you.

From a letter I received last fall from Mr. Dixon, I learn that my dear Harriet is now both a wife and a mother. Tender and endearing relations! May you ever prove worthy of the confidence and affection of your husband, and a tender, wise and judicious mother, and never forget that you are training immortal spirits for an eternal world. If you have never read "Alcott's Young Wife and Young Mother," I beg you will procure and read them. You will derive great benefit from them. You cannot begin too soon to study your duty as a mother. It is a responsible station, and doubtless you feel it to be so. Be sure and make it your business to train them for the Lord, and hold them not as yours, but His, to be called away at His bidding. This is an interesting theme to me.

When you write, please tell me about your maternal association. I want to know all about them, and how the cause prospers. We have an association here consisting of the missionary mothers and two native mothers, who are the wives of the gentlemen of this country. We find it a great comfort to meet together, to pray and sympathise with and for eath other in this desert land where we have so few privileges. Please remember me to your association, and solicit an interest in the prayers of those praying mothers for the missionary mothers of Oregon.

I hope by this time you have had a good visit with your brother Marcus. I presume it has been a short one. Tell me, you that have enjoyed the sweets of connubial bliss long enough to know the happiness it affords, how would you like to be so widely separated and for so long a time. Think you, it is no trial, no sacrifice of feeling? For what would you be willing to make such a sacrifice? Is there anything in this lower world that would tempt you to it? I presume not; at least I can see no earthly inducement sufficiently paramount to cause me voluntarily to take upon myself such a painful trial. Painful, I say? Yes, painful in the extreme to the natural heart. But there is one object, our blessed Saviour, for whose sake, I trust, both you as well as we are willing if called to it, to suffer all things. It was for Him, for the advancement of His cause, that I could say to my beloved husband, "Go; take all the time necessary to accomplish His work; and the Lord go with and bless you," Sacrifice made for Him will not go unrewarded. Believe me, this same Heavenly Friend so manifests himself to me, sustains, upholds, and comforts me, and that, too, almost continually as to enable me to "glory in tribulation," yea to rejoice that I am counted worthy to suffer for His sake. He has been preparing me for the self-denial for some time past, and no time more effectually than when he was pleased to take my beloved child from me. Once I could not have borne it without the same measure of grace I now enjoy. But blessed be His Holy Name, it is from Him I receive all things, and I desire to be wholly consecrated to Him. I feel that I am nothing — Jesus is my all, His righteousness alone I plead; in Him my guilty soul expects to find a full and free salvation.

I hope the hand and the heart that has got possession of my beloved Harriet's will please accept of a sister's love, although we have never been privileged with an acquaintance, and may never meet in this world. May I not hope to receive letters from you both, and frequently, too? Can such a thing be under the sun that my husband will prevail on you to come to Oregon to spend your days? I know you would say, I cannot leave pa and ma to go so far.

Give much love to sister C. and her husband; tell her to please consider this as written to her, if I am unable to write her by this opportunity. I think of sister Mary Ann as being a guardian angel to me sometimes. When shall I be one to you? I think sometimes it will not be long. Again I send love to J.G. and all the family. Many kisses for all the babies.

Your affectionate sister,

NARCISSA.

Mrs. John W. Jackson,
    Cuba, Allegheny Co.,
        New York, U.S.A.

Letters

WASKOPUM, March 31, 1843.

My Dear Brother: — Why is it that I never receive a letter from you? Have you no time to write, or have you forgotten me? I will not think it; not that you do not love me, for this would make me unhappy. Could you see my heart and know how much I love and think of you and sympathize with you, should I not receive a communication from you and thus be assured of your love and remembrance of me? It is not for the want of a heart that I do not write more and oftener to all my brothers and sisters, but for the want of health and strength to do it. Now I am deprived of the society of my beloved husband, I realize more than ever your situation; yet not its keenest pang, for ourselves is a voluntary and temporary separation, while yours is — I hardly know what to call it — an unwilling and unnecessary separation, at least on your part; yet I hope not a perpetual one. O that I could hear that you were once more united and happy in all the sweets of domestic bliss, for they are many, and when given us from the Lord, how we should prize them. Those are tender ties to be separated and hang bleeding all our life, but the Lord permits us thus to be afflicted. We should lean on Him for support. And may you, dear brother, realize as much of the blessed Saviour's gracious presence as I do in my lonely situation, and have it continued to you constantly. I, too, know the blessed effects of affliction to purify the heart and sanctify the soul; and notwithstanding their keen smart and writhing pang, yet it is good to be afflicted; they are choice mercies to us, for when He has tried us, my brother, we shall come forth as gold. Our greatest care should be, not to murmur or complain of His trying dispensations towards us, but feel always more anxious to have them sanctified to us than to be delivered from them — for then "patience will have her perfect work."

O what would I give could I see you, for then I could pour a full heart into your bosom; but you have seen my better self, I hope, and enjoyed a sweet visit with him, for me as well as for him. You will write me, I know, by him. You will doubtless see my letter to father and mother. I have given the particulars of the past to them.

Recently, intelligence has come to us from above that the Indians are talking and making preparations for war. The visit of the government's agent last fall has caused considerable excitement. All decisive measures and language used to them they construe into threats, and say war is declared and they intend to be prepared. They have heard many unwise remarks which have been made by designing persons, especially a half-breed that came up with the agent last fall. Such as troops are coming into the river this spring and are coming up with Dr. White to fight them. It is the Kaiuses that cause all trouble. There are no tribes in all the country but what are more quiet and peaceable to live with than they are. If any mischief is going ahead they originate and carry forward. They are more difficult to labour among than the Nez Perces. They are rich, especially in horses, and consequently haughty and insolent. A large assemblage is expected in less than a month to meet in the valley of Walla Walla. What the result of it will be, time will determine. From the excitement and talk that has been going on all winter we have reason to fear that it will not be a very quiet time. The Indians of the Buffalo country have been sent for by the high chief of the Nez Perces, Ellis.

Narcissa Whitman

WALLA WALLA, April 14th, 1843.

My Dear Brother: — I arrived here last Saturday. Left Wascopum Monday early April 3rd, and came with Mr. Grant, who was in charge of the company's boats, three in number; had a pleasant and safe voyage; arrived greatly exhausted with fatigue but feel much benefited by the trip. Two days after I received a letter from Sister Littlejohn at Lapwai (Mrs. Spalding's), giving the afflicting news of the death of her only son by drowning. He fell into the mill floom and floated down out of sight into a deep pit and was not found until it was too late to bring him to life.

This makes the sixth person that has been drowned since November in this infant country; four adults and two children. Mr. Olley, of the Methodist mission, was drowned in the Willamette about two months before Brother Rogers, and those with him.

What the Lord means by the removal of so many, we know not, but feel admonished to be also ready. Brother and sister Littlejohn feel their affliction deeply, but are mercifully supported under it.

The excitement among the Kaiuses has abated considerable from what it was when I commenced this letter. Mr. McKinlay of this fort has been to Vancouver and brought back word to them from Dr. McLoughlin that they, the British, do not, neither have they intended to make war upon them. This relieves them considerably. Now their fear is the Americans. They have been led to believe that deceitful measures are being taken to rob them of their land, to kill them all off. Language like this has been told them, and at the meeting last fall, "that if you do not make laws and protect the whites and their property, we will put you in the way of doing it." They consider this a declaration to fight and they have prepared accordingly. We hope no depredations will be committed upon us or the mission property, and think the difficulties can be removed and adjusted to their minds, but not without the most prudent and wise measures. The agent is quite ignorant of the Indian character and especially of the character of the Kaiuses. Husband's presence is needed very much at this juncture. A great loss is sustained by his going to the States, I mean a present loss to the station and Indians, but hope and expect a greater good will be accomplished by it. There was no other way for us to do. We felt that we could not remain as we were without more help, and we are so far off that to send by letter and get returns was too slow a way for the present emergency.

I intend to go to Waiilatpu as soon as the water falls; it is so high now and is rising so that I cannot cross the rivers. I shall write some of the family by the mountain route; this I send by the express to Montreal.

Would it be a strange thing if I should see you coming to this country with my husband? You will write me to pay for this I hope. Remember I have not heard a word about the death of that sister, and perhaps still greater inroads have been made in the dear circle that I have yet to be informed of. It will not be many years before we shall all be transplanted, and O may it be into the paradise above, and not one of us be missing.

I want very much to hear about your little daughter, yourself and all your affairs, and how you feel and live from day to day, and what you are doing for the cause of Christ. How does the doctor appear to you? How have you enjoyed your visit with him? Living alone in the midst of a savage people, without seeing much company, we lose our polish and doubtless would appear quite uncouth to the uncivilized world. This is one of the missionary's trials, because he is apt to be despised for it.

Love to all. Pray for your loving sister,

NARCISSA.

Your spectacles are of great use to me. I should not know how to do without them. My eyes have failed me almost entirely. I think sometimes I have reason to think of you pretty often. I should like a pair of green double plain glasses. Hope doctor will bring some.

Farewell.

N.

Jonas Galusha Prentiss, Esq.
    Angelica, Allegheny County,
        New York,
            U.S.A.

Narcissa Whitman

SHAWNEE MISSION SCHOOL,
NEAR WESTPORT, May 27, 1843

Dear Brother Edward:—I take this opportunity to write you a few lines before I leave the border. I was sorry not to see you when I was at Quincy, but was glad to hear so much about you. It gave me great pleasure to see Sister Jane.

I suppose you think yourself a man now, and perhaps are not anxious for advice. I will venture, however, to let you know how anxious I am for you to complete your education. Entering the ministry a year or two sooner will not avail for any good purpose. We ought to aim at the greatest usefulness. I trust your manhood will only add to your firm determination to do all in your power for the glory of God, and good of his cause. I do not feel that I shall never see you, but I cannot tell how it will be likely to be, except you come to Oregon. I am sorry I have not got a letter from you for Narcissa. I need not tell you that she loves you, for I have no doubt she spoke for herself in the letter I brought you.

I cannot tell you very much about the immigrants to Oregon. They appear very willing, and I have no doubt are generally of an enterprising character. There are over two hundred men, besides women and children, as it is said. No one can well tell, until we are all on the road and get together, how many there are. Some have been gone a week and others have not yet started. I hope to start tomorrow. I shall have an easy journey as I have not much to do, having no one depending on me.

Lieut. Fremont, of the United States Engineers Corps, goes out with about thirty men to explore for the government, and expects to return this fall. His men are Canadian voyageurs mostly, and himself a Catholic. Two Papal priests and their lay helpers are along, and Father DeSmet has gone back in order to go to Europe to bring out others by ship.

I think, however, the immigrants who are going out will be a good acquisition. It will call on Christians to labor for their good. What a pity a good minister was not with us to go along at once. My expectations are high for that country. I believe it must become one of the best of countries very soon.

Let us hear from you as often as you can. If you send letters for crossing the mountains, direct to the care of Boone & Hamilton, Westport, Missouri. You can send letters every fall by merchants to be left with them; Rev. Doctor Armstrong, in New York, at the office of A.B.C.F.M., or to Boston, as the Mission House of the A.B.C.F.M., care of Rev. David Greene. Ships mostly sail in the fall, so that fall letters should go by ship and spring letters come the other way. Tell Jane two or three young lawyers will be in the party for Oregon, but I hope this will not deter her from coming if she has an opportunity.

I should not be surprised if I saw a number of your father's family west of the mountains before long. Jackson and Galusha may come. I hope to start to-morrow. It is very late starting, but I hope to go on fast after I cross the mountains, and have no more dangerous Indians.

With best regards and brotherly affection I am, dear brother,

Yours truly,
MARCUS WHITMAN

Mr. Edward Prentiss,
Quincy, Illinois.

SHAWNEE MISSION, May 28th, 1843.

Dear Brother Galusha:—You will be surprised to learn that I am here yet. I have been, as it were, waiting for three weeks. When I got to St. Louis I found I had time and so I went to Quincy and saw Sister Jane, but Edward was not there. Jane was well and seemed happy. She was teaching school. Edward was away teaching music. I had a fine journey all the way and have been here nearly two weeks. I shall start to-morrow or next day. Some of the emigrants have been gone a week and others are just going. Lieut. Fremont is camped about two miles off for the night. The number of emigrants will be over two hundred men, besides women and children. This tells well for the occupation of Oregon. A great many cattle are going, but no sheep, from a mistake of what I said in passing. Next year will tell for sheep. I do not know what to say to you about sheep; there can be no difficulty in their traveling. They have been proved to travel as well through the prairie as pack horses. My plan, you know, was to get funds for founding schools and have good people come along as settlers and teachers, while others might have sheep of their own along, also.

It would be a fine thing if Esq. Divin would open his eyes to Oregon and see if he could not get some of the offices, such as Judge or Indian Agent, or Commissioner to form trades with Indians. You will be best Judge what can be done and how far you can exert yourself in those matters and whether the secret service fund can be obtained.

It is now decided in my mind that Oregon will be occupied by American citizens. Those who go only open the way for more another year. Wagons will go all the way I have no doubt this year. It should be remembered that nothing should be taken across the mountains but provisions. All goods should be sent by ship. Sheep and cattle, but especially sheep, are indispensable for Oregon. One man goes with us who thinks he is soon to be an Indian Agent over there. I mean to impress the Secretary of War that sheep are more important to Oregon's interest than soldiers. We want to get sheep and stock from government for Indians instead of money for their lands. I have written him on the main interests of the Indian country; but I mean still to write a private letter touching some particular interests. I want you to get Dr. Smith's *Indian Sketches*. It can be found at the Catholic Book Store. You will see what way the Society of Jesus do their missionary work and what we have to contend with in Oregon.

I hope to be expeditious in traveling. After we get to Fort Hall I shall try to go on rapidly, if not before. Grass has not been in a good state quite a week yet, but is very fine now. I think I shall find that grass has been two months earlier in Oregon. Fremont and most, if not all, his men are Catholics. He intends to be back this fall. If so, you may hear from me after I get home. Give my love to your father and mother, brothers and sisters. I shall by no means be surprised to see some, if not all, of you on our side of the mountains. Jackson talked favorably. Let me hear from you. Letters sent to New York by merchants in the fall and left at the office of the A.B.C.F.M., will find a ready passage. Letters sent in the spring to the care of Boone & Hamilton, Westport, Missouri, will come if they are here by the first to tenth of May. Wishing you peace and happiness, I am in the best of bonds,

Your brother,
MARCUS WHITMAN.

VANCOUVER, June 8th, 1843.

My Beloved Brother and Sister Perkins:—I have but a moment's notice of an opportunity of sending to you. Your trunk was forgotten by us all and brought on. I would send it now if I could, but Iatin says his boat is too small for that and his sheep. I felt very sad after leaving you, particularly as my visit had been so marred with what transpired while passing. I was grieved to see it affect you, as it was very natural it should. But there is this consolation to comfort you, and in this case it is yours to rejoice when you are persecuted for righteousness' sake.

I had a very fatiguing journey down; came near drowning in the portage once. One of the boats upset, but no lives lost. The boat I was in just escaped capsizing. We arrived here just before sunset, Sabbath; displeased with myself and every one around me because of the profanation of the holy day of the Lord.

Brother Hinds left this Tuesday morning. Dr. Barclay advises that I remain here nearly a month that he may be able to satisfy himself respecting my case.

This is but a poor return for the two good long letters I have received from Brother P. and the one from sister, yet I have a heart filled with gratitude and Christian sympathy and love for you and those little ones associated with you.

Do write as often as you can, both of you.

Ever yours,

NARCISSA WHITMAN.

Do not pay for these letters.

Letters

VANCOUVER, July 11th, 1843.

My Beloved Sister Jane: — Your letters of March and April,' 42, I received about three weeks since, and can assure you I was not a little rejoiced in hearing from you, they being the first I have received from you since March '40, by Mrs. Littlejohn. I have written you and Edward several times since — indeed, I always write you every opportunity, whether you get them or not. I heard of the death of dear sister Judson last September through Lawyer Divin, but no particulars until your letter came. About the same time one came from poor brother Judson, the only one I have received from him or Mary Ann since '39. My last from dear parents and Harriet was in September '40; so you see I have not the means of knowing but little about you all, yet I trust that I am truly thankful for that little. It is a great cordial to me. I love you all with an undying love, and every fresh breeze I receive fans it into a burning flame. I feel not the least disposition to shed a tear on dear sister Judson's account, but rather do rejoice that she is safely harbored in the bosom of her and our Saviour's love; but for the sake of those who still live and whom she might be the means of leading to Christ, I could mourn and weep in bitterness of soul. I rejoice, too, that the sustaining grace of God was so manifest to her beloved bereaved husband, and our dear parents, as well as you all, under the afflictive dispensation. My first thought when I heard of her death was that I should be the next to go; but it may be otherwise, the Lord only knows. This I do know, His time will be the best time, and my chief concern is, and shall be, to be ready and have my work done and well done. But O, what a poor weak creature I am; how little I can do to glorify His great Name. What poor returns I make daily for His unbounded goodness to me. If I am saved I am sure it will not, it cannot, be because of any intrinsic worth in me, or any of my friends, but solely and alone for His sake who gave His own life a ransom to save a lost world.

Dear Jane, I have the privilege of once more addressing you from Vancouver where I am spending a little time very pleasantly, and where I am favored with the medical advice and treatment of two very able physicians, Doctors Barclay and Tolmie. It will soon be seven years since I first saw this place. I should not be here now if my husband had not gone home and left me, or, I should have said, if my health had been sufficient for me to have continued at my post of labor among the Indians. Doctor White, the government Indian agent of this country, advised me to avail myself of this opportunity to rid myself from care and labor, come here and attend to the advice of Doctor Barclay for the perfect restoration of my health, and I have no reason to regret it so far. I feel that my health is improving, I hope permanently.

You speak of Mr. and Mrs. Abernethy. I have seen your letter to them and have only seen him a short time since I have been here. I hope to see them both in a few days, for I am waiting convenient opportunity to go to the Willamette, where I expect to visit the different members of the Mission and spend a pleasant season among them. The two Missions are three hundred miles apart and it is not easy to visit back and forth, especially where all hands are full of business each in his own field of labor.

You almost make me feel, from your letters, that you will accept of my invitation and come over and live with me and help me teach the poor Indians. Indeed! Are you not now almost here with my beloved husband? The time draws near when I hope to see his dear face again, and O! Am I to greet a beloved sister with him, and, perhaps, a dear brother too? I know not what inexpressible joys or sorrows are before this frail, trembling heart of mine; I feel that I could not survive an excess of either, my nervous system is so much impaired. But I know assuredly that the same grace that has sustained me hitherto under fiery trials, is able and will sustain in time to come. I am in His hand. The nine months past that I have been separated from my precious husband, have been months of His special favors to me in this dreary land of heathenish darkness. The sacrifice, if I may call it so, has been a great one — much more so that I at first thought it could be, ever to exceed that of leaving my native land and beloved friends, and coming to dwell among the heathen. But the precious promises have been fulfilled in my case leaving all for Christ's sake, as I trust I did in coming to this country, and freely consenting to be left so feeble and lonely in such a lonely situation, by my earth protector, my husband. I feel that I have indeed received manifold more in this present time with an assured hope of receiving in the world to come, life everlasting.

I am pleased to hear so good an account of dear E.'s progress in study and piety, and sincerely hope he will be a useful and devoted Christian minister. I wish he would write me more, for his own sake as well as mine.

Miss Jane A. Prentiss
Cuba, Alleghany County,
New York, U.S.A.

FORT GEORGE, August 11th, 1843.

My Dear Parents: — I am now at the mouth of the Columbia river. I came down with Rev. Daniel Lee of Waskopum, where I spent the last winter, and Mr. Leslie. He and his family are expecting to leave in the ship, that is now on its way down the river for the states. Doctor Babcock and his family of the same mission are going on the same vessel to the Islands, also Mr. Frost and family are leaving the missionary field, by the same opportunity and going home. Thus one after another of our Methodist brethren leave the country and go to the States. This is very discouraging to those who remain. Some of our number have done the same: — Mr. Smith and Mr. Gray and their families. Ministerial and missionary work is increasing in the country, and the labourers are decreasing.

My beloved parents may think it strange that I should wander about the country so much when my dear husband is absent. The Lord is very merciful and of great kindness to me in showing me so many favours in my lonely situation. It serves to occupy my mind and keeps me from undue anxiety concerning him; and besides this, journeying is beneficial to my health. I have come down to enjoy the benefit of a sea breeze, and visit the mission station at Clatsop on the Pacific coast. I am now enjoying a friendly visit in the family of Mr. Birnie at this fort. When the ship leaves I shall accompany Rev. Jason Lee to Clatsop, where I expect to spend a few days and return with Mr. Lee and Mr. Leslie to the Willamette and finish my visit there. Everywhere I go I find attention and kindness far more than I deserve. I believe I wrote to pa and ma while I was at Wascopum. I left them and went up the river in the company's boats in charge of Mr. Grant, the first of April, and arrived in safety after a voyage of five days. I went home and arranged affairs, attended upon the company of Doctor White and his party, which consisted of Revs. Hinds and Perkins, who came up to hold a meeting with the Indians. When the meeting closed I accompanied them to Walla Walla, and on the first day of June left there in the brigade for Vancouver, Mrs. McKinlay accompanying me. In coming, Dr. White recommended me to the attention of Dr. Barclay, an eminent physician of the fort. I remained there about two months and attended faithfully to his directions; feeling it is a great favour to have so good an opportunity to attend to my health, and to be so free from care and labour. I left two of the children in the care of Mrs. Littlejohn and Mrs. Eells. Helen I have with me. About the last of July, I went to the Willamette Falls and spent most of my time in the families of Mr. Abernethy and Mr. Waller. The latter one says he knew pa well; his circuit was in that region and he resided in Friendship. Last Monday, at sundown, I left them to come down the river to see the mission families leave.

It is very trying to part with dear Brother and Sister Lee. I have enjoyed such sweet religious privileges with them the past winter that I feel very much endeared to them. I cannot feel very willing to have them go. It is but very recently that they have talked and made up their minds to go, and it was very surprising to us. They are pious, devoted missionaries, but Mrs. Lee's health has failed, and they feel it their duty to go home. They were from the New England states and very probably pa and ma will not see them. Brother Lee says he will write to pa when he gets home for me. I send this by him. Doctor Babcock goes to the Islands to return again; it is possible he may not. He is from Avoca. I do not know when I shall see my dear husband again. I hope in a few weeks to receive letters from him and then I shall know when to expect him. The Lord be merciful to me and return him to my arms again in peace. I forbear to think much of the future, but rest it with the Lord. I have written this very poorly. The house if full of company and it is difficult to keep my thoughts. My most dearly beloved and excellent parents, please accept of my heartfelt thanks for all your love and kindness to me, and be assured of the sincere, devoted love of your unworthy daughter.

NARCISSA.

Hon. Stephen Prentiss,
   Cuba, Allegheny Co.,
      New York, U.S.A.

WAIILATPU, Jan. 30th, 1844.

Beloved Sister: — I received your kind letter and the accompanying book, a short time since and enjoyed to hear that the blessings of our kind Heavenly Father are still resting upon you and yours. May they still be continued and your precious lives be preserved long for the poor heathen's sake.

I will do as you desire and forward the memoir of Mrs. Smith to Mrs. Eells, as I shall have a good opportunity by my husband when he goes to attend upon Mrs. Walker, the last of next month.

After I arrived at Walla Walla last fall, I spent a week there, and during the time I wrote several letters and sent back by the express. Since that time I have not been able to write to any one. I was not well when I left W.W., yet I thought I could endure to ride here in one day in a wagon, but it proved too much for me. We were in the evening late before we could reach home, as they had to go slow on my account, and I took cold. For six weeks after, I scarcely left my room and most of the time was confined to my bed more or less; — could take no care of my family, or but little. Indeed, I was in a much more miserable state than I was last winter while with you. About the twentieth of Dec. I was taken very suddenly with the inflammation of the bowels, and for a few days my life was despaired of. But the Lord in His infinite mercy directed and blessed means for my restoration in answer to prayer.

Since that time I have gradually gained my usual strength so that I am able to see to my domestic concerns more than I have any time since my return. I have not suffered from the disease I took medicine for last summer, but a new and more precarious one has discovered itself, since my return, yet of long standing. It consists of an organic affection of the main artery below the heart, a beating tumour which is liable to burst and extinguish life at any moment. There is no remedy for it, so I never expect to enjoy better health than I do at present; never do I expect to continue long on the earth.

You expressed an assurance that I enjoyed the presence of my Saviour in my affliction. It has, indeed, been so for the most of the time. I feel that His mercies are very great to me and that I can say with the Apostle, "For me to live is Christ, and to die is gain," So long as it pleases Him to spare my life, I should like to live for my family and the poor Indians' sake. Notwithstanding I felt such a dread to return to this place of moral darkness, after enjoying so much of civilized life and christian privileges, yet now I am here, I am happy and love my work and situation and desire to live long to see the cause of Christ advanced in this dark land. Indeed, I think I never enjoyed the privilege of being a missionary, better than this winter, although I cannot do but little if any more than instruct my family and pray for and sustain the hands of my dear husband in his labours.

My family consists of six children and a Frenchman that came from the mountains and stops with us without invitation. Mary Ann, however, it with Mrs. Littlejohn now. Two English girls, Ann and Emma Hobson, one 13 and the other 7, of the party stopped with us; husband engaged to take them in the first part of the journey, but when they arrived here they went directly to W. Walla, being persuaded not to stay by some of the party on account of the Indians. When I arrived at W.W. they saw me and made themselves known to me and expressed a desire to come home with me. The girls were so urgent to stop that I could not well refuse them, and their father was obliged to give them up. I felt unwilling to increase my family at that time, but now have no reason to regret it, as they do the greater part of my work and go to school besides. I should like to keep on and tell you how I found things when I reached home; but this sheet is full; I will, however, take another and direct it to Sister Perkins, and as it is but the continuation of this, I presume she will allow you the privilege of reading it. I sympathize with you and Mrs. M. in the affliction of a broken breast. Please remember me to her if with you.

We send you a bunch of twine and desire to exchange it for some shoe thread if you are willing and can spare it.

I often think and dream of you and the scenes of the past. Neither do I forget you in my weak supplications at a throne of grace and the people for whom you labour; but especially at the seasons of our mothers' meetings do I feel a meeting of hearts around the mercy seat clearer and sweeter to me than all this earth can afford.

Kind regards to your dear husband, and please give many kisses to the sweet babes for me.

Your sister,
N. WHITMAN.

Mrs. L.L. Brewer,
    Wascopum.

Narcissa Whitman

WAIILATPU, Jan. 31st, 1844.

Beloved Sister: — My story was so long that I could not put it all on one sheet, so I told sister Brewer I would take another and direct it to you, for I presume you would allow her the perusal. Before I begin, however, I will speak of the interest of this day to us as mothers, it being the last Wednesday of the month, and according to our constitution we have agreed to observe it as a day of fasting and prayer on our own account and our children's. It did not occur to me last winter while I was with you. It is a change that has been recently made in our constitution. It is a pleasing thought to feel that on this day our hearts center at one point, namely, the Mercy Seat, with all our interesting charges in our arms as the mothers of old were agreed in bringing their children to the Saviour while on earth. Although we are so widely separated in person, yet we meet there and feel that our hearts are one for our object is one, and a dear one, too, to every mother's heart. O when shall we be permitted to see these heathen mothers as anxious and enjoy as much comfort in bringing their children to the Saviour in such meetings as is their privilege to? Perhaps you may live to see it, but I have no reason to think I shall. I have written to Sister B. the particulars concerning my health to which I must refer you. I must begin my story, or I shall not be able to finish it even on this sheet.

When I arrived home, I found Mr. and Mrs. Littlejohn occupying my bedroom. She was sick, having been confined a few days before I came. The room east of the kitchen, Mr. East and family occupied — four children, all small. Mr. Looney, with a family of six children and one young man by the name of Smith, were in the Indian room. My two boys, Perrin Whitman and David, slept up-stairs. Alex., the Frenchman, in the kitchen, and Mary Ann and Helen in the trundle-bed in the room with Mr. Littlejohn. The dining room alone remained for me, husband and my two English girls, all of these were fed from our table except Mr. Looney's family, and our scanty fare consisted of potatoes and corn meal, with a little milk occasionally, and cakes from the burnt wheat. This was a great change for me from the well furnished tables of Waskipom and Willamette.

Thus it continued for four weeks with the exception of the slaying of a lean hog as often as required. Besides those fed at our table, there were three families in Mr. Gray's house that were supplied with provisions by us; one by a widow woman with three children, whose husband was drowned in crossing the Snake river, and another with four, and an aged couple. These constitute the foreign inhabitants of Waiilatpu.

In about five weeks after my return, Mr. L. and family removed into a room prepared for them over the cellar, Mr. Looney to the Prince's house up the river, and Mr. East to Mr. Spalding's, taking with them one of the daughters of Mrs. Eyers, the widow, to live with Mrs. S. During all this period and for some time after I was too sick to make any effort at arranging my house, or to have the care of my family, and the confusion and noise distressed me exceedingly, for every child about the house, my own with the rest, were as wild and uncontrollable as so many wild animals.

As soon as Mrs. L. recovered her health and got settled, she opened a school for the children of the white inhabitants which numbers fifteen scholars. Now our children are quite tame and manageable and we feel that they are all enjoying a great privilege. How many times I have thought of Henry and Ellen and wished they could enjoy the same. For about a month past my health has so much improved that I have had the strength to set some part of my house in order by degrees and to relieve my husband in his care of the family in a good measure. He never expects me to be anything more than an invalid, consequently my labours will be circumscribed.

I hope your dear husband will favour us with his presence at our expected meeting, accompanied by Mr. Lee.

In all things I desire to be submissive to the will of my Saviour, although at times I have felt that it was trying to be taken away in the midst of my days and without accomplishing more for Christ. The Lord's time is the best for us if we can always feel it to be so, which I desire to do.

        Do pray for your unworthy sister,

                                    N. WHITMAN.

Mrs. Elvira Perkins,
    Waskopum.

Narcissa Whitman

WAIILATPU, OREGON TERRITORY
April 12th, 1844.

My Beloved Father:—I was coming up the Columbia river from the Willamette and Vancouver with Rev. Jason Lee when your welcomed letter reached me. My husband had each of the stations of the mission to visit before he could come after me. Mr. Lee brought me on my way home as far as the Dalles, to Mr. Perkins, one of their stations, where I spent the winter of my husband's absence. I remained there a few days, and my long absent doctor came for me. It was a joyful and happy meeting and caused our hearts to overflow with love and gratitude to the Author of all our mercies, for permitting us to see each other's faces again in the flesh. We came home immediately after a short visit with friends there. My health, which had been quite poor some of the time of his absence, was somewhat improved, but the voyage up the river, or rather the exposure of rain, cold and fatigue, and also the journey from Walla Walla here, proved injurious to me. I was so unwell when I reached home that I could scarcely get about the house for several weeks. I continued to decline, or, rather, had two attacks of remittent fever until the last of December, when I was taken with a very severe attack of inflammation of the bowels and bloating which threatened almost immediate death. The second night of the attack, we almost despaired of my living. From the first, I was taken with excruciating pain and spitting bilious fluid from the stomach, and could keep nothing down, nor effect a motion of the bowels sufficient to afford a permanent relief, a clyster of salts was introduced into the bowels with a long tube and stomach pump the second night, and followed by a portion of the same medicine in the morning, which soon gave signs of relief. The cathartic operated favorably and thoroughly, and I recovered almost immediately so as to be able to sit up and be about the room. Previous to this, and almost as soon as husband returned and inquired into my case, he discovered a beating tumor near the umbilicus and fears it is an aneurism of the main aorta below the heart. If what he fears is true, he says there is no probability or possibility of a cure, or of my ever enjoying anything more than a confortable degree of health, and I am liable at any moment to a sudden death. While I was at Vancouver, I placed myself under Doctor Barclay's care, a surgeon of the H.B. Company's. He discovered that I had an enlargement of the right ovary and gave me iodine to remove it. I was very much improved by his kind attentions for that complaint, and had it not been for the other difficulty of the aorta which was not at that time discovered by Doctor Barclay, although it existed, I might have recovered my health. But the medicine I took for the cure of one tumor was an injury to the other, and for three months after my husband's return, my situation was a source of deepest anxiety to him and he greatly feared that he was about to be bereaved. But the Lord dealt in infinite loving kindness to us both, and in answer to prayer, raised me up again. Yes, beloved parents, while I was in that precarious state, and almost without hope that I should survive many hours, dear brother Littlejohn, who is now with us, prayed for me with the full assurance that the prayer of faith shall save the sick, and the Lord heard and answered.

I am now much more comfortable than at that time husband expected I ever could be. I am able to take the whole care of my family and aid in doing the most difficult part of the work, or that I cannot get done by others. During the first three months after my return to the station, husband was confined with the care of me and was obliged to have the whole care of the family upon his mind at the same time with his other duties. Our family was large and at the time I arrived, there were two large families of the emigrants in our house besides Mr. Littlejohn's, and our own consisted of six children and two hired men. We have written about our half breed children, those we had before the doctor left; in addition to those is Perrin, our nephew, and two English girls of the emigrating party of last year. One of them is thirteen and the other six; they are motherless; they have both returned with Mr. J. Lee and Mr. Leslie to the Willamette Falls, and immediately proceeded up the river to the upper Mission and visited the families of Rev. Mr. Hinds, Mr. Beers and others, and also Mr. and Mrs. Gray, my old associates. While there a camp meeting was held near by, which I attended and a precious season it was to my soul. To witness again the anxious tear and hear the deep-felt inquiry, "What must I do to be saved?" as I once used to, filled me with joy inexpressible. It continued four days and resulted me in the conversion of almost all the impenitent on the ground. From this precious season, after a week or two, we came to the Falls where a protracted meeting was held. While that was in progress, the news came that my husband was on his return with a hundred and forty wagons containing an immense party of emigrants, and that probably he was now at Waiilatpu. This was cheering news, as I had just heard from the Islands through Mr. Hall that in recent news from the States to the Islands down as late as April, 1843, no mention was made of his arrival. This had given me much anxiety, but it was not long before the other intelligence came. The last week in September, I left the Falls for Vancouver and The Dalles in company with Mr. J. Lee, the Superintendent of that Mission, and turned my back upon many dear friends in Christ with whom I was permitted to form an acquaintance and a Christian attachment never to be forgotten.

Having been so long secluded, I was well prepared to enjoy society and I may well say that some of the moments spent here with Christian friends were among the happiest in my life. We made a short stay at Vancouver and then proceeded on our way up the river. Passing the Cascades and making the portage, we had continual rain, and before we reached The Dalles, I took cold to my great injury, as it afterwards proved. Between the Cascades and The Dalles, I received father's letter with several others from friends, also sisters Jane, C. and H; I am greatly obliged to them for writing. Mr. Lee waited at The Dalles until the doctor came. It was pleasing to see the pioneers of the two Missions meet and hold counsel together. Soon we parted and I turned my face with my husband toward this dark spot, and dark, indeed; it seemed to be to me when compared with the scenes, social and religious which I had so recently been enjoying with so much zest.

When we parted with Mr. Lee, we little thought that our first news from him would be, that he had set his face toward his native land. But it was, indeed, so. He has gone again and I should rejoice if dear father and mother would see him. He has shown me great kindness during my lonely state, and may the Lord reward him for it. He has been deeply afflicted in his domestic relations. He has buried two excellent wives, and a little son. A little daughter of his last wife, still survives to comfort and cheer him in his loneliness. She has gone with him to the States; and so has Rev. Mr. Hinds and his wife. As they are from the region of Allegheny county, I hope father will see them.

It must appear singular to friends at home to hear of the return of so many missionaries from Oregon. So it seems to us; but we have not the discouragements which our friends of that Mission have. The Indians of the Willamette and the coast are diminishing rapidly; but they have another work put into their hands. Settlers are coming into the country like a flood and every one of these need the gospel preached to them as much as the heathen. That Society have been and are doing a great deal of good in the lower country. Mr. Clark and Mr. Griffin, ministers of our denomination, are settled near on the Tualatin plains and are doing much good in the way of schools and preaching. I did not visit them, although greatly urged to; on account of my health I could not ride there, as it was some distance from the river.

I was greatly disappointed in not seeing Jane when the doctor returned. I fancied he would bring her, and so he would have done had a family been coming with whom it would have been prudent for her to come. I still hope some day to see her. But I know not how. This I do know, that no one of my friends at home know how much comfort she would be to me if she was here.

Sister Littlejohn is a great comfort to me. She acted the part of a sister to me during my sickness, but I do not always expect to keep her. Mr. Littlejohn is in poor health and unable to labor. His mind suffers greatly from dejection and melancholy, and he longs to go back to the States again.

Mr. and Mrs. Spalding and two children have been deeply afflicted the past summer, just before the doctor's return, with sickness, especially Mrs. S. She lay for several days expecting every moment would be her last, and no physician near. Mr. and Mrs. Littlejohn was there at that time, and as soon as possible Mr. Geiger, who was at this station, was sent for, also Mr. Walker, to preach her funeral sermon—expecting she would die before he reached there. Her husband and children were sick at the same time and all must have perished had it not been that Mr. and Mrs. Littlejohn were providentally there, having a short time before returning from Mr. Walker's. God in mercy spared them all and restored them back to health again. But Mrs. S. is feeble, and like myself, we feel cannot be expected to live long.

Since my return to the station, Mrs. S. has written me very kindly, showing that her feelings have undergone a change during her sickness, while in the near view of death and expecting every moment to enter the dark valley. This is a great consolation to us, and we hope and believe that they both feel different toward us from what they did, and surely they have great reason to, from husband's account of his visit to the rooms in Boston.

I desire never to pass through such scenes of trial as I have done, and God grant that I may never be called to. We both have spent a happy winter in each other's society. Having those unhappy difficulties removed makes a change in our every day feelings. We are happier in each other and happier in God and in our work than we could have been while laboring under those exciting difficulties—yea! Soul-destroying difficulties, I may well say.

For more than a year past I have enjoyed an unwonted quiet resting upon God my Redeemer, especially during my husband's absence. Truly my Saviour was with me in those trying hours, and sustained me far beyond what I deserve. A calm, peaceful sense of His abiding presence was what I almost daily realized. Being free from any distracting cares of my family and the station, I had nothing else to do but rest myself in my Saviour's arms; and it would be well for me now if I were to do the same, instead of attempting to shoulder my cards, as I often do—to cast them on Him who has said "Cast they burdens upon the Lord and He will sustain thee." I know this, and believe it, too, for I have sometimes realized it. But to have the constant habit of doing so is what I would gladly obtain, and I know I may with diligence and prayerful watching thereunto.

I see I have almost exceeded my limits, and must think of closing. Father's letters are choice gems to me, and I hope he will continue to write as long as I live. O! that dear mother would put some of her thoughts on paper for the consolation of my heart. She does not know what joy it would give me. I am a thousand times thankful for all the favors I receive from home, and shall write to all as many and as much as my weak state will admit.

Love to all, in which husband unites. I am sorry he did not have time to make a longer visit after going so far. Farewell, dear father and mother, and if I never write again till we meet in heaven,

Your ever affectionate daughter,

NARCISSA WHITMAN.

Hon. Stephen Prentiss,
 Cuba, Allegheny Co.,
  N.Y., U.S.A.

My Dear Father and Mother:—A little more than a year has elapsed since I had the pleasure of seeing you. The remembrance of that visit will never be effaced from my mind. I did not misjudge as to my duty to return home; the importance of my accompanying the emigration on one hand and the consequent scarcity of provisions on the other, strongly called for my return, and forbin my bringing another party that year.

As I hold the settlement of this country by Americans rather than by an English colony most important, I am happy to have been the means of landing so large an emigration on to the shores of the Colulmbia, with their wagons, families and stock, all in safety.

The health of Narcissa was such in my absence and since my return as to call loudly from my presence. We despaired of her life at times and for the winter have not felt she could live long. But there is more hope at present, although nothing very decisive can be said. While on the way back, I had an inflammation in my foot which threatened to suppurate, but I discusses it and thought nothing more of it until I got home, when I found I had a tumor on the instep. It appears to be a bony tumor and has given me a good deal of apprehenseion and inconvenience, but is now some better, but not well.

It gives me much pleasure to be back again and quietly at work again for the Indians. It does not concern me so much what is to become of any particular set of Indians, as to give them the offer of salvation through the gospel and the opportunity of civilization, and then I am content to do good to all men as "I have opportunity." I have no doubt our greatest work is to be to aid the white settlement of this country and help to found its religious institutions. Providence has its full share in all these events. Although the Indians have made, and are making, rapid advance in religious knowledge and civilization, yet it cannot be hoped that time will be allowed to mature either the work of Christianization or civilization before the white settlers will demand the soil and seek the removal of both the Indians and the Mission. What Americans desire of this kind they always effect, and it is equally useless to oppose or desire it otherwise. To guide, as far as can be done, and direct these tendencies for the best, is evidently the part of wisdom. Indeed, I am fully convinced that when a people refuse or neglect to fill the designs of Providence, they ought not to complain at the results; and so it is equally useless for Christians to be anxious on their account. The Indians have in no case obeyed the command to multiply and replenish the earth, and they cannot stand in the way of others in doing so. A place will be left them to do this as fully as their ability to obey will permit, and the more we can do for them the more fully will this be realized. No exclusiveness can be asked for any portion of the human family. The exercise of his rights are all that can be desired. In order for this to its proper extent in regard to the Indians, it is necessary that they seek to preserve their rights by peaceable means only. Any violations of this rule will be visited with only evil results to themselves.

The Indians are anxious about the consequence of settlers among them, but I hope there will be no acts of violence on either hand. An evil affair at the Falls of the Willamett, resulted in the death of two white men killed and one Indian. But all is now quiet. I will try to write to Brother Jackson when I will treat of the country, etc.

It will not surprise me to see your whole family in this country in two years. Let us hear from you often. Narcissa may be able to write for herself. We wish to be remembered with your other children in your prayers.

Your affectionate son,
MARCUS WHITMAN.

Hon. Stephen Prentiss,
   Cuba, Allegheny Co.,
      New York.

WAIILATPU, April 24, 1844.

Dear Sister Brewer: — I hear that you are alone and I thought I would write a little to comfort, or at least to assure you that I have not forgotten you or yours, although I am unable to write as much as I would like to. Your letter, together with the accompanying ones, came in a good time when they did as much good, and I have wanted very much to reply to them earlier, but have felt too unwell most of the time, or had so much care I could not find time when I was able. You have had the trouble of entertaining our winter visitors, and longer, too, I fear, than you knew how. I sympathize with you and hope provisions have not been as short with you as us, but fear they have been more so. We were greatly in hopes that we should have one of your number to visit with us this spring, but it seems Mr. and Mrs. P. and family have gone below. I hear nothing from Sister Abernethy nor any of them below; I desire to very much. I wish you could visit us this summer — will you not try? It would be so refreshing. Do come — all of you. How I do desire to enjoy another refreshing season of divine worship and social privileges, such as I used to last summer. But I do not know as I may ever in this world.

Our Indians have been very much excited this spring, but are now quiet. The influx of emigration is not going to let us live in as much quiet, as it regards the people, as we have done.

I must close. This is a miserable letter and not worth reading; I have written in such haste. But this one thing be assured, I still love and think of you with increased interest, and if we meet no more in this world, it gives me joy to think we may meet in Heaven and there, being washed white in the blood of the Lamb, Praise Him continually.

      Affectionately yours,
           N. WHITMAN.

Mrs. L.L. Brewer,
 Waskopum.

WAIILATPU, OREGON TERRITORY.
May 18th, 1844.

Mrs. Lydia E. Porter, My Dear Sister: — It is impossible for me to describe the many pleasing associations that entwined around my heart as I perused the three tokens of affectionate remembrance received by the hand of my husband, from the friends of my early youth, the dearest friends of my heart, and friends of my Saviour, too. It would have been an indescribable favour to have participated with him in the visit; but this could not have been, short as it was. It is a great satisfaction to me and was to him to have seen your faces again in the flesh. That I shall ever be permitted to visit my dear native Prattsburg again is very uncertain. I do not desire to, so long as my poor inefficient services are needed here, much as I should enjoy the visit. I had rather try to induce my friends to come and see me and seek a home in Oregon. A wide door of usefulness is open here to the philanthropic and benevolent heart. Multitudes are flocking to this land and will continue to in still greater numbers, and for every purpose. And our anxious desire is that the salt of the earth should be found among them, also that this entire country may be seasoned with heavenly influence from above. The powers of darkness have long held their undivided sway over this land, and we feel that Satan will not quietly yield his dominions to another. He is on the alert with all his hosts, and in as many ways as he has numbers employed to gain the entire victory to keep and drive from the field all who molest or disturb his quiet. Many souls are here for whom Christ died, and multitudes more unconcerned are hastening to this far-distant land to seek their fortune of worldly goods, regardless of their treasure in heaven. But thanks be to the hearer of prayer, many already have found Christ in Oregon, who have long rejected him in a gospel land. Last summer while husband was absent, I had the unspeakable happiness of attending two meetings of days at different places — while on a visit to the Willamette among our Methodist friends. Almost every soul was affected with divine truth and many, we trust, found peace in believing.

I left the station soon after husband's departure and spent the winter with Messrs. Lee, Perkins and Brewer's families, of the Methodist mission. My health was quite poor, indeed I was unable to ride to any of the stations of our mission, and being invited and desirous of visiting them, I availed myself of the opportunity of a passage down the river in the express boats. In April, returned to the station, and in June went to Vancouver and the Willamette on a visit, as there was no female society at the station. I enjoyed my visit much; having been so long from the civilized world, it seemed good to get among Christians once more. I was in the Willamette when husband arrived at this place. He could not come for me as he had to visit Brother Spalding's on an express, as Sister S. was then at the point of death and had been dangerously ill for some time. But she has been mercifully spared to us, and is now enjoying comfortable health. From Mr. S. he returned to the station to make arrangements for imparting provisions to the emigrants, which took all the station raised the past year, leaving us to obtain our supplies from Brother Spalding. Immediately he was obliged to go a hundred and sixty miles to Brother Eells to attend Sister E. in her expected confinement. Before he returned I was making my way up the river under the protection of Rev. Jason Lee, superintendent of that mission, who was coming up as far as their mission at the Dalls. It was at this place we met after a separation of little more than a year, rejoicing in the mercy of God to us both in sparing our lives and permitting us to see each other again. We came home immediately and re-organized our family which had increased considerably. My health, which before had been very feeble, was most precarious for three months after my return. At one time I was brought very near the gates of death. I am at present by no means perfectly well, but am more comfortable than I feared I ever should be. I desire to spend the remnant of my day to the glory of God, and to be in constant readiness for my departure, for I feel that it is not far distant.

Truly you and your dear husband have been deeply afflicted in the death of so many members of your beloved families. I feel to sympathize with you and your truly bereaved and aged father. Please present my love and kindest remembrances to him. I could not keep from weeping in hearing my husband's interesting description of him. Surely, what has he to bind him to earth when the most of his beloved family is in heaven. I love to think of them there as my own dear friends, for I hope soon to be with them.

Husband has been writing to Father Hotchkiss concerning this country, what I hope your dear husband will see, and with other friends be prevailed upon to come to this country and adopt it as your own. Be assured nothing would give us greater pleasure than to see some of our Prattsburg friends here in Oregon.

I sincerely hope you will write me often, for I am anxious to hear more particulars concerning Mrs. Leland's death and her surviving family. You know not how much I enjoyed the reading of the Pastor's Wife which Mr. Malin kindly sent me. I had written to her, also Mrs. O.L. Porter, but have received no answers.

Please remember me affectionately to each member of your family, your Brother V. and P.'s family, and all Christian friends who may inquire. Forget not to write concerning your own dear children and your maternal association, for I desire much to know of its prosperity; also of the cause of Christ generally.

Yours sincerely and affectionately,

NARCISSA WHITMAN.

Mrs. Lydia C. Porter,
    Prattsburg,
        Steuben County, N.Y.
Favour of W. Gilpin.

Narcissa Whitman

WAIILATPU, OREGON TERRITORY,
May 20th, 1844.

My Dear Clarissa: — I am glad you have begun to write me. I hope it will not be the last one I shall receive from you. You cannot do me so much good in any way, except by praying for me, as in writing me all about yourselves and beloved children. I want to see how you look and how you live. I try to be faithful on my part, although I have not so much time as you, and many more correspondents. My husband's visit was very short, too much so to gain all the information I was in hopes he would bring me. Yet I am glad he has seen you, although I have not had the privilege. It would give me great enjoyment to visit you once more, but I cannot expect it; I am a missionary, and therefore cannot seek after comfort merely, but must be content to stay where I am and do the Lord's work. Believe me, dear sister, I am most perfectly so. I would not be otherwise situated so long as the Lord wants me here.

You and sister Harriet seem anxious to make me laugh. Perhaps if you could see me you would not desire to. I feel but little disposition to, I can assure you, for I have more around me and within, to make me cry than to make me laugh. In the first place, my health is poor, and I feel as if I was not very far from Eternity. My family cares are numerous. I feel sometimes as if I had almost as many children as mother, although they are not my own. Besides these, I have a sluggish heart within that requires constant watching. I desire to be cheerful, because that is a duty; but I find it hard work always to be so, especially when husband was gone. But the Lord supported me, else I could not have been at all.

For two weeks past Mrs. McKinlay has been here. She came to stay during her confinement, as there are no females at the Fort. She boards with Sister Littlejohn, who lives in the east wing of our house over the cellar. This morn we were called about four o'clock and in a short time she was delivered of a fine son. This is her second child born in this house. She had a daughter born two years ago now that died last fall with the croup.

Dear C., do you think we shall ever see you in Oregon? Husband has been writing to father and others, to hold out inducements for our friends to come into this country.

The Indians are roused a good deal at seeing so many emigrants, but they are foolish enough to wish to sell their lands.

Husband tells me that you and mother are in the same house together and that Harriet is close by. I think you must be happy in so many of you being so near together and having father and mother with you.

I wish they would come and live with me. True, they are considerably advanced, and you think too old to cross the Rocky mountains. We wintered an old couple last winter that had followed their children to this country, for the sake of benefiting them in the things of this world. They were considerably older than father and mother. They came in wagons all the way, and was sick, particularly the woman, most all the way. But the past winter she has fleshed and regained her health, better than it had been for years, notwithstanding our living was very plain — good beef, potatoes and cornmeal — no milk nor butter through the winter. We find it very good to dispense with horse beef and have plenty of cow beef in its place.

I do not know as I should be more surprised to see them than to see many that I have seen. True, it would be very fatiguing and distressing to both mind and body, for them both. I cannot say that I desire they should endure so much fatigue and suffering in their old age as they would necessarily to come and see me, unless there was a more ennobling object; but for a young couple just beginning in life, perhaps there is not a place where they would do better. Please tell Harriet that I shall not be able to answer her letter at this mail, as I have my Rushville friends to answer yet. Soon we hope to have a monthly mail to pass back and forth from here to the States, then I hope to receive letters often.

Remember me affectionately to your husband and all the friends there.

Ever your affectionate sister,

N. WHITMAN.

Mrs. Clarissa P. Kinny,
    Cuba, Allegheny Co.,
        New York.
Favour of W. Gilpin.

WAIILATPU, Aug. 5th, 1844.

My Dear Mrs. Brewer: — Tilaukikt is about starting for the Willamette, and I take the opportunity of replying to yours of June 10th, which was thankfully received. We know well how to sympathize with you in having such boys as Eli and Thomas about you, and for the trouble of those families in passing. We are all of us, I suppose, on the eve of another such scene as last fall — the passing of emigrants — and as it falls the heavier upon my friends at the Dalles, I hope they have laid in a good stock of strength, patience and every needed grace for the siege. We have had no news from that quarter as yet, but cannot think it will be long before we shall hear.

We hear Mr. and Mrs. Gary are visiting you. Last week we sent an invitation to Mr. G. in a letter to Mr. Perkins, to have him visit us accompanied by Brother P. and any other member of your mission who could conveniently come, and we have been looking for and anxiously desire to see them. Perhaps our letter may not have been received. By the by, we never heard in all of our correspondence from the lower country, that there was a Mrs. Gary until our letters and papers from the Islands arrived. If she is still with you, please do me the favor to present her our Christian salutations and a hearty welcome to Oregon, our adopted home.

We should be happy to have her visit us at the present time, if convenient. I can imagine myself with you; particularly in your enjoyments, both social and spiritual, and if it would be right, could envy you. Are Brother and Sister Waller there? We have heard that they were coming to the Dalles, but not that they were come. Do write us when you can. It does us good to know that you all are enjoying such privileges, if we must be deprived of them. I think my husband would have made you a visit if he could have known that it was not convenient for any of your number to come to Waiilatpu.

I wrote Sister Perkins last week. The Indian leaves this morning, and as I write in haste, you will please excuse the brevity of this note. I should like to hear the result of the late camp meeting.

Love to you all, in which the doctor unites.

Sincerely and affectionately yours,
NARCISSA WHITMAN.

WAIILATPU, Oct. 9th, 1844.

Beloved and Honored Parents:—I have no unanswered letters on hand, either from dear father and mother or any of the family, yet I cannot refrain from writing every stated opportunity. The season has arrived when the emigrants are beginning to pass us on their way to the Willamette. Last season there were such a multitude of starving people passed us that quite drained us of all our provisions, except potatoes. Husband has been endeavoring this summer to cultivate so as to be able to impart without so much distressing ourselves. In addition to this, he has been obliged to build a mill, and to do it principally with his own hands, which has rendered it exceedingly laborious for him. In the meantime, I have endeavored to lighten his burden as much a possible in superintending the ingathering of the garden, etc. During this period, the Indians belonging to this station and the Nez Perces go to Forts Hall and Boise to meet the emigrants for the purpose of trading their wornout cattle for horses. Last week Tuesday, several young men arrived, the first of the party that brought us any definite intelligence concerning them (having nothing but Indian reports previous), among whom was a youth from Rushville formerly, of the name of Gilbert, one of husband's scholars.

Last Friday a family of eight arrived, including the grandmother, an aged woman, probably as old, or older than my mother. Several such persons have passed, both men and women, and I often think when I gaze upon them, shall I ever be permitted to look upon the face of my dear parents in this land?

25th—When I commenced this letter I intended to write a little every day, so as to give you a picture of our situation at this time. But it has been impossible. Now I must write as briefly as possible and send off my letter, or lose the opportunity. The emigration is late in getting into the country. It is now the last of October and they have just begun to arrive with their wagons. The Blue mountains are covered with snow, and many families, if not half of the party, are back in or or beyond the mountains, and what is still worse, destitute or provisions and some of them of clothing. Many are sick, several with children born on the way. One family arrived here night before last, and the next morn a child was born; another is expected in the same condition.

Here we are, one family alone, a way mark, as it were, or center post, about which multitudes will or must gather this winter. And these we must feed and warm to the extent of our powers. Blessed be God that He has given us so abundantly of the fruit of the earth that we may impart to those who are thus famishing. Two preachers with large families are here and wish to stay for the winter, both Methodist. With all this upon our hands, besides our duties and labors for the Indians, can any one think we lack employment or have any time to be idle?

Mr. and Mrs. Littlejohn left us in September and have gone below to settle in the Willamette. We have been looking for associated this fall, but the Board could get none ready, but say, they will send next year. Am I ever to see any of my family among the tide of emigration that is flowing west?

Our mill is finished and grinds well. It is a mill out of doors or without a house; that we must build next year.

We have employed a young man of the party to teach school, so that we hope to have both an English school and one for the natives. My health has been improving remarkably through the summer, and one great means has been daily bathing in the river. I was very miserable one year ago now, and was brought very low and poor; now I am better than I have been for some time, and quite fleshly for me. I weigh one hundred and sixty-seven pounds; much higher than ever before in my life. This will make the girls laugh, I know. Mrs. Spalding's health is better than last year. She expects an increase in her family soon.

This country is destined to be filled, and we desire greatly to have good people come, and ministers and Christians, that it may be saved from being a sink of wickedness and prostitution. We need many houses to accommodate the families that will be obliged to winter here. All the house room that we have to spare is filled already. It is expected that there are more than five hundred souls back in the snow and mountains. Among the number is an orphan family of seven children, the youngest an infant born on the way, whose parents have both died since they left the States. Application has been made for us to take them, as they have not a relative in the company. What we shall do I cannot say; we cannot see them suffer, if the Lord casts them upon us. He will give us His grace and strength to do our duty to them.

I cannot write any more, I am so thronged and employed that I feel sometimes like being crazy, and my poor husband, if he had a hundred strings tied to him pulling in every direction, could not be any worse off.

Dear parents, do pray earnestly for your children here, for their situation is one of great trial, as well as of responsibility.

Love from us both to you all. I am disappointed in not getting letters from some of the dear ones this fall, but so it must be and I submit.

Your affectionate daughter
NARCISSA.

Hon. Stephen Prentiss,
    Cuba, Allegheny Co.,
        New York.

My Dear Father: — it gives me pleasure to write you at this time, as I know you will be anxious to hear how we prosper. The health of Narcissa is very much improved from what it was when I came home and the winter following, yet it is not good, nor is it likely to be again. She is, however, able to take the charge of the family, and to perform much important labor. Our family had the important addition of an orphan family of seven children whose parents both died on the road to this country. The two oldest are boys, the oldest is fourteen, and the rest are girls; the youngest was only five months when she came here. It did not seem likely the little one could have lived many days more, but she is now strong and healthy, as are all the rest.

I have thought much for the last winter that I should be glad if you were in this country. The immigrants are benefiting themselves much by coming here, as they take each a mile square of land and will hold it, as they make such a regulations among themselves, in accordance with the bill of Mr. Linn, formerly in the Senate of the U.S.

No country now open to settlers presents such a field for enterprise, as this near vicinity to the Pacific ocean offers large promise of commercial advantage. The salubrity of the climate is such here that I am every year only the more and more admiring it. Flowers have been in blossom in this valley this year since the middle of January, and the grass is as fine for the whole winter as in almost any other country in June.

I have had much to do with supplying immigrants for the last two years.

My mill was burnt soon after I left for the States, but I have rebuilt it, and have a saw-mill in a state of forwardness, which I hope to start soon after planting. It is about twenty miles from the house and situated in the Blue mountains. It is necessary to have a saw-mill, as we are in want of conveniences, and our houses are to be roofed anew, as we have only dirt roofs at present, and besides we have no house over our flour-mill, and we need storehouses.

We must also use a saw-mill for fencing, as a timber is so scarce except in the mountains. The Indians are doing more this year at farming than before and fencing much better — a thing much needed, for most of them are now getting more or less cows and other cattle. I have killed nineteen beeves, of course mostly to supply immigrants. The last was but two years old when killed the 10th of March and weighed six-hundred, and the tallow, after one hind quarter was sold, weighed 65 lbs. This will show a specimen of my stock, as we never feed either to raise or fatten, and he was only an ordinary animal. I have four two year old heifers (this spring only) which have each better yearling sucking them, probably than any that can be shown in the state of New York, except they have had more than one cow's milk.

We have above eighty sheep, a large part ewes, as we kill the wethers — besides all that have been killed by dogs, wolves, etc., and besides a good many furnished the Indians. All these came from one ewe brought from the Sandwich Islands in '38 and two more brought in '39. We shall have more than a hundred when the spring lambs have come.

Let us hear from you, and if any of you think to come here.

I have had many a rebuke by Narcissa, because I did not bring Jane with me when I came back. Edward might do well in this country, and we shall be glad to see him when his education is completed, is he is to complete it; but if not, still let him come, but only with a wife. You can come in wagons all the way, but bring nothing but provisions and necessary clothing — nothing. Accept our love for you all. And believe us,

Your affectionate children,

MARCUS WHITMAN.

My Dear Parents: — I have now a family of eleven children. This makes me feel as if I could not write a letter, not even to my dearest friends, much as I desire to. I get along very well with them; they have been to school most of the time; we have had an excellent teacher, a young man from New York. He became hopefully converted soon after entering our family, and mother, I wish you could see me now in the midst of such a group of little ones; there are two girls of nine years, one of seven, a girl and a boy of six, another girl of five, another of three and the baby, she is now ten months. I often think of mother when she had the care of Henry Martin Curtis.

It would make me indescribably happy to have father and mother and some of the children come to Oregon; but it is such a journey I fear Mother would be sorry she undertook it, if she should conclude to come, but if once here I think there would be no cause of regret. Families can come quite comfortable and easy in wagons all the way. But why should I wish thus? It cannot be possible that I shall see my beloved parents again — is it? — Until I meet them in heaven. The Lord only knows; I will leave it with Him to direct all these things. We have had some serious trials this spring with the Indians. Two important Indians have died and they have ventured to say and intimate that the doctor has killed them by his magical power, in the same way they accuse their own sorcerers and kill them for it. Also an important young man has been killed in California by Americans; he was the son of the Walla Walla chief and went there to get cattle, with a few others. This has produced much excitement also. We are in the midst of excitement and prejudice on all sides, both from Indians and passing immigrants, but the Lord has preserved us hitherto and will continue to, if we trust Him. Love to all, as ever and forever.

Your affectionate daughter,
NARCISSA.

Miss Jane A. Prentiss,
   Cuba, New York.

WAIILATPU, Feb. 10th, 1845.

My Dear Mrs. Brewer: — I do not recollect that I am indebted to you, but having a favourable opportunity of sending, and feeling desirous of a social chat with you, I have seated myself to write, although my baby is whining and the children are busy about me like so many bees.

I am anticipating very much enjoyment from your contemplated visit to us this season. I hope you will not disappoint us. Please let me know about the time when you will probably come.

I have had a very happy winter in labouring for my family of orphans, and other reasons. The Lord so mercifully provided me with a fellow labourer that I feel I never can be sufficiently thankful. I think I mentioned when I wrote last that we had an excellent school, and that our children were improving rapidly; and perhaps I spoke, too, of the conversion of the teacher to God. A kind Providence brought him to our door, and he had not been here many days before, like the prodigal in a far country, he came to himself, and remembering the many prayers and admonitions of parental love, his former convictions and strivings of the Spirit, together with the long suffering patience and loving kindness of is Heavenly Father, he resolved to return, and in deep contrition, consecrated himself to his divine Master. Now he contemplates studying for the ministry, and with this view remains with us for a season and will teach school, or, at least, give one lesson a day through the summer, and next winter keep a regular one.

Since his conversion, Mr. Hinman has laboured indefatigably in Sabbath-school and otherwise for the benefit of the youths and children that have been with us the winter past, and much good seed has been sown which we doubt not will be felt after.

I write in so much confusion that I shall be obliged to stop before I have said what I wish to.

Husband is so much engaged in fitting out and settling with the immigrants that he wishes me to apologize to your husband for him. He would write, if possible. He sends some corn as Mr. B. requested. He has none that has been particularly saved for seed; but will, next fall, if desired, save and send some New York corn, which we find to be very suitable for the country. Some beets and acorn squash seeds are in the bag with the corn. The others you requested, we have none.

Please give my love to Brother and Sister Waller, to your husband and self and all the dear children, and believe me, in haste,

Yours affectionately,
N.W.

Mrs. L.L. Brewer,
  Wascopum.

Narcissa Whitman

WAIILATPU, May 19th, 1845.

My Dear Mrs. Brewer:—My husband and our dear Brother Hinman are about to visit you, and I wish very much I could enjoy it with them. I have been looking for a visit from you and Brother Brewer, and regret very much that you have not been here at the time you mentioned, for both Mr. Walker's and Mr. Eell's families have been here. Why did you not come? I am afraid now you will not let me see you this summer; do come if you can when the doctor returns. How I should like to converse with you about your trials, hopes, fears and prospects in the missionary work. I cannot write much now, but hope you will enjoy the company of those who go from here and be of mutual benefit to each other. We were permitted while the mission was here to receive Brother Hinman into our church. It was an interesting time not soon to be forgotten. Please give my love to Brother and Sister Waller, your dear husband, and kiss the dear children for me. Have you heard from Brother Perkins lately? and also, Mr. J. Lee, is he coming back?

Yours in love,

NARCISSA WHITMAN.

Mrs. L.L. Brewer,
    Wascopum.
Favour of Mr. Hinman.

Letters

WAIILATPU, August 9th, 1845.

My Dear Sister:—Your sympathizing letter came in just the time to do me much good. I thank you for it, and for the information it contained concerning Francisco, and the feelings of the party with whom he traveled, about the orphan children with us. I read your letter to John; he seemed quite hurt about Mr. P.'s charge, and said that he (Mr. P.) asked him several times if he did not wish to go to the Willamette. I saw nothing to make me think that John wished to have his brother to go; but, on the contrary, he and all the sisters tried to keep him and appeared to feel very bad about his going. If it were otherwise, his actions deceive me very much.

You are right in saying that I "feel indifferent to what is said about me, so far as I am concerned individually." I endeavour in all things to act towards the children as if they were my own. My sincere, ardent and abiding wish is to train them up for God and eternity, and not for their transient existence in this life. I try to study my duty towards them in every respect, both carefully and prayerfully. We felt it our duty to have them baptized, as many as were willing to be, and accordingly we did so, the girls only consenting. I felt it a great privilege to do so still, and am greatly strengthened in spirit to labour for them.

I do not think them difficult children to manage, neither do I have occasion often to use the rod. The little one, as all other little children do, manifested a stubborn disposition at first, which required subduing; since she has appeared well—obeys promptly when spoken to. I have no reason to regret the course I have pursued with her, when I consider the effects upon her disposition, naturally very obstinate, as well as all the others. Doubtless this is what has occasioned the remarks, for it took place about the time Francisco went away. Louise, the next older, I have not been able to subdue so completely; but she is much better than when she first came. They were said to be very bad children when they were left; but there was a reason for that. Left without restraint in such a journey, it could not be expected otherwise. Putting them all in school immediately under such a good and faithful disciplinarian as Mr. Hinman, I was entirely relieved of the difficult and hard task of breaking them in to habits of obedience and order. I feel that I never can be too thankful for the mercies of the Lord in placing such a good young many in our family to do this work for us when my health was so inadequate to the work, and the doctor so entirely taken up with other duties with emigrants and Indians. He has also, accomplished the tedious task of starting them all in a, b, c, and ba, be, etc. They are so well advanced and have been trained to such good habits of study, that my labour is comparatively easy, and I am now taking new delight every day in teaching. All except Louise read and spell well. She is in words of three letters. Some, or all the older ones, are showing considerable mind and rather seriously inclined: Our Sabbath-school is always an interesting season with us—increasingly so. I am desirous to see them Christians. What I do I feel that I ought to do immediatley; and will you pray for me, my dear sister, that our instructions may not be lost upon them? I could write much more upon this subject, but have not time. I wish I could see you, then we could open our hearts freely to each other. Do come if you can and see us.

I do feel, as I have every reason to believe you do, that the receipt of our Mother's Magazine is an unspeakable favour. Situated as we are, away from other help, what a blessing to possess such a pleasing auxiliary in our labours as mother, I hope and pray that its introduction into this country will be the means of much good. Husband sent the one that came to Mrs. Perkins to Mrs. Willson. Perhaps Mrs. Waller would have preferred to have had it continued to her in the room of Mrs. Perkins. I do not know as Mrs. Willson wishes to become responsible for it; if not, and Mrs. W. would, it can be sent to her. Other numbers can be ordered if desired.

I received from the editor receipts for each subscriber. Yours I will enclose and forward at this time. If husband had opened my package, he would have been able to have distributed them to all. You will see that it is given for a little more than the doctor settled for, the bound volume being twenty-five cents more than the unbound ones. Mrs. McKinlay has all the back bound volumes sent to her order.

But I must close. If you can read this poorly written letter, I shall be glad. It would be no more than justice to your good sense to copy it, but inability from poor health and numerous cares, pleads to be excused. Please give my love to Brother and Sister Waller and your husband in which husband unites. Please accept our united thanks for your kindness to him in passing. He enjoyed his visit with you and in the Willamette very much.

Affectionately yours,
NARCISSA WHITMAN.

P.S. —John send an invitation to his brother, and a horse to have him come back. I hope it will have the effect to prevail on him to do so. I feel much for him and wish him to return, as all of us do, and pray the Lord to restore the wanderer to our arms again.

Letters

WAIILATPU, Nov. 28th, 1845.

My Dear Mrs. Brewer:—I seize a moment this morning to write you, although it is in the midst of bustle and Indian excitement. Mr. Rinearson will hand you this. He has been engaged by us in teaching an Indian school. He is very agreeable and good young man in every respect, except the one thing needful. He will be our living epistle to you concerning the state of things with us. It may be that we shall be obliged to leave here in the spring. The state of things looks now very much as though we should be required to.

We have long been anxious to hear from you. From Indian reports, we fear that you have been through a season of trial and distress the season past before unknown. It so, I hope the strength and grace of God has been your support and consolation through all your afflictions.

I feel greatly worn out, both physically and mentally, so that I scarcely feel strength enough of mind left to dictate any thing that will be worth reading. But I felt that I could not let this oppotunity pass without just saying to you that we often think and speak of you both, and Brother and Sister Waller, too; love and sympathize with you as fellow sharers in the same labour, trials, faith and patience, in the work of our Divine Master.

For the poor Indians' sake and the relief of future travelers to this country, I could wish to stay here longer if we could do it in peace. We fear, sometimes, as if our quietness was past this country, at least for a season. It may be that you are suffering under the same commotions that affect us, and perhaps more so. If so, you will understand me. Mr. Rinearson has a full view of the subjects agitated, takes a deep interest in our situation and prospects, as well as the interest of the Indians and country.

I received your letter by Mr. Spalding and was much refreshed by it, and I believe I have not written you since.

Please give my love to Brother and Sister Waller, and accept for yourself and husband our assurances of continued esteem and affection.

Your sister in Christ,

N. WHITMAN.

Mrs. L.L. Brewer,
    Wascopum.
Favour of Mr. Rinearson.

WAIILATPU, April 2nd, 1846.

My Dear Edward:—You can imagine better than I can describe how glad I was to receive your token of remembrance, together with the letters from yourself and Jane last September, as two of the emigrants called on us to deliver them. Your letters, Edward, were just the thing for me. I like such kind of letters as show me the spirit and make of the writer. I cannot see how it should be so difficult for you or the girls to write me, and should think you might write me five or six times a year instead of once in two or more years. I really believe if you were situated as I am you would never write at all. Think of me now while I am attempting to write—half a dozen children making a noise around me, and to put on the climax, the doctor must come in, and taking a paper sit down and read aloud or talk to Mr. Rogers, who is sitting in the room; then in comes an Indian woman or two to sell some dry berries, and I must stop to attend to them, until I am quite lost and scarcely know what I am thinking about, especially when I have nearly twenty letters to write, and but little time to accomplish it in; but enough of this.

I have just asked the doctor what I should say to you about your coming to Oregon. He says there is no want of inducement for you to come, and he intends to write you some of them at least; but the only qualification you need, he says, is a *wife*, and then you must bring Jane. I do not know what you will say to that. If there were any here to be had, I should prefer to have you come without; but as there is none, and to make the trip twice to get one would be dubious; for this reason, if you could find a good one, by all means get her and come on, and bring Jane with you. You cannot tell how anxious I am to see you. I have been looking for you more or less for several years past. You know now how disappointed I was that the doctor did not bring Jane with him. He wants to have her here as much as I do; but the reason he did not bring her was—(you will laugh when I tell you)—the Indians would say that he had got tired of me and taken another wife, as they do, or was wishing to have two wives. Don't be frightened by this, Jane, and stay away, but by all means come, both of you. We have work enough for all of you to do, and want your help very much. It is a pleasant, healthy country to live. When once here you will not wish to go away again. It is a bad job to get here, but make the best of that you can and come. I do wish Mr. Pope and his lady would come. Good men are needed here and he would do well for himself. Jane might have come with husband if he had known in season of some good family for her to come in, but it will be pleasanter for her to come with her brother.

The journey is a trying one to the faith and hopes of Christians. Should you come I hope you will look well to the exercises of your own heart and never neglect to watch and pray. Hold sweet communion with God every day. Make it a point not to neglect this duty and you will be assisted to make the journey without having to experience the bitter reflection after your arrival of dishonouring God and your profession by the way.

Dear brother, this is the most important subject to be looked at in making a journey to ths country. "See that ye fall not out by the way," was Joseph's advice to his brethren. And it would be well if it were written on every Christian's wagon, or to say the least, his heart, to be called to mind every day or every hour of the day as need be. You will be tried in every point and in many ways you never were before. You may be persecuted and reviled, "but if you suffer for Christ's sake, happy are ye;" but if for your own faults, then it will be trying. Much of this will be avoided if you have a select few who are devoted Christians, united in all points for each others, interest, especially in keeping the Sabbath and social worship, etc. If you come together and keep together all the way, it may be made very agreeable. This, perhaps, may be difficult to find a party sufficiently large to be safe. There are several gentlemen going back this spring that left their families last year and intend returning next year, I believe. I hope you will have an opportunity of seeing some of them, from whom you may learn more about the journey than I can write. I am not concerned but that you will get here well enough if you start with any suitable arrangements; but I am more anxious lest you should not at all times bring honour upon Christ, our dear Redeemer, who died to save us. The excitement is great and objects of faith are too apt to be lost sight of in objects of sense, and our duty of prayer and watchfulness neglected. When you have experienced what I have, and heard and seen what I have in others, you will believe me if you do not feel the importance now.

Hoping the Lord will bring you safely here and that we shall be permitted to see each other's faces in the flesh and enjoy His unspeakable favours together in glorifying Him while we live.

So prays your devoted sister,

NARCISSA.

P.S. — There were many very useful articles in the box you sent me for all of which I thank you. I was in hopes of finding one little article more that is needed more than most of any other because it cannot be obtained here; namely a pi-la-ain, as the Indians call it (louse trap). You will understand me, I suppose — the finest fine combs cannot be obtained here, for that reason I was in hopes of finding one in the box. I know you would have sent me some if you had known my need. At any rate, I was very proud to get what I did from you, because it came from you, dear brother.

WAIILATPU, April 2, 1846.

My Dear Jane: — The season for sending letters has nearly arrived, and I begin to feel as if I must be about writing to some of my friends or they will complain of my negligence or forgetfulness. I believe I have written very few letters since the doctor returned. My health has been so poor, and my family has increased so rapidly, that it has been impossible. You will be astonished to know that we have eleven children in our family, and not one of them our own by birth, but so it is. Seven orphans were brought to our door in October, 1844, whose parents both died on the way to this country. Destitute and friendless, there was no other alternative — we must take them in or they must perish. The youngest was an infant five months old — born on the way — nearly famished and but just alive; the eldest was 13 — two boys and five girls; the boys were the oldest. The eldest daughter was lying with a broken leg by the side of her parents as they were dying, one after the other. They were an afflicted and distressed family in the journey, and when the children arrived here they were in a miserable condition. You can better imagine than I can describe my feelings under those circumstances. Weak and feeble as I was, in an Indian country without the possibility of obtaining help, to have so many helpless children cast upon our arms at once, rolled a burden upon me insupportable. Nothing could reconcile me to it but the thought that it was the Lord that brought them here, and He would give me grace and strength so to discharge my duty to them as to be acceptable in His sight. The Lord at the same time sent us a very good young man, originally from New York, whom we employed to teach an English school. He was of great assistance to me in bringing the children into good habits and advancing them in reading, as well as in the government of them. He was not pious when he entered the family, but the influence of being once more in a Christian family, called to his mind the feeling and many prayers and tears of a pious mother and deceased father for him, and overwhelmed him. He went to a retired spot just below the house on the river side and wept bitterly and poured out his soul to God in prayer and consecrated himself to His service. He immediately engaged in religious duty and was my associate in instructing and labouring with the children in Sabbath school and otherwise. At the annual meeting of our mission he united with the mission church. He is now in the Willamette teaching in the Oregon Institute. This was the winter of 1844 and 1845.

I received no letters from you or Edward that fall and thought it surprising that in all that great company you could not have sent us a single letter. I think I wrote you in the spring by Overton's party; hope you have got it by this time. It seems to me the immigration might bring me letters from my friends every year. I have not had a letter from mother in a great while, and I most envy you your privilege and wonder why you did not send it to me, so that I might have the reading also; the last from father was when doctor returned. I have just been writing to Edward how much we wish to see you both here and hope you will three of you come; there is work enough for you to do. We could give you a school all the time—an English school—our children and the children of the other families of the mission and perhaps some others; also, and Indian school some part of the time.

Dearest Jane, you know not what special tokens of our dear Redeemer's love and mercy we have been receiving the last three months. Last Saturday, however, was a day of all days never to be forgotten by me, while I live. And can you think what it was, beloved sister? It was this: The triumphant death of a dear brother in Christ. I wish I could enter into particulars and lay out the whole scene before you so that you could see and feel it as I do and those who were witnesses of his glorious departure. The individual was Joseph L. Finley from Illinois, who came over with the last immigration for his health; his disease was consumption, and deep-seated when he left the states. He was advised to stop here for the winter because it would be so unfavourable for invalids in the lower country in the winter. You will wonder how I could have the care of him in my feeble state of health and large family. He kept about until about the middle of January and during that time boarded with a cousin that stopped for the winter; when he became confined to his room, I opened my bedroom to him, as there was no other on the premises suitable for a sick man, and a cousin, a young woman, came and took care of him until the families left for the Willamette, the first of March. Mr. Rogers, our school teacher, had the principal care of him, as also during the journey. He was without a well-grounded hope when he came here, and the Lord was pleased to bless our efforts for his salvation. He afterwards desired to unite with our church, and accordingly did Feb. 26th, in company with Mr. Rogers, who had formerly been a member of the Seceders. Being in my family, I was very much with him and read and prayed with him almost daily towards the close of his life. He grew in grace steadily and felt that he was over-privileged to die in such a quiet place, where he could have the society of those who cared for his soul. Dear sister—he was a stranger, moneyless and friendless, in one sense—no relative who felt the reponsiblity of caring for him. He was just such a one as the Saviour says, "Inasmuch as ye have done it unto the least of these, my brethren, ye have done it unto me."

Mr. Finley was nearly 32 years of age—was never married.

We felt, that is Brother Rogers and myself, that we were abundantly rewarded for all the care and labour we had bestowed upon him. It was such a glorious sight, especially to Brother Spalding and Brother Rogers, who had never seen the like before. Husband and myself saw much the same in Mrs. Satterlee, at Liberty, when we were coming to this country. Let us praise the Lord, dear sister, and live so that our death may be as triumphantly glorious.

            Affectionately your sister,
             NARCISSA WHITMAN.

Mr. Edward W. Prentiss,
  Quincy,
    Illinois.

WAIILATPU, April 9th, 1846.

My Dear Mother: — It is now ten years since I left the paternal roof of my home east of the Rocky mountains, and how much have I been thinking of the scenes that transpired at that time, and of the dear, dear friends, I have left behind. My father, my mother, venerable friends — shall I ever behold your faces again in the flesh? O, how I long to see you, yet I dare not indulge the thought lest I should be found to murmur. If it would give such joy and satisfaction to meet again in this world, to interchange thoughts and feelings, what will it be to meet above, when we shall be free from sin and sorrow, in the immediate presence of our Savior to adore and wonder together and praise God and the Lamb before the throne. My thoughts have been very much in heaven, on heavenly subjects for two or three months past, having been permitted to accompany a fellow travelor down to the gates of death and to see him pass the dark waters triumphantly and enter joyfully the New Jerusalem above. O, what a glorious sight, and I may say that reluctantly I turned away, mourning that I was not permitted to follow him in reality as with an eye of faith. The individual I refer to, was not a relative, or I could not have stood and looked on with such composure and quietness, he was a young man nearly thirty-two years of age; far gone in the consumption when he arrived here last fall, as one of the last immigration — Joseph S. Finley, from Illinois, and without friends and money, left here to die among strangers. His brother went on past to the Willamette, and he stopped here because it was more unfavorable for an invalid there in the winter time than here. We had assistance, however, in taking care of him until the last month of his life, when the sole care devolved on me and the children; my health very poor all the time. You can see, beloved parents, what my work was, when I tell you that when he came here, he was without a Saviour. This gave deep anxiety of mind and earnest prayers, until the Lord was pleased to bring him to himself, but the evidence was not always so clear as to feel very confident in his case, so that, during the whole time, I felt a tender anxious watchfulness for him, which led me to be constantly seeking an opportunity of nourishing and cherishing him as I would a little child. Blessed be the Lord, he did not suffer me to labor in vain, but from time to time gave me evidence to believe that the good which he had begun, was progressing. Along in February he manifested a desire to unite with the church. An opportunity was presented.

Mr. Spalding and family visited us the last of February, and on the 26th, he with Mr. Rogers, another young man that had been employed as teacher of our children, offered themselves and were received most joyfully into our little church here in the wilderness. He was unable to sit up, consequently we were gathered around his sick and dying bed, to commemorate with him for the first and last time the dying love of our blessed Redeemer before he left us to join the church triumphant above. From this time on his evidence of an acceptance grew brighter and stronger, yet it never exceeded a calm and steady trusting in the Saviour, sometimes doubting almost that such a sinner could be saved. I never could discover anything like ecstasy, joy, or rejoicing at any time in his state of mind. He never had received very much religious instruction in his youth, his mother having died when he was quite young.

Many, very many, precious seasons I have spent with him, reading, conversing, and praying with him, and I have been very much refreshed myself in doing it. Although I had more work and care on my hands than I could do, without him, in the care of my eleven children, yet I felt that it was work that the Lord put in my hands and He would and did give me strength to do it. He died on Saturday, 28th of March, few minutes past one. He was more than two hours dying. Mr. Spalding was providentially present at the time of his death. When I discovered a change had taken place in his breathing, I went to him and told him that I thought Jesus was about to take him away, and asked him if he did not rejoice? He said he did, if he knew what rejoicing was. Soon he said, "Lord, help me now," and then asked Mr. Spalding and myself if we thought he was smothering, meaning that he was distressed to get his breath; we told him we thought he was dying, and asked if he did not wish Mr. Spalding to pray? He said, "Yes," and we united in fervent prayer that the Lord would not forsake him now in this trying hour, and commended his departing spirit into the hands of his Saviour.

The family were called in. I asked him if he felt the Saviour present with him now? He said deliberately, "I think He is," Occasionally ejaculations like these would be heard from him as we stood watching around him, "Lord, help me now; Thy will be done." After a little he looked up and around and said, "Farewell to this world;" then, some moments after, "Father, Thy will be done." Afterwards he reached his hand to husband and I, with a look of gratitude and thankfulness for the kindness he had received from us. Soon after Mr. Spalding asked him if the Saviour was with him? After a moment he said, "I think so." Shortly after he ejaculated, "Jesus, save me." Mr. Rogers stood by him holding his hand. In a few minutes he looked at us with inexpressible sweetness depicted in his countenance, and said, "Sweet Jesus! sweet Jesus! sweet Jesus!" as if anxious that we should receive the evidence of his Saviour's presence with him and the token he had just received from Him. It was like a ray of glory bursting through him upon our minds. It completely melted us all. From this time on he lay breathing still more and more laborious, and he desired us to try and turn him to see if he could not find relief; but the change of position made it still more difficult, and he wished to lie back again as he was before, exclaiming, "Sweet Jesus! sweet Jesus!" as if the Saviour had again given him another taste of His sweetness, and assurance that the rest or ease was not for him in this world. After this the occasional uttering of these words, "Sweet Jesus!" led us to think that his communion was more with the inhabitants of the heavenly world than with us, although he was most perfectly conscious of everything that passed up to the last moment. A little after one o'clock he uttered "Sweet Jesus! sweet Redeemer!" and then "Farewell, farewell, farewell!" and, indistinctly, "I am going!" and thus expired, sweetly yielding up his spirit into the hands of his Redeemer.

This was new and unexpected to Mr. Spalding and Mr. Rogers, they having never seen the like before. As for me, I had been asking that the Lord might be glorified in his death, and thus we were left without a doubt that our brother, on whom we had bestowed so much anxious care, had gone to be forever with the Lord; feeling, too, that we had been more than amply rewarded for the labor bestowed upon him. He was always so grateful for the attention shown him, particularly for the instruction and religious help he received—said if he had ever in his life had such instruction, he would never have lived so far from the Saviour as he had done. He felt that I had been a mother to him, for he never received such attention before from any one, and he said it weeping. But it was all of the Lord to dispose my heart in kindness toward him when I am always so weak and burdened with cares. "I was a stranger, and ye took me in; sick, and ye ministered unto me"—these and similar passages all the way through were my support; and I pray God I may always be in a frame of mind to apply this scripture, "Be not forgetful to entertain strangers, for thereby some have entertained angels unawares."

Letters

April 10th, 1846.

My Dear Father: — I have received no letters from father, mother or any the sisters or brothers in Allegheny county since husband returned. I wonder why, sometimes, and feel a little like complaining. Nothing I receive from the United States gives me so much comfort as letters from my dear parents. I am sure those sisters and brothers might write oftener if they would think so. It may be that you are feeling as if I had not been as faithful lately as formerly; true, I have not, but it is not for the want of a disposition. The greatest reason is want of health, then the care of a large family of eleven children, aside from our complicated duties to the Indians. Think of our being the sole instructors spiritually and mentally of so many children, except during the winter, we hire a teacher; otherwise all these mental and physical instructions devolves upon us, and no responsibility is greater than the care of so many immortal souls to train up for God, and we must be the ministers, Sabbath school teachers, parents and all to our children. I am sometimes about ready to sink under the weight of responsibility resting upon me, and should, were it not that an Almighty hand sustains me. Bringing up a family of children in a heathen land, where every influence tends to degrade rather than elevate, requires no small measure of faith and patience, as well as great care and prayerful watchfulness. Under such circumstances, how comforting could I call in the superior wisdom and experience of my beloved parents to aid us in times of emergency. As a substitute for this, however, and for it I desire to be thankful, the influence of the impressions made upon my young mind by those beloved ones are now being called forth and acting upon other minds to a degree that astonishes me many times, and I may say that almost always those impressions are of such a nature, that if faithfully carried out, would greatly tend to promote the honor and glory of God. Children of such parents have much, very much, to praise God for, and if it should be found at last that any of them have not borne fruit to His Names' glory, how great will be their condemnation.

There has been considerable evidence of the movings of the Holy Spirit upon the minds of the children since the first of January, as well as upon some that wintered here. For ourselves, we feel that our own souls have been greatly revived, and I hope and pray that we may never again relapse into such a state of insensibility and worldly-mindedness as we many times have found ourselves in. This may seem strange to my dear father, that missionaries should ever become worldly-minded; and it should be strange, for it never ought to be; but situated as we are, with every thing of a temporal nature to see to, in supplying our own family with food and clothing, to try and save expenses to the churches, and also to relieve as much as possible a starving immigration as they pass, together with the temporal and spiritual calls of the Indians — what time is there left for the care of one's own heart? If there is any, it may all be required to restore our over-exhausted natures, which often groan under their burden and will sooner or later tumble and fall down. I would not plead any excuse; if there is fault any where it is in undertaking to accomplish too much of a worldly nature. When I say this, a thought comes in: Where shall we draw the line? As it is, we but just make the ends meet, and sometimes with the greatest difficulty, too. Much, very much, is left undone that might be done to make us more comfortable and save labor. Thus we struggle on from year to year.

How cheering under such circumstances, when the heart is weighed to the earth with a burden too heavy for mortal man to sustain, to have an aged Christian, a minister whose heart is always glowing with love to God and for the souls of men, call in, sit and converse awhile and draw the mind to heavenly things and sympathize and pray with us. To me it would seem to fill my soul with such ecstacy that I should want nothing more. It would be a heaven on earth. Perhaps, dear father will say that I can draw a richer draught from the fountain head, Jesus, oftener and easier than that. True, I may; but that requires effort and energy of mind more than I at all times possess, laboring as I am under the infirmity of a debilitated nervous system. But why should I be indulged in such a melancholy strain? Can it be that I wish to excuse myself for negligence on my part? This, I confess, is too often a fault; for if it were otherwise, I should not be mourning for my beloved Jesus as I often find myself now, notwithstanding His permitting me to speak of His faithfulness and of His tender care and love for me, unworthy as I am. He gives me now and then streams from which to gather refreshing sweetness. But the fountain head oftener pours its healing waters into my weary, sin-sick soul. Instead of complaining that I enjoy so little, rather let me rejoice than my mercies and spiritual comfort and enjoyments are so many and great.

If my dear father and mother were here, I think they would be very well contented, for we could give them a very comfortable home and enough to eat and do, and if the distance were not so great, I should hope they would come and finish their days with us. But it is a dreadful journey to perform to get here, and I ought not to ask such a sacrifice of them for my own comfort, merely; but if there could be a design worthy of the sacrifice and fatigue to such elderly people, I should ask it with all my heart, if there was a willing mind. I know father once used to think he should come to Oregon; but if I recollect right he wrote me that he had given it up. It is not so difficult to get here now as when I came, for families come in wagons all the way. The fatigue is great, however, and the dust from Fort Hall here is very afflicting; aside from that, with food enough and teams enough, no loading except necessary clothing, it would not be difficult.

Father, if you would send word from Fort Hall we could send and meet you and assist you on. But the greatest affliction would be to the pious soul—it is so continually vexed with the ungodly conversation and profanity of the wicked, and is so often brought into straitened circumstances with regard to his own duty in obeying the commands of God, such as keeping the Sabbath, etc., that he often is wounded to that degree that it requires many months, if not years, before he is restored to his wonted health again. To be in a country among a people of no law, even if they are from a civilized land, is the nearest like a hell on earth of anything I can imagine. I do not say that the journey cannot be performed and the Christian enjoy his peace of mind and continued communion with God all the way. But this I know, that the experience of all proves it to be exceedingly difficult, if not impossible. It is often said that every Christian gets so that he can swear before the journey is completed. One thing has been true of almost every party that have crossed the mountains; Christians are not warned of their danger before starting, and are consequently off their guard. If I had to ever again, I should try and pray more, both in secret, family and social meetings, but above all in secret, for if faithful there the soul is kept alive and in health, Generally speaking, every religious duty has been neglected and probably none more so than reading the Bible, consequently dearth prevails over the whole mind.

If I am not permitted to see my dear parents here, I hope I shall hear from them often. I love to have them both write; when they receive this, they will know how to pray for us, and will I trust most fervently.

From your most affectionate child,
NARCISSA.

Hon. Stephen Prentiss,
  Cuba, Allegheny Co.,
    New York.

CATHERINE SAGER PRINGLE, ELIZABETH SAGER HELM, and MATILDA SAGER DELANEY

WAIILATPU, April 13th, 1846.

My Dear Harriet:—I believe I have not written you since the Lord brought this orphan family under our care. How could I, for I have been so unwell and had this increase of care upon my mind, that I have written to no one in the States, as I recollect. I find the labor greater in doing for so many, especially in instructing them—where they come in all at once—than if they had come along by degrees and had received a start in their education, one before the other; whereas all their minds appear to be alike uninstructed, especially in the great truths of Christianity.

I would like to know how you and Clarissa get along in unfolding the minds of your little ones. I hope you both feel that the immortal part is of the greatest moment in all your strivings for them, and to educate the physical in such a way as to give the immortal part the utmost vigor and energy possible.

I used to think mother was the best hand to take care of babies I ever saw, but I believe, or we have the vanity to think, we have improved upon her plan. That you may see how we manage with our children, I will give you a specimen of our habits with them and we feel them important, too, especially that they may grow up healthy and strong. Take my baby, as an example: in October, 1844, she arrived here in the hands of an old filthy woman, sick, emaciated and but just alive. She was born some where on the Platte river in the first part of the journey, on the last day of May. Her mother died on the 25th of September. She was five months old when she was brought here—had suffered for the want of proper nourishment until she was nearly starved. The old woman did the best she could, but she was in distressed circumstances herself, and a wicked, disobedient family around her to see to.

Husband thought we could get along with all but the baby—he did not see how we could take that; but I felt that if I must take any, I wanted her as a charm to bind the rest to me. So we took her, a poor distressed little object, not larger than a babe three weeks old. Had she been taken past at this late season, death would have been her portion, and that in a few days. The first thing I did for her was to give her some milk and put her in the cradle. She drank a gill, she was so hungry, but soon cleared herself of it by vomiting and purging. I next had a pail of warm water and put her in it, gave her a thorough cleansing with soap and water, and put on some clean clothes;—put her in the cradle and she had a fine nap. This I followed every day, washing her thoroughly in tepid water, about the middle of the forenoon.

She soon began to mend, but I was obliged to reduce her milk with a little water, as her stomach was so weak she could not bear it in its full strength.

Now I suppose you think such a child would be very troublesome nights, but it was not so with her; we put her in the cradle and she slept until morning without waking us more than once, and that only for a few of the first nights. Her habits of eating and sleeping were as regular as clock-work. She had a little gill cup which we fed her in; she would take that full every meal, and when done would want no more for a long time. Thus I continued, giving her nothing else but milk, she only required the more until her measure became half a pint. In consequence of the derangement of her digestive powers, which did not recover their healthy tone, she had a day of sickness some time in Dec. when we gave her a little oil and calomel; this restored her completely, and since that time, and even before, she has nothing to do but to grow, and that as fast as possible; she is as large or larger than her next older sister Louisa was when she came here, then nearly three years old. She now lacks a month and a half of being two years old. She is strong, healthy, fleshy, heavy, runs any where she is permitted, talks everything nearly, is full of mischief if I am out of the room. She is energetic and active enough and has a disposition to have her own way, especially with the children, if she is not prevented.

She contended sharply for the mastery with her mother before she was a year old, but she, of course, had to submit. Since then she has been very obedient, but frequently tries the point to see if her parents are steadfast and uniform in their requirements or not. She will obey very well in sight, but loves to get out of sight for the purpose of doing as she pleases. She sings a little, but not nearly as much as Alice C. did when she was of her age. Thus much for my baby, Henrietta Naomi Sager. She had another name when she came here, but the children were anxious to call her after her parents. Her father's name was Henry and her mother's name was Naomi—we put them together.

What I call an improvement upon mother's plan is the daily bathing of children. I take a child as soon as it is born and put it in a washbowl of water and give it a thorough washing with soap. I do this the next day and the next, and so on every day as long as the washbowl will hold it; when it will not, then I get a tub or something larger, and continue to do it until the child is able to be carried to the river or to go itself. Every one of my girls go to the river all summer long for bathing every day before dinner, and they love it so well that they would as soon do without their dinner as without that. In the winter we bathe in a tub once a week at the least. This is our practice as well as the children. I do not know but these are your habits, but if they are not, I should like to have you try them just to see the benefit of them. I never gave Henrietta any food but milk until she was nearly a year-and-a-half old. She never wanted any thing else. I avoid as much as possible giving my children candies, sweetmeats, etc. such as many parents allow their children to indulge in almost all the while; neither do I permit them to eat cakes and pies very often.

It is well to study these things with regard to our children, for it saves many a doctor bill; and another thing with our children, we never give medicine if we can help it. If children complain of the headache, or are sick at the stomach, send them to bed without their supper or other meals; they are sure to get up very soon feeling as well as ever.

My husband says many times when a physician is called to see a patient he finds nothing ails him but eating too much. If he is told this he will be offended, so he is obliged to give him something, when all he needs is to do without a meal or two and to fast a day or two and drink water gruel.

Doubtless you will think this a strange letter, Harriet, but you must take it for what is worth and make the best of it.

We sleep out of doors in the summer a good deal—the boys all summer. This is a fine, healthy climate. I wish you were here to enjoy it with me, and pa and ma, too. We have as happy a family as the world affords. I do not wish to be in a better situation than this.

I never hear as much as I wish about Stephen's children. I should think Nancy Jane might write her aunt now—tell me something about them.

O, how I wish you were all here. I could find work enough for you all to do; and every winter we have a good school, so that our children are learning as fast as most children in the States.

Harriet, I do want you and that good husband of yours to come here and bring pa and ma. I know you will like it after you get here, if you do not like the journey. There are many of the last immigration that came without their families, that are now going back to bring them as quick as possible, and are only sorry they did not bring them last year. Bring as many girls as you can, but let every young man bring a wife, for he will want one after he gets here, if he never did before. Girls are in good demand for wives. I hope Edward and Jane will come. I have written to them to come. Judson wants to come, too. I hope he will, and many other Christians. Where is Jonas G.? Why does he not come? Poor man, I never can think of him without sorrow.

Love to all, and a kiss for all those little ones.

NARCISSA.

Letters

TSHIMAKAIN, April 22, 1846.

Miss Prentiss:—An apology is due in my attempting to write to you, being an entire stranger, although I feel almost as though I had been well acquainted with you for years, having become so much attached to Mrs. Whitman.

Some days before I left Dr. Whitman's for this place, Mrs. Whitman was speaking of having a great number of letters to write to the States, and in her pleasant way wished to know if I would not write some for her. To which I replied, I would rather engage her to write for me, as she could do it so much better; but said, finally, that I would write one to any of her friends, if she would do the same for me.

To this she agreed and gave me her name. I desired her to write to my mother, who is living near Monmouth, Warren county, Illinois, where I have been living for the last ten years before the spring of '45, at which time I left home with the desire of seeing the far West.

As I learned from Mrs. Whitman that you and your brother had some thought of coming to this country, you will doubtless feel more or less interested in some of the difficulties and trials that one has to encounter on the way. One of the greatest trials that a religious mind has to encounter on the way is the company one is often compelled to travel with. There is no place where one can better see all the varieties of civilized life than here. You can see from the highest to the lowest grade. You may see all these at home, it is true, but you can't see them all brought so closely together, and under so many vicissitudes of life as have to be passed through on the way—hunger and thirst and fatigue, cold and wet weather. Now you have bad roads and no grass for your cattle; now, perhaps, some one will tell you there is much danger from Indians. After traveling all day through dust that is almost insupportable, you will come into camp at 9 or 10 o'clock at night and feel almost as though you did not care whether scalped before morning or not. And to make the trouble greater the cattle have almost nothing to eat, and may be you have no water within a mile, and perhaps no wood. Under such circumstances who is there among the sons of men that would not be likely to feel somewhat peevish, so much so that almost anything would throw him off his balance, and be likely go to beyond the bounds of propriety. Sure I am that nothing but "much of the mind of Christ," will support one under such trials. You must not think that the whole journey is just such as I have described. By no means. I have given you about as dark a picture as is likely to be met with on the road. But I must confess that I endured more fatigue during the six months we were on the way than I had ever before undergone in the same length of time. No one need think that it is like traveling in the stage or on the steamboat; yet one is not often vexed with high prices, nor are they in danger of being robbed as they are on steamboat.

One is not likely to spend a great deal by the way, without he does it in gambling, which he may do here as well as any where if he wished, as it is almost always the case that some one was thoughtful enough to bring a deck of cards with him; and if they have none of them, they bet on the distance to some hill, or on the distance traveled during the day, or that my oxen can draw more than yours.

Another trial that one has often to meet on the way is disregard for the Sabbath. I suppose there was about as much contention arose on that subject in the company in which I came as any another. A good part of the company cared nothing about that, or any other religious question, and if it suited them they wished to travel on that day as well as any other. And even when they did stop on that day it was only to mend their wagons, or wash their clothes. I do not say that all did so, for there were some of the company that were devotedly pious. There were three ministers in the company, one a Seceder minister from about Burlington. The other two were Baptist ministers, one from Iowa, the other from Rock Island county, Ill., whose name was Fisher, and who was formerly of Quincy, and is doubtless well known there. He manifested more of the true spirit of Christ while on the road than any other man with whom I was acquainted. Sometimes one is compelled to travel on the Sabbath, even if the company were willing to stop, as it happens that pasture cannot be found in sufficient quantities, though this does not often occur, but it often made a plea for traveling on that day when there would be plenty if they wished to stop to hunt buffalo. The company in which I came, traveled, may be, half the Sabbaths on the way. We had preaching most of the days on which we stopped. But I am dwelling too long on this subject, perhaps.

I desire to say to you, if you have any influence with respect to this country, I hope you will use it in endeavoring to have it settled with pious Yankees. Although not one myself, yet, as western people say, "I have a mighty liking for them." I do hope that it may be another New England, and I would to God that the mothers of this country could only be from Yankee land. Perhaps I have said more than I ought, but such are the sentiments of my heart, and I have ventured to express them. Let me but have the choice of the mothers of any country, and I will feel well satisfied as to the destiny of that country, either as to its moral, literary or civil aspect. But the moral prospect of this country is not very encouraging at this time. The "man of sin" appears to be making considerable progress in the lower settlements. One thing that makes much in his favor is, he has the influence of the H.B. Company, though it is to be hoped that God will thwart his plans, and that He will "overturn, overturn till He come whose right it is to reign." "Till the stone cut out of the mountain shall fill up the whole earth." May God hasten it in His day, is my earnest desire and prayer.

It may be interesting to you to know any one with whom I have been formerly acquainted. Mr. Bacon used to be my preceptor in music, whom I suppose you have often seen. I would like much to be remembered to him, if he is living there.

I have, perhaps, said more now than you will think worth sending more than two thousand miles, but I must say in conclusion, that Dr. and Mrs. Whitman seem very near to me. It appeared almost like parting with my mother when I left there to come to this place (which you will find marked on the map of Oregon in the November number of the *Missionary Herald*.) I have spent many very pleasant hours in her company and hope to spend more ere life closes.

Should you ever receive this, a letter as long as you wish to write would be most acceptable. News from the States is always scarce at Tshimakain and Waiilatpu.

Miss Jane A. Prentiss,
   Quincy, Adams Co.
      Illinois, U.S.A.

Your true friend,
ANDREW ROGERS, JR.

Letters

WAIILATPU, May 15th, 1846.

Edward and Jane Prentiss, My Dear Brother and Sister:—It gave us much pleasure to receive your letter by the last emigration, but it would have given us more to have seen you both here. If I could have known more when I was home I would have tried to have had you both come out with me. It is now, however, still favourable for you to come. Narcissa wants Jane to come and I want Edward, but it is not for us that you should come but for yourselves and the Lord. Edward would do well to have a wife and then come, and Jane will be agreeable with or without a husband, as suits her best; but if she comes without one, I shall try to convince her of her duty to marry. This country needs those who are able and willing to found and support society, religion, and schools. There are the best inducements to young men to come and locate a mile square of first-rate land in a better climate than in any of the States, with the broad Pacific Ocean to open in prospect before them. A good title will be secured to all who located and reside on or occupy land or mile squares, according to the Oregon laws.

You must see how fine it is for a settler not only not to have to fed his stock as a general thing, but when he first comes, his poor stock can winter the first winter without the need of providing for them. We want a school teacher every winter, and shall like to employ you the first winter, at least, until you can look around. We had a good, pious teacher last winter and may have him the next. He adds instruction to music. I believe he wrote Jane on the spur of Mrs. Whitman's promising to write his mother in case he would write one of her friends. He is studying for the ministry with one of the ministers of our mission, Rev. Elkanah Walker.

It cannot be much for you to come the rest of the way now you are so near, and more since you have become weaned from favorite spots of your youth. If Father and Mother Prentiss should consent to come with you, I think they would be rejoiced in their old age. A light wagon with an ox team is the best for families, as all must keep company on the road. Let provisions so far as can be, be the only loading. Necessities for the journey are all you want, unless you have special reasons for bringing something particular. The intimations in your letter that you might come if we would write you, give us hope to look for you in the next year. In the meantime, get Brother Jackson and Kenny, etc., to come with you, as also Galusha and Father and Mother Pentiss.

It is a hurried letter I have to give you, but I hope it will be taken as a token of our love to you both, with desire to see you.

With our united love to you both,

I am your affectionate brother,
MARCUS WHITMAN.

Jane, you need not fear what my husband says. I am not anxious you should without you find a good husband and desire to. But come and see us at any rate. Mr. Rogers has written you and given you much interesting information about the journey, etc. Don't take it amiss that he has written you—he has only helped me to tell a part of my story. I should have written to his mother if I could, but I have had to write such a long letter to Mr.

Finley's father—the young man that died here—that I could not get the time. I wish you could see it. He lives in the same town that Mr. Roger's parents do, so if Edward ever travels there he can inquire for it if you please, and they are willing to show it. E. and Jane where are you now? Have you gone back to see mother again? I wish I could see her, too but you will not thank me for writing so. I am in a hurry and cannot do otherwise; so this or none. Goodbye; come and see us as soon as you can. Love to all inquiring friends.

Your sister,
NARCISSA.

Mr. Edward W. Prentiss,
    Quincy,
        Illinois.
Care of Mr. Pope.

Letters

WAIILATPU. July 17th, 1846.

My Dear Mrs. Brewer:—A long silence has prevailed of late between us as to letter writing, and it is perhaps my fault as much as any one. I find it increasingly difficult for me to command a sufficient relief from the cares of so numerous a family of children to write as many letters as I desire to. Another reason—I have been looking for a visit from you all summer long, and do not yet feel willing to give it up. We have heard you started once and came part way and was obliged to return on account of sickness. I regret this very much, for had you come at that time you would have met Mr. and Mrs. Eells here, who would have rejoiced very much to see you. Will you not make another effort when Mr. S. returns and accompany him. I should be so delighted to see you and yours once more, and also to become acquainted with Mr. and Mrs. Gary of whom I have heard much. This is a dry and thirsty land for Christian communion and fellowship. I do long for the society of some Christian sisters.

We have had a quiet time for a few weeks past, and a precious season of rest it has been to us. We seem to be renewing strength for the season of burthen and trial that generally falls upon us the other portions of the year. I have been trying to read a little, for I find my mind suffers without more food than I am able to give at some seasons, especially when we are thronged with company, and many and complicated duties are pressing upon our hands.

But seasons of rest and quiet are of but short duration both for you as well as us. The Indians tell us that more Americans are coming, so that we shall soon be thronged again. We are looking with some interest for an associate to be among them, and hope we shall not be disappointed.

The Indians are very quiet now and never more friendly. There has been some deaths among them of the most important Indians, the past winter and spring, and we are not without hope that some of them have gone to be with the Saviour. So far as the Indians are concerned our prospects of permanently remaining among them were never more favourable then the present. I feel distressed sometimes to think I am making so little personal effort for their benefit, when so much ought to be done, but perhaps I could not do more than I am through the family. It is a great pleasure to them to see so many children growing up in their midst. Perrin, the eldest, is able to read Nez Perces to them and when husband is gone, takes his place and holds meetings with them. This delights them very much. I have much to write you, but I am still waiting, hoping to see you. But I will give you a specimen of my eligible situation for writing. I have six girls sewing around me, or rather five—for one is reading, and the same time my baby is asking to go and bathe—she is two years the last of May, and her uneasiness and talk does not help me to many very profitable ideas. Now another comes with her work for me to fix. So it is from morning until evening; I must be with them or else they will be doing something they should not, or else not spending their time profitably. I could get along some easier if I could bring my mind to have them spend their time in play, but this I cannot. Now all the girls have gone to bathe and this will give me a few moments to close my letter in peace; they are very good girls and soon will be more help to me than they are now, although at present they do considerable work. Please give my love to all your missionary friends and believe me, as ever,

Sincerely yours,
N. WHITMAN.

Narcissa Whitman

WAIILATPU, Sept. 11th, 1846.

Mr. Harvey P. Prentiss, Mrs. Livonia L. Prentiss, My Dear Brother and Sister:—It is but a few days since I received that good family letter bearing the date of March, 1836, [1846?]. Since that time my mind has been much upon you for this reason: I hear you are removing to the South for the sake of a warmer climate. I had much rather you would come this way, and have been studying ever since to see if I could not induce you to come. There are many reasons why we wish you to come, but my time is so limited that I can give you but a few of them now. I shall write again this fall to some or all of you, if permitted. We wish you were here to assist us in our work; we have more than we can do and if you were here now we could give you both labor and support and would be glad to do it. I know you would like this mild and healthy climate better than the one where you have gone, at least we think so. Take the map, if you please, and just look at our situation on this Western coast. The Sandwich Islands and China are our next door neighbors. I see I cannot enlarge upon this subject. I was going to speak of the facilities for acquiring competency, if not wealth, in this country, but my time will not permit.

A little reflection will show you what I wish to say and I hope induce you to come. If you will only manage to get here, we are here to assist you all you need to get a start, if you should not wish to continue with us. Do not be anxious for your children; here is a good place for them to do well for themselves, both as to education and getting a living. We have a good English school here every winter and eventually intend to have an academy or college. Do come. I say this will all my heart. You will find the journey a trying one, but there is no difficulty in getting here. A good wagon with an ox team, and cows to change with, will in time bring you here, and then I wish you would bring Jane. I want her here very much as a teacher, and Edward, too. If you come they will come, I have no doubt, for last year they wrote us proposing to come if we wanted them. The Board had rather we would employ a farmer than appoint one and send to us. We expect the line will be settled with England soon, if it is not already, and that the United States will extend her jurisdiction over us; when that is done, we expect there will be a flood of emigrants rolling this way. For three years past there has been large companies of from 500 to 700 wagons each year to Oregon and California.

Brother Kinny says he would come to Oregon, if he had no wife. Please tell him he is in a much better situation for coming to Oregon as a settler than if he had none, for nothing makes bachelors feel so much like getting a wife as to come here and find none to be had. Many are often disposed to degrade themselves enough to take a native.

I see congress is talking about starting a mail across the mountains. When that is accomplished I shall hope to hear from home friends oftener and more regular. Mother thinks if she should come here she would be afraid of the Indians. It might be, yet I think she would soon get over it. They never were more quiet and peaceable than now, and appear to be getting more so. We feel that your going to Virginia will not be in the way of your coming, for we think you will be more likely to come here, for having come thus far. I hope you will write us and tell us all about it. As I know not where to direct this letter, I shall send it to father to have him forward it. I have written this in great haste, for the Indian post is waiting to take this, with many other letters, to Walla Walla, where the boats will leave to-morrow morning.

My health is quite good for me. All of the family are well; indeed, we have no sickness at all in the family scarcely, although the orphan family, before they came here, were quite subject to sickness.

Please give our united love to all our dear friends, and believe me

Affectionately your sister,
NARCISSA WHITMAN.

Hon. Stephen Prentiss,
  Cuba, Alleghany Co.,
    New York.

WAIILATPU, Oct. 19th, 1846.

Dear Sister:—I have been trying to write you some time, but find it difficult on account of bustle and necessary care, and even now it is not much better. By Mr. Littlejohn we wrote you and Brother Waller, inviting you to send your children to school; as you said nothing about it in your last, we think perhaps you did not receive the letter. Be that as it may, we would glad to have you send your child if you think she is not too young, and particularly Brother and Sister Waller, as they have expressed a wish to Brother Spalding when he was there. We have an excellent school, taught by Mr. Geiger, and when he leaves, Mr. Rogers will continue. We have been looking for Brother Waller to bring his children for some time, and hope he will yet do it.

I have much to say to you and would be glad to write much longer, but you must excuse me for the present as I have been washing today and am now coloring madder. I send this by some young men of the immigrants who are to leave today, and are the last, among whom there is one from Massachusetts; you will find him intelligent and learn, perhaps, news about your home. He is a member of the Congregational church and returns next spring for his father's family.

Affectionately yours,

N. W.

Please excuse so short a letter; I hope to do better soon. Because it is so difficult for husband and self to write, I persuaded Mr. R. to write to your husband. Adieu.

Mrs. L.L. Brewer,
    Wascopum.
Favour of Mr. Imbree.

Letters

WAIILATPU, OREGON TERRITORY
Nov. 3rd, 1846.

Mrs. Clarissa Prentiss, Honored and Beloved Mother: — It is with indescribably pleasure I received and perused those excellent lines, penned by that hand that has been so much of my life devoted to my comfort, and dictated by that heart that has so often beat with emotion for my good, too deep for utterance. It really seemed as if the very fountains of my heart were broken up and my whole soul was filled with emotions indescribable. O, my mother, my dear mother, and father! How I love to dwell upon these blessed sounds. Do I love these dear ones less, as I grow in years and as separation widens? Surely not. Yea, my heart clings to them with an undying grasp; and I bless God that we have the assurance that this union is not to end in this life, but will exist, yea, and increase, too, through an unending eternity.

It was but a few mornings ago that I was reading mother's letter to the children, and husband was sitting by. Afterwards I handed it to him, and looking at it, he said (the tears filling his eyes), "Mother writes well for one that writes so seldom;" said he "she writes better than any of her daughters." And so I think, too. I hope mother will be encouraged, when she finds her letters so acceptable and doing so much good, to write oftener, at least once a year, if not twice.

I have not yet received father's promised letter; it may be it failed to be in time for the opportunity of a transport across the mountains. Mother's, dated march 26th, 1846, was sent from Boston to Westport and reached me in about five months after it was mailed. This brings me very near home. Indeed, it is the first I have received since those sent by husband. It would be well to send everything direct to Westport, to the care of Boone & Hamilton, and in the summer and fall to Boston, and they will be most sure to reach us. there is a prospect of a monthly mail to be established soon from St. Louis to Oregon — so we judge from movements in Congress; when that is accomplished a new era will commence in our western world and a happy one, too, to us, if our friends will write us often.

Since writing the above we have been assembled for our Tuesday evening concert, established more than seven years ago by the two Missions, to pray for the cause of Christ in Oregon. We have evidence to believe that this concert of prayer has been greatly blessed to us, and this infant country. We feel that God has heard prayer, for many precious souls give evidence of having passed from death to life, some among the Indians and many more among our own countrymen. The standard of piety and morals in the Willamette is good for so new a country. Many pious people and professing Christians have found their way here, and many ministers of different denominations; yet there is a want of able ones. Mother asks what sort of people come to this country. There are very many intelligent and excellent people, and also many others who are lawless and ignorant. It would be well for the Home Missionary Society, in her benevolence, to look this way, for this country is destined to exert an influence that will be felt the world over. The Papists are at work with all their might to get the control of the country, and have been ever since we have been here, nearly. We hope they will not succeed. Protestants need to be up and doing in order to save this the only spot of the whole western coast of North America from their iron grasp. God grant we may. For this purpose we need more active Christians, teachers, and ministers to come to this country from the East, and my dear father will, I hope, use all his powers in persuading such to come. I cannot bear the thought that my brothers and their families should go to Virginia to settle. Why will they not come here? It is both warm and healthy. Here they would be exerting an influence that would be felt for good, and here they would make a comfortable living without so much hard labor. I have written to Brother H. urging him to come here. We want him to help us very much. I hope he will get the letter. Brothers H. and C. I think would like the country, if once here. His being a married man is no objection, but rather a good reason why he should come, for with his family here, he would be worth something to the country. O, how I have desired, and still desire, to have Jane and Edward come as teachers. The Lord grant that they may, and that soon, too. I could wish that the Prattsburg colony might be turned this way, instead of going to Virginia. They are much needed here, and in the end would be much better satisfied, we have no doubt. I would ask father to come, but mother says she would be afraid of the Indians. I have a widow lady in my family who came over this fall that is fifty-seven years old. She is an excellent woman, so kind and motherly. She makes me think of my own dear mother every day, and what it would be to have her here.

Mother wishes me to write about my children. I wrote last spring very fully about them all, and if I had room I might again say much more.

We have a good school taught by Mr. Geiger, son of Deacon Geiger, formerly of Angelica. He is an excellent young man and superior teacher—children all happy and learning fast. Brother Spalding's two eldest board here and go to school, and we are expecting three from Brother Walker's. We set the table for more than twenty every day three times, and it is a pleasing sight. Mr. G. serves the children. Mr. Rogers, the young man that taught last winter, is still with us studying the ministry. He is a good young man and his Christian society affords me much comfort. He is an excellent singer and has taught the children to sing admirably. When they came here not one of them could make even a noise towards singing; now they constitute quite a heavy choir. None of them could read except the three eldest very poorly; now they are quite good scholars and are making good progress.

Six families of immigrants winter with us, and some young men. Three of them are at the saw-mill twenty miles from here. The children of the three families that remain here go to school; when they arrived here, several were quite sick; one woman remains so still, having been afflicted with the inflammation of the lungs.

Last Saturday, Marcus was called to attend a woman at the mill at the birth of a son. We find it quite agreeable to have neighbors to winter with us, but this may be the last, as a good southern route is now open into the head waters of the Willamette, and all will wish, probably to go that way, as it will be much nearer and better.

I must tell mother of a luxury we enjoy very much, and one that has a tendency to make us very cheerful and happy. For me it has done much toward restoring my health to be so much better than it has been for several years. It is daily cold bathing. Our students and teachers go out every morning, winter and summer and jump into the river. Husband does it frequently, but not so regular, on account of his business. The children all delight in it. Both would be glad to, all winter, if we had conveniences. In the summer I go with them to the river, and now when it is warm enough, and when it is cold we take the tub in the house. I know father would like to live here on that account, and he would enjoy it so much, too, as some of our folks do. The climate is so mild and exhilarating. Husband is doing all he can to induce friends to come. He has written to Father Hotchkiss inviting him, and requested him to copy and send the letter to father, and many others.

I see I must soon stop for want of room. The children all send their love to their grandparents, and aunts and uncles; some of them will be able to write soon to some of you.

I have spoken of many things and subjects, but one still remains about which I should like to write, and that is the other half of self. I wish mother was more acquainted with him; he is all benevolence, has amazing energy of thought and action, nothing is too hard or impossible for him to do, that can be done. I often think he cannot last always; indeed, his strength is not what it used to be, although his health is quite good.

We try to do good to our neighbors that winter with us. I hold a prayer meeting with the females on Wednesday, which is precious to us. Thursday evening is the children's meeting, which is precious to us. Thursday evening is the children's meeting, which I superintend, also. Saturday evening, Mr. Rogers has a Bible class, in which the children bring forth the text of Scripture they have selected on a given subject. Last week it was "Prayer"; the present week it is the "Sabbath." Besides this, the children commit a verse a day which is got in the morning as their first lesson to be recited in Sabbath school.

By this mother will see that both my hands and heart are usefully employed, not so much for the Indians directly, as my own family. When my health failed, I was obliged to withhold my efforts for the natives, but the Lord has since filled my hands with other labors, and I have no reason to complain; when I am not overburdened with work and care, I am happy and cheerful, but as I many times am straitened with more than I can do and no one to assist but my chindren, I become fretful and impatient. I am most happily provided for now. I have a good girl in the kitchen, and the old lady, which relieves me a great deal; and Mr. Geiger is such a good governor and teacher, that the children give me little, if any, trouble as to that part. Of course I take the place of moderator out of school. We pay the girl one dollar and a half a week; the widow is a boarder, but does a great deal in keeping things straight in the kitchen; do not charge her for her board.

If this goes from the Islands to Panama and across the Isthmus, mother will receive it in a short time; if otherwise, it may be some time before it will reach home, if it ever does. I would be glad to speak of the Indians, but one sheet is too small to contain all. I would be glad to say to my dear parents, the Indians are kind and quiet and very much attached to us, none the less so for having so many children about us. Many that were on the stage when we came here, are dead and new ones have taken their places. And as husband has just written to our Board, he says he never has felt more contented and that he was usefully employed than for the last year and the present. May the Lord incline the hearts of my dear parents and friends to pray especially for us this winter that He would send His Spirit urging us that new sould may be born into His Kingdom.

We send much love to all our relatives and friends.

Ever your dutiful and affectionate daughter,

NARCISSA.

Mrs. Clarissa Prentiss,
   Cuba, Allegheny Co.,
      New York, U.S.A.

Letters

WAIILATPU, Nov. 5th, 1846.

Rev. L. P. Judson, My Dear Brother:—I have a last moment to spare in writing, and I have resolved to write you, inasmuch as you have given me the hint by the note you appended to a family letter from Mrs. Whitman's friends. I am going to write plainly to you, for we love you and do not like to see your influence and usefulness abridged. I have known you long and well—better perhaps than you me. I esteem you for your warm affections and ardent temperament, but although these are aminable qualities, they are like the health of an infant, of so high and excitable a nature that it is but a step between them and derangement of disease. Mental disease is not suspected by the person who is the subject of it. But do not be surprised at what I am intimating. There are but few who are possessed of perfectly balanced minds. I have felt and acted with you on points to which the public mind was not awake, nor ready for action. It is well to be awake on all important points of duty and truth, but it can do no good to be ultra on any of these points. Why part friends for an opinion only, and that, too, when nothing is to be gained for truth or principle, and much lost of confidence, love, usefulness, enjoyment and interest.

Why trouble those you cannot convince with any peculiarity of your own sentiment, especially if it is likely to debar you from the opportunity of usefulness to them. By one part of your own confession let me confute your ultra perfectionism; that is, you complain of not being perfect and pray for more sanctification." If you could arrive at the point where you felt you were perfect, of course you would no longer pray for sanctification, and what would be your prayer after that? Let the thought awe you, for such cannot be the prayer of mortal in the flesh. Prayer becomes us, and we shall not be fitted in this life to join in the song of praise triumphant, of Moses and the Lamb. And now for Millerism.

I was in Boston when the famous time came for the end of the world, but I did not conclude that as the time was so short I would not concern myself to return to my family. But I did conclude that inasmuch as you had adopted such sentiments, you were not prepared for any work calling for time in its execution, and thinking the work of time so short with you that it would be in vain to call forth any principle to your mind that would involve length of time for its execution, I was contented to pass you in silence. For to my mind all my work and plans involved time and distance, and required confidence in the stability of God's government and purpose to give the heathen to His son for an inheritance, and among them those uttermost parts of the earth for His possession.

I had adopted Oregon as my country, as well as the Indians for my field of labour, so that I must superintend the immigration of that year, which was to lay the foundation for the speedy settlement of the country if prosperously conducted and safely carried through; but if it failed and became disatrous, the reflex influence would be to discourage for a long time any further attempt to settle the country across the mountains, which would be to see it abandoned altogether. Now, mark the difference between the sentiments of you and me. Since that time you have allowed yourself to be laid aside from the ministry, and have parted with tried friends for an opinion only, and that opinion has done you nor no one else any good. Within the same time, I have returned to my field of labour, and in my return brought a large immigration of about one thousand individuals safely through the long and the last part of it an untried route to the western shores of the continent. Now that they were once safely conducted through, three successive immigrations have followed after them, and two routes for wagons are now open into the Willamette valley.

Mark, had I been of your mind I should have slept, and now the Jesuit Papists would have been in quiet possession of this the only spot in the western horizon of America not before their own. They were fast fixing themselves here, and had we missionaries had no American population to come in to hold on and give stability, it would have been but a small work for them and the friends of English interests, which they had also fully avowed, to have routed us, and then the country might have slept in thier hands forever.

Time is not so short yet but it is quite important that such a country as Oregon should not on one hand fall into the exclusive hands of the Jesuits, not on the other under the English government. In all the business of this world we require time. And now let us redeem it, and then we shall be ready, and our Lord will not come upon us unawares. Come, then, to Oregon, resume your former motto, which seemed to be onward and upward—that is in principle, action, duty and attainments, and in holiness. Dismiss all ultraism, and then you will be co-operative and happy in the society of acting and active Christians. I say again, come to Oregon; but do not bring principles of discord with you.

This is a country requiring devoted, pious labourers in the service of our Lord. There are many and great advantages offered to those who come at once. A mile square, or 640 acres of land such as you may select and that of the best of land, and in a near proximity to a vast ocean and in a mild climate where stock feed out all winter, is not a small born. Nor should men of piety and principle leave it all to be taken by worldlings and worldly men.

A man of your stamp can do much by coming to this country, if you adopt correct principles and action. Should you come, the best way is to take a raft at Olean, if you are near Cuba at the time of starting. You will need to bring bedding with you for the journey, so that you can come on a raft, and also take a deck passage on the steamboat if you wish to be saving money. A piece of cloth painted suitable to spread under a bed will be most useful. Do not bring feathers, but let your bed be made of blankets, quilts, etc. If you want any goods after you get into the country, be sure and have them come around by water, if you do not like to trust the shippers in the country. A train of oxen will be the best with a light wagon; no loading except provisions. Good sheep are excellent stock to drive, and travel well. Some sheep we imported from the Sandwich Islands in 1838, have increased one hundred and twenty-five per cent in eight years. think of what a few good men could do to come together into the country. On the way they could make a party of their own and so rest on the Sabbath. With 640 acres of land as bounty, they could, by mutual consent, set apart a portion for the maintenance of the gospel and for schools and learning in such form as they felt disposed.

A large country to the south as far as the California line is now open by the new wagon route made this fall.

You have a good faculty to be a pioneer and lead out a colony; that is to start people to come. But when once on the way do not over-persuade, but remember that the best of men and women when fatigued and anxious by the way will be very jealous of all their rights and privileges and must be left to take their own way if possible. Restraint will not be borne under such circumstances.

As I do not know where to send to reach you, I will direct this to the care of Father Prentiss, who will forward it to you, after reading it himself.

The Indians are doing very well we think in their way and their habits of civilization. A good attention is paid to religious instruction. Morning and evening worship is quite general in their lodges, and a blessing is strictly regarded as being a duty to be asked upon taking food.

I do not think you can be ignorant of the advantages of this country, nor of its disadvantages. I wrote a letter to Father Hotchkiss, which I hope was copied and sent to Father Prentiss, which you may have seen. That applies to this section and climate. The country best suited for settlement are the Willamette valley and the coast west. Then the valley of the Umpqua on the south, and still south the Klamath which takes you south to the California line.

North of the Columbia, you know, is in dispute between the British and the States; you may early learn the result.

The greatest objection to the country west of the Cascade range is the rains in winter. But that is more than overbalanced by the exemption from the care and labour of feeding stock. It is not that so much rain falls, but that it rains a great many days from November to April or May. People that are settled do not find it so rainy as to be much of an objection. It is a climate much like England in that respect.

I hope you will excuse the freedom with which I have written. If we shall see each other, we can better bring our thoughts to harmonize.

Narcissa's health is on the gain, and is now pretty good. She joins me in love to yourself and wife, hoping to see you both in due time.

In the best of bonds,

Yours truly.

MARCUS WHITMAN.

Dear Brother Judson: — Husband has written you a long letter, for which I am glad, for he can write so much better than I can. I do hope you will accept of his invitation and come to Oregon. We want to see you very much, and there is much good to be done for this country in the cause of Christ. Your heart is here, I believe, and ever has been, and you are just the one to come. Wife and children need be no hindrance, but will be a great comfort — true it is some.

We feel a deep interest in you and love you still, and ever shall, not only for your own worth, but for her sake who was so dear to both you and us. It is a cause of great gratitude that, although the Lord has broken your heart, he has, as it were, bound it up again, and given you still to enjoy the endearing relation of wife, and what is not a small consideration, that of father to a beloved son. Bless the Lord for these great mercies, my brother, for we never know the full strength of them until they are severed. Should you be called to lay that little son in the grave you would then know the depths of a father's love

Please remember me affectionately to your dear wife, and say to her that I should be most happy to receive a letter from her. I would have written you both by this opportunity upon a separate sheet, but for the want of time.

My family is large and I have much to see to in the care of so many children. Although they are not mine by birth, yet I am interested in them and am much better pleased than if I had not the opportunity of acting the part of a mother. It is a satisfaction to feel that we are doing good and saving many individuals from being worse than useless in this world and lost in the world to come.

Henrietta, my baby, is a sweet, interesting child, and loves me as my own Alice used to, and I love her dearly; but that tender anxiety, so peculiar to mothers for their own offspring, is not for me to feel toward her, because it is impossible. She is now two years and five months old, and attends school and is very happy.

For some reason I feel assured that you will come to Oregon, and that I shall live to see you and converse with you face to face here in our cheerful, happy home. Till then adieu, my dear brother and sister, and may the Lord bless you and make you perfect unto every work through Him that loved us and gave himself for us.

As ever, your affectionate sister,

NARCISSA WHITMAN.

Rev. Lyman P. Judson, or
Hon. Stephen Prentiss,
    Cuba,
        Allegheny County,
            New York.

Letters

WAIILATPU, OREGON TERRITORY, UNITED STATES,
April 15, 1847.

My Dear Jane:—I received your letter of March 27th, 1846, a week ago yesterday, and for a whole day I could think of nothing else but you and weep. Not a letter that I have ever received from home has ever given me such intense feelings as this last of yours. I am glad you wrote me so much about yourself. If you had said a great deal more I would have been much better satisfied. True, we are strangers to each other as it regards our situation and circumstances; but dear and beloved as ever. Scarcely a week or day passes without some incident or other bringing you to mind, and we often converse about you. Oh! how we wish you were here now, this very moment. It seems to me as if you would be happier than ever in your life before. Perhaps it is because I feel that I should be so, which makes me think that you would be; at any rate, I have every reason to feel that you would be far more so than where you now are. There are many happy little beings that would delight to call you Aunt Jane, and some larger ones, too. Why did you not come with Mr. and Mrs. Thornton? Had you not the means? Oh! if you could only get here in some safe way, we would be willing to pay most any price for bringing you. You say, "you shall have to see our dear mother first." I do not blame you, I would see her if I could. But seeing you cannot go home, you had better come here than stay there and perhaps after a while we may go together and see our beloved parents. Even now while I am writing I feel that perhaps my dear Jane and Edward are starting, or are on thier way here. Oh! if I might indulge this feeling. I do, notwithstanding the improbabilities, and that, too, perhaps, to be disappointed. There is work enough here for you, and E., too, and just such work as you delight in, and we have not the afflicting trials of which you speak, opposition from those who ought to support and sustain us. True, we have our trials, but they can be born without so sorely afflicting us. If we could only know when you would come, we would send horses to meet you at Fort Hall. As it is, I feel so confident that you may be on your way now that I intend writing this spring to a friend of ours, Mr. McDonald of Fort Hall, and request him to find you and assist you down, if you are not so well provided as not to need his assistance. This encouragement we take from dear Edward's letter writeen in '45, and we wrote you last spring and particularly insisted on your coming immediately. Those letters I think you must have received, as they were put in the hands of Mr. Palmer, who designed to reach the States as soon as possible; and he gave me some encouragement to believe that he would call on you and deliver the letters with his own hands. He said he should return this spring with his family, and if I had known as much of your circumstances as I now do, we could have said more to Mr. P. about you, and even engaged him to bring you, and we would have satisfied him for it.

The Lord bless you, my dear sister, and reward you an hundred-fold even in this life for all the trials and afflictions. He calls you to meet with, in your efforts to promote His glorious cause, and blessed be His name that He gives you grace to withstand temptation, and a time-serving spirit.

My dear husband is gone to Vancouver and has been absent for several weeks. But I am now looking for him every moment. Indeed, dear Jane, you know not how much of the time he is away, necessarily, from home. That is one very good reason why I want you here. True, I am not without my comforts, even when he is away. The Lord has sent us a dear good brother who has now been with us more than a year, in whose society I find much enjoyment and satisfaction. He is the same who wrote you last spring, and you may judge from his letter something of what he is. We talk, sing, labour, and study together; indeed, he is the best associate I ever had, Marcus excepted, and better than I ever expect to get again, unless you and Edward come and live with me. He has always seemed to me very much like Brother Stephen, and I have often fancied myself enjoying his society again. I can assure you it is no small comfort to have some one to sing with who knows how to sing, for it is true, Jane, I love to sing just as well as ever. From what I have heard of Edward, it would be pleasant to hear him again; as for you, *kala tilapsa kunku* (I am longing for you continually to sing with), and it may be, put us all together, with the violin which Mr. Rogers plays, we should make music such as would cause the Indians to stare.

May 18th — *My Dear Jane:* — The time has nearly arrived for sending this. I have just been writing Mr. McDonald at Fort Hall requesting him to find you out and assist you down. Don't go the southern route as Mrs. Thornton did and nearly lost her life by it. They lost everything they had and suffered untold hardships. If I had time I could tell you more about it. I am just now preparing to go to Tshimakain station with Messrs. Eells and Walker to attend a meeting of mission. It is 180 miles north of us. I have not made a journey on horseback for six of seven years, and you will doubtless be pleased to hear that my health is so much improved as to be able to undertake a journey again. I am going to start in the care of Mr. Rogers, expecting to overtake Mr. Eells, who has just been here on a visit and gone to Walla Walla for some goods. Husband can go much quicker than I like to ride, and as he is obliged to settle with and see to the starting of the immigrants that wintered here, he does not leave home until several days after I do, and then goes by way of Mr. Spalding's, to notify him and see to some business there. So you see my dear Marcus is almost always on the move. A head and heart more full of benevolent plans, and hands more ready in the execution of them for the good of the poor Indian and the white population of the country, you have probably never seen. I would write you several pages, but if this should meet you on the way, and you are soon to be here as we most earnestly desire, I had much rather talk with you than write; but if otherwise — if this still finds you in Quincy — then be sure and come next year. Do not wait to go and see mother first; come and see me and then let us go together, or perhaps she may come and see us. If you are destitute of the means, then get some one to bring you and we will pay them in provisions or any thing else that we have to spare when they arrive. If you had a good horse and a good side-saddle, it would be better for you than to come without. I shall not be able to write to father, mother, or any of the family now, but if there is time after we return I may do it then. Husband is equally pressed and cannot write to any one more than the Board. He would like to write to Mr. Foote, but cannot now. We should have been happy to have had Mr. and Mrs. Thornton to winter with us, but they did not come this way. How many will go the southern route this year I cannot tell, but I could wish my friends would not.

I should like to say much about the Indians, but cannot. Our prospects for usefulness among them never have been more encouraging than at present. The field is white for the harvest and labourers are needed to enter in and reap. The Lord has inclined the heart of Brothers Rogers to devote himself to the work, and he is now engaged in studying the language. We have just received a letter from the Dalles, a station of the Methodist mission, wishing this mission to take that station as they judged best to abandon it. To this mission it is a very important station, and the brethren will probably think it best to occupy it; but we shall need more help still, and God grant to send labourers into His harvest.

All unite in sending much love to you both, praying and hoping that we may be permitted to see you both here soon, dear sister and brother.
Affectionately yours,

NARCISSA WHITMAN.

Miss Jane A. Prentiss,
    Quincy,
        Illinois.

Narcissa Whitman

WAIILATPU, OREGON TERRITORY,
July 4th, 1847.

My Dear Mother:—It was not convenient for me to write to any of my friends in the States, the past spring by the returning of immigrants except sister Jane. To her I wrote briefly, in answer to the one received in March by the hand of Mr. and Mrs. Thornton, who came from Quincy, Illinois. It was nearly a year in reaching me in consequence of Mr. and Mrs. Thornton taking the southern route with the majority of the immigrants. What would dear mother and father think if they knew how anxiously and eagerly I am expecting Jane and Edward to come with the immigrants this season. It is, indeed so. We are looking for them with deep solicitude, and hope and pray that we may not be disappointed. From what she wrote me last spring, I think she would have come with Mrs. Thornton, except for her mother; she desired very much to see her first. It was the same with her when Marcus was there. She could not come with him without seeing mother first. Although I think she might have been prevailed upon at that time to have come with him, if he could have seen a way to have brought her, when he was in Quincy. He learned afterwards that she might have come very safely and comfortably with one of the families that were coming at that time. I was greatly disappointed and felt almost inclined to reproach my husband for not making more effort to bring her. But it was all right; he did the best he could under existing circumstances. Since that time I have rather been waiting in hopes Edward would complete his course of study and be appointed by the Board to come and bring her with him.

From their letters it appears he has not been making that progress desirable, and in his last he intimated that he desired to come to this country and wished to know of us if we would encourage it. Accordingly, last spring a year, we wrote to them both and set before them every possible inducement to have them come immediately. Consequently we are looking for them and shall be not a little disappointed if they should not come. Perhaps my beloved parents would wish to know some of the reasons why, or the object for which we wish to have them here. I need not speak of the comfort and enjoyment their society would afford us here in this far-distant land. That is self-evident. In a temporal view, we feel that they would be better situated here than where they now are. As it regards their usefulness, perhaps no place could be found where they could do more for the advancement of the precious cause of our dear Redeemer, and with better success, than here, whether it be as missionaries to the Indians or as Christian teachers among the white population of this country. Good help of every kind is needed here in our missionary work, and if they were now here we could fill thier hands (or the Lord could) and their hearts, too, with just as much missionary work as they could well do. If E. still desires to finish his preparation for the Gospel ministry, we would certainly do all in our power to facilitate him, and at the same time he could render himself useful in teaching a part of the time and be of great service to us. We have now in our family a young man of real worth (and he has been with us almost two years), who came to this country principally for the benefit of his health, thinking to return again after a season, but finding it improving he has for more than a year past been pursuing a course of reading and study with a view to the ministry. He had commenced studying before leaving home, but had been obliged to desist on account of his health. Since living with us, he has had his mind much drawn towards the subject of devoting his life for the benefit of the heathen, and last spring came to the determination of doing so; consequently, he is now pursuing the study of Nez Perces language in connection with his other studies. Thus the Lord has had compassion on us and inclined the heart of one dear youth to enter this field of missionary labour.

We have often asked for more associates of the Board, and they have met our solicitations with encouragement and many promises, and at one time had an individual appointed for this station; but he failed to meet his engagements and went over to the Presbyterian Board and was sent by them to some other part of the world. At present we have no encouragement that any will be sent very soon. There seems to be a great destitution of laborers at the present time, or of those who are qualified and willing to go forth to the missionary work. This mission is needing another missionary very much to occupy a new station just offered us by the superintendent of the Methodist Mission. It is the Waskopum station, situated at the Dalles, where I spent the winter while my husband was absent to the States. It is an interesting and very important station, particularly so with reference to its locality to this mission, as well as to the cause of civilization and Christianity in the country at large. Our mission have appointed Mr. Walker, of the Tshimakain station, to occupy it for the present, until some other one can be obtained.

Tuesday, July 15th — While engaged in writing the above, I was interrupted by the arrival of Mr. Hinman from the Willamette. He is the young man that taught our school the winter of 1844, of whom I wrote as becoming a Christian and uniting with our church. He has come up to try to obtain the use of the mission press for the purpose of printing another paper in the Willamette. He has now gone on to see the other members of the mission, and will probably visit both stations before he returns. He has given us much intelligence concerning the lower country. Five ships are now in the river from different parts of the world.

Christians of all denominations are trying to do something for the upbuilding of Christ's kingdom in the land; but the enemies of the cross of Christ are doing much faster.

If I had time I might write much concerning the lower country that would be of interest, but for the present I desire to speak of our own prospects as a mission, which we feel were never brighter than at the present moment. Shortly after closing my letter to Sister Jane, I took a journey to Tshimakain to attend a general meeting of our mission. It is now six years this month since I made the same journey. Since that time I have been obliged to avoid journeying on horseback, on account of my health until the present season. I am happy to inform you that my health has so much improved that I endured the journey well, even much better than for three years previous to relinquishing the saddle altogether. For this I desire to be thankful. I was absent from home a little more than three weeks. Our meeting was an interesting one. Never probably since our existence at a mission has a meeting been characterized by so great a manifestation of the influence of the spirit of God upon each member, as at that time. All seemed to feel that we had come to an important crisis and that God alone could and must direct us. Our Board had written and advised to abandon the Tshimakain station in consequence of the discouragements under with our brethren of that station were laboring. Mr. Eells as advised to remove to this station, and Mr. Walker to go to Kamish, the station Mr. Smith formerly occupied. This advice, however, was accompanied with discretionary power. Soon after the arrival of Mr. Green's letters, came the offer of the station at the Dalles. This all acknowledged to be an important acquisition; but who of our limited number should occupy it? After much deliberation and consultation, it was finally determined not to abandon altogether the station at Tshimakain, but that during the winter Mr. Eells with his family remove to this station to act as a minister in the English language for the benefit of our own families and those who may winter with us, and that during the summer his time be spent at Tshimakain, and in internerating among the Indians in that language. This arrangement is very much in consequence of the severity of the winter with them, it occupying so much of their time and strength in caring for themselves and their animals. Mr. Walker is recommended to occupy the station at the Dalles for the present, at least, or until it is thought best to make some other arrangements.

August 23—*My Dear Parents:*—I see I cannot finish my letter without interruptions, and long ones, too. Another resolution of the meeting was that husband see to getting houses built for the mothers of the mission families, so that they could spend the winter here for the sake of having the children attend school. This would relieve me greatly of having to board them as I have done.

Since I commenced this letter many changes have taken place, which entirely prostrate the plans and resolutions of the meeting. Mr. W. is unwilling to remove with his family this year, on account of Mrs. W. being in a state of pregnancy, which was known at the time of the meeting, but not made an objection. Mr. Eells and family must remain with them throughout the winter, and consequently will not need a house here as was expected. Mrs. S. and children expect to come and winter here unless circumstances prevent. Marcus has now gone to Vancouver on business to bring up the property of the mission and see to the occupancy of the Dalles station. We are unwilling to let it pass out of our hands and fall into the hands of Catholics. He expects to hire Mr. Hinman, as he has a wife now, and both are pious, to take the charge of the secular affairs of the station, and in case we can do no better, let Perrin (the little boy that was with us in Cuba, but now grown to be quite a young man), his nephew, spend the winter with Mr. Hinman, as he is very successful in speaking the language, and can read and talk to them a little. Perrin, with one of our good Indians and Mr. Hinman, we think, will do very well in keeping up the station until a missionary can be sent. Perrin also indulges a hope.

Husband has been absent more than two weeks and it will be three more probably before he returns.

For the last two weeks immigrants have been passing, probably 80 or 100 wagons have already passed and 1,000 are said to be on the road, besides the Mormons. Sixty have gone the southern route that proved so disastrous last year to all that went that way. I have heard that an individual passed us who had letters for us and others, so that we are deprived of hearing from our friends as soon as we otherwise should. It was just so last year, Mother's letter was carried by the Dalles and brought up again after a week or two by Mr. Geiger and Mr. Littlejohn, who came up here on a visit. Mr. G. spent the winter and taught school. Mr. Littlejohn and family have gone home to the States; they started this spring and came here while I was absent at the meeting. I was very sorry not to see her. She was Adeline Saddler; I presume you knew her. She was very unwilling to leave the country, but her husband has become such an hypochondriac that there was no living with him in peace. He wanted to kill himself last winter. It is well for him that he has gone to the States, where he can be taken care of. Poor woman; she is disconsolate and sad, and greatly changed from what she used to be. It is difficult to define the cause of his malady. He seems to be very much like Mr. Munger, the individual we had here that became crazy, and at last caused his own death by driving two nails into one of his hands, and afterwards putting it into a hot fire until it was burnt to a crisp, as was supposed, to work a miracle.

I said in the commencement of my letter that I was expecting to see Jane and Edward this fall; but from those who have already passed we can hear nothing from them, notwithstanding they may be on the road, for among so many, it is not expected that all will be known to each other.

It is difficult to imagine what kind of a winter we shall have this winter, for it will not be possible for so many to all pass through the Cascade mountains into the Willamette this fall, even if they should succeed in getting through the Blue Mountains as far as here. From the Dalls on to the Willamette is considered the worst part of the route from the States to the end, that is, to the Willamette valley. We are not likely to be as well off for provisions this season as usual—our crops are not as abundant.

Poor people—those that are not able to get one, or pay for what they need—are those that will most likely wish to stop here, judging from the past; and connected with this, is a disposition not to work, at any rate, not more than they can help. The poor Indians are amazed at the overwhelming numbers of Americans coming into the country. They seem not to know what to make of it. Very many of the principal ones are dying, and some have been killed by other Indians, in going south into the region of California. The remaining ones seem attached to us, and cling to us the closer; cultivate their farms quite extensively, and do not wish to see any Sniapus (Americans) settle among them here; they are willing to have them spend the winter here, but in the spring they must all go on. They would be willing to have more missionaries stop and those devoted to their good. They expect that eventually this country will be settled by them, but they wish to see the Willamette filled up first.

We wish to employ a teacher for the winter. If J. and E. do not come, we must look out for some one among the immigrants. We should prefer an accomplished young lady from the Eastern States, if such could be found to teach the children of our families. Young ladies are greatly needed in this country as teachers—also female help of all kinds. Many more men than women come into the country. Almost every body has been sick in the Western States which is said to be the cause of so large influx this way. When I heard that dear brother Harvey was going to Virginia, I could not help desiring him to come this way. O, if he was here now to take our farm, how much better it would be for him and us, too; we need just such a man. I would that he would come and two or three others just like him, for their help is greatly needed. I wrote him to come, but do not know that he got my letter. Husband is wearing out fast; his heart and hands are so full all the time, that his brethren feel solicitous about him, but cannot help him; his benevolence is unbounded, and he often goes to the extent of his ability, and often beyond, in doing good to the Indians and white men.

It is probably not right for me to desire to have father and mother here; but still I cannot help thinking all the time, O, if they were here. God grant that they may live long to pray for their unworthy children among the Indians.

We hear that a monthly mail route is to be, or already is, established on the coast south — a steamer to take packages from Panama, that come across the Isthmus of Darien. I hope it will not be so difficult to hear from home as formerly. I intend to send this that way for an experiment. I send this by our man and John, one of the orphan boys, who go with two ox teams to the Dalles to bring up the threshing machine, cornsheller, ploughs for Indians, and other goods for the mission, also books for Mr. Rogers, the pious young man of whom I have spoken, that husband brings up in a boat from Vancouver.

Now I have the care of two additional boys for a year, who are left here by their fathers for the benefit of school; they are native half breeds. May the richest of heaven's blessings ever rest upon my beloved father and mother.

From your ever affectionate daughter,
NARCISSA.

Letters

WAIILATPU, Oct. 12th, 1847.

Dear Jane: — Two men are at this place on their way to the States. One of them, Mr. Glenday, intends to return to this country next spring with his family. I have importuned him, and made an arrangement to have you accompany them to Waiilatpu. Now Jane, will you do it? I know you will not refuse to come. As least I feel that you must and will come. I wrote you last spring and told you that I was expecting you and E. this fall, and I have been looking for you in every company that have passed. But I have not seen you nor received any letter from either of you. But a week or two ago when I was on the Utilla river, I saw an individual that told me that he had seen a brother of mine that was near Independence with his family, that he was intending to come to Oregon this season, but could not get ready, but would come next year. He furthermore told him that he wished to send a package to us, and would go to his house and get it, which was five miles distant, if he would bring it. This individual said he promised to bring it and would have waited for it had it been possible, but the company with whom he traveled started before he expected and he was obliged to leave before he returned with the package. From his description, I was confident that it was Brother Harvey, and you can better imagine than I can describe, the joy I felt on receiving such intelligence. I have also received a letter from father and Brother J.G. They tell me that H. was in the West and that you were with him. Mr. Glenday tells me that there is a teacher in Monticello Seminary of the name of Prentiss, and he thinks it must be you. I am at a loss to know where you are. I write you every spring, but I am not informed if you ever receive my letters.

I will now give you the arrangements we have made with Mr. Glenday to have you come immediately and directly to us. He says when you receive this letter, he wishes you to get into a boat or stage and go directly to St. Charles and see Mrs. Glenday and make her acquaintance. She is a pious woman and he is highly pleased with the idea of your accompanying them to be company for her on the way. He says he will bring you free of all expense. Of course we shall satisfy him when you arrive. We are confident that you could not have so good an opportunity to come to this country in any other way as with Mr. G. He is accustomed to travel in an Indian country, and knows how prefctly. I am satisfied that if Brother H. and his family and E. and yourself would make the arrangement to come wth him and would submit to be controlled by him (as he is coming in a small party by himself), you would be the gainers by it in the end. Perhaps you would think that for so small a party it would be dangerous traveling through the Indian country. It would be for persons entirely unacquainted with the Indians and with traveling in the Indian country. But you may rely upon Mr. Glenday; that he knows how to travel and can escort you here quicker and safer and with less annoyance from dust and fatigue and worn out cattle and with half the expense that you would be at to come any other way. You will always hear it said by every one who knows anything about the way, "Bring as few things as possible." I would advise you and my brothers and Sister L. to be governed by Mr. G.'s advice about what you bring, as well as the amount. I will add however, that I would prefer you would not encumber yourself with anything except what you need on the way, and to bring your minds to need as little as possible. I consider Mr. G. capable of giving you directions upon this subject, and such, too, as will meet my mind more fully than I can express by writing. We have enough to supply you when you get here; and if we have not we can get it here.

You know not how much you are all needed here this present moment; yes, I may say, we are suffering and shall suffer for the want of your assistance and presence here this winter.

Dear Jane, I have written in great haste, as I have but a moment to write, and a hurried one at that; for it is all confusion as usual when immigrants are about us. I would write Brothers H. and E. and Sister L., but Mr. G. wishes to be burdened with as little as possible, for he may have to go on snow shoes a part of the way. He wishes to return next spring, and about the last of August encourages me to think that, it spared and prospered, he will set you down at our door. I cannot help feeling rejoiced that Providence has opened up a way, to appearance so favorable, for the safe, easy and speedy transport of my dear Jane to my arms. I long to see you all, and should much prefer to have you all come with him if you felt it best. But he seems to think that my brothers would not be willing to come with him on account of traveling in so small a party.

Wednesday morn—*Dear Jane and Edward*:—I have been talking this morning to Mr. Glenday about you coming with him. I am at a loss how to direct him to find you. I do not know where Brother Harvey is. Father says he is in Quincy and that you are with him and that Edward is in Hazel Green, Wisconsin. He is confident, however, that He will find you all and Brother H. as he goes in, especially if he is anywhere in the vicinity of Independence. I expect husband will write Harvey if he gets away from his cares long enough; but lest he should not, I will suppose you all together and talk to you en masse, for it is impossible to write separate letters. We, that is husband and self, think it best for you all to come with him; and he is willing, provided you all would be willing to submit to his laws. He is a rigid mountaineer, and the principal laws in an Indian country are to be particular in guarding your animals lest you be robbed of them and left on foot. You cannot imagine the distress such an event would occasion. Many events of that kind have happened to the immigrants of the present year. It is hard work to cross the Rocky Mountains in the easiest way it can be arranged. If I had the journey to make, and knew as much as I now do about traveling, I should by all means, prefer to travel in the camp of such a man as Mr. Glenday. If E. comes as a single man he will employ him and pay him wages to assist in driving sheep; consequently he could come without its costing him anything. If he has a wife in view, he had better marry (that is if he has found a good one)—let his motto be "a good one or none." Mr. G. says he will be to the expense of Jane's outfit, and I think you may rely upon it. When you get this letter you must write him and direct to St. Charles post office, then he will write you and invite you to come.

It may not be strange for you to be a little unbelieving and think it not true that we have sent for you, but when you see the big mule that we have sent for you, Jane, your heart may faint within you, and you will feel that it is, indeed, so. The name of the big mule is Uncle Sam. He was left here by Fremont when he was here on business for Uncle Sam. Mr. Rodgers is expecting a brother-in-law, sister and parents, some time next summer.

Jane, there will be no use in your going home to see ma and pa before you come here—it will only make the matter worse with your heart. I want to see her as much as you. If you will all come here it will not be long before they will be climbing over the Rocky Mountains to see us. The love of parents for their children is very great. I see already in their movements, indications that they will ere long come this way, for father is becoming quite a traveler. Believe me, dear Jane, and come without fail, when you have so good an opportunity.

Farewell,
N.W.

Narcissa Whitman

OREGON CITY, April 6, 1848.

To Stephen Prentiss, Esq., and Mrs. Prentiss, the Father and Mother of the late Mrs. Whitman of the Oregon Mission—My Dear Father and Mother in Christ:—Through the wonderful interposition of God in delivering me from the hand of the murderer, it has become my painful duty to apprise you of the death of your beloved daughter, Narcissa, and her worthy and appreciated husband, your honored son-in-law, Dr. Whitman, both my own entirely devoted, ever faithful and eminently useful associates in the work of Christ. They were inhumanly butchered by their own, up to the last moment, beloved Indians, for whom their warm Christian hearts had prayed for eleven years, and their unwearied hands had administered to their every want in sickness and in distress, and had bestowed unnumbered blessings; who claimed to be, and were considered, in a high state of civilization and Christianity. Some of them were members of our church; others candidates for admission; some of them adherents of the Catholic church—all praying Indians. They were, doubtless, urged on to the deadful deed by foreign influences, which we have felt coming in upon us like a devastating flood for the last three or four years; and we have begged the authors, with tears in our eyes, to desist, not so much on account of our own lives and property, but for the sake of those coming, and the safety of those already in the country. But the authors thought none would be injured but the hated missionaries—the devoted heretics, and the work of hell was urged on, and has ended, not only in the death of three missionaries, the ruin of our mission, but in a bloody war with the settlements, which may end in the massacre of every family.

God alone can save us. I must refer you to the *Herald* for my views as to the direct and remote causes which have conspired to bring about the terrible calamity. I cannot write all to every one, having a large family to care for; Mrs. Spalding is suffering from the dreadful exposure during the flight and since we have been this country—destitute of almost every thing, no dwelling place as yet, food and raiment to be found, many, many afflicted friends to be informed, my own soul bleeding from many wounds; my dear sister, Narcissa, with whom I have grown up as a child of the same family, with whom I have labored so long and so intimately in the work of teaching the Indians, and my beloved Dr. Whitman, with whom I have for so many years kneeled in praying, taking sweet counsel, have been murdered, and their bones scattered upon the plains—the labors and hopes of many years in an hour at an end, the house of the Lord, the mission house, burned, and its walls demolished, the property of the Lord to the amount of thousands of dollars, in the hands of the robbers, a once large and happy family reduced to a few helpless children, made orphans a second time, to be separated and compelled to find homes among strangers; our fears for our dear brothers Walker and Eells of the most alarming character; our infant settlements involved in a bloody war with hostile Indians and on the brink of ruin—all, all, chill my blood and fetter my hands.

The massacre took place on the fatal 29th of November last, commencing at half past one. Fourteen persons were murdered first and last. Nine men the first day. Five men escaped from the Station, three in a most wonderful manner, one of whom was the trembling writer, with whom I know you will unite in praising God for delivering even one. The names and places of the slain are as follows: The two precious names already given, my hand refuses to write them again. Mr. Rogers, young man, teacher of our Mission school in winter of '46; since then has been aiding us in our mission work and studying for the ministry, with a view to be ordained and join our Mission; John and Francis Sager, the two eldest of the orphan family, ages 17 and 15; Mr. Kimball of Laporte, Indiana, killed second day, left a widow and five children: Mr. Saunders of Oskaloosa, Iowa, left a widow and five children; Mr. Hall of Missouri, escaped to Fort Walla Walla, was refused protection, put over the Columbia river, killed by the Walla Wallas, left a widow and five children; Mr. Marsh of Missouri, left a son grown and a young daughter; Mr. Hoffman of Elmira, New York; Mr. Gillan of Oskaloosa, Iowa; Mr. Sails of latter place; Mr. Bewley of Missouri. Two last dragged from sick beds eight days after the first massacre and butchered; Mr. Young, killed second day. Last five were unmarried men. Forty women and children fell captives into the hands of the murderers, among them my own beloved daughter, Eliza, ten years old. Three of the captive children soon died, left without parental care, two of them your dear Narcissa's, once a widow woman's. The young women were dragged from the house by night and beastly treated. Three of them became wives to the murderers. One, the daughter of Mrs. Kimball, became the wife of him who killed her father—often told her of it. One, Miss Bewley, was taken twenty miles to the Utilla and became the wife of Hezekiah, a principal chief and member of our church who, up till that time had exhibited a good character. Eight days after the first butchery, the two families at the saw-mill, twenty miles distant, were brought down and the men spared to do work for the Indians. This increased the number of the captives to forty-seven, after the three children died. In various ways they were cruelly treated and compelled to cook and work late and early for the Indians.

As soon as Mrs. Spalding heard of my probable death and the captivity of Eliza, she sent two Indians (Nez Perces) to effect her deliverance, if possible. The murderers refused to give her up until they knew whether I was alive, as I had escaped their hands, and whether the Americans would come up to avenge the death of their countrymen. Should the Americans show themselves, every woman and child should be butchered. The two sick men had just been beaten and cut to pieces before the eyes of the helpless children and women, their blood spilled upon the floor, and their mangled bodies lay at the door for forty-eight hours, over which the captives were compelled to pass for wood and water.

Eliza says when she heard the heavy blows and heard dying groans, she stopped her ears. Such was and such had been for several days the situation of Eliza, when the two Nez Perces, particular friends to our children, told Eliza they must return without her. The murderers would not give her up. She had given up her father as dead, but her mother was alive and up to this hour she hoped to reach her bosom, but now this hope went out and she began to pine. Besides, she was the only one left who understood the language, and was called up at all hours of the night and kept out for hours in the cold and wet, with almost no clothing left by the hand of the robbers, to interpret for whites and Indians, till she was not able to stand upon her feet, and they beset her lying upon the floor—bed she had none—till her voice failed from weakness.

I had reached home before the Indians who went for her returned, and shared with my wife the anguish of seeing the Indians return without her child. Had she been dead, we could have given her up; but to have a living child a captive in the hands of Indians whose hands were stained with the blood of our slain friends, and not able to deliver her, was the sharpest dagger that ever entered my soul. Suffice to say, we found our daughter at Fort Walla Walla with the ransomed captives, too weak to stand, a mere skeleton, her mind as much injured as her health. Through the astonishing goodness of God she has regained her health and strength, and her mind has resumed its usual tone.

The captives were delivered by the prompt interposition and judicious management of Mr. Ogden, Chief Factor of the H.B. Co., to whom too much praise cannot be awarded. He arrived at Walla Walla Dec. 12th. In about two weeks he succeeded in ransoming all the captives for blankets, shirts, guns, ammunition, tobacco, to the amount of some five hundred dollars. They were brought into the fort on Dec. 30th. Myself and those with me arrived on the first of January. Oh, what a meeting—remnants of once large and happy families; but our tears of grief were mingled with tears of joy. We had not dared to hope that deliverance could come so soon and so complete.

For some time previous to the massacre the measles, followed by the dysentery, had been raging in the country. The familes at Waiilatpu had been great sufferers. I arrived at Waiilatpu the 22nd of November; eight days before the dreadful deed. All the doctor's family had been sick, but were recovering; three of the children were yet dangerously sick; besides Mr. Osborn, with his sick family, were in the same house. Mrs. Osborn and three children were dangerous; one of their children died during the week. A young man, Mr. Bewley, was also very sick. The doctor's hands were more than full among the Indians; three and sometimes five died in a day. Dear sister Whitman seemed ready to sink under the immense weight of labor and care. But like an angel of mercy, she continued to administer with her ever-ready hand to the wants of all. Late and early, night and day, she was by the bed of the sick, the dying, and the afflicted. During the week, I enjoyed several precious seasons with her. She was the same devoted servant of the Lord she was when we enjoyed like precious seasons in our beloved Prattsburg many years ago, ready to live or die for the name of the Lord Jesus Chirst. Saturday the Indians from the Utilla, sent for the doctor to visit their sick. He wished me to accompany him. We started late, rode in a heavy rain through the night, arrived in the morning. The doctor attended upon the sick, and returned on the Sabbath on account of the dangerous sickness in his family. I remained till Wednesday. Monday morning the doctor assisted in burying an Indian; returned to the house and was reading—several Indians, as usual were in the house; one sat down by him to attract his attention by asking for the medicine; another came behind him with tomahawk concealed under his blanket and with two blows in the back of the head, brought him to the floor senseless, probably, but not lifeless; soon after Telaukaikt, a candidate for admission in our church, and who was receiving unnumbered favors every day from brother and sister Whitman, came in and took particular pains to cut and beat his face and cut his throat; but he still lingered till near night. As soon as the firing commenced at the different places, Mrs. Hayes ran in and assisted sister Whitman in taking the doctor from the kitchen to the sitting-room and placed him upon the settee. This was before his face was cut. His dear wife bent over him mingled her flowing tears with his precious blood. It was all she could do. They were her last tears. To whatever she said, he would reply "no" in a whisper, probably not sensible. John Sager was sitting by the doctor when he received the first blow, drew his pistol, but his arm was seized, the room filling with Indians, and his head was cut to pieces. He lingered till near night. Mr. Rogers, attacked at the water, escaped with a broken arm and wound in the head, and rushing into the house, shut the door. The Indians seemed to have left the house now to assist in murdering others. Mr. Kimball, with a broken arm rushed in; both secreted themselves upstairs. Sister Whitman in anguish, now bending over her dying husband and now over the sick; now comforting the flying, screaming children, was passing by the window, when she received the first shot in her right breast, and fell to the floor. She immediately arose and kneeled by the settee on which lay her bleeding husband, and in humble prayer commended her soul to God and prayed for her dear children who were about to be made a second time orphans and fall into the hands of her direct murderers. I am certain she prayed for her murderers, too. She now went into the chamber with Mrs. Hayes, Miss Bewley, Catharine, and the sick children. They remained till near night. In the meantime the doors and windows were broken in and the Indians entered and commenced plundering, but they feared to go into the chamber. They called for sister Whitman and brother Rogers to come down and promised they should not be hurt. This promise was often repeated, and they came down. Your dear Narcissa, faint with the loss of blood, was carried on a settee to the door by brother Rogers and Miss Bewley. Every corner of the room was crowded with Indians having their guns ready to fire. The children had not been brought down and huddled together to be shot. Eliza was one. Here they had stood for a long time surrounded by guns pointing at their breasts. She often hear the cry "Shall we shoot?" and her blood became cold, she says, and she fell upon the floor. But now the order was given, "Do not shoot the children," as the settee passed through the children over the bleeding, dying body of John. Fatal moment! The settee advanced about its length from the door, when the guns were discharged from without and within, the powder actually burning the faces of the children. Brother Rogers raised his hand and cried, "my God," and fell upon his face, pierced with many balls. But he fell not alone. An equal number of deadly weapons were leveled at the settee and, oh! that this discharge had been deadly. But oh! Father of Mercy, so it seemed good in thy sight. She groaned, she lingered. The settee was rudely upset. — Oh, what have I done? Can the aged mother read and live? Think of Jesus in the hands of the cruel Jews. I thought to withold the worse facts, but then they would go to you from other sources, and the uncertainty would be worse than the reality. Pardon me, if I have erred.

And now, shall I attempt to sooth your bleeding hearts? It would be like one drowning man stretching out his hand to hold up another. I, myself, am in the deepest waters of affliction. My dear brother and sister Whitman no more; their mission house demolished; myself and family driven from our first own home, and the little church which we had been gathered around; our brothers, Walker and Eells, perhaps, slain and their wives and children captives in the hands of the murderers. "But why art thou disquieted, oh my soul?" "Even so, Father, for so it seemeth good in Thy sight." "This world is poor from shore to shore." There is no place like heaven, and it has seemed doubly precious since the day my dear associates ended their toils, and left this world of blood and sin to enter upon the unending song of Moses and the Lamb. I know where you will go, my honored father and mother in Christ, when you have read this letter, you will go to the Mercy Seat, and there you will find balm for your deeply wounded soul, for you know how to ask for it. And when there, you will not forget the scattered sheep and the trembling lambs of our broken mission.

At the same time of the massacre, Perrin Whitman nephew of Dr. Whitman, was at The Dalles in the family of Mr. Hinman, whom we had employed to occupy the station which had been lately transferred to our mission by the Methodist mission. On hearing of the bloody tragedy, they left the station and came to the Wallamette. He is here. The little half-breed Spanish boy by the name of David Malin was retained at Walla Walla. I fear he will fall into the hands of the priests who remain in the country. Catherine, Elizabeth, Matilda, Henrietta and Mary Ann, we brought with us to this place; Mary Ann has since died. For the other four we have obtained good places and they seem satisfied and happy. Catharine is in the family of the Rev. Mr. Roberts, Superintendent of the Methodist mission.

Three Papists, one an Indian formerly from Canada and late from the state of Maine, had been in the employ of the doctor a few weeks; one a half breed with Cayuse wife, and one a Canadian who had been in the employ of the doctor for more than a year, seemed to have aided in the massacre, and probably secured most of the money, watches and valuable property. The Canadian came down with the captives, was arrested, brought before a justice bound over for trial at next court charged with having aided in the murders. The night before he was arrested, he secreted in the ground and between the boards of a house considerable of Mr. Hoffman's money and a watch of one of the widows. The Canadian Indian, Jo Lewis, shot Francis with his own hand and was the first to commence breaking the windows and doors; is now with the hostile Indians. The half-breed named Finley was camped near the station, and in his lodge the murderers held their councils before and during the massacre. He was at the head of the Cayuses at the battle near the Utilla; managed by pretended friendship, to attract the attention of our officers, while his warriors, unobserved, surrounded our army. As soon as they had gained their desired position, he wheeled and fired his gun, as the signal for the Indians to commence. Although they had had the advantage of the ground, far superior in number, and the first fire, they were completely defeated, driven from the field and finally from their possession of the country, and expect to fortify at the mission station at Waiilatpu. The Cayuses have removed their families and their stock over Snake river into the Palouse country in the direction of brothers Walker and Eells. Our army came upon them at Snake river as they about were to cross. About 1,500 head of cattle and the whole Cayuse camp were completely in their hands. But here our officers were again for the third and fourth time outwitted by some Indians riding up to them and pretending friendship, saying that some of their own cattle were in the band, and begged time to separate them. Our commander having received orders not to involve the innocent with the guilty, gave them till morning. It is said his men actually wept at the terrible mistake. Next morning, as might be expected, most of the cattle and nearly all the Cayuse property had been crossed over and were safe. Our army started away with some 500 head. The Indians with the pretended friendly ones at the head, fought all day. At night, being double the number of the whites, the Indians retook their cattle. The whites were obliged to retreat to the station. The Indians continued to fight them through the night and the next day. The third day the officers reached the station, none killed, but seven wounded. The commander and half of the army immediately started for this country for provisions, ammunition and more men. If the few left are not soon reinforced, and supplied, they will be in danger of being cut off, and the Indians will be down on the settlements. The commander was accidentally killed on his way down.

The Lord has transferred us from one field of labor to another. Through the kindness of Rev. Mr. Clark, Mr. Smith and others, we have been brought to this place, "Tualatin Plains." Mrs. Spalding has a large school, and I am to preach, God assisting, at three stations through the summer.

As I cannot write to all, I wish this letter printed and copies of the papers sent to Rev. David Greene, Mission House, Boston, Mass.; Dudley Allen, M.D., Kinsman, Trumbull Co., Ohio; Rev. C.F. Scoville, Holland Patent, Oneida Co., New York; Calvin C. Stowe, Lane Seminary, Cincinnati, Ohio; Mr. Seth Paine, Troy, Bradford Co., Penn.; Mr. G.W. Hoffman, Elmira, Chemung Co., New York; Hon. Stratton H. Wheeler, Wheeler Steuben Co., New York, and Christiam Observer, Philadelphia, Penn.

Yours in the deep water of affliction,

H.H. SPALDING.

Hon. Stephen Prentiss, Esq.,
    West Almond,
    Allegheny Co., New York.

MORE ABOUT THE WHITMANS

Clifford M. Drury

History is never static. As new information of the past becomes available, former evaluations need to be reappraised and accepted horizons must be broadened. My *Marcus and Narcissa Whitman and the Opening of Old Oregon,* published in August 1973, was as definitive a study of these two important historical characters who played such important roles in the opening of the Old Oregon country for white settlements, as available documentary sources then provided. Among other contemporary sources used in this writing of this two-volume work were 302 letters written by either Marcus or Narcissa Whitman, a list of which is given in an appendix to that work.

Since the publication of *Marcus and Narcissa Whitman,* four more Whitman letters have become known to me which I wish I had been able to use when writing the two-volume work. Two of these letters, written by Narcissa Whitman, January 16, 1840 and September 30, 1842 were received recently by the Steilacoom Historical Association, Steilacoom, Washington, from a private individual whose family had owned the letters for many years. The other two were written by Marcus Whitman, October 22, and November 8, 1847, and probably were the last letters that Dr. Whitman ever wrote. These were located in some uncatalogued archives in the library of Whitman College by Larry Dodd, Curator of Manuscripts and Special Collections.

Although these four letters do not contain any information which is dramatically new, they warrant publication because they throw interesting spotlights on certain contemporary events which were taking place at Waiilatpu, Whitman's mission station near present-day Walla Walla. This new and supplemental information is welcomed.[1]

THE TWO NARCISSA WHITMAN LETTERS

The letter that Narcissa Whitman wrote on January 16, 1840 was addressed to one of Narcissa's younger sisters: "Mrs. Mary Ann Judson, Pembroke, Gennessee County, New York." An alternate address was to a younger brother:" or J.B. Prentiss, Angelican, Allegany County." Mary Ann was the wife of the Rev. Lyman Judson who had been a Presbyterian minister. Unknown to Narcissa at the time she wrote this letter, he had left the Presbyterian Church and become a Seventh Day Adventist.

Characteristic of that day when envelopes were not in common use, the letter was so folded that a space was left for the address. In this area two notations: "N(arcissa) W(hitman), Oregon, April 1840" and West Port, Mo., Sept. 4," which indicate that the letter had been carried across the country and mailed at Westport. Also on this space was written the cost of postage, "25" which indicates the amount paid by the person who received the letter. Angelica, where J.B. Prentiss lived, was the place where Marcus and Narcissa had been married on February 18, 1836.

A note on the back of the letter states: "This is a copy of original letter written by Mrs. Marcus Whitman." Since the handwriting appears to be Narcissa's, there is doubt as to whether the letter is a copy or a duplicate.

In this letter to Mary Ann, Narcissa refers to four instances when her husband attended missionary women in childbirth: Mrs. W.H. Gray, Mrs. E. O. Hall,[2] Mrs. H.H. Spalding, and Mrs. Elkanah Walker. During the eleven-year history of the Oregon Mission, sixteen children were born to five of the missionary wives. With but few exceptions, Dr. Whitman was the attending physician. In addition, Dr. Whitman administered to Mrs. Pierre Pambrun of Walla Walla, the wives of the independent missionaries, and later some of the incoming immigrant women. Dr. Whitman had to spend an inordinate amount of time in making long horse-back rides to distant places as Lapwai (near present-day Lewiston, Idaho) and Tshimakain (near Spokane) to assist missionary wives in their confinements. Often after arriving at his destination he would have to wait days for the baby to arrive.

Up to the time Narcissa wrote the 1840 letter, she had received but two communications from any of her family in New York State, and she had left her home in February, 1836! A letter from her sister Jane arrived at Waiilatpu on July 11, 1838 and another from Mary Ann in the fall of 1839. It is hard to understand why her relatives to did not write or, if they had written, what had happened to the letters in transit. "I cannot write so much & receive no answers," she bemoaned. "It seems like talking to the wind, or that I am entirely out of the reach of your hearing."

Another interesting comment in this letter is that which refers to her endeavors to raise chickens and turkeys, so that they could provide a substitute for horse meat which she did not relish. Dr. Whitman, in a letter to the American Board dated May 10, 1839, reported that up to that date, they had butchered "twenty-three or four horses" for their table use.

The text of Narcissa's letter written at Waiilatpu on January 16, 1840, follows. Where words have been omitted, these are added in brackets to clarify the meaning.

My dear sister Judson. O how I wish you and brother Judson would call in and see how pleasantly situated [I am] this evening. Pleasantly I say, but rather lonely for my better half has gone to Clear Water to assist in making and printing a book.[3] He and Bro. Hall & Mr. Pambrun[4] of Walla Walla left here on Tuesday noon and will be absent probably some time. Although I always love to have my husband at home & particularly when we have company, yet should you be induced to favor us with your society, I think I should not feel so lonely.

Sister Hall and I live together & sleep together. She is [a] feeble body and suffers much constantly. Nov. 5th [1839] she gave birth to a daughter, her third child, but second living one. She recovered from her confinement very well. The babe is very well and strong and grows rapidly. They will call her Caroline Alice, the latter name after my sweet babe whom we have laid in the grave.[15] *Mrs. Hall's afflication is an affection of the spine and the prolapses of the womb, a complicated and difficult disease to effect a cure rapidly. Since her confinement, she has commenced blistered her back for although she has applied but three - yet she realized a benefit from [it] already.*[6] *She expects to apply one tomorrow. Previous to her confinement, her situation rendered it [impossible][7] impracticle for much to be done for her and now they expect to leave us next month. the arrived here in April [1839].*

The following updated postscript was evidently written early in May 1940 shortly before Dr. and Mrs. Whitman left for Tshimakain to attend Mary Walker at her coming confinement. A daughter, named Abigale, was born on May 24th.

A week from next Monday we expect to start for Mr. Walkers & [Fort] Colville. Husband and myself to attend upon Mrs. W. in her confinement. It is 160 miles to Mrs. W's & 200 to Colville.[8] *He is obliged to go and I [will] accompany him for the benefit of my health, which has been quite poor this spring owing to our uncomfortable house.*[9] *As soon as we can return, which must be by the 13th of June, one sister here expects to be confined, Mrs. Munger.*[10]

In Nov. after the birth of Mrs. Hall's child, Husband went immediately to Mrs. Spalding to attend Mrs. S. at the birth of her second here in Oregon, a son.[11] *They call him Henry after the father. So you see we have much of this kind to do as well as our folks at home. You will recall [that] Mrs. Walker had a son born in Dec. after they arrived in 1838. I have but little time to write letters home & much less disposition for I begin to feel that I cannot write so much and receive no answers. It seems like talking to the wind, or that I am entirely out of the reach of your hearing. Perhaps you have all forgotten me. Clarissa*[12] *I have received no letter from her since I have been here.*

One hen has just come off with nine chickens. She is the first. We have 24 more setting hens on hen and turkey eggs.[13] *I do not like to eat horse [meat] beef very well as I am trying to do away with the necessity by raising hens and turkeys. We are beginning [to have] and increase in hogs very well and hope we [will] have a cow beef to kill if so many is not gone to need it alive.*[14] *I must write to father and mother - so good bye.* N.W.

We will meet in heaven and then with far more exalted views than we now have. We can talk of his kind dealing toward us & his great love in our situation.
Your affectionate though afflicted sister.
Narcissa Whitman

Dr. Elijah White, the newly appointed Indian Agent for Oregon, arrived at Waiilatpu on September 9, 1842, and delivered to the Whitmans some letters that he had carried across the country. Among these was one from Secretary David Greene of the American Board, dated February 25, 1842. Because of dissensions within the mission of several years' standing, the American Board had decided to recall Spalding, Gray and Smith.[15] and to close the work at Waiilatpu and Lapwai and have the Whitmans move to Tshimakain.

The drastic instructions of the Board were out-of-date before they arrived in Oregon. Smith already had resigned from the mission and Gray was about to do so. The difference between Whitman and Spalding had been resolved. Spalding's station at Lapwai was the most prosperous of the three then under the American Board and it was folly to close it. Moreover, with the beginning of Oregon immigration, Waiilatpu took on new importance because of its strategic location near the Oregon Trail. Whitman concluded that the circumstances demanded that he go to Boston to intercede for Spalding and to persuade the Board to rescind its order.

Among the letters that Narcissa received was one which carried the news of the death of her sister Mary Ann. On September 30, just three days before Marcus was to leave for Boston on mission business, Narcissa wrote a letter of condolence to her brother-in-law, Lyman Judson. This was carried east by her husband and is the second letter held by the Steilacoom Historical Association. It is here published.

Perhaps the most significant statement in this correspondence is that which refers to the decision of Dr. Whitman to go East - a decision that was reached several weeks before the special Mission Meeting was held on September 26-28. Knowing that his associates probably would object to his leaving Waiilatpu for so long a journey,[16] Whitman tactfully said nothing about going until the morning of the 28th when Spalding, Walker, and Eells were making preparations to return to their respective stations. Although Narcissa refers to the "hearty sanction" given for his trip, actually Walker and Eells were opposed.[17] No doubt Spalding, whose status was involved, gave his hearty approval.

Waiilatpu, Sept. 30th, 1832.

My Dear Brother Judson:

We have just heard of your heart rending affliction & ours too for she was dear to us all but the particulars we know nothing about. We hope by ship to get the information which we so much desire in a few days.[18] *May you be as I trust you are, supported & feel that is is "good to be afflicted" - As I have but little time to write, I cannot say much more by way of comfort to your broken [heart], but be assured of this, we know how to sympathize in the trial of committing a loved & idealized subject into the grave.*[19]

You will be surprised to learn that the bearer of this is my own dearly beloved Husband[20] *whom I hope you will find & go hand & hand together untill he returns to my arms again & then perhaps you will come with him for Oregon needs home* missionaries for the settlers as well as missionaries for the Indians. He can tell such a history of the past as you would never hear from us by letter & I hope you will see him long enough to learn his whole heart - it will take you a long time however, go with him to father's if you can.

I must refer you to him for all intelligence concerning the Mission, country, Catholics[21] &c for I have not time. It is less than a month since he first contemplated the journey & our Mission were together the three first days of this week & gave their hearty saction to his undertaking.[22] It is a hazardous one but the subject to be accomplished demands it. He hopes to get to the borders [of the States] by the first of Dec. - he expects to start the 3d of Oct.[23] May the Lord speed his way & give him favour in the eyes of the churches & the Board. He wishes to go directly to Boston before he calls on a single relative[24] - indeed he does not wish to be recognized in passing that is the papers untill he sees the [Prudential] Committee.[25]

May you have all the interchange of views & feelings that you & he & I desire - & if you do not conclude to return with him, will you not spend some time in writing several sheets of intelligence about yourself [and the] dear one that is in heaven & any other news of interest for I have not heard a word from either of you since [18]39, the time we received the barrels of clothing[26] you sent us.

My husband will not remember to tell me everything I may wish to hear from you for he will have his mind so full of business & plans for the benefit of the cause that I shall not expect him to give me much from my personal friends.

I must close & write a line to some other ones. Accept of much love & sympathy. From your affectionate sister.

Narcissa Whitman

Please give my love to your father's family, especially your Mother if living & other friends whom you may see. You have a cousin Butler at Oberlin, [Ohio], so he writes me.

N.W. Adieu.

Following Narcissa's letter, on a part of the last page which was left blank, is the following note written by Narcissa's father, Stephen Prentiss, dated Cuba, New York, May 2, 1843:

My Dear Son.[27] I have taken the liberty to open your letter to explain some things written in it. You will perceive by the letter that the Doc. expected to get across the mountains by the first part of Decr., but on account of the winter snow is so early, he did not get across until Febr. That cut him short nearly three months time that he [had] expected to have had to visit, consequently he could not visit any friends, only those that came in his way. He came home on Saturday night [April 15] and left Tuesday morning in order to meet the company at Missouri to cross the Mountains.[28] So he is gone again... Your Father, Stephen Prentiss.

There follows a postcript in which Stephen gave some local news which has no relevancy to the Whitman story.

Narcissa's hope that her brother-in-law, the Rev. Lyman Judson, might return with her husband and join them in their missionary labors was completely nullified when Marcus discovered that Judson had abandoned his Presbyterian ordination and had become a devoted follower of the visionary New England prophet, William Miller, who had preached the second coming of Christ and the end of the world. Miller's first effort to set a definite date when this cataclysmatic event would occur failed. He then set a second date, March 31, 1843.[29] Whitman was approaching either Washington or was in the city on Miller's day of doom, and again nothing happened. When Whitman learned of his brother-in-law's involvement with Millerism, he dismissed the thought of trying to persuade Judson to return with him to Oregon.

On November 5, 1846, about three years after Whitman had returned to Waiilatpu, he wrote to Judson and mentioned the fact that he was in the East at "the famous time" when the end of the world was at hand. Whitman then stressed the point that he refused to permit such a prophecy to prevent him from proceeding with his plans. "I did conclude," Whitman wrote, "that inasmuch as you have adopted such sentiments, you were not prepared for any work calling for time in its execution...I was content to pass you in silence. For to my mind, *all my work & plans involved time & distance &* required confidence in the stability of God's government."[30]

The words italicized in the above quotation were engraved, in a slightly different version, on the base of the Whitman statue which now stands in Statuary Hall of the Capitol in Washington, D.C.: MY PLANS REQUIRE TIME AND DISTANCE

Design for the Marcus Whitman window in the Stewart Memorial Chapel, San Francisco Theological Seminary, San Anselmo, California. Mr. John Wallis, artist.

Design for the Narcissa Whitman window in the Stewart Memorial Chapel, San Francisco Theological Seminary, San Anselmo, California. Mr. John Wallis, artist.

THE WHITMAN LETTERS AT WHITMAN COLLEGE

The following two letters written by Marcus Whitman, copies of which are now in the archives of Whitman College, were not known to me when I was writing my two-volume *Marcus and Narcissa Whitman*. As previously stated, these letters are dated October 22nd and November 8, 1847, and may have been the last letters that Whitman ever wrote. Both were addressed to Alanson Hinman, then in charge of the former Methodist mission at The Dalles, known as Waskopum. Whitman College has no record as to the time or from whom the typed transcriptions of the originals were acquired, or where the original manuscripts, if still in existence, might be.

Whoever made the typed transcriptions was not always able to read Whitman's handwriting, which often became a scrawl. The typed copies are peppered with question marks after some words, occasional blanks, and some evident mispellings. For instance, the name of Whitman's nephew, Perrin, was spelled as Penira in the October 22nd letter. Even though these two typed Whitman letters have these evident blemishes as historical documents, their contents do throw some interesting sidelights on events then taking place at both Waiilatpu and The Dalles on the eve of the Whitman massacre.

Some understanding of the historical background is needed to appreciate the contents of these letters. The Rev. George Gary, who succeeded Jason Lee as Superintendent of the Methodist Mission in Oregon, arrived in the Willamette Valley on June 1, 1844, with definite instructions from the Methodist Mission Baord in New York to liquidate its property in Oregon as quickly as possible. The last station to remain in Methodist control was Waskopum at the Dalles. After some prolonged negotiations, the Methodists transferred the title to this property to the American Board in the summer of 1847.

Whitman was delighted with the prospect that the American Board would take over the station at the Dalles. He appreciated its strategic location as being an important way station for immigrants bound for the Willamette Valley. When the four male members of the Oregon Mission of the American Board gathered for the annual meeting at Tshimakain on June 2, 1847, Alanson Hinman arrived unexpectedly at Waiilatpu. Hinman had served as teacher of the school for white children at the Whitman station during the winter of 1844-45, after which he had moved to the Willamette Valley. Dreaming of the possibility of publishing a newspaper, Hinman traveled to Waiilatpu to get permission from the members of the Oregon Mission to borrow the printing press at Lapwai. No use had been made of this press following the publication of Spalding's translation of the Gospel of Matthew in Nez Perce in 1845. Whitman was agreeable to Hinman's request. Hinman then visited Spalding at Lapwai and Walker and Eells at Tshimakain to obtain their consent. Having secured the necessary permission, Hinman took the press either to The Dalles or to some other place in the Willamette Valley. Thus, it escaped the destruction and loss of mission property which followed the Whitman Massacre.[31]

Sometime before July 25, Whitman received a letter from Walker which stated that he and his wife had decided not to move to The Dalles. Whitman was deeply disappointed. Negotiations with the Methodists had proceeded to such a point that he believed he could not honorably withdraw. The season was too late for another Mission Meeting to be called. The only course opened to Whitman was to hire someone to take temporary possession of Waskopum with the hope that the American Board would send additional personnel to occupy the station.

Hinman was at Fort Walla Walla early in August 1847 with the mission press. Whitman met him there and persuaded him to accept the responsibility of taking care of The Dalles station. Whitman also assigned his seventeen-year-old nephew, Perrin, to go with Hinman. Perrin had lived with his uncle at Waiilatpu since the fall of 1843, during which time he had acquired good knowledge of the Nez Perce language, spoken by the Cayuses. Whitman, Hinman, and Perrin arrived at The Dalles sometime before September 7. Having made the best possible arrangements for the occupation of Waskopum, Whitman hastened back to Waiilatpu to make such preparations as he could for the incoming immigration of that year.

The Oregon emigration of 1847 was larger than that of any preceding year. According to the best estimates, between four and five thousand people with their one thousand or more wagons made the westward trek that year.[32] According to a letter that Narcissa Prentiss wrote on August 23, the advance party of this immigration arrived at the Umatilla[33] as early as August 10. Because Waiilatpu lay some twenty-five or more miles north of the Oregon Trail, which followed the Umatilla River, only a few of the incoming immigrants found it necessary to make the detour to the Whitman station. Those who did were the sick, the needy, the weary, and those who for a variety of reasons wanted to spend the winter at the Whitman station. These were the people for whom Whitman felt a special responsibility. At the time of the Whitman massacre there were fifty-two men, women and children who had crossed the country that year, staying at Waiilatpu. In addition, there were twenty-three others including the Whitmans, the seven Sager orphans, seven half-breeds, the Osborn family of five, and young Elisa Spalding. This brought to seventy-five those who were present at the time of the massacre.

The two letters reveal the multiplicity of concerns which were demanding Whitman's time and attention. Special mention must be made of the Osborns. Josiah Osborn, with his wife and three small children, migrated to Oregon in 1845. The family spent the following winter with the Whitmans. Osborn was a skilled carpenter and render valued service in repairing Whitman's gristmill, making furniture, etc. Needing a good mechanic, Whitman called on Osborn at his home in the Willamette Valley in

August 1847 and persuaded him to return to Waiilatpu. Whitman promised to pay him $300.00 a year if he would stay for a two year period.[34]

The Osborn family with their four children arrived back at Waiilatpu on October 18. They were housed in what had been called the Indian room of the large "T" shaped Whitman home. Shortly after their arrival, one of the Osborn children died of the measles. At the time of the massacre, the family lifted some of the floor boards of their room and hid underneath, thus escaping the attention of the murdering Indians. After suffering incredible hardships, the family succeeded in fleeing to Fort Walla Walla.

Whitman's last letter to Secretary David Greene of the American Board was dated October 19, 1847. He had just returned from a trip to the Umatilla where he had seen hundreds of immigrants and scores of wagons streaming westward. Consequently, the subject of Oregon immigration was very much on his mind. In this letter, Whitman again urged the Board to induce colonies of Protestant church people to migrate to Oregon with their ministers. He returned to another subject about which he had previously written to Greene, that of establishing a college somewhere in the upper Columbia River country. He wrote: "I know of no place so eligible as at the Dalles, close by our station."[35]

Whitman's letter of October 23, 1847, was written at Waiilatpu and addressed to Alanson Hinman at the Dalles. With the exception of the addition of some punctuation marks, the following text is an accurate copy of the typed transcript at Whitman College.

My Dear Sir:

I am sorry things are so badly arranged for it gives me no chance to take advantage of the movements. Mr. Osborn got to Walla Walla the day before yesterday, but I did not know of it until noon today. I cannot on that account send anything to go down in the boat as I have no doubt the Indians will be off. Besides had Mr. Osborn waited as was expected and had you wrote me by Raymond,[36] I might have been at the Dalles and back by this time.

I an sure Penire[37] [?] knew my plan and knew that I hold two boat loads of goods to come up. In my letter to you, I intimated I am sure my wish to meet Mr. Osborn at the Dalles. But when I saw your letter stating when he was to start, it put it out of my power to be there.

I hope the boat has not come without the salt[38] and things for us. We are out of salt nearly. I see no mention of any load at all having come in the boat. You will have to pay the Indians as you can for I am not likely to see them. I am going to start for the Dalles on Monday or Tuesday at all risk had I not heard from Mr. Osborn. But I cannot now say when I shall be able to come. I must see if he has brought us anything such as we so much need. I want much to be at the Dalles.[39]

A Mr. Brawley[40] is here, sick with his wife. He is a minister of Cumberland

Presbyterian order. We may have him to stop at the Dalls for a time. If he comes, I will write by him. The last of the immigrants are to be on the Umtilla[?] today. They must come here for part of the week. There are ten families and two will join them from here. I hope the boats will hold over for them to arrive.

We have a school. A Mr. Saunders[41] formerly from Saratoga, New York, is the teacher. He is an experienced teacher, a lawyer with a family. I think I may stop a blacksmith out of the party now at the Umtilla[42] Helen[43] may come with Mr. Brawley.

I hope the Indians will be encouraged to regard the land on the lower plains as the place where they are to plant and not let the Papists have it. I want much to see them before they give their leave to the Papists for a station.[44]

Tell Thomas, John and Luxilo I want to see them. So also the old man Kergusin and Tilitson. If an opportunity offers, try to council with Wilaptulikt[45] although he has long been a Papist.

I write this in haste, the waggon[46] having gone allready. Do not wait for an opportunity to write but have a letter ready to send at the first chance. I am not able to give you much direction not knowing how you are situated. The field ought to be sowed to wheat but I do [not] know as you have obtained any team to do it with.

I wrote, I think, to buy cattle if possible so as to pay after the first of April at Vancouver. I will write fully by Mr. Brawley.[47] Mr. Brawley's oxen will be able to help some if you do not finish before he comes down.

We have the measles[48] all about us [?]. Give my respects to   and tell him I would like some tinware if the tin can be got to make it of. I would like to write to   [?] but must wait a little. Love to him, Mrs. Whitman and yourself.

          Yours truly
          Marcus Whitman

The second letter at Whitman College was written just three weeks before Whitman was killed. The massacre, which took the lives of the Whitmans and twelve others, began on a Monday morning, November 29, 1847. This letter, also addressed to Alanson Hinman at The Dalles, deals largely with mission business. Whitman refers to the measles epidemic which was affecting both the Indians and the white people. He gives directions to Hinman regarding the transportation of supplies bound for Waiilatpu. Evidently, such supplies were sent up the river from Fort Vancouver by boat to The Dalles, then carried by wagon around the Columbia River rapids, and then transshipped by boat or canoe to Fort Walla Walla.

Whoever made the typed transcription of this second letter had difficulty with interpreting Whitman's spelling of the name given as "Wisin," and it may be that Whitman was referring to the notorious hald-breed Joe Lewis. We know that Joe Lewis arrived at Waiilatpu with one of the last groups of immigrants and that he was thoroughly disliked by those with whom he had traveled. Mrs. Saunders wrote that when he arrived he was sick and destitute, and that Dr. Whitman gave him medical care, clothed him, and then sent him away with a family bound for Willamette Valley.[49] In all probability, Lewis traveled to The Dalles with the Braley family.

Whitman's warnings to Hinman about this "worthless vagabond" might have caused Lewis, if indeed he was the person involved, to return to Waiilatpu in desperation, having no other place to go. We do have contemporary evidence that when Lewis returned to Waiilatpu, he lived with another half-breed, Nicholas Finley, and that he was active in stirring up the Indians against Dr. Whitman. Mrs. Saunders commented: "He returned in three days and refused to leave. It was a case of warming a viper in one's bosom."[50]

Following is Whitman's letter of November 8, 1847, written from Waiilatpu:

Mr. Alonson Hinman
My Dear Sir:

As our family are having the measles, I am not sure of being able to come down to the Dalles. Stikas[52][?] is here and says he desired to come to the Dalles as soon as his family get over the measles. In the meantime it will be well for you to buy four of Mr...[?] pounded salmon of the Indians to store it up for any use we may have in voyging or otherwise feeding the Indians. Be careful not to pay too much at first. If Mr. Brawley stays at the Dalles, it might be well to let some man take one or both the cannoes to go down with. If the Indians are hired for the trip, they might bring us back some flour from Mr. Abernathy[53] or from Vancouver. If one set of Indians will not [?do], right, let them along and go to the Chutes[54] of some way get others.

Indians ought not to have better pay and more of it than whites at least until they become more trusty and efficient than they are now. They will make you think you are obliged to pay largely [?] and if you do pay exhorbitantly, you will always be obliged to do so.

Never employ Wisin [?][55] again if it can be avoided. Tell him from me, he is a worthless vagabond, not worth the food he eats. Let pay be out of the question. He did not treat Mr. Osborn well. It may not be safe to let more than one canoe go as I may want the other. In an extreme case both might go but they should hurry back as soon as possible. I am sorry you did not take a waggon to bring most of the load for a canoe to the Chutes River. The team might easily have been taken back. It was a severe exposure to put upon the lives of Mr. Osborn and his family to sent them through the Dales [sic].[56]

I wish always to be able to send all but the boat and a little, it may be, for ballast in the boat, by a wagon to the Chutes. I suppose you are not aware of the danger. I promised Mr. Osborn if he came in a boat to send him by land to the Chutes. Indeed I feel it to be so important that I think of keeping a boat for the lower part of the river and one never to pass the Chutes.

I enclose two notes which may possibly be put in for the purchase of butter as the drivers [?] pass along. Do not crowd them too much but still if it comes night, let them stay. With best respects to Mrs. Hinman and yourself,
Yours truly
Marcus Whitman

THE AFTERMATH OF THE MASSACRE

The Whitman massacre which began with the killing of both Marcus and Narcissa Whitman on Monday, November 29, 1847, took a toll of fourteen lives, including one of the immigrants who evidently was drowned in the Columbia River while trying to reach The Dalles, Those killed at Waiilatpu included ten men, one woman, and the two Sager boys, ages 17 and 15. Joe Lewis,[57] who was the prime instigator of the massacre, is known to have killed Francis Sager. He may have participated in the murder of the others.

Spalding had accompanied Whitman on his trip to the Umatilla where the Doctor called on some Indians sick with the measles. Spalding did not return to Waiilatpu with Whitman on Sunday, November 28. Instead, he tarried for two days at the Umatilla and then started back. While within only a few miles of Waiilatpu, Spalding was told by a Catholic missionary, Father J.B.A. Brouillet, what had taken place and was warned that the Cayuse murderers were looking for him. Thus alerted, Spalding was able to escape and made his way back to Lapwai.

William McBean, then in charge of Fort Walla Walla, first learned of the massacre on Tuesday morning, November 30. He at once dispatched one of his employees, a man called Bushman, to carry the dreadful news to Fort Vancouver. For some inexplicable reason, McBean gave Bushman strict orders not to tell those at The Dalles of what had happened. Bushman reached The Dalles on the following Saturday morning and left at once for Fort Vancouver. Since Hinman decided to accompany Bushman down the river, Perrin Whitman was left in charge with five other Americans — Mrs. Hinman and her small child, an immigrant couple, and Dr. Henry Saffarans, who had but shortly before been appointed Indian Agent for the Indians at The Dalles.

After Bushman and Hinman had left for Fort Vancouver, Perrin heard about the massacre from the Indians and on December 12 a friendly Nez Perce called and gave the details. Perrin also learned that the Cayuse chiefs had offered a reward of 100 horses for his scalp. Being warned, Perrin and his companions made such preparations as they could to defend themselves. On the morning of the 13th, Perrin heard a party of Cayuses stealthily approaching the house. Being able to understand their conversation: "We must have the boy," one said. "He knows us all." Just at that opportune time, a party of friendly Nez Perces came riding into view and the conspirators fled. Otherwise, Perrin would surely have been killed.

The Whitman massacre brought the Oregon Mission of the American Board to a sudden and tragic end. After a month, the fifty captives held by the Cayuses at Waiilatpu were released. The Spaldings escaped and traveled down the Columbia River with the former captives to begin life anew in the Willamette Valley. The Walker and the Eells families, who had taken refuge in Fort Colville out of fear for their safety, were escorted out of the Spokane country by a company of Oregon Volunteers in May 1848. Their departure marked the end of the Oregon Mission.

The massacre also marked the doom of the Cayuse tribe even though not more than fourteen of their number were actually responsible for the massacre.[58] Decimated by the measles epidemic, the small tribe which had not numbered more that 300, suffered additional losses in the spring of 1848 in the hostilities which followed the arrival of the Oregon Volunteers, who sought to apprehend the murderers. Finally, five of the ringleaders were captured and, after a trial at Oregon City, were hanged in June 1851.

Whitman's dream of establishing a thriving mission station at The Dalles and possibly of establishing a college there was a fleeting dream, and nothing more.

FOOTNOTES

1. The Text of the four Whitman letters herein published has been printed with the permission of the Steilacoom Historical Association and Whitman College.

2. Mr. and Mrs. E.O. Hall, members of the American Board's Mission in Hawaii, arrived at Waiilatpu in the spring of 1839. Hall, a printer, brought the small printing press which had been given by the Hawaiian Mission to the Oregon Mission and which was set up at Lapwai,

3. The small book being printed was a Nez Perce primer. See Drury, *Marcus and Narcissa Whitman*, Vol. I:190.

4. Pierre Pambrum was at this time Chief Trader in charge of the Hudson's Bay Fort Walla Walla.

5. Alice Clarissa was the only child born to Marcus and Narcissa Whitman. On June 23, 1839, she drowned in the Walla Walla River which flowed near their home. She was then two years and three months old.

6. Blisters were sometimes then applied as a counter irritant.

7. This word is in parenthesis in the original letter.

8. The distance from Waiilatpu to Fort Colville was closer to 230 miles than that indicated by Narcissa.

9. The Whitmans were still living in their first small adobe house at the time Narcissa was writing this letter. They moved into the larger "T" shaped house in the spring of 1840 after their return from Tshimakain.

10. Mr. & Mrs. Asahel Munger and two other couples, all independent missionaries not having been appointed by any mission board, arrived at Waiilatpu in August 1839. The Mungers spent the following year with the Whitmans.

11. The baby was named Henry Hart Spalding. I had the pleasure of calling on his widow, Mary, at Almota, Washington, in August 1934.

12. Clarissa was one of Narcissa's younger sisters.

13. The Whitman's were able to get chickens and turkeys from Fort Walla Walla. Narcissa's experiment in trying to raise poultry was not successful. Other missionary wives, as Mary Walker at Tshimakain, complained about the Indian dogs killing her chickens. Perhaps Narcissa had the same problem

14. The meaning is somewhat obscure. Since Marcus was trying to encourage the natives to raise cattle, he was either selling or giving some of his American stock to the natives, thus postponing the time when he could butcher a beef. Writing to her parents on October 6, 1841, Narcissa stated: "We killed a very fat beef a short time ago." Drury, *Marcus and Narcissa Whitman*, Vol. I:448. She also reported that on that day her husband had butchered seven hogs. The Whitmans had a smokehouse so that some of the meat could be cured. Also, salt had been imported from Hawaii, so some meat

could have been salted down. Narcissa's letter indicated that for nearly five years they had been obliged to eat horsemeat.

15. The Oregon Mission of the American Board had thirteen members. Dr. and Mrs. Marcus Whitman, Rev. and Mrs. Henry H. Spalding, and W.H. Gray went across country to Oregon in 1836. Gray returned East in 1837, was married, and in 1838 brought out his bride, Mary, and three other newly wedded couples: Rev. and Mrs. Elkanah (Mary) Walker, Rev. and Mrs. Cushing (Myra) Eells, and Rev. and Mrs. Asa B. (Sarah) Smith, and a single man, Cornelius Rogers. The Smiths opened a branch station at Kamiah in 1839 and remained there until the spring of 1841 when they left for Honolulu. Both Gray and Smith were trouble-makers, being especially severe in their criticism of Spalding.

16. Whitman left Waiilatpu on October 3, 1842 and returned on September 28, 1843. He brought back with him his thirteen-year-old nephew, Perrin B. Whitman. Whitman was the guide for the 1843 immigration of about 1,000 people after it had reached Fort Hall, near present-day Pocatello, Idaho. This was the first great Oregon emigration.

17. The account of the special Mission Meeting of September 1842, which gives evidence of the great reluctance of both Walker and Eells to agree to Whitman's proposed journey to Boston, is found in Drury, *Marcus and Narcissa Whitman*, Vol. I:pp. 463 ff.

18. It usually took a year or more for a letter to arrive in Oregon from Boston if it were sent by ship around Cape Horn. Oregon bound mail had to be left at Honolulu to await some vessel going to Fort Vancouver.

19. Here Narcissa was referring to the death of their child, Alice Clarissa. See footnote 5.

20. Narcissa was facing the fact that her husband would be gone for at least a year. During this time, she spent a few months with the Methodist missionaries at The Dalles and then with friends in the Willamette Valley.

21. The arrival in Oregon of two Roman Catholic priests in 1839 - Fathers A.M.A. Blanchet and Modeste Demars - greatly complicated the work of the Protestant missionaries. One reason why Whitman went east in 1842 was to induce Protestant settlers to migrate to Oregon.

22. Emphasis, the editor's.

23. Whitman had persuaded Asa Lovejoy, who had arrived with the 1842 Oregon immigration, to travel with him over the mountains. The winter snows had already fallen on the Blue Mountains before they started.

24. Narcissa gives no indication of her husband's intention to visit Washington, D.C., before going to Boston. Her letters show that his primary purpose in going was on mission business.

25. The Prudential (or Executive) Committee of the American Board had charge of

Indian Missions.

26. The letters of the missionaries contain occasional references to the "missionary barrels" which were sent by sea to Oregon by interested individuals or churches. Since the missionaries received no salaries from the Board, only the basic living expenses, these barrels which contained clothing, books, and other items were deeply appreciated.

27. Although Narcissa's letter was addressed to Lyman Judson, a son-in-law of Stephen Prentiss, evidence indicates that Narcissa's father had received the letter and then had forwarded it to his son, J.G. Prentiss.

28. Because of Indian hostilities along the Oregon Trail, Whitman and Lovejoy found it necessary to make a detour to Santa Fe. The winter proved to be unusually severe and the two men nearly lost their lives. They were obliged to swim the Colorado River, then nearly frozen over, at what is now Grand Junction, Colorado. They did not reach Westport, Missouri, until February 15, 1843, two and one-half months later than Whitman had planned. This unexpected delay cut Whitman's visit to his relatives short, for he was expecting to be back at Westport by the middle of May in order to join the Oregon-bound emigration of that year.

29. William Miller was one of the founders of the Seventh Day Adventist Church although he, himself, did not stress the importance of keeping Saturday as the Sabbath.

30. See Drury *Marcus and Narcissa Whitman*, Vol. II:68

31. This historic press is now in the museum of the Oregon Historical Society, Portland.

32. Drury, *Marcus and Narcissa Whitman,* Vol. II:192-3.

33. *Ibid*, Vol. II:193.

34. *Ibid*, Vol. II:196.

35. *Idid*, Vol. II:198.

36. Unidentified but possibly one of the employees of Fort Walla Walla.

37. Undoubtedly a reference to Perrin, Whitman's nephew.

38. Members of the American Board's Mission in Hawaii often sent quantities of salt to their fellow missionaries in Oregon. This was needed especially for the salting down of meat. Also, Whitman might have been able to purchase salt from the Hudson's Bay Company at Fort Vancouver.

39. Possibly Whitman was referring to some goods which had been taken to The Dalles which he wanted moved.

40. The Rev. James E. Braley arrived in Oregon in 1847 but moved on to California in 1849. *Oregon Historical Quarterly*, Vol. 40, 1939, p. 270. Braley and the Rev. J.A. Cornwall organized the first Cumberland Presbyterian Church in Oregon at Tualatin in the late fall of 1847.

41. L.W. Saunders, his wife, and five small children arrived at Waiilatpu during the

first week of October. Having once served as a Probate Judge, he was often referred to as Judge Saunders. He was one of the first victims in the Whitman Massacre. His wife, Mary, was the only adult at the time of the massacre who later wrote a detailed account of the tragedy. The only known copy of her posthumously published pamphlet, *The Whitman Massacre, A True Story by a Survivor,* Oakland, California, 1916, is in the Library of Congress.

42. Waiilatpu was so crowded with its normal population plus the fifty-two immigrants that Whitman was obliged to utilize his blacksmith shop for living quarters. Eight of the immigrants were housed there at the time of the massacre. Drury, *Marcus and Narcissa Whitman,* Vol. II:202. There is no indication that Whitman was successful in finding a blacksmith to assist him at Waiilatpu, although one of the immigrant men whom he received may have been one.

43. Unidentified.

44. Whitman was concerned with the possibility that the Roman Catholics would secure a foothold at The Dalles.

45. Possibly one of the chiefs of the local Indian tribe.

46. Whitman, following the common spelling of his day, always spelled "wagon" with a double g.

47. Evidently Braley and his family were about to leave Waiilatpu for the Willamette Valley.

48. During the late summer and fall of 1847, a virulent form of measles and dysentery spread with devastating effects throughout all of Old Oregon. We have evidence that the epidemic had struck the Walla Walla area even before the arrival of the immigrants. It has been estimated that about one-half of the Cayuse tribe died of this disease. The epidemic may be considered a basic cause for the Whitman Massacre, for the Indians believed the false rumor that Whitman was poisoning them in order to get their lands and their horses. Drury, *Marcus and Narcissa Whitman,* Vol. 11: pp. 82 ff.

49. Drury, *Marcus and Narcissa Whitman,* Vol. II:201.

50. *Ibid.*

51. Several of the white children at Waiilatpu were sick with the measles at the time Whitman wrote. One of the Osborn children died of this disease on November 16.

52. Stickus, a Cayuse chief who lived on the Umatilla, was one of Whitman's most loyal friends among the Indians. Stickus warned Whitman a few days before the massacre began that he might be killed.

53. George Abernethy, a former Methodist missionary, was Oregon's first governor, 1845-49.

54. An abbreviation for the Deschutes River which empties into the Columbia about ten miles upstream from the Dalles.

55. Possibly an error in transcribing Whitman's poor handwriting. Whitman might

have been referring to Joe Lewis. It is not difficult to see how Whitman's "L" could be read as a "W" if he made a "u" before and after the letter "l." It is easy to see how "ewis" could be read as "isin." The time element involved and the harsh characterization of the man as here given provide circumstantial evidence to support the conclusion that Whitman was referring to Joe Lewis.

56. Possibly the Osborn family had been advised to negotiate one of the Columbia River rapids rather than making a land detour.

57. Joe Lewis escaped capture following the massacre and fled to Montana, where he was joined by Nicholas Finley. Lewis is reported to have been killed in 1862 in an attempted stagecoach robbery. Drury, *Marcus and Narcissa Whitman*, Vol. II:310.

58. The identification of each of the fourteen conspirators and their final fate is given in Drury, *Marcus and Narcissa Whitman*, Vol. II:pp. 321 ff.

My dear sister Judson

O how I wish you and brother Judson would call in and see how pleasantly situated this evening — Pleasantly I say — but rather lonely for my better half has gone over to Clear Water to assist in making and printing a book. He and brother Hall & Mr. Pambrun of Walla Walla left here on Tuesday noon and will be absent probably some time. Although I always love to have my husband at home & particularly when we have company yet should you be induced to join us with your society, I think I should not feel so very lonely. Sister Hall and I live together and sleep together. She is feeble body and suffers much constantly. Nov. 5th she gave birth to a daughter — her third child — but second living one — She recovered from her confinement very well — The babe is very well and strong and grows rapidly. They call her Caroline Alice. The latter name after my sweet babe whom we have laid in the grave. Mrs. Halls affliction is an affliction of the spine and the prolapse of the womb a complicated and difficult disease to affect a cure rapidly. Since her confinement she has commenced blistering her back for although she has applied but three — yet — she realized a benefit from already she expects to apply one tomorrow. Previous to her confinement her situation rendered it impossible for much to be done for her and now they expect to leave us next month which gives her but a short time to apply remedies for her cure. They arrived here in April.

(On reverse side fold)
"This is a copy of original letter written by Narcissa P. Whitman"
(On middle fold - reverse side)

Our hen has just come off with nice chickens she is the first. We have 24 more setting hens on hen and turkey eggs. I do not like to eat horse (meat) beef very well so I am trying to do away with the necessity by raising hens and turkeys. We are beginning an increase in hogs very well now and hope soon to have a corn beef to kill if so many is not gone to need it alive. I must write to father and mother so good bye.

      (seal)   NW

(on inside fold)

A week from next Monday we expect to start for Mr. Walkers & Colville. Husband and myself to attend upon Mrs. W. in her confinement — It is 160 miles to Mrs. W. & 200 to Colville. He is obliged to go and I accompanying him for benefit of my health — which has been quite poor this spring owing to our uncomfortable house. As soon as we can return which must be by the 18 of June our sister here expects to become confined. Mrs. Munger in Nov — after the birth of Mrs. Halls child Husband went immediately to Mrs. Spalding to attend Mrs. S. at the birth of her second here in Oregon. A son they call him Henry after the father, so you see we have work of this kind to do as well as our folks at home. You will recollect Mrs. Walker had a son born in Dec. after she arrived in 1838. I have but little time to write letters home & much less disp (unclear, possibly dispositioned) for I begin to like talking to the wind or that I am entirely out of the

reach of your hearing. Perhaps you have all forgotten me. Clairissa I have received no letter from her since I have been here.
(On reverse fold)

We meet in heaven and then with far more exalted veins than we now have ere we can talk of his kind dealings toward us & his great love in our salvation.
Your affectionate though afflicted sister
Narcissa Whitman

N.W.
Oregon
April 1840

West Port Mo.
Sept 4

Mrs. Mary Ann Judson
Pembroke
Gennessee County
New York

Or J.G. Prentiss
Angelica (difficult to read)
Allegany County

Letters Index

A

Abernethy, Mr. 165
Abernethy, Mr. and Mrs. 163
Abernethy, Sister 175
Adams, Glen 8
Adeline 116
Alice 76, 81, 92
Alice Clarissa .... 7, 8, 49, 50, 55, 58, 60, 61, 74, 79; death of, 82, 95, 132, 140
Alice Clarissa's disposition 52
Alice, little 73
Allegheny Mountains 9, 13
Allen M.D., Dudley 235
Allis, Mr. 16, 19
Alts, John 25
American Board of Commissioners for Foreign Missions 5, 8, 99, 162
American Falls on Snake River 25
American Fur Company 6, 20
American Rendezvous 76, 108
Americans 143, 225
Angelica, N.Y. 11, 56, 67, 111
Ap-ash-wa-kai-kin (Indian) 111
Armstrong, Rev. Doctor 160
Avoca 165

B

Babcock, Dr. 164, 165
Bacon, Mr. 204
Barclay, Brother 162
Barclay, Dr. 163, 165, 170
Bayette, Monsieur 143
Bear Creek 22
Beardsley, Mr. and Mrs. 113
Beaver, Rev. Mr. 37, 38
Beecher, Dr. 11
Beers, Mr. 171
Bellview 10
Bewley, Mr. (killed) 231
Bewley, Miss 231, 233
Big Head's land 72
Big Wood River 7, 28
Birnie, Mr. 165
Blackfeet country 24
Blackfeet tribe 23
Blue Mountains 7, 28, 30, 181, 225
Board 97, 100, 110, 117, 223
Board (American) 67, 129, 131

Boise, Fort 181
Boone & Hamilton 160
Boston 57, 93, 211, 215
Brewer, Brother 186
Brewer, Mr. 186
Brewer, Mrs. 185
Brewer, Mr. and Mrs. 150
Brewer, Mrs. L.L. 135, 167, 175, 185, 189, 210
Bridger, James 120
Bridger, Mary Ann 128
Bridger, Sister 105
Brigade 65
Brigman, Mr. and Mrs. 63
Brother Augustus' shoe store 14
Brother Gray 14, 61
Brother Henry 22
Brother Hull 61
Brother Judson 61
Brother Rudd 61
Brother Spalding 12
Brother Whitman 11
Brother and Sister Hull 11
Buffalo 15, 21
Buffalo country 157
Butler, Jeremiah 89

C

California 108, 121, 208
Camas 30
Canada 53, 136
Cantonment Leavenworth 19
Captain Dandy 36
Captain Home 53
Captain Royal 36
Captain Thing 23
Cascade mountains 225
Cascade range 217
Cascades 36, 44, 171
Catherine (Sager) 233, 234
Catholic Book Store 161
Catholic church 230
Catholic priest 89
Catholics 108, 224
Cattle, 1500 head 234
Cayuse girl 48
Cayuse Indians 7, 8, 30, 39, 47, 58, 150, 151, 152, 234
Cayuse property 235
Celam, Mr. 16
Chariton (steamboat) 5, 12

Chariton, town of 13
Charles 143
Chester, Illinois 10
Chief Factor Black 124
Chief Factor McLoughlin 126
China 208
Chinook 122
Church of England 37, 39
Chute 35
Cincinnati (Ohio) 9, 10, 11
Clarke, Mr. 113, 116
Clark, Rev. Mr. 99, 100, 105, 235
Clarissa 58, 153, 178, 200
Clatsop 165
Clatsop Indians 152
Clearwater River 54, 74, 80
Cook, Mr. 132
Columbia, mouth of 114, 164
Columbia River 7, 34, 36,
  53, 82, 110, 150, 170, 231
Columbia River, valley of 31
Colville 38, 41, 58, 65
Compo, Charles (interpretor) 56, 65, 70
Contagion 8
Copendel, Mrs. 37
Cornish, Giles, death of 69
Council Bluffs 14, 117
Cowlitz 124
Cuba 214
Curtis, Henry Martin 184

D

Dalles 45, 110
Dalles, other 45
Dalls 176
Dandy, Captain 36
David (Indian boy) 58
Deborah 143
Des Chutes 110
Diana (steamboat) 10
Diggers 26
Dixon, Mr. 155
Doctor, the 71
Douglas, Mr. 36
Douglas, Mrs. 36
Douglass, Mr. 49
Dr. McLoughlin 36
Dr. McLoughlin's barn 38
Dr. Tolmie 36
Drayton, Mr. 117
Dryer, Mr. 61
Dunbar, Brother 20
Dunbar, Mr. 16, 49

E

East, Mr. and family 168
Edward 68, 69, 96,
  110, 116, 130, 133, 134, 161, 190, 192, 205,
  212, 220, 225, 228
Eels, Brother 134, 230, 233, 234
Eels, Mr. 39, 87, 121,
  133, 143, 145, 146, 186, 220, 224
Eels, Mr. and Mrs. 71, 207
Eels, Mrs. 121, 165, 166
Eliza (Spalding) 55, 231, 233
Elkhorn River 20
Ellis, Nez Perce chief 144, 157
Elmira 27
England, ship from 78
Ermatinger, Mr. 47, 76, 106, 145
Ewing, Mr. 54

F

Fairfield, Herkimer Co., N.Y. 57
Falls of the Willamette 174
Feather beds 38
Feathercap 143
Fee-low-ki-ke (friendly Indian) 47
Finley, Joseph L. 194
Finley, Joseph L. (death of) 192
Finley, Mr. 193
Fisher, (minister) 204
Fitzpatrick, Mr. 15, 16, 108
Fitzpatrick, Thomas 6
Flathead country 48, 108
Flat Head language 68, 71
Flatheads 22, 78
Fleas 7, 25, 94
Flour mill 151
Foote, Mr. 220
Fort Boise 7
Fort George (Astoria) 164
Fort Hall 6, 7, 24, 25,
  106, 108, 123, 144, 145, 162, 181, 198,
  219, 220
Fort Walla Walla 7, 124, 231, 232
Fort William 6, 24, 28
Four Years in the Rockies (book) 6
Francis (Sager) 234
Francisco (Sager) 187
Fremont, Lt. 160, 161, 228
Frost, Mr. 164
Fur caravan 19
Fur Company 15, 16, 21

G

Galliger, Mr. 11
Galusha 160, 161, 205
Gary, Mr. and Mrs. 180, 209
Geiger, Brother 151
Geiger, Deacon 212
Geiger, Mr. 88, 151, 172,
  210, 212, 213, 225
Gillan, Mr. 231
Gilpin, W. 177
Glenday, Mr. 226, 227, 228
Clenday, Mrs. 227
Grande Ronde 29, 39
Grande Ronde River 125
Grande Ronde Valley 7
Grand Round 74
Grant, Mr. 147, 158, 165
Gray, Brother 128, 131
Gray, Joe, (half breed Iroquois) 124
Gray, Mr. 5, 15, 19,
  24, 29, 32, 45, 46, 47, 48, 62, 65, 70, 71, 76,
  98, 105, 121, 123, 142, 147, 151, 164
Gray, Mr. and Mrs. 68, 171
Gray, Mrs. 64, 153
Gray, Sister 75, 109, 130, 132, 133
Greene, Mr. 48, 61
  118, 119, 121, 224
Greene, Rev. David 121, 160, 235
Green River 108
Griffin, Mrs. 100
Griffin, Rev. Mr. 88, 98, 116

H

Hale, Mr. 117, 122
Hall, Brother 90
Hall, Brother and Sister 96
Hall, Mr. 89
Hall, Mr. and wife 77, 88
Hall, Mrs. 77, 78, 80,
  86, 87, 94, 171, 231
Hall, Sarah 57
Hannah 142
Harmoney Stattion 121
Harriet (Mr. Pambrun's daughter) 58,
  69, 96, 117, 119, 121, 154, 155, 163, 179
Harriet, Sister 178
Harris, Major 16
Harvey, Brother 226, 228
Hayes, Mrs. 232, 233
Hazel Green, Wisconsin 228
Helen 142, 144
Helen (Marr Meek) 129, 131

Helen Mary 120
Henrietta (Sager) 234
Henry and Ellen 169
Henry, Brother 22
Herald 230
Hezekiah (Indian) 231
Him-in-il-il-ip (Indian) 111
Hinds, Brother 162, 172
Hinds, (colored man) 46
Hinds, Rev. 171
Hinman, Mr. 185, 187,
  223, 224, 234
Hobson, Ann 166
Hobson, Emma 166
Hoffman, Mr. G.W. 235, 231;
  his money, 234
Home, Captain 53
Home Missionary Society 211
Hotchkiss, Father 177, 213, 217
Hudson's Bay Company 5, 7,
  53, 57, 119, 124, 170, 204
Hull, Judge 116
Hull, Mr. and Mrs. 63
Hull, Mrs. 66, 97
Hull, Sarah (Indian girl) 65

I

I-a-tin (Indian) 121, 122, 162
Idaho 6
Il-hich-kais-kais (Indian) 117, 127
Immigrants 224
Indians 7, 35, 36, 67, 76,
  84, 92, 93, 101, 108, 110, 117, 118, 121, 123,
  126, 137, 143, 144, 147, 150, 151, 157, 164,
  175, 181, 183, 207, 213, 221, 115, 234, 235
Indians of the Willamette 172
Indian school 189
Indian Sketches (book) 161
Ipuantatawiksa (Indian) 142
Ithaca 14
Ithmus of Darien 64, 226

J

Jackson, Brother 205
Jackson, John W. 156, 160
Jane, Aunt 219
Jane (Prentiss) 13, 77, 116,
  130, 190, 192, 208, 212, 219, 225, 226, 227,
  229
Jane, Sister 119, 163

Jefferson City (Missouri) 13, 314
Jesuit Mission 117
Jesuit Papists 314
Jesuits 108, 214
John (Indian boy) 20, 21, 29, 39, 142, 143, 144
Johnson, Henry 73, 74, 88
Jonas G., Brother 119
Joseph's death 98
Journal of a Trapper (book) 6
Judd, Mrs. 77
Judson, Brother 61, 68, 97, 153, 163, 217
Judson, Brother and Sister 77
Judson, Mr. Lyman P. 218
Judson, Sister M.A. 119, 141
Julia, Sister 22
Junious (steamboat) 5

K

Kaiuses 157, 158
Kayuses 74, 134, 136
Keith, James, Esq. 119
Kenny, Brother 205
Kentuck 24
Kimball, Mr. 233
Kimball, Mrs. .... 231; (killed), 231
Kimball, Rev. Milton 12
Kinny, Mrs. Clarissa P. 179
Klamath 217
Kooskooska (Clearwater) 40

L

Lachine 119
Lapwai 98, 109, 151, 152, 158
Laramie Fork of the Platte 24
Lawyer Divin 163
Lee, Brother and Sister 165
Lee, Messrs 37
Lee, Mr. 15, 43, 59, 61, 64, 72, 78, 150, 165, 170, 171, 176, 177
Lee, Mrs., death of 65, 67
Lee, Sister 106
Lee's school 66
Leland's death, Mrs. 177
Leslie, Mr. 65, 153, 164, 165, 171
Lewis, Jo. 234
Liberty (Missouri) 5, 6, 10, 11, 15, 16, 19, 61
Linn, Mr. 183
Little Dalles 44
Littlejohn, Brother 105
Littlejohn, Mr. 99, 107, 116, 140, 150, 151, 170, 171, 172, 225
Littlejohn, Mr. and Mrs. 100, 168, 172, 181
Littlejohn, Mrs. 106, 158, 163, 165, 166, 178
Littlejohn, Philo 99
Little Spokane River 8
Livonia, Sister 119
Lone Tree 29
Loomis, Mother 21
Looney, Mr. 165
Louisa 201
Loup Fork 20
Lovejoy, Mr. 12, 140, 142
Lower Canada 119
Lysander 97

M

Mahi, Joseph and wife 70
Majestic (steamboat) 5, 9
Maj. Dougherty's brother 19
Malin, David (Spanish boy) 234
Malin, Mr. 177
Marcus 21, 130, 155, 212, 220, 222, 224
Margaret 79, 84
Maria 74
Maria, Miss 37
Marian (Dr. McLoughlin's daughter) 58
Mark 214
Marsh, Mr. 231
Marshall (small boy) 130
Mary Ann 120
Mary Ann (Bridger) 131, 166, 234
Mather, Mrs. 66, 147
Matilda (Sager) 234
McCoy, Rev. Josesph 93
McDonald, Mr. 65, 72, 145, 146, 150, 158, 219, 220
McDonald, Mr. and Mrs. 41
McDonald, Mrs. 58
McKay, Mr. 22, 23, 24, 59, 74, 76, 124, 126, 143
McKay, Thomas 6, 7
McKay, Thomas 57
McKinlay, Archibald 126

McKinlay, Mr. 124, 125, 126, 142, 144
McKinlay, Mr. and Mrs. 144
McKinlay, Mrs. 165, 178, 188
McKinlay's letter 117
McLeod, John L. 6, 7
McLeod, Mr. 22, 23, 24, 25, 26, 28, 29, 32, 33, 44, 48, 76
McLeod's party 29
McLoughlin, Dr. 36, 38, 39, 40, 48, 53, 56, 126, 158
McLoughlin, Miss 72
McLoughlin, Mrs. 36, 40
Measles 232
Meek, Helen Marr 128
Meek (Joe), mountain man 120
Merrill, Brother 20, 50
Merrill, Sister 50
Methodist brethren 137, 164
Methodist friends 67
Methodist Mission 150, 152, 158, 176, 221, 234
Methodist missions 116
Methodists 119
Mill, burned by Indians 150
Misner, Dr. and Mrs. 11
Mission, ... 118, 174, 231
Mission House 160, 235
Mission school 230
Mississippi (River) 9, 12
Missouri (River) 10, 12, 108, 114
Monmouth, Warren Co., Ill. 203
Monticello Seminary 227
Montreal 57, 150, 158
Montreal Express 40
Mormons 224
Mother Loomis 21, 33
Mother's Magazine 59
Mount Hood 31
Mount Pleasant 31
Mount St. Helens 31
Munger, Asabel 94
Munger, Brother 105
Munger, Mr. 99, 108, 112, 116, 225
Munger, Mr. and Mrs. 88, 91, 96, 106, 116
Munger, Mrs. 98, 107, 147
Mungo 121, 142, 143, 144

N

Narcissa 6, 99, 103, 113, 129, 148, 156, 159, 165, 173, 182, 184, 191, 199, 202, 206, 214, 226
Neirede (ship) 53
Neriade (ship) 36, 37, 38
New York 13, 57, 162
New York City Association 131
New York Observer 135
Nez Perce county 75
Nez Perce hymns 62, 74
Nez Perce Indians 6
Nez Perce Indian boys 5
Nez Perce (language) 74, 151, 207, 223
Nez Perces 39, 47, 58, 77, 110, 122, 128, 138, 157, 181
Nez Perces Mission 87
Northwest Coast 37

O

Oahu 37, 53
Obakili's history 48
Oberlin 89, 91
Oberlin Institute 88
Observer (publication) 12
Observer, Christian 235
Ogden, Peter Skene 8, 232
Ohio 34
Ohio River 6
Olley, Mr. 158
Onondaga 31, 78
Oregon 6, 43, 88, 118, 155, 161, 172, 176, 177, 190, 198, 208, 211, 214, 215, 217, 218, 227
Oregon City (Oregon) 8, 230
Oregon Concert 137
Oregon, immigrants 160
Oregon laws 205
Oregon, occupation 161
Oregon, rivers of 152
Oregon Trail 7, 8
Osborn, Mr. 232
Osborn, Mrs. and children 232
Otoe agency 19, 20
Otoes 117
Owynees 48
Oxen 214
Ox team 208

P

Pacific Northwest 8
Pacific Ocean 183, 205

Packett 111, 121
Paine, Mr. Seth 235
Pa-la-is-ti-wat (Indian) 124, 125
Palouse country 234
Pambrun, Mrs. 47, 65
Pambrun, Pierre Chrysologue 7, 32, 33, 34, 39, 41, 45, 47, 70 73, 74, 86, 106, 108, 109, 116, 145
Panama 213, 226
Papists 211, 234
Parker, Mrs. 14, 70, 72
Parker, Rev. Samuel 5, 14, 17, 24, 29, 37, 39, 40, 54, 70
Patrick, Mr. and Mrs. 63
Pawnee agency 19
Pawnees 20
Pawnee village 21
Peacock (ship) 115, 118
Pend O'Oreille 108
Perkins, Brother 105
Perkins, Brother and Sister 162
Perkins, Mr. 67, 88, 105, 145, 146, 150, 170, 176, 180
Perkins, Mrs. Elvira 43, 65, 73, 75, 80, 169, 188
Perkins, Rev. H.K.W. 42, 81, 150, 165
Perkins, Sister 135, 167, 180
Perrin (Whitman) 171, 207, 224
Pitamianinmuksmuks (Indian) 123
Pitiitosh's wife 143
Pittsburg (Penn.) 6, 9
Pittsburgh (Pennsylvania) 11
Platte River 6, 10, 15, 19, 20
Pope, Mr. 190
Poris, Mr. 118
Porter, Mrs. Lydia C. 177
Porter, Mrs. O.L. 177
Porter, O.L. 112
Port Neuf 25
Prattsburg (Steuben County, N.Y.) 5, 31, 212, 232
Prentiss, Edward W. 206
Prentiss, Father 217
Prentiss, Father & Mother 205
Prentiss, Jonas Galusha 159
Prentiss, Harvey L. 208
Prentiss, Miss Jane A. 78, 113, 164, 184, 204, 221
Prentiss, Livonia 112
Prentiss, Livonia L. 208
Prentiss, Mr. Stephen 11, 69, 103, 154, 165, 173, 174, 182, 193, 199, 209, 218, 230, 235
Prentiss, Mrs. Clarissa 97, 211, 214
Prentiss, Narcissa 5, 17
Presbyterian Board 223
Printing press 77, 89
Protestants 117, 212

R

Rae, Mr. 58, 72
Rag babies 129
Raymond, Mr. 144, 152
Red River 24, 117, 121
Red River School 110
Rendezvous (in Wyoming) 5, 21, 22, 23, 26, 48, 56, 67, 116
Richard (Indian boy) 20, 21, 29, 30, 39, 72
Rinearson, Mr. 189
Rivers of Oregon 153
Roberts, Mr. 61, 234
Rocky Mountains 6, 22, 29, 64, 76, 120, 178, 194, 229
Rogers, Andrew 204
Rogers, Brother 109, 152
Rogers, Edward 113
Rogers, Mr. . . . . 68, 112, 114, 126, 134, 140, 151, 158, 190, 193, 194, 195, 205, 206, 210, 212, 213, 220, 221, 226, 230, 233 (killed)
Rogers, Mrs. 153
Rolla, Deacon and Mrs. 14
Roman Catholic 10, 106
Roman Catholics 39
Romanism 136
Roman priests 73
Rose, Isaac P. 6
Royal, Captain 36
Rudd, Brother 61
Rushville (New York) 5, 14, 89, 97
Russell, Osborne 6

S

Saddler, Adeline 225
Sadler, Miss 100
Sager, Francis 231
Sager, John (killed) 231, 233
Sails, Mr. (killed) 231
St. Charles 227
St. Louis (Missouri) 9, 12, 13, 61, 108, 116, 117, 140, 161

St. Peters 121
Sak-ah-too-ah, Richard 17
Sa-ki-aph (Indian) 123, 124, 125
Samuel (Indian boy) 20
Satterlee, Dr. 13
Satterlee, Mrs. 13, 19
Saunders, Mr. (killed) 231
Saunders, Mrs. 231
Saw mill 36, 183
Scoville, Rev. C.F. 235
Seven orphans 191
Shawnee Mission 161
Shawnee Mission School 160
Sheep 161, 183, 216
Shepherd 39
Siam (steamboat) .... 5, 9, 13 (wreck of)
Simpson, Governor 124
Sister Allen 11
Sister Bridgemen 61
Sister Jane 97, 102, 161
Sister Julia 22
Sister Patrick 11
Sister Perkins 41
Sister Spalding 22, 54, 55, 75, 90
Smith, Dr. (an error for Fr. De Smet) ... 161
Smith, Father 117
Smith, Brother and Sister 75
Smith, Mr. 61, 76, 86, 87, 99, 105, 109, 116, 164, 235
Smith, Mr. and Mrs. 68, 114
Smith, Mrs. 61, 166
Smith's Creek 22
Snake Fort (Boise) 7, 24
Snake Indians 22
Snake River 6, 25, 27, 28, 36, 53, 54, 63, 70, 74, 77, 88, 97, 114, 129, 183, 108, 214, 234
Snake tribe 26
Sniapus (Americans) 225
Snow shoes 129, 130
Society of Jesus 161
Southern route 224
South Pass 6
Spalding, Brother 9, 80, 128, 176, 210
Spalding, Eliza 5
Spalding, Mr. 5, 13, 14, 20, 28, 32, 40, 48, 54, 65, 68, 70, 72, 86, 88, 98, 101, 112, 120, 143, 146, 150, 189, 194, 220, 235
Spalding, Mr. and Mrs. 11, 14, 33, 34, 87, 172

Spalding, Mrs. 6, 7, 13, 21, 28, 40, 182, 230, 231, 235
Spalding's station 98
Spokane Falls 72
Spokane House 8
Spokane (River) 8
Spokanes 136
Squire Crocker 152
Squire Gray of Wheeler 60
Stephen, Brother 220
Steuben 30
Stewart, Mr. 15
Stick-as (Indian) 51
Stowe, Calvin C. 235
Suckling calves 26

T

Tanatua 147
Telaukaikt (Indian) 232
Te-lou-ki-ke (Indian) 94
Te-wat (Indian doctor) 49
The Dalles 7, 35, 44, 65, 88, 150, 170, 171, 180, 221, 223, 224, 225, 226, 234
The Dalles Station 224
Thomas (boy) 180
Thornton, Mr. and Mrs. 219, 220, 222
Thornton, Mrs. 220, 222
Til-au-ka-ik (Indian) 124, 125, 126, 127
Til-ka-na-ik (Indian) 122
Timothy 76
Tolmie, Dr. 36
Too-en-too's lodge (Young Chief) 49
Townsend, John Kirk (naturalist) 7, 32, 33, 36
Tshimakain 203, 220, 223, 224
Tualain Plains 235
Tukanon 74, 77

U

Umpqua 217
Umtippe 49, 50, 57, 59
Umtippe's wife 49
Um-tip-pi (deceased) 117
Uncle Sam (mule) 228
United States Engineers Corps 160
U.S. Ex. Squadron 115, 117, 122
Utilla 232, 234

V

Vancouver 29, 33, 34,
   36, 37, 39, 44, 46, 49, 51, 58, 65, 68, 72, 73,
   89, 97, 109, 117, 137, 146, 147, 151, 162, 163,
   170, 171, 176, 219, 224, 226
Victoria (ship) 145
Virginia 212, 226

W

Wagons 161
Waight, Robert 61
Waiilatpu Mission 7, 8
Wailatpu, O.T. 90, 97, 100,
   104, 106, 128, 133, 136, 140, 146, 158, 166,
   168, 170, 175, 176, 178, 181, 185, 186, 187,
   190, 191, 194, 200, 207, 208, 210, 211, 215,
   219, 222, 227, 232, 234
Walker, Brother 128, 130,
   210, 212, 230, 233, 234
Walker, Mr. 68, 72,
   88, 94, 96, 172, 186, 220, 223
Walker, Mr. and Mrs. 71
Walker, Mrs. 76, 98
Walker, Rev. Elkanah 205
Walker, Sister 130, 133
Wallamette 234
Walla Walla 22, 24, 28,
   29, 36, 38, 39, 41, 45, 46, 48 49, 50, 51, 54,
   65, 71, 80, 86, 89, 97, 109, 126, 128, 129,
   142, 146, 149, 150, 157, 158, 170, 220, 234
Walla Walla chief 184
Walla Walla (Fort) 34,
   117 (burned)
Walla Walla River 7, 14,
   46, 82, 88
Walla Wallapoos Indians 47
Waller, Brother and Sister 180, 189, 210
Waller, Mr. 165
Wallula (Fort) 32
Wap-tash-tash-tak (Indian) 125
Wap-tash-tok-mahl (Indian) 117, 126, 127
Wascopum 73, 75,
   81, 105, 149, 150, 155, 157, 158, 165, 167,
   168, 175, 185, 189, 210
Washington (D.C.) 140

Waskopum station 223
Westport 93, 160, 211
Wheeler, Hon. Stratton H. 235
White, Dr., physician 67,
   151, 152, 157, 163, 165
White, Mrs. 64, 67
White, Sister 74
Whitman, Brother Augustus 60, 117
Whitman, David 168
Whitman, Dr. and Mrs. 14, 65, 204
Whitman, Marcus 5, 7, 8,
   127, 134, 161, 162, 174, 183, 205, 217
Whitman, Marcus and Narcissa 89
Whitman massacre 8
Whitman Mission 7
Whitman, Mr. 20
Whitman, Mrs. 32, 124, 203
Whitman, Mrs. (friends) 215
Whitman, N. 42, 81, 105,
   107, 134, 141, 167, 169, 175, 179, 207
Whitman, Narcissa 8, 11, 14,
   41, 43, 51, 66, 69, 72, 78, 80, 87, 90, 96, 103,
   135, 145, 149, 173, 177, 186, 188, 189, 193,
   209, 218, 221, 230
Whitman, Perrin 168, 234
Whitman, Sister 61, 232, 233
Whitney, Mrs. 77
Wielatpoo, O.T. 43, 53, 60,
   61, 64, 67, 70, 73, 76, 79, 81, 82, 85, 91, 93,
   94, 114
Wieletpoos 77
Wieletpu, O.T. 98, 145, 149, 150
Willamette 73, 88, 109,
   114, 115, 116, 122, 151, 153, 163, 165, 170,
   176, 181, 187, 193, 194, 212, 223, 225
Willamette Falls 165, 171
Willamette River 152
Willamette settlement 121
Willamette valley 7, 214, 217, 225
Williamsport 27
Willson, Mrs. 188
Wyeth, Captain 24
Wyeth, Nathaniel J. 6

Y

Young, Mr. (killed) 231

COLOPHON

The LETTERS OF NARCISSA WHITMAN — 1836-1847 *was printed in the workshop of Glen Adams, which is located in the quiet country village of Fairfield, southern Spokane County in Washington state and one township removed from the Idaho line. We printed this one in 1986 and when every copy sold a decision was made to print a second edition. This differs from the first printing only in that there is a slight change in the title page, adding the "1836-1847" dates, and also adding five more Narcissa Whitman letters supplied by Washington State Historical Society in Tacoma, and the National Park Service, Waiilatpu Museum, which is located seven miles west of Walla Walla at the site of the Whitman mission. Type for the pages of the first printing was set by Kristy Frisbie and Sharyn Brown, using a Compugraphic 7300 Editwriter computer photosetter. Added material for this slightly expanded edition was set by Pat Nigh. The pages are set in 11 point Baskerville with running heads and page numbers in Mahogany Script. The original camera/darkroom work was done by Tami Van Wyk. Added camera/darkroom work was by Shellie Stevens, using a Model 660C DS (Japanese) camera. Added material was stripped by Shellie Stevens who also made the printing plates used in the second printing. The sheets were printed by Vern Stevens using a 28 inch Heidelberg press Model KORS. Folding is by Garry Adams using a 22x28 three stage Baum folding machine. The paper stock is 80 pound Embossed Matte. Assembly was by Gracie Kohler. Paperback books were bound in house by Garry Adams and Glen Adams. Hard case binding was by Willem Bosch of Oakesdale, Washington. The books were sewn by Juanita Hurlbert using a National book sewing machine. Gold foil stamping of the cases was by Willem Bosch, Jr. of Spokane. This was a fun project. We had no special difficulty with the work.*

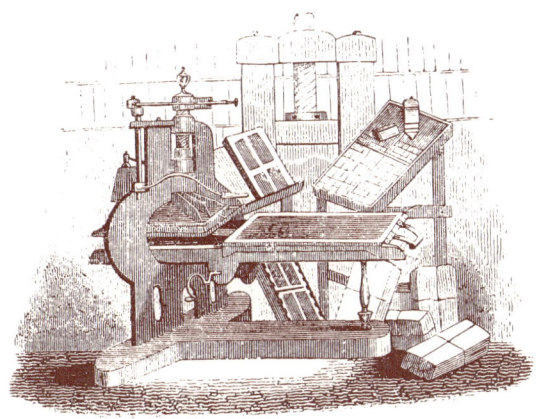

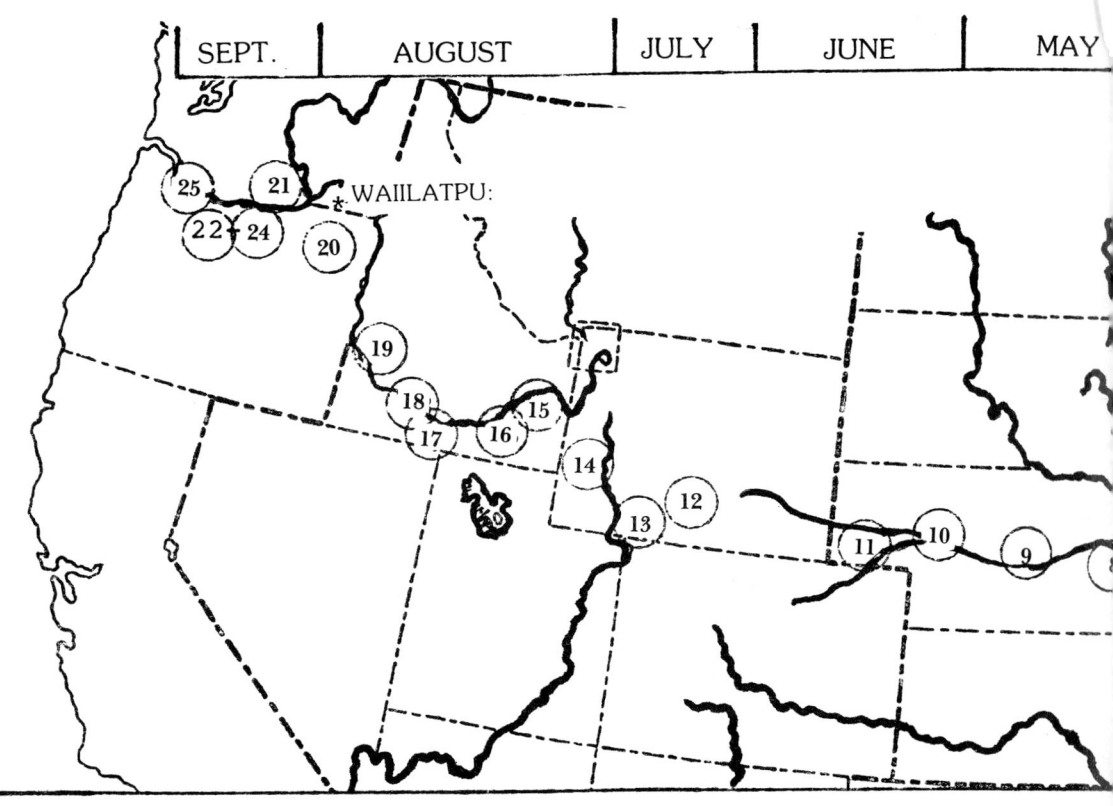

1.	Angelica, N.Y.	Narcissa Prentiss (age 28), & Marcus Whitman (age 34) were married in the Angelica Presbyterian Church, Thur. February 18, 1836. Departed Angelica, Fri., Feb. 19, for visits to Ithaca & Rushville before heading west.
2.	Rushville	Departed for Oregon Terr., Thur., Mar. 3.
3.	Williamsport	Sunday, Mar. 6.
4.	Pittsburgh	Sat., Mar. 12 - Tue., Mar. 15.
5.	Cincinnati	Thur., Mar. 17 - Tue., Mar. 22.
6.	St. Louis	Tue., Mar. 29 - Thur., Mar. 31.
7.	Liberty	Thur., Apr. 7 - Wed., Apr. 27.
8.	Platte River Crossing	Wed., May 18 - Fri., May 20.
9.	Joined Caravan	Thur., May 26 (1 a.m.).
10.	Forks Platte R.	Fri., June 3.
11.	Fort William (Fort Laramie)	Mon., June 13 - Tue., June 21.
12.	South Pass	Mon., July 4.
13.	Rendezvous	Wed., July 6 - Mon., July 18.

| APRIL | MARCH | FEB. |

"We arrived here on the tenth, distance twenty-five miles, from W.W.; found a house reared & the lean-to enclosed, a good chimney & fireplace & the floor laid. No windows or door except blankets. The siding is made of split logs fitted into grooved posts, & the spaces filled with mud. . . ."
Narcissa Whitman letter, dated December 10, 1836.

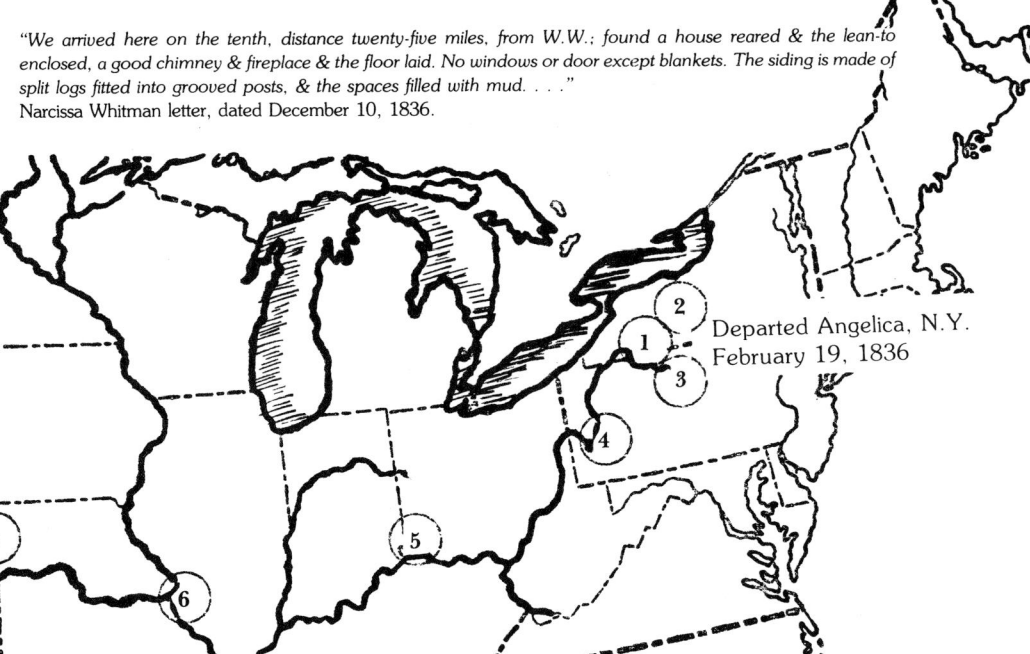

Departed Angelica, N.Y. February 19, 1836

14.	Soda Springs	Sat., July 30.
15.	Fort Hall	Wed., Aug. 3 - Thur., Aug. 4
16.	American Falls	Fri., Aug. 5.
17.	Salmon Falls	Fri., Aug. 12.
18.	Three Island Crossing Snake River	Sat., Aug. 13
19.	Snake [Boise] Fort	Fri., Aug. 19 - Mon., Aug., 22.
20.	Blue Mountains	Sun., Aug. 28 - Mon., Aug. 29.
21.	Fort Walla Walla	Thur., Sept. 1 - Tue., Sept. 6.
22.	The Chutes (Celilo)	Wed., Sept. 7.
23.	The Dalles	Thur. Sept. 8.
24.	The Cascades	Sun., Sept. 11.
25.	Fort Vancouver	Mon., Sept. 12 - Thur., Nov. 3.
	Fort Walla Walla	Sun., Nov. 13 - Sat., Dec., 10.
	Waiilatpu	Arrived Sat., Dec. 10, 1836.

After 295 days and about 2,500 miles, Narcissa Whitman arrived at her new home in the Walla Walla Valley.